A World in the Making

Living in a Globalised World

A Demanding World

Edited by Clive Barnett, Jennifer Robinson and Gillian Rose

A World in the Making

Edited by Nigel Clark, Doreen Massey and Philip Sarre

These publications form part of an Open University course DD205 *Living in a Globalised World*. Details of this and other Open University courses can be obtained from the Student Registration and Enquiry Service, The Open University, PO Box 197, Milton Keynes, MK7 6BJ, United Kingdom: tel. +44 (0)870 333 4340, email general-enquiries@open.ac.uk

Alternatively, you may visit the Open University website at http://www.open.ac.uk where you can learn more about the wide range of courses and packs offered at all levels by The Open University.

To purchase a selection of Open University course materials visit http://www.ouw.co.uk, or contact Open University Worldwide, Michael Young Building, Walton Hall, Milton Keynes MK7 6AA, United Kingdom for a brochure. tel. +44 (0)1908 858785; fax +44 (0)1908 858787; email ouwenq@open.ac.uk

Cover: transition between forestry plantation and semi-natural heather moorland with native pines, Scottish Highlands, UK, autumn.

A World in the Making

Edited by Nigel Clark, Doreen Massey
and Philip Sarre

The Open University
Walton Hall, Milton Keynes
MK7 6AA

First published 2006

Edited and designed by The Open University.

Typeset by The Open University

Printed and bound in the United Kingdom by the Alden Group, Oxford.

ISBN 0 7492 6790 9

1.1

Contents

The Open University course team

Course Team Chair of Production

Gillian Rose, Professor of Cultural Geography

Course Team Chair of Presentation

Chris Brook, Senior Lecturer in Geography

External Assessor

Peter Jackson, Professor of Human Geography, University of Sheffield

Faculty of Social Sciences staff

John Allen, Professor of Economic Geography
Clive Barnett, Lecturer in Geography
Nick Bingham, Lecturer in Geography
Nigel Clark, Lecturer in Geography
Caitlin Harvey, Course Manager
Michele Marsh, Secretary
Doreen Massey, Professor of Geography
Giles Mohan, Senior Lecturer in Technology
Karim Murji, Senior Lecturer in Sociology
Steve Pile, Professor of Human Geography
Mike Pryke, Senior Lecturer in Geography
Parvati Raghuram, Lecturer in Geography
George Revill, Senior Lecturer in Geography
Jennifer Robinson, Professor of Urban Geography
Philip Sarre, Senior Lecturer in Geography
Dave Turton, Staff Tutor in Geography

Other Open University staff

Melanie Bayley, Media Project Manager
Karen Bridge, Media Project Manager

Martin Chiverton, Sound and Vision
Stephen Clift, Media Developer (Editor)
Janis Gilbert, Media Developer (Graphic Artist)
Lisa Hale, Compositor
Jo Mack, Sound and Vision
Margaret McManus, Picture Research and Rights
Diane Mole, Media Developer (Graphic Designer)
Howie Twiner, Media Developer (Graphic Artist)

Consultant authors

Klaus Dodds, Royal Holloway, University of London
Owain Jones, University of Exeter
David Lambert, Royal Holloway, University of London
Owen Logan, University of Aberdeen
Roger Silverstone, London School of Economics, University of London
Sarah Whatmore, University of Oxford

AL consultants

Eluned Jeffries, Associate Lecturer, Region 2 South
Jenny Meegan, Associate Lecturer, Region 12 Ireland
Richard Morgan, Associate Lecturer, Region 10 Wales
Isobel Shelton, Associate Lecturer, Region 5 East Midlands
Lorraine Wild, Associate Lecturer, Region 2 South

DVD/audio production

Michael Burke, Executive Producer, 186 Media
Nick Gray, Producer, 186 Media
Rebecca Fleckney, Researcher, 186 Media
Angela Hind, Producer, Pier Productions

Preface

This book and its companion volume, *A Demanding World* (Barnett et al., 2006), are part of the Open University course *Living in a Globalised World*. Both books explore key characteristics of globalisation today.

That the world is now globalised seems an incontrovertible fact. There are thousands of books analysing what globalisation is and hundreds of thousands of newspaper articles reporting its various aspects. There are commissions on the state of the world economy, scares over the state of the planet's climate and campaigns against certain forms of globalisation; resources and commodities travel thousands of kilometres and television pictures can show almost any part of the world instantaneously. Why then two more books on the phenomenon?

Globalisation today has a paradoxical form. On the one hand, it seems to saturate our everyday lives in ways it never has before. Many ordinary, seemingly trivial aspects of people's lives now involve some kind of connection with places far away. The clothes we buy, the food we eat, the music we listen to and the television we watch (not to mention the set we use to watch it on), these are more and more likely to come from distant places. More people are migrating now than ever before in human history. Everyday life has gone global for many people around the world. But on the other hand, that greater involvement in some of the processes bringing distant parts of the world together does not always seem to lead to a greater understanding of globalisation. Indeed, globalisation can seem rather baffling. Moreover, it seems clear that even among those people who do claim some understanding of contemporary forms of globalisation there are debates and arguments about the implications of various globalising processes. Globalisation is at once deeply familiar and hotly contested.

These two books concentrate on this paradox of contemporary globalisation. In doing so, they examine both how global processes are now so pervasive and why globalisation is so debated.

Both books examine the four things that most commentators agree are fundamental to the way globalisation has become part of everyday life. They both examine the global economy, looking at patterns of trade, work and finance; they both look at various global political institutions and campaigns; they both examine the way new technologies are increasingly networking the world; and they both explore migration as a particularly important globalising process. In exploring these four processes, both books suggest that the geography of globalisation – the pattern of where things are and why – is crucial to understanding how it now works. Thinking geographically is a necessary part of understanding globalisation.

To understand some of the key debates about that rich and surprising global geography, *A Demanding World* and *A World in the Making* focus on three things that are especially important to globalisation today. The first of these aspects is the importance to globalisation not only of the connections that make the world globalised, but also of the *disconnections* that characterise the contemporary world. Not even global capital flows everywhere; there are borders and boundaries that limit flows and movements of all kinds. There are also places seemingly left out of the globalisation club; places with only a few connections to the internet, places with no resources to sell, places ignored by the big global players, places kept distant from elsewhere. Both books explore this very uneven geography of globalisation. Secondly, *A World in the Making* especially looks at the importance of the *non-human* to globalisation today (and indeed to globalisation in the distant past). One reason that globalisation is challenging is that its non-human, or natural, events and processes seem often to disrupt or to challenge human ways of going global. New viruses, climate change, volcanoes, earthquakes and tsunamis are a reminder that humans are not the only actors on the planet: planet earth itself is also active. Taking that action seriously is a necessary part of understanding contemporary globalisation. Finally, the two books examine how globalisation is made and remade in all sorts of different ways by the *different sorts of actions* of political organisations, institutions and campaigns. This is a particular theme of *A Demanding World*, which explores a range of demands to take responsibility for global issues.

Together, we think that these two books can help us to understand a great deal about the paradoxical nature of living in a globalised world. After reading one or both of them, we hope you will agree.

The Open University course *Living in a Globalised World* was produced as a collaborative effort by a large team of people. In relation to these two books in particular, some of them deserve special thanks. Professor Peter Jackson from Sheffield University was an extremely helpful External Assessor, providing us with very good advice at all stages of the course. Following preliminary work by Fiona Harris, Stephen Clift coordinated the editing and production of these volumes. Diane Mole was responsible for the lovely design, and Janis Gilbert and Howie Twiner produced the maps and other figures. Karen Bridge was a great Media Project Manager and Michele Marsh an excellent course team secretary. Finally, coordinating the authors and much more besides was our wonderful Course Manager Caitlin Harvey. Caitlin worked extremely hard with unfailing goodwill, extraordinary efficiency and sound advice, and without her the quality of these books, and the course, would have been greatly diminished.

Gillian Rose, Chair of Production
Chris Brook, Chair of Presentation

Barnett, C., Robinson, J. and Rose, G. (2006) *A Demanding World*, Milton Keynes, The Open University.

Introduction

Doreen Massey and Nigel Clark

The title of this book – *A World in the Making* – may seem both strange and obvious. Strange because we so often imagine ourselves as living in the world as though the world came to us ready-made. Obvious because of course the world is constantly being made and remade by a whole variety of forces. However, by choosing this title we are trying to get at a very particular argument which is the dominant theme of the book. In the companion volume to this book **Barnett et al. (2006)** explore the variety of ways in which living in a globalised world presents us with demands. From the possible feelings of responsibility towards those who, in sometimes dreadful conditions, produce the commodities (clothes, shoes, food, mobile phones and so forth) through which we live our lives, through the appeals that stare out at us from photographs in charity campaigns for peoples elsewhere in the world, to the dilemmas of when and whether to intervene to ameliorate horrors being perpetrated in other sovereign countries, we *live in* a world full of demands that make us ponder our responsibilities.

This volume builds on those insights and takes them a step further. Or perhaps, rather, it looks at them from a slightly different angle. Here, our argument is that as well as being faced with already existing demands, we are also, necessarily in an interdependent world, part and parcel of the *production* of the world in which those demands exist. **Allen (2006)** has written of the long chains of people and practices that connect the purchaser of a pair of trainers, say, to those in a factory on the other side of the planet who spend their lives producing them. As he pointed out, we can analyse this situation, and respond to it, in a number of ways. The angle that we want to stress in this volume is that in any decision about that purchase, and in the act of purchasing (or not), we are influencing the way the world is. We are truly involved in *making it*. Whether we like it or not, our actions (and our inactions) have effects. Sometimes in big ways, more often in small ones, we are implicated in the production of this world.

However, that is just one example, and it is focused on 'us' as individuals. Yet, of course, the making of the globalised world involves much more than this: it involves the actions of nation states, the strategies of multinational institutions, the campaigns and protests that would challenge this globalisation, the manoeuvrings of financial corporations, the migrations of peoples and cultures, and much more. We shall focus, in the course of this book, on some of the most significant of these agents who are responsible for the making of the globalised world. One of the reasons for working like this, for emphasising in this way the making of the world, is that it highlights the fact that, in many cases, the world could have been made *differently*, and – perhaps – could be made differently in the future. Indeed, this book pays special attention to a wide range of efforts actively and consciously to make the world differently. From attempts to create new nations in a recently decolonised world to campaigns for notions such as a global commons, we shall explore such initiatives here. On the other hand, through the very way we live our lives we are part of making the world in the first place, and therefore we need to think responsibly about that as well. The things in our shopping bags, to return to our initial example, say quite a lot about what *kind* of a globalised world we want to participate in making. This raises a further argument: that it is not just 'disasters' that warrant our attention but the normal everyday production of the problems and pleasures of this world.

Given this emphasis on the making and remaking of a globalised world, what kind of geographical thinking might best help us explore it? **Barnett et al. (2006)** introduced the geographical concepts of proximity and distance, and of presence and absence. In this volume, we shall explore another, complementary, pairing: that of territory and flow. Once again, we select these concepts both because they are vital elements of the debate about globalisation and because they are essential tools for analysing the geography of the globalised world.

One of the ways in which a 'globalised world' is frequently characterised is in terms of a planet in which all borders and boundaries have dissolved and in which flows of people, money, cultural influence, communications and so on flow freely. It is this feature of globalisation that can give rise to feelings of being bombarded from all directions. Certainly, it is in the context of this aspect of living in a globalised world that we can feel pressured by a host of demands **(Barnett et al., 2006)**. The physically very distant can suddenly seem close.

Yet, even as this image of a globalised world becomes ever more powerful, it is clear that the world does still have its borders and distances, that it is still in many ways divided up into territories; indeed, that new enclosures are being erected in the very midst of the production of powerful new flows. Nation states still exist; there are fierce debates over international migration; the rich may try to seal themselves off against the poverty outside; and aboriginal peoples may fight to protect their lands from invasion by multinational corporations. It may even be that the very process of opening up which is implied in so many stories (and realities) of globalisation itself encourages a need to build protective boundaries, to define areas of privacy – territories which can be controlled in some way or another.

On the one hand, there is the continuing fact and formation of territories; on the other hand, an increasing intensity and speed of flows. One of the central arguments of this book is that this constant interplay between territory and flow is a crucial aspect of a globalised world. Both territory and flow may occur in many forms. A 'flow' might be the instantaneous transmission of finance, or the massive physical movements of traded goods and commodities. Or it might be the movement of ocean currents; and, in the current period of climate change, plant and animal migrations are happening again as, for instance, some species find it increasingly difficult to survive in the islands of the UK, and yet others arrive. All these movements we refer to as flows.

'Territory', in the way we use it, might refer to something very obvious such as the nation state (so long our dominant way of organising the political world) or to a continent or island. It might also refer simply to a local place, to a campaigning group or to a spatially defined culture or ecology. While flows may range from hugely powerful currents, through hesitant journeys, to broad, slow movements, territories may be loose constellations, weavings together of people and things, or they may be fiercely bounded exclusivities. Some of the debates about different kinds of globalisation arise precisely from the differences between these forms and the need to take them seriously.

Moreover, as you can see from these examples, both the human and non-human are part of how we think about territories and flows. The objects, energies and processes that make up territories and flows very often have both human and non-human aspects, and this mix too can fuel debates about globalisation. This is an important theme of this book, and all chapters here discuss it in one way or another.

Thus, the interplay between the tendencies to flow and to territorialise is at the centre of the analyses in this book. As the chapters progress, we examine the concepts of territory and flow, show how they can be useful in an analysis of this world, and develop the complexities of their forms and of the relations between them. Understanding the world through these concepts enables us to raise, and in some measure address, some of the most difficult ethical and political issues with which the emerging world presents us.

It becomes evident that there is contest over the making of this globalised world. The financial institutions' view of the future is hotly contested by a global congeries of protest groups, arguing for a differently globalised world. The financiers themselves have changed their own views and proposals about financial organisation of the planet, and there is still dispute among them. There is debate, and fierce contest, over how to address issues that plainly affect and involve the whole planet. There are contesting visions: of a planet that belongs to us all without any dividing borders; and of a planet of territorially organised communities in which local people have their local rights. How far can we really tear down borders? What happens to the need to feel part of definable communities or places?

Furthermore, if we take seriously the notion of a world in the making, there is no way that 'we', as individuals or as members of collectivities, can evade these issues because we are inevitably part of this world and inevitably involved in producing it. We are thus in some measure 'responsible' for it. However, as is clear in the chapters that follow, this power to make the world is distributed unequally. The capacity of nation states, tectonic plates or international institutions such as the World Bank is far greater than that of the individual, 'ordinary' person. Nonetheless, we want to argue, careful analysis helps to escape a feeling of powerlessness. Thus, for instance, we are often led to believe that the 'big' global changes in the world are inevitable, that there is nothing we can do. Clearly, some things may be impossible – or extremely difficult – to change. Yet there is perhaps a need to bring some of these 'big' things down to earth, to see how they are made. This immediately makes them more accessible to influence and to change. We shall explore a range of efforts, proposals and campaigns to put such changes on the agenda.

Chapters 1 and 2 set out some of our basic arguments. As well as laying out the concepts of territory and flow (and exploring both of them a little), they immediately engage us with big 'global' processes. Chapter 1 straightaway sets the 'non-human' centre stage. When we speak of 'the ground beneath our feet' it is often to evoke a sense of stability: *terra firma* is the reassuring term, sometimes in contrast to the flows of human globalisation. We begin this book by engaging with the fact that the land is not in fact stable. In so many ways, from earthquakes, through climate change, to the slow movements of the continents, this is a dynamic planet upon which we live, and we need to take this seriously in our analyses. We make our territories in a world on the move. Chapter 2 forms a counterpart to this. Perhaps the things most often referred to in descriptions of the globalised world are money and finance. They seem to be the epitome of mobility and flow: transactions (it is so often said) can be made instantaneously around the world. Yet, as Chapter 2 argues, such flows could not happen without territorial bases from which to operate. Once again, then, there is a relationship between territory and flow, and the one is always accompanied by the other.

Chapters 3 and 4 consolidate and develop these arguments. In Chapter 3, we examine the movement of plants and explore how the human-induced transport of biological material has involved much work of territorialisation, cutting the plants and genetic material off from their surrounding ecologies in order to make them transportable. In Chapter 4, we turn to Antarctica – the earth's land area not submitted to nation-state control – and explore the often inadequate attempts to turn its shifting nature into a human territory.

In all of these chapters, we encounter contests and arguments over which architecture of territory and flow might be most appropriate: arguments for and against 'neo-liberal' market forces; arguments about who should have rights over genetic plant material – the peoples in the area where the plants have long been used or the multinational companies that have further developed the science of their use; and arguments about how the continent of Antarctica might be considered, and protected, as a place and a resource for all. In many of these battles, the forces raised on the different sides are of unequal power – their capacities to make things happen are unequal. There are confrontations between rich and poor countries, and between the interests of Western medicine and science and those of aboriginal groups in Peru.

Nevertheless, in these chapters the vantage point from which we address these issues is that of powerful forces – financial institutions and nation states, for instance. In the second half of the book, we shift perspective and examine some of the ways in which we are all, often in quite everyday ways, bound up in this production of territories and flows. Chapter 5 turns to the way in which, in this world of global connections, many people feel strong affection for particular local places – a desire for a local territory in the midst of global flows. Yet, as the chapter argues, these very 'local' places, while remaining special and particular, are themselves the product of long years of global connections. In a sense, Chapter 6 moves to the other side of this question: given the global movement of people, how are local identities established, at the same time as connections are retained, by internationally dispersed cultural groups? Throughout the book, we draw from our analyses some of the questions and dilemmas that such globalised geographies produce, but as the book nears its conclusion we take up more and more explicitly the question of the active political responsibility we may have, and the initiatives we may take, as producers – makers – of this globalised world. In Chapter 7, we examine explicit proposals and campaigns to rethink current territories and flows with the aim of making a more equal world: potential, and actual, geographies of solidarity. In the final chapter, we explore how the different arrangements of territory and flow, evident in fairly traded and ethically produced foodstuffs, have developed from a heightened sense of responsibility towards the other people, plants and animals that inhabit planet earth with us.

Our case studies range widely – from Antarctica to Ghanaian migration to the UK; from fair trade campaigns to financial institutions; and from nation states to an argument over a local wood. These topics have been chosen because of their intrinsic interest, because they are in themselves important or are representative of important issues, and because they are good settings for exploring and developing our arguments. The aim is for you to be able to wield these arguments yourself, in a whole range of other situations.

As well as presenting analyses of the recent past and of the present, this book is also forward looking. It asks us to engage with how we *should* be making the world. Moreover, it is, in the midst of all these challenges, positive. Positive partly in its recognition of the incredible variety of forces at play in the world and positive too in its argument that being rigorous about how we think about the world, and about the geographical thinking and themes that we bring to bear ('making', the 'non-human', 'territory' and 'flow'), can be truly enabling.

References

Allen, J. (2006) 'Claiming connections: a distant world of sweatshops?' in Barnett, C., Robinson, J. and Rose, G. (eds) *A Demanding World*, Milton Keynes, The Open University.

Barnett, C., Robinson, J. and Rose, G. (eds) (2006) *A Demanding World*, Milton Keynes, The Open University.

Chapter 1

Climate changes: island life in a volatile world

Nigel Clark

Contents

1   Introduction

A good globe can set you back quite a lot of money. Of course, I don't mean the little moulded plastic planets or the globes you can blow up as if the world were a beach ball, but the decent sized ones that sit solidly on turned wooden bases and quietly emanate authority from the corner of a room. Yet these days, it hardly seems worthwhile making such an investment. Countries appear to change their colour, their shape or their name with remarkable rapidity.

It has become a cliché to point out that globes and maps that date back to the middle of the last century and earlier featured vast swathes coloured in pink or red to signify lands that belonged to the British Empire. Not only has the British Empire broken up, but over recent decades we have also seen the dissolution of the Soviet Union into a number of new states. Other countries like Czechoslovakia, Yugoslavia and Ethiopia have split themselves into two or more pieces. Meanwhile, in the western Pacific, a cluster of islands that was once a British colony called the Gilbert and Ellice Islands has become two republics: the Gilbert group are now known as Kiribati, while the Ellice Islands are now Tuvalu.

How we divide the planet's surface up into recognisable units reveals ongoing changes: territorial reshufflings that may render a map or globe out of date before it has even left the production line. More importantly, such transformations are often contentious and painfully wrought at the 'ground level' where people live, frequently leaving some people unsettled or uncertain as to where they belong. But amid all this relentless activity, it can be tempting to think of the land masses themselves, the continents and the islands, as maintaining the same shape, even as their names, colours or subdivisions change.

While there may be some comfort in the idea that land endures while all else changes, it is a rather dubious assumption. For several decades it has been generally accepted in the earth sciences that continents 'drift', usually at the rate of inches or fractions of an inch each year. More recently, a growing body of evidence suggests that much more rapid physical changes in the surface of our planet are also beginning to take place. Since the 1980s, intensive research by climate scientists collaborating internationally has built up a picture of the earth's weather systems being transformed by human activities. These changes are often referred to, in a kind of shorthand, as 'global warming'.

The prospect of global climate change and what it might mean for the way we experience and imagine our planet is the theme of this chapter.

As we will see, it is not easy to predict the extent or severity of future changes in the world's climate, and it is just as difficult to anticipate how people, organisations and nation states will respond to these potentially changing conditions. Many climate scientists are now predicting that a generalised warming now under way will lead to gradually rising sea levels throughout this century. This would impact on coastlines around the world, but it would have particularly serious implications for small islands or atolls.

Within the span of a single lifetime, islands which now support dense and vibrant populations could become too prone to climatic extremes to remain habitable. Some low-lying coral islands might even disappear completely beneath the surface of the sea.

Figure 1.1   Boy with model outrigger canoe, Nukulaelae Atoll, Tuvalu

Activity 1.1

Turn now to Reading 1A by Mark Lynas (2003) entitled 'At the end of our weather', which you will find at the end of the chapter. Lynas, a journalist, felt moved by personal evidence of changing climate to seek out its impacts at 'ground level', and to give an impression of what it is like to live through these changes. While you are reading, you might want to pause and think what it would feel like to lose your whole country, never to be able to come back for a visit. Do you think you would try to stay even if weather events were potentially life-threatening? If you chose to evacuate your country, where would you go? What would you try to take with you? Would you want all your friends and family, or all your compatriots to go to the same place?

These are emotionally charged issues, and perhaps you are being asked to think about things which are so life-changing as to be almost unthinkable. However, these are also questions or dilemmas that some people, including the islanders of Tuvalu, have to live with in an everyday way. **Steve Pile (2006)** has written about disturbing events in the past that come back to haunt people in the present; the issue of climate change suggests that there are possible future events that can 'haunt' us here and now.

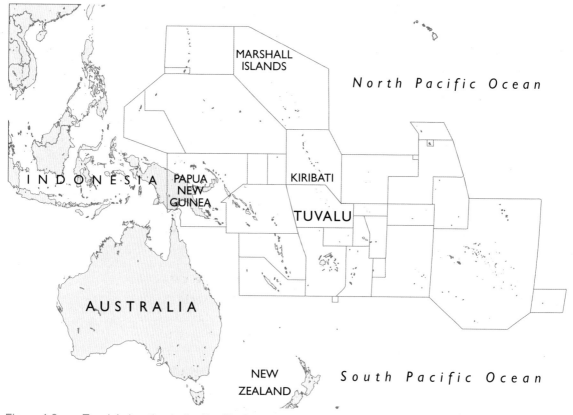

Figure 1.2   Tuvalu's location in the Pacific Ocean

In this way, the phenomenon of climate change, and the possibility of people displacement that it raises, impels us to think afresh about the ground beneath our feet, and the air and sea around us. It prompts us to question the permanence of what we may once have taken to be stable and enduring. The changes that are now being predicted are linked to patterns of energy use in the modern world. Accelerating industrial growth over the last two and a half centuries has relied predominantly on fossil fuels that release carbon into the atmosphere, which scientific evidence suggests is contributing to an enhanced greenhouse effect that is warming the planet as a whole.

Recognising that industrial processes act cumulatively on climate focuses attention firmly on human activity as a potent force acting on the physical world. Indeed, some social theorists have argued that human-induced climate change, along with other damaging consequences of industrial activity on the environment, has now eclipsed natural disasters as a source of popular concern and anxiety (Beck, 1992).

However, amid this growing acknowledgement of the severity of human-induced or 'anthropogenic' environmental issues, we should not forget that physical processes are highly variable, and sometimes extremely volatile, even without human input. Recent years have seen a number of sharp and shocking reminders of the forcefulness of the natural world, including earthquakes in Kobe, Japan (1997), Bam, Iran (2003) and the underwater quake off the island of Sumatra, Indonesia (2004) that triggered the devastating tsunami in the Indian Ocean.

Defining the enhanced greenhouse effect

The greenhouse effect is a natural part of the functioning of the earth. It involves certain atmospheric gases (termed 'greenhouse gases') absorbing solar energy which has previously passed through the atmosphere and been reradiated back from the earth's surface. This has the effect of keeping the planet many degrees warmer than would otherwise be expected from the amount of solar energy coming in. There is strong evidence that this natural greenhouse effect is now being enhanced as a result of human activity. Burning fossil fuels and other activities change the composition of gases in the earth's atmosphere – adding significantly more greenhouse gases like carbon dioxide – which results in an overall warming of the planet.

Events on the scale of the Indonesian earthquake and tsunami can also alter the contours of land and sea – even more rapidly than changes triggered by human activity. In the worst affected regions, whole towns and villages were destroyed and, even after the surges had receded, areas of coastline remained transformed. You may recall from news coverage that within days of the disaster in 2004, satellite photos taken before and after the event revealed sudden, dramatic changes, as can be seen in Figures 1.3a and 1.3b. Within a few weeks, images from satellites and other sources had been compiled to produce a new atlas of the region which provided topographic information of the transformations as well as documenting the immediate social impacts of the disaster.

Human activities – such as clearing away mangroves that once offered protection for coastlines – may have contributed to the extent of the destruction caused by the Indian Ocean tsunami. Nonetheless, the earthquake itself, and the waves it triggered, was a natural event caused by shifts in the earth's crust that remain beyond human influence.

This chapter starts by looking at the issue of human-induced change in global climate and its potential social impacts, but we will see that this

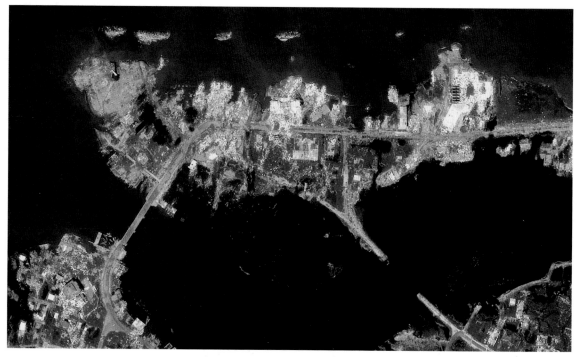

Figures 1.3a and 1.3b   Satellite images of the northern shore of Banda Aceh, Indonesia before and after the 2004 earthquake and tsunami

issue soon draws our attention to ongoing changes in the world that are not directly attributable to human action. Concern with the human making and remaking of the world inevitably draws us to consider those other processes and events that have shaped our planet – and will continue to shape it in the future.

As Lynas's (2003) account (see Reading 1A) of the predicament of Tuvalu makes clear, the climate change issue raises questions about which particular groups or sectors of humanity have had the most impact, and which groups are most likely to suffer the worst consequences. Section 2 of this chapter looks at the way that climate change as a global process implicates people who are literally oceans apart. It introduces the notion of 'territory' as a way of coming to a clearer understanding of what is under threat when we talk about serious changes in the world, and why people feel so strongly about threats to the places they live. Yet the very idea that one part of the globe can be affected by activities elsewhere on the planet also suggests that territories are connected in some way. This section also introduces the idea of 'flows' that move through and between territories, connecting them to the world beyond.

Thinking through territories and flows helps us to build up a sense of the different forces that come together to make and remake the world. In particular, it offers us a way of looking at both human and non-human forces, and how they work together. In Section 3, we will consider the long and rich story of human involvement in the making of islands, including the often awe-inspiring journeys that island settlers have undertaken to arrive at their new homelands far out in the ocean. Humans, however, are not alone in settling islands, and they are rarely, if ever, the first to arrive. Therefore, in this section we will also examine the other forms of life that make their way to islands, and their contribution to island territories. Section 4 continues the theme of the importance of non-human forces in the shaping of islands, this time looking beyond the movements of human beings and other forms of life to the shifts and changes that take place in the earth itself and in the sea and sky around us.

We delve beneath the issue of human-induced climate change, and its impact on low-lying islands like Tuvalu, in order to explore the long and profound entanglement of humans and non-human forces in the making of the world. Moreover, we begin to ponder what this entanglement might mean when addressing problems like climate change – urgent and far-reaching problems that call out for some response.

2　Island territories, ocean flows

The aftermath of the 2004 Indian Ocean tsunami saw an unprecedented aid effort to assist the affected regions. In the early days after the disaster, pledges of financial assistance from overseas governments were often outstripped by the generosity of their own populaces. This was a case when ordinary people around the world saw and were moved by the tragic circumstances of others far away **(Rose, 2006)**, and they responded with gifts of money and provisions, and even with offers of their own skills or labour.

There has yet to be a crisis of this magnitude that has been pinned to anthropogenic climate change, though warnings of large-scale catastrophes from scientists and activists now abound. In contrast to natural disasters, however, climate change raises the issue of a different sort of responsibility: an obligation to others that arises not simply out of an upwelling of sympathy, but out of a feeling of being implicated in the lives of island peoples and the predicament in which they find themselves.

Iris Marion Young (2003) has written of a kind of responsibility that comes about when we recognise that we are connected by our own actions to the suffering or injustice experienced by others who may live far away from us (see **Allen, 2006**). What concerns us in this section is the way in which these connections operate in a case where the actions in question transform the physical world on the global scale. To begin to grasp the issues of responsibility this raises, we must also grapple with these transformations. As this section will also argue, the concepts of territory and flow help us make sense of how the world changes, offering an understanding of events that might otherwise seem too vast, complex and chaotic to pass into the realms of political consideration.

2.1   Climate change in a globalised world

As you will recall from Reading 1A, the people of Tuvalu are now arguing that larger and more affluent nations should take responsibility for the climatic changes threatening their country. As Paani Laupepa from the Tuvalu environment ministry put it: 'We are on the front line ... through no fault of our own. The industrialised countries caused the problem, but we are suffering the consequences' (Lynas, 2003). Before we look more closely at this charge, and the scientific evidence that is being compiled to support it, it is important to appreciate how the problems faced by Tuvalu form part of a much larger issue that implicates other countries or regions in different ways.

Activity 1.2

I would like you to turn to Reading 1B by Molly Conisbee and Andrew Simms (2003) entitled 'Environmental refugees: the case for recognition', which you will find at the end of the chapter. The aim of this piece is to gain recognition for people displaced by what the authors claim is accelerating environmental degradation. It addresses the issue in a general sense, gathering evidence from around the world.

As you are reading, note how often the terms 'global' or 'international' or some variants of these words appear. What kind of relationships do you think the authors are attempting to establish between distant places? What kind of image of the world are the authors seeking to convey?

Many claims are made in Reading 1B. You may have come across similar pronouncements in news media reporting. There are quite a lot of 'ifs' and 'mights' in the reading, and you should be mindful that some of the arguments are hotly contested (as we will see later in Section 4.3), although the references to Oxford University analysts, world organisations and international panels of scientists are intended to lend them a certain authority.

At the heart of Conisbee's and Simms's argument (2003) is a sense that the planet is being transformed in its entirety by human activity. The term 'global', as it prefixes the issue of climate change, points to flows or interconnectivities that link people and places over vast distances. Like Paani Laupepa from the Tuvalu environment ministry in Reading 1A, Conisbee and Simms make a strong case for the argument that what some people do on one side of the world has serious implications for the lives of others on the other side of the world.

Human-induced climate change, then, is not simply a process that takes place in a globalised world. It also helps bring the question of what we mean by 'globalised world' into focus, adding a powerful new dimension to the idea of an increasingly interconnected planet. The issues revolving around climate change do more than simply enfold all of us into a single, unified world. The geographical imagination suggested by Readings 1A and 1B is one that draws connections across great distances, yet also makes important distinctions between the conditions of life of people in different parts of the world. The issue of climate change prompts us to take account of flows around the globe, but also impels us to think in new ways about the countries or territories where most people live, most of the time.

2.2   Divisions that matter: thinking through territories

Without losing our focus on the planet as a whole, it is time now to return to what Paani Laupepa from Tuvalu refers to as the 'front line' of climate change: those islands that are particularly vulnerable to rising sea level and associated climatic hazards (Lynas, 2003). It has often been said that low-lying coral islands like Tuvalu or Kiribas in the Pacific Ocean, or the Maldives in the Indian Ocean, are acting as a kind of early warning system for global climate change. Sea level is expected to rise with even a modest increase in global temperatures, both because of the contribution of melting glacial ice to the world's oceans and because water expands when its temperature rises.

As Conisbee and Simms (2003) remind us, the Intergovernmental Panel on Climate Change (IPCC) predicts a sea level rise over this century of somewhere between 9 and 88 cm. These figures seem at once strangely precise and wildly divergent, and it is not surprising that they provoke uncertainty and fear in the inhabitants of low-lying islands. Moreover, islanders and coastal dwellers in tropical regions face the prospect not only of gradually rising seas, but of an increase in the incidence and intensity of cyclones along with the temporary surges in sea level that accompany these storms. In Tuvalu, as we can see in Figure 1.4, high tides can also produce flooding.

Figure 1.4   Tuvalu: flooding during a very high tide

As we saw from Reading 1A, the island republic of Tuvalu has begun legal proceedings against some of the nation states it considers especially responsible for generating the hazards associated with anthropogenic climate change.

Activity 1.3

Now turn to Reading 1C (Reuters News Service, 2002a) entitled 'Tiny Tuvalu sues United States over rising sea level' and Reading 1D (Reuters News Service, 2002b) entitled 'Tuvalu seeks help in US global warming lawsuit', which you will find at the end of the chapter. Both of the news items in the readings emerged from the second Earth Summit, a gathering of representatives of countries from around the world which convened in Johannesburg, South Africa in 2002 to pick up on discussions about environmental issues in a worldwide context. What do these reports tell us about divisions or differences within the 'globalised world'? In the light of this information, and what you have already read about Tuvalu and its people, where do you think the loyalties or attachments of the Tuvaluans lie?

The idea of 'tiny Tuvalu' (Reuters News Service, 2002a) – officially the world's second smallest nation – taking on much larger countries like the USA has a kind of 'David and Goliath' feel to it. If the threat to Tuvalu has a clear global framing, the way in which the problem is being couched and responded to also seems to rely upon, if not to reinforce, a sense of separate countries or nation states. Indeed, there is a kind of 'us' and 'them' division which appears to be taking shape around the distinction between those who are likely to suffer the most from global climate change and those who have contributed the most to the problem. Statistics about energy consumption and contribution to carbon emissions add substance to this division.

Taken together, the four readings we have looked at suggest that the people of Tuvalu – or at least their spokespeople – tell a story which brings together a sense of the interconnectedness of global processes with a clear focus on the predicament of their own nation and other small island nations who are similarly at risk. It is interesting to note that Tuvalu only joined the United Nations (UN) in 1999, and did so in large part to draw attention to the islands' vulnerability to climate change. The expense of being a UN member was easily covered by Tuvalu selling its internet domain address extension – which happened to be '.tv' – the equivalent of the United Kingdom's '.uk', or Russia's '.ru'. In 1998, a Californian company, Idealab, agreed to pay the government of Tuvalu US$4 million each year for the next 20 years in return for selling on the .tv address code to media companies who want to signal their role in television (such as 4kids.tv, hollywood.tv and bollywood.tv).

The Kyoto Protocol mentioned in Readings 1A, 1C and 1D was an agreement of the majority of the world's nations to limit their carbon emissions, with the onus on the most developed or heavily industrialised economies. Though it was non-binding, the Kyoto Protocol nevertheless articulated a basic consensus that use of fossil fuels and other carbon-emitting activities were in the process of affecting global climate change. Negotiations were extremely complex, but at its simplest the Kyoto Protocol was based around the premise that countries or nation states should not persist in activities that are known to damage or threaten other countries.

Although global climate change raises new issues, the principle of nation states not impinging in harmful ways on the territories of other nation states is an old and familiar one (Batty and Gray, 1996). At the same time, it is often tensions or disagreements between nation states that bring the nation states' distinctiveness and defining characteristics into clearer focus. In the case of Tuvalu, which achieved independence from UK rule in 1978, the issue of climate change seems also to be giving the people an opportunity to speak of their attachment to their islands and to voice what it is they find important about the place in which they live. As Tuvalu Finance Minister Bikenibeu Paeniu said: 'we are not encouraging people to leave because of climate change. It's our land. It's where we live' (Reuters News Service, 2002b).

Consequently, in a paradoxical kind of way, the very threat to the territory of Tuvalu also seems to be helping define this territory, for the people who live there, and in the eyes of the wider world. But what exactly *is* under threat? Or to put it another way: what do we mean by 'territory'? In Section 1, I talked about changes on a globe or map and the possibility of seeing areas of land alter their shape or even disappear completely. This scenario conveys a sense of 'territory' that may well feel quite familiar: that is, territory as a particular area or parcel of land. Viewed in this way, we can think of the territory of Tuvalu as the nine coral atolls lying in the South Pacific, a combined land area of around 10 square miles (26 square kilometres), which is inhabited (in 2005) by some 11,600 people.

When we view territory as a specific area of land, the kind of outlines or borders that we can see depicted on a map take on a special importance, for they play a major role in defining the territory in question. By identifying a border on a map, we can usually tell quite quickly and easily what belongs within a particular territory (an area, country or region) and what doesn't. In other words, we can make a distinction between what is included and what is excluded: between an inside and an outside. But borders are not only important on maps. They also tend to play a big part in defining a territory at 'ground level', in the lived experience of those people who inhabit a particular piece of land. This border may be some recognisable physical feature, such as a river, mountain range or coastline. Or in other instances, especially in the case of a country or nation state, it might well be a human-made demarcation, such as a fence or wall.

A border, however, does more than simply *divide* a territory from the world around it. There is also an important sense in which it *connects* a territory with its surroundings, which is to say that it also functions as a zone of transition or a point of passage from one place to another (Figures 1.5 and 1.6). In this regard, passing through or crossing a border can be quite a momentous event, for it often marks a significant change in the conditions or circumstances under which people live. We can see this with particular clarity in the case of people who are desperate to cross from one country to another, those for whom a safe transit across a border can be a life-changing experience. But it is not only human beings whose lives may be transformed by passing through borders. As we will see in Section 3.2, crossing a border, such as the beach that separates land from ocean, can also mark an important transition for other, non-human, forms of life.

Figure 1.5   Border crossing at Tuvalu: carrying supplies across the beach

Figure 1.6   Border crossing from the USA to Mexico: queuing for customs

Borders, then, tend to play a practical and meaningful part in defining territories. But there are ways of defining territories other than through a consideration of boundaries or outlines. And there are ways of conceiving of, or experiencing, territory other than as a simple area of land. As accounts of the threat to Tuvalu seem to suggest, there is more at risk than changing outlines or diminished land area; something more is at stake than a certain area of land distributed among a certain number of people. Indeed, with the funds coming in from the sale of their internet domain address, the Tuvaluans could probably purchase some fairly substantial real estate elsewhere in the world.

What comes through in the voices of the people of Tuvalu is an attachment to their islands: the affirming of a whole way of life that is bound up with the place they live. And this points to a way of thinking about and experiencing territory not simply as a pocket of land, but more as a set of relationships. You might recall that in Reading 1A journalist Mark Lynas (2003) spoke of 'a world that seemed to be unravelling'. 'Unravelling' suggests that a whole weave of ties or connections is being undone, evoking a sense of territory as a kind of pattern or fabric in which many different things are bound together.

In this sense, we might still conceive of territory as a particular parcel of land along with the borders around it, but we should keep in mind that there is a lot more going on as well: an interweaving of land with all its inhabitants and their ways of life. Viewed in this more complex sense, territory is not so easy for maps to depict. While a map, a globe or a satellite photograph of a region might give us the broad outlines of territories, it is difficult for such static images to reveal relationships between different elements and the patterns they form. But together with land areas and borders, it is this tangle of relationships that holds a territory such as the islands of Tuvalu together, giving it coherence and a character or identity of its own. In this regard, we might think of the various problems associated with changing climate as tugging at the weave of island territories, their increasing severity raising the chance that the whole might undo or come apart. In the extreme case, the scenario that former Prime Minister Toaripi Lauti talks of in Reading 1A, the people of Tuvalu may shift elsewhere. More than a simple move to another land, this could be viewed as entailing an unravelling and re-weaving of relationships.

In this section we have used the concept of territory as a way to help make sense of what it is that climate change threatens; what it is that people rally together to defend against such threats. The territory we have focused on is a group of atolls in the midst of the Pacific, which can be viewed at once as discrete pockets of land bordered by ocean, and as a weave of different elements. Each of the subsequent chapters in this book will look at other examples of territory, on a range of different scales – some much larger than these islands, others very much smaller. And in each case, we will see that what defines a particular territory is not just its size or shape and the borders which surround it, but also the relationships among the various things or 'ingredients' that make it up.

But once we start to think about territories as having borders, which are points of passage as well as barriers, and once we begin to consider the different elements of which territories are comprised, it soon becomes apparent that there is little sense in looking at territories in isolation. What are also important are the things which come and go – the movements and connections that link territories with the world around them. You will recall that we came to consider the notion of islands as territories under threat through the issue of the interplay between connectedness – on a global scale – and what it felt like to be at the 'ground level' of climate change in a particular place. Just as it is helpful to have a sense of how territories have their own distinct identities, which can really matter to all those who live there, it is important to understand how connections or flows play a part in the lives of territories. Section 2.3 explores this notion of 'flow', and what it means for our understanding of island life.

2.3   Worlds in motion: the importance of flows

'The sea had welled up suddenly through thousands of tiny holes in this atoll's bedrock of coral.' Do you recall this passage in Lynas's (2003) account of his first days on Tuvalu in Reading 1A? For me, this gives an impression of the islands being quite literally porous, a solid ground that reveals itself, now and again, to be not so solid after all. Lynas offers this particularly striking example of the island's openness to the world around it as evidence of a growing vulnerability that results from global climate change. How else are islands open to the goings-on in the wider world? And just how novel are the openings or susceptibilities that climate change might bring to island territories?

Activity 1.4

Now take another quick look through Readings 1A–D at the end of this chapter. From what you have read in these excerpts, and in the chapter so far, what are the different ways that the islands of Tuvalu are open to or connected with the world beyond their shores? You may have to use your imagination a little and read between the lines. As you come up with ideas, it is worth pausing for a moment and considering what difference global climate change makes to these relations or connections. Are these new connections – or are they connections that have been in place for a long time?

In the readings, there seems to be a number of new connections or flows that are closely related to the climate change issue – especially the beginning of a new movement or migration of people, starting with the resettlement of some Tuvaluans in New Zealand. There is also the participation of representatives of Tuvalu in international institutions such as the UN, the International Court of Justice and the Earth Summit. In each case, climate change has been an important impetus to the Tuvaluans establishing or extending their connections with global communities.

There are other forms of interconnection that you may have picked up on, such as air travel which is related to climate change through its contribution to carbon dioxide emissions, and internet connections which bear less of a direct relation to climate change issues though they may play a part in communicating these issues. You may also have thought about the economic goods or products that enter Tuvalu or are exported to other countries – whether by air or sea. This serves as a reminder that the sea is not simply an element or force that threatens the islands, but also a medium of connectivity. In a simple, intuitive way, it is the sea that separates the islands of Tuvalu from other islands or land masses, forming an obvious border or edge in a territorial sense. Nevertheless, the sea is also a way of travelling to and from the islands, and in this sense it has long played a vital role in island life, as we will see in Section 3.

Furthermore, of course, climate itself is a matter of connections. Climate change, as we have seen, implicates Tuvalu in flows of air and water that may be in the process of transformation because of anthropogenic inputs. At the same time, it is important to keep in mind that weather or climatic systems must already have been operating 'globally' in order for these transformations to take place, a point we will be returning to in Section 4.

Connection!

Islands and other territories may have discernible boundaries, then, but a great many things pass into, out of, over or through these boundaries. Such flows implicate the lives of those in each territory with those living in other territories in many different ways. The flow of economic goods from one country or territory to another, for example, draws the people of these countries together. As **John Allen (2006)** argues, the everyday lives of those who live in affluent countries are entangled with the working lives of people in relatively poorer countries through such practices as shopping for clothes and other goods that have been manufactured in sweatshop conditions.

In a similar sense, current understandings of human-induced climate change point to entanglements between people in distant territories. Changing flows brought about by altering the composition of the earth's atmosphere connect distant places in a very physical way. Climate science makes the case that every single unit of non-renewable energy that is consumed, anywhere in the world, makes a small, cumulative addition to the planet's overall energy budget – therefore impacting on the global climatic system as a whole.

Hypothetically, the energy consumed by the people of any one particular territory has an effect on every person in every territory across the planet's surface, though in practice, the actual amount of this impact may be infinitesimal. This, as you may imagine, is a very complicated kind of entanglement indeed. It can be difficult enough to trace all the different transactions that bring a consumer of a manufactured item in one part of the world into contact with the person who produces the item in a faraway country. Yet the lines of connection or flow that link all of us together across the planet through our respective energy use are almost unthinkably complex.

For all that the precise lines of connection between our lives and the lives of distant others may be difficult to disentangle, global issues like climate change may be helping to transform the way we experience our world – contributing to new feelings of shared problems and common interests that span oceans and hemispheres. An understanding of how changing flows can threaten distant territories, gnawing at their boundaries and unravelling their fabric, can give a powerful emotional charge to such a sense of connection or entanglement. However, we have to be careful that the attention given to new and far-reaching flows – especially those flows that may endanger territories – does not leave us with the impression that these territories were once free of outside influence or disturbance.

Some of the flows we have looked at are certainly disturbing, but some of them are also sustaining and generative. Indeed, it is difficult to imagine any territory maintaining itself without such flows. Similarly, your own body, although it is discernibly individual and distinct from other people's bodies, remains utterly reliant on things passing into it, flowing through it and passing out of it. In this sense, it is more useful to conceive of flows as having an ongoing and dynamic relationship with territories. Just as there are many different forms and compositions that territories take, so too are there many different kinds of flow. While some of these flows may help territories to form and consolidate themselves, others may exert stress and pressure upon them.

Summary

- There is growing evidence that island territories are vulnerable to changes in climate triggered by the actions of people living in other parts of the world.
- One way of conceiving of a territory is as an area of land surrounded by a border. This border serves both to divide the territory from the world around it, and to connect it with this wider world.
- Another way of viewing territory is as a kind of pattern or weave composed of the relationships between different elements.
- Different kinds of flow move within and between territories, keeping them in contact and in ongoing interchange with the surrounding world.
- Territories and flows interact dynamically; flows can help to generate territories but can also destabilise them.

3 Settling islands

In Section 2, we saw that there are momentous new and recently transformed flows that are impacting on island territories. Some flows have important precedents, and others may not be quite as novel as they first appear. In this section, we look more closely at some of the flows that have helped make, remake and sometimes unmake islands.

This takes us away from the flows that have captured recent attention, such as movement of goods or human-induced changes in climate, drawing us into the longer-term process of the formation of island territories. Beginning with the journeys that have taken human explorers and colonists to oceanic islands, we move on to other acts of settlement that are no less wondrous and impressive.

3.1   Voyages of discovery and settlement

The people of Tuvalu, as we have seen from Readings A–D, are contemplating leaving their islands and shifting permanently to higher and drier ground elsewhere in the Pacific. Consequently, some islanders have already left for New Zealand. Migration, at least in this context, is a kind of flow which occurs as a response to a territory felt to be under threat or pressure. If some of the predictions presented by Conisbee and Simms (2003) in Reading 1B turn out to be accurate, the flow of migrants triggered by climate change and other forms of environmental degradation will dramatically increase over coming decades. Even without additional movements propelled by environmental causes, current rates of migration are already often referred to as 'floods' by people in receiving countries. Nevertheless, while there may be many new pathways and intensities of movement in the contemporary world, migration is far from being a novel form of flow.

Activity 1.5

While you have been reading the story of the threatened existence of the Tuvaluans, have you stopped to wonder how they came to be living on these islands in the first place?

1   How did the Tuvaluans come to be hundreds of kilometres from any other land, out in the wide open waters of the western Pacific?

2   Did the Tuvaluans' ancestors once discover these islands? And, if so, where did they come from?

Europeans often talk about having 'discovered' many oceanic islands during an era of maritime exploration between the sixteenth and nineteenth centuries, when voyagers like Ferdinand Magellan and James Cook and their crews sailed through the Pacific. However, this is rather misleading for, as anthropologist Greg Dening (1992) reminds us, by this time the Pacific had already been thoroughly explored. As he tells the story:

> There are more than 25,000 islands in the Pacific. Yet any one of them can be lost in an immense ocean that covers a third of the globe. Remarkably, in the central Pacific where a canoe or a ship could sail for months or for 5,000 miles and never make a landfall, every mountaintop that had pushed from the ocean bed, every coral reef that had grown above the ocean surface had been discovered before the European strangers had had the courage or the knowledge or the technology to discover the sea.
>
> (Dening, 1992, p.307)

Evidence suggests that the people who first populated the Pacific, whom anthropologists refer to as 'Austronesians', departed from eastern-most Asia and the islands off Southeast Asia. As geographer Patrick Nunn points out, leaving the mainland, or islands that are densely-packed and often visible one from another, and heading out into the open ocean where islands are hundreds or thousands of kilometres apart, would have presented an enormous challenge (Nunn, 2003). Moreover, as he reminds us, such voyages would have commenced in the context of a very different geographical imagination than the one many of us share today. As Nunn puts it: 'It is difficult today to imagine ourselves without our knowledge of the world. We know the geography of the earth's surface, we have only to flick open an atlas to know instantly the bounds of the Pacific Basin, but the first islanders did not' (Nunn, 2003, p.222).

It is now believed that Austronesian peoples were the first in human history to master long-distance ocean sailing, and that they began to colonise the islands of the western Pacific some 3000–4000 years ago. Those who later continued to journey eastwards into the Pacific settled the islands of Polynesia. Known today as 'Polynesians', these people continued their way eastwards across the Pacific as far as South America and southwards as far as New Zealand (Aotearoa). Other Austronesians headed westwards across the Indian Ocean, eventually settling in Madagascar, off the coast of Africa (see Figure 1.7).

For a long time, Western anthropologists and historians toyed with the idea that most islands were discovered and settled accidentally, by sailors swept away from familiar waters. However, the fact that enough men and women arrived on newly discovered islands to create viable populations, and that there is evidence that they usually arrived with a whole range of plants and animals which they relied upon for food

Figure 1.7   The Austronesian diaspora with estimated dates of colonisation

Source: based on Pyne, 1997, p.419 and Fischer, 2002, Ch. 1

and other needs, suggests a much more organised pattern of settlement (Hau'ofa, 1993, p.9).

Flying over the Pacific, I have looked out of the aeroplane window, trying to spot small islands. It seems like you can fly for hours without seeing even the tiniest speck of land, which makes you wonder how those early navigators ever found their islands or, having left, ever found them again. This is especially intriguing in the case of Tuvalu and other atolls which are, in the most part, no more than a few metres above sea level.

Those who have studied traditional Pacific navigation give accounts of seafarers gradually building up, over thousands of years, knowledge of swell patterns, wave refraction, currents, prevailing winds and the position of stars. Seafarers were also familiar with more ephemeral signs – phosphorescence, the colour or shape of clouds, the presence of certain fish or birds. By reading such signs, traditional navigators could precisely locate a speck of land in a vast ocean – a practice known in nautical terms as 'dead reckoning'. Moreover, they could still sail home in this way in cases where their vessels were storm-blown hundreds of kilometres off course (Lewis, 1994).

Marshall Islands stick 'charts', such as the one in Figure 1.8 (opposite), are used for teaching about wave refraction around islands. Unlike most modern Western charts or maps that attempt to give a one-to-one correspondence with the area they represent, the stick chart is not intended to be in proportion to actual oceans and islands, and it does not necessarily refer to any specific area. Instead, it depicts the processes or dynamics by which swells hitting an island are refracted back into the ocean. It is for learning purposes only and is not taken to sea. It is said that traditional Marshallese seafarers could lie in the bottom of their canoes and navigate using the feel of waves and the current on the hull. This suggests that they relied less on visual recognition and cues than do most modern Western mariners.

Figure 1.8   Stick chart from the Marshall Islands

Amid all the contemporary talk of accelerating long-distance migration, tourism and other flows of people around the world, it is easy to overlook how far and how frequently people travelled hundreds or even thousands of years ago. In the late eighteenth century, Captain Cook noted that Polynesian ocean-going canoes could sail far faster than his own ships, and he judged that they could 'with ease sail 40 Leagues [120 miles] a day or more' (cited in Lewis, 1994, p.70). More recent evidence supports Cook's estimates, pointing not only to long-distance journeys around the Indian Ocean and across the Pacific, but also to very frequent trips between neighbouring island groups.

Pacific scholar Epeli Hau'ofa speaks of Pacific islanders, prior to European contact, engaging in a constant movement of ideas, goods and people which linked distinct island groups or territories. As he explains: 'Fiji, Samoa, Tonga, Niue, Rotuma, Tokelau, Tuvalu, Fatuna and Uvea formed a large exchange community in which wealth and people with their skills and arts circulated endlessly' (Hau'ofa, 1993, p.9). After much of the Pacific was colonised by Europeans, colonial administrators tried to restrict inter-island voyaging in an attempt to pin down and firm up the boundaries of various island territories. Hau'ofa tells of an earlier time: 'the days when boundaries were not imaginary lines in the ocean, but rather points of entry that were constantly negotiated' (Hau'ofa, 1993, p.9).

Hau'ofa seems to be saying that islands, though they may be bounded in some respects, were certainly not closed or isolated. These were territories that were permeated by flows. Therefore, centuries and, in some cases, millennia before Europeans made their way across the world's oceans, Pacific navigators were already reworking sea and islands into a space in which human beings 'flowed'. Although it is unlikely that they would have been able to imagine the world to be a single place – in the way it is now possible to think of the globe in its entirety – Austronesian and Polynesian voyagers succeeded in forging connections that spanned more than half of the planet's surface. In fact, with hindsight, it has been argued that these seafaring peoples made greater leaps towards globalising the world than any others, before or since (Gould, 1992, p.109).

Looking at this long history of oceanic journeying helps to give a sense of the way human beings have been generating new flows – sometimes over very long distances – for thousands of years. These flows have been vital in establishing new territories by opening up lands for settlement. Nonetheless, it is important to see that the settling of new islands has not been achieved by humans alone. As was suggested above, Polynesian settlers travelled with a 'portmanteau' of useful animals and plants. Along with seedlings of the plants they needed for food and clothing, island colonists across much of the Pacific also introduced their traditional 'feasting' animals – pigs, dogs and chickens – to their new homes (Dening, 1992, pp.307–8). In the case of Tuvalu, such staple foodstuffs as breadfruit, taro and banana would probably have been brought to the islands on board the canoes of inter-island voyagers.

It is worth considering more closely the dynamic relationship between territories and flows in the case of oceanic islands. We have seen in Section 2.2 how the concept of territory helps us to conceive of islands as a weave of many different strands. Like other territories, islands are inconceivable without the input and throughput of flows and, as with the notion of territory, one of the advantages of thinking through the concept of flow is that it can be inclusive of both human and non-human elements. Thus, when we consider the ways in which territory and flow are interrelated, it is possible to address the human and the non-human together, and to recognise that they often share similar dynamics.

Considering the interaction of territory and flow encourages a view of islands as having been made, rather than simply discovered or awaiting discovery. This making is ongoing: islands remain open to the possibility of being unmade or remade. However bounteous and balmy tropical islands may sometimes appear, we should not forget that making islands is difficult and often dangerous work. Every new arrival to an island – either human or non-human – has to find some way of weaving itself into the existing fabric of island life if it is to make itself at home. On smaller islands especially, newcomers may struggle to find enough of the things they need to sustain them, while the existing pattern of island life may be deeply disturbed by even a few impetuous new arrivals. In many cases, not only have new groups of human settlers caused much damage to the islands on which they have settled, but so too have the rats, pigs, cats and other predatory species that have accompanied such humans on their oceanic voyaging (Quammen, 1996).

Yet is it enough to think of human beings, working together with their companion species, as the producers of viable island territories? Human colonists did not settle barren rocks or bare coral in the middle of the ocean. They, and the useful species they brought with them, could never have settled themselves were the islands they found not already a rich weave of living and non-living things. If the story of how the earliest oceanic voyagers established new flows between distant lands is an awe-inspiring one, no less epic are the achievements of all the other life forms which had already made themselves at home on even the most isolated oceanic islands.

3.2   Migrations of life

As biologist and pioneer environmentalist Rachel Carson once wrote: 'the stocking of the islands has been accomplished by the strangest migration in earth's history – a migration that began long before man appeared on earth and is still continuing' (Carson, 1953, p.66). Austronesian voyagers may have been the first people to venture far into open water, but many other species, as Carson suggests, have also found ways of negotiating passages across the ocean. Arriving at pockets of land thousands of kilometres out in the Pacific, the first human voyagers encountered plants, insects, crustaceans, birds and sometimes even reptiles and mammals.

Activity 1.6

In the same way that Activity 1.5 asked you to ponder how the people of Tuvalu came to inhabit their islands, now give some thought to how other forms of life may have reached oceanic islands before they were able to hitch lifts on human vessels. It may take a little imagination, and an ability to take low odds and sheer fluke into account, but see if you can come up with some ideas.

This is indeed a challenging problem, and biologists, including Charles Darwin, have spent a great deal of time trying to answer it. Back in the mid nineteenth century, when Darwin was still working on his theory of evolution, biologists, or 'natural historians' as they were usually called, often relied on theories of land bridges to explain how different organisms found their way to islands. At this time it was already widely accepted that sea level had varied considerably over long periods of time, so that present-day islands may not always have been encircled by sea. As Darwin wrote in *The Origin of Species*, 'authors have thus hypothetically bridged over every ocean, and have united every island to some mainland' (Darwin, 1996, pp.288–9, first published 1859). While agreeing that these submerged connections might explain the populating of some islands, particularly those closer to the mainland, Darwin was dubious about their extension to oceanic islands – in part, because he was well aware that many of these islands were volcanic in origin, rather than being detached outcrops of once larger continents.

This left Darwin speculating over, and experimenting with, the ways that various forms of life might have made it across oceans. He proposed that seabirds must have played a major part in the dissemination of plant life by unintentionally dispersing seeds. Following an intuition along this line, Darwin once plucked a ball of mud from the plumage of a seabird, and extracted from it enough seeds to grow 82 separate plants from five different species (Carson, 1953). He performed similar experiments with seeds that had passed through the digestive system of birds, and also gathered evidence that nuts, fruit and other seed-bearing propagules could endure lengthy immersion in sea water and still germinate successfully (Darwin, 1996, pp.290–3, first published 1859). Later researchers have gone on to identify lightweight seeds equipped with feather- or parachute-like appendages that enable them to ascend high into the sky and to be wind blown across vast distances, as Rachael Carson (1953) recounts.

While sea-going birds and ocean and air currents could explain the dispersal of plant life, many members of the animal kingdom have posed thornier problems. The presence of land-based and frequently flightless birds on oceanic islands – such as the ill-fated dodo of Mauritius – was especially baffling. That is, until Darwin's theory of long-term evolutionary change offered a way of explaining how birds that were once capable of long-distance flight had subsequently adapted physically to a more terrestrial life. While some insects have likewise arrived with their own wing power, others have evolved ways of hitching lifts with seabirds or drifting on air currents, such as the numerous species of spider known to float or 'balloon' across the sea on their own silken filaments (see Figure 1.9) (Winchester, 2004; Carson, 1953).

In the case of many land-based life forms, which could not conceivably have relied on wings, fins or floating ability, it was Darwin's contemporary, Alfred Wallace, who offered evidence from the field of some intriguing modes of maritime voyaging. Among the islands between the Pacific and Indian Oceans, Wallace observed large clumps of drifting vegetation, and speculated that all sorts of organisms – including mammals and reptiles – could raft across hundreds of kilometres of open sea in this way, eventually colonising new islands. However, he also recognised that this was an incredibly chancy affair, especially considering that many species rely on sexual reproduction, and that it would require a pair of organisms to complete the journey (Quammen, 1996, p.145). Subsequent researchers have lent support to Wallace's speculations. It is now widely acknowledged that not only uprooted trees and matted vegetation but also volcanic rock, such as the eminently buoyant pumice, operate as a 'sea going transport system' for the propagation of island life (Barnes, 2002, p.808).

Figure 1.9   *Nephila maculata*: a 'ballooning' spider

Many of the ocean-crossing or island-hopping journeys that have brought new species to islands must have been so rare that their contribution to island life only makes sense if great reaches of geological time are taken into account. Being so discontinuous and fitful, it may be stretching the use of the concept to refer to all such forms of mobility as 'flows'. What is remarkable about these dispersals of non-human life is their continuity with some of the different modes or means of human migration. Polynesian seafarers, you may recall, found their way to new islands by taking advantage of winds and ocean

Defining colonisation

Colonisation refers to the process by which organisms become established in an area where they were not previously found. It is a normal and vital part of the changing distribution of life across the planet. In this sense of the word, there have been many times when human beings, like any other species, have established themselves in areas where there were previously no people. In cases where human colonisation involves the establishment of a new group of people at the expense of people previously inhabiting an area, colonisation takes on other, political meanings, not usually associated with colonisation as a biological process **(Barnett, 2006)**.

currents, as well as taking pointers from seabirds and ocean-going life forms. These are much the same physical or elemental forces that other species have relied upon to reach new islands, albeit in a more haphazard fashion. Consequently, we might also refer to the prevailing winds and ocean currents, as well as the more regular movements of living things, as forms of 'flow' – flows which can be tapped into by opportunistic travellers, both human and non-human.

Islands have been shaped and woven into territories through a combination of flows of very different kinds. Without the many other organisms that have made it over the ocean, crossed the beach and performed the difficult task of weaving themselves into a workable web of life, new human arrivals could not have made a home of these islands.

Summary

- Early seafarers developed the skills to take advantage of flows of wind and sea in order to colonise oceanic islands, as well as creating their own flows between islands.
- Other forms of life have also taken advantage of flows of wind and sea in order to cross the sea and colonise oceanic islands.
- Every new arrival – whether human or non-human – that crosses the ocean must weave itself into the existing territory if it is to become established on an island.
- Human and non-human beings often share similar dynamics in the utilisation of flows to find and shape territories.

4   Volatile worlds

We have seen that human-induced climate change poses a challenge for people who live on islands. Such changing patterns and extremes of climate also put pressure on the other living things that are part of the make-up of island territories. However, long before human beings became aware that they could transform the flows that constitute climate, they and other species were already taking advantage of these same flows to help create the very territories that are now under threat. But have these flows themselves changed over time, even without human input?

As mentioned in Section 3.2, it has been known at least since Darwin's day that sea levels have changed dramatically over time. This raises some interesting questions about contemporary changes in climate, and how we respond to their effects. In this section, we explore some of the ways in which the earth itself shifts, including the flows we call 'weather' or 'climate', and the very ground beneath our feet. This takes us into the realm of momentous changes that occur even without human impact or influence, which in turn raises some thorny questions for the issue of responsibility.

4.1   When climate changes

As you may recall from Section 3.1, anthropologists suggest that the early settlers of the Pacific probably departed from eastern Asia, perhaps via the islands off Southeast Asia. From here, they set out into the world's largest reach of open water, with little way of knowing what they might find.

Activity 1.7

In Activity 1.5, the question was posed of how the Tuvaluans came to be on their islands in the first place. You may now have some idea of how they got there, but we have not really considered the question of why. Why do you think the distant ancestors of the people who eventually arrived in Tuvalu (most likely after hundreds of years of island-hopping) left their original homelands?

Hau'ofa (1993) and other scholars familiar with the traditions of Pacific seafaring present a good case that sheer adventurousness has played a large part in Pacific voyaging. Yet this claim refers to people who have had thousands of years of experience in deep-water sailing and navigation. It may not be so useful in accounting for those first forays into the ocean, away from the sight of land.

Perhaps some pressure or stress helped to push people seawards – possibly a shortage of land or other resources. Something along these lines has been suggested by Nunn (2003), and his explanation turns out to have rather a surprising relevance to contemporary islanders threatened by the effects of climate change. Nunn proposes that it might have been the stress brought on by changing climate that first propelled people out into the 'blue water' of the Pacific.

irony
originally settled the islands due to climate change now forced them to abandon them due to climate change

It is, of course, very difficult to piece together the motivations of people who lived thousands of years ago, and so speculation is called for. Nevertheless, based on a combination of evidence from archaeology and climatology, Nunn (2003) propounds that rising sea levels caused by a cycle of long-term climatic warming may have been a major push factor.

In the aftermath of the last ice age (about 10,000 years ago), the receding and melting of glaciers would have led to rising sea levels all around the world, with serious repercussions for people who had settled into agricultural life on coastal lowlands. One likely area of displacement, a region where it is known that there were early farmers, was the coasts of East Asia, especially on the rich alluvial plains around the mouths of large rivers like the Huanghe and Yangtze in present-day China. Some of these people, Nunn suggests, may have headed out into the ocean: 'In this scenario the first true Pacific Islanders were "environmental refugees" rather than the bold, curious adventurers they are sometimes portrayed as having been' (Nunn, 2003, p.220).

However, it is unlikely that everybody left the coasts and set out into the oceans, so we might amend Nunn's view and say that they may have been bold and adventurous as well as being under pressure! If we keep in mind, as Nunn encourages us to do, that those setting out into the Pacific had no way of knowing what the world into which they were heading was like, then it is conceivable that those people who ventured out into the open ocean may have been hoping to find places where the sea was not rising (Nunn, 2003, p.22).

Another way to express this would be to say that as a certain territory came under pressure, or began to destabilise or come undone, some people began an outward flow that would eventually lead them into making new territories. As Lynas (2003) observed in Reading 1A, under current conditions of climatic change the world 'seemed to be unravelling'. One implication of Nunn's (2003) view is that the world may have also felt like it was 'unravelling' in the past, perhaps many times before. Nunn's argument makes a strong claim for the ongoing impact of climatic change on the peoples of the Pacific. For the people of Tuvalu, and many other low-lying islands, climate change indeed appears to have been decisive in the past. As Nunn explains, it was only after a colder period 2000 or 3000 years ago, with resultant falls in sea level, that the land that became Tuvalu surfaced from the ocean, enabling the accumulation of sand and gravel, and coral growth that helped make the islands.

Subsequently, from around AD 750 to 1250, the Pacific experienced a phase of gradual warming known to climate change scientists as the 'Medieval warm period' (Nunn, 2003, p.223). As temperatures rose, so too did sea level. Rising sea levels would have brought salt into the fresh water beneath the ground of many islands, as it is doing at present, while declining rainfall would have increased aridity. Although such conditions would have impacted harshly on island life, there may have been some compensation as clear skies and decreased storminess seem to have encouraged long-distance voyaging – increasing inter-island contact and leading to the discovery and settlement of new islands.

Around AD 1300, this warming came to a close and a period of rapid cooling followed. In Europe, this was known as the 'Little Ice Age'. Global cooling meant more water locked up in ice as well as a general lowering of sea water temperatures worldwide, with the result that sea level may have fallen by as much as 1.1 m between the thirteenth and sixteenth centuries. There are paintings and prints from this period of English history showing people ice-skating or walking on a frozen River Thames. While this spell of coldness may have caused considerable hardship in Europe and other temperate regions, global cooling had rather different implications for the island peoples of the Pacific. Nunn (2003) describes the likely effects of what he calls the 'AD 1300 Event':

> Almost all Pacific Islanders at the time lived along island coasts and, although they may have had inland food gardens, they would also have depended on crops (including coconuts) growing on coastal lowland areas. As sea level fell, so water tables fell, and many such crops would have grown and yielded less well. More importantly, these people would have been accustomed to acquiring food from nearshore coral reefs but when the sea level fell the most productive parts of these reefs would have been exposed above sea level and would have died. Likewise these people would have routinely exploited lagoonal resources for sustenance or trade, but when the sea level fell and exposed the surfaces of the nearshore reefs, this would have inhibited lagoonal water circulation resulting in turbidity and sluggishness, which in turn would have caused a deterioration in the health of lagoon ecosystems and a decline in their organic productivity.

The cooling and the increased storminess during the AD 1300 Event would have exacerbated many of the effects described above, largely through increasing stress on various food-producing ecosystems. It is thought that within 100 years of the AD 1300

Event, the food resources readily available to coastal dwellers in the reef-fringed Pacific Islands fell by around 80 per cent.

(Nunn, 2003, pp.223–4)

It is difficult to piece together all the factors involved, but such changes are likely to have brought great stress and loss of life: what we might describe as a serious undoing and remaking of many Pacific island territories. Moreover, in the case of very low-lying islands like Tuvalu there was no option, as there was on larger islands, of moving inland to exploit new resources. One redeeming factor is that falling sea levels would have brought new islands and atolls to the surface, some of which were then settled (Nunn, 2003, p.224). Such islands, however, would have been poor in resources, having not had time to develop a rich web of living organisms.

Nunn's (2003) research reminds us that climate fluctuates and varies, even without human impact. More than this, the evidence he presents makes the point that climate changes not just over millions or thousands of years, but sometimes over timescales short enough to be registered in human lifetimes or in memories passed between generations. While changing flows of air and water might currently threaten island territories like Tuvalu, we need also to consider that earlier changes have not only disrupted island life before, but may have played a pivotal role in initiating the exploration of oceans and settlement of islands. Changing climate contributes not only to the unmaking of islands, but also to their making.

We have seen that there were very different, but nonetheless parallel, experiences of cooling in the AD 1300 Event in northern temperate countries like Britain and on the tropical islands of the Pacific. It is worth considering what the implications of this might be for the way we imagine our world. In both places, at the same time, climate change exerted considerable stress. Yet, from a human perspective, these far apart territories did not share a common world. It was only towards the end of the cold phase that the first European explorers ventured into the Pacific Ocean, and it was not until several centuries later that contact between Europeans and Pacific islanders became ongoing and sustained. Therefore, in the imaginary geographies of the era – of both Europeans and islanders – it was not yet possible to experience climate change as a fully global phenomenon.

Nonetheless, as we can see through the lens of a contemporary world view, climate change in the AD 1300 Event and all other major fluctuations in climate are fully global phenomena. Climate in temperate Europe and climate in the tropical Pacific was as connected and mutually implicated then as it is now, as it has been for the estimated 4.5-billion-year existence of our planet. Thus, knowledge of human-induced climate change may be contributing to a new experience of entanglement between faraway people or places, but in another sense – a purely physical sense – our planet has always already been fully globalised.

An understanding of the globalised climatic flows that impact on oceanic islands adds further weight to the idea that the making of territories is a much more than human process and, indeed, a much more than biological or organic process. This awareness of forces and energies that are literally larger than life becomes even more pronounced when we turn to the physical processes that bring islands into existence.

4.2   Shifting ground

In Section 3 and in Section 4 so far, we have begun with the questions of how and why humans found their way to oceanic islands, and how other living things have come to make themselves at home on these same islands. The question we have yet to consider, the one that in a way underpins these other questions, is how there came to be isolated tracts of land in the middle of a vast ocean in the first place. To answer this, we need to turn to the insights of the earth sciences.

There are hints that have surfaced in previous sections of the chapter about the formation of islands. As you may recall from Section 4.1, falling sea levels facilitated the accumulation of sand and gravel, and the coral growth that helped form the islands that are today's Tuvalu. However, in order for these processes to occur, there must already be a significant protrusion from the seabed, and it is the formation of such irregularities that directs our attention to some of the most powerful forces that have shaped, and continue to shape, our planet.

As most earth scientists now agree, it is the movement of the vast rigid plates that make up the earth's crust – the process of plate tectonics – that is behind the formation of the major peaks and ranges that rise up from the surface of the planet. The location of these plates, and their direction of movement, can be seen in Figure 1.10 (overleaf).

Defining earth science

Earth science (also known as 'geoscience') is an all-embracing term for the sciences related to the study of the origin, structure and physical phenomena of the planet earth. It includes the study of rocks, oceans and fresh water, ice and the atmosphere, as well as the dynamics that connect these parts of the planet together.

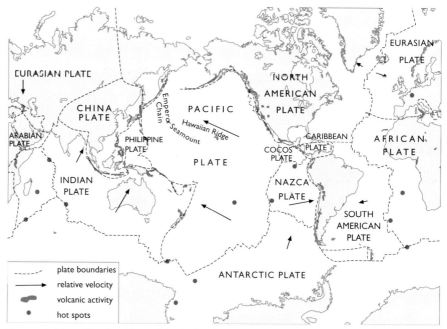

Figure 1.10   The location of tectonic plates, showing direction of plate movement and sites of volcanic activity

Source: Colling et al., 1997, p.113

The molten rock (or magma) that creates these tectonic plates wells up from beneath the earth's crust along submarine ridges on the seabed. In turn, this creation of new crust pushes the existing plates sideways, where they collide with other plates. When plates converge in this way, one of them will be forced downwards, deep below the earth surface, in a process of plate destruction that balances out plate creation. The immense force of one plate being driven under the other melts the crust into magma. When this occurs on continental land masses, this magma tends to erupt into volcanic mountain ranges; when it occurs under the sea, the resulting eruptions tend to give rise to an arc of volcanoes which forms the basis of oceanic islands such as those found in the western Pacific (Colling et al., 1997, pp.114–15). These processes are depicted in Figure 1.11 (opposite).

In the warmer reaches of the oceans, some of the work that brings the peak or 'cone' created by volcanic activity to the surface can be carried out by life itself. Coral, attracted to a submerged volcano, lives out its life just beneath sea level. The skeletons of coral polyps build up into solid structures of limestone over many generations, which may then be pushed above the waves by further tectonic activity to form an island or atoll.

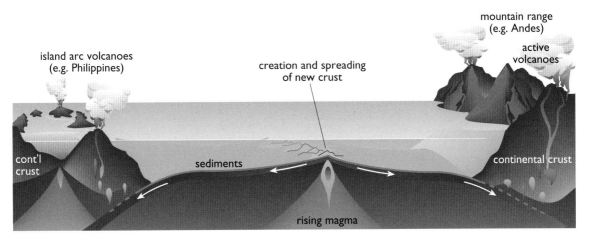

Figure 1.11   The action of plate tectonics, showing the formation of volcanic island arcs at the meeting point of plates

Source: Colling et al., 1997, p.115

Once a cone rises above the sea's surface, it begins to attract wandering life forms, as we saw in Section 3.2. Yet the same processes that produce the ground on which organisms can gain a foothold can also extinguish this life, reverting a verdant island to barrenness with a later coating of ash and lava, or annihilating the island altogether in a violent outburst or subsidence (Carson, 1953; Winchester, 2004).

The Indian Ocean tsunami of December 2004 was a reminder of the immense force of the ongoing process of plate tectonics. The waves were generated by an earthquake just north of the island of Sumatra, at a point along the juncture where the Indian Plate is being driven under at a rate of around 2.5 cm or so a year as a result of its convergence with the China Plate (often included as part of the larger Eurasian Plate). While a string of active volcanoes in the region usually provides a release for the energy generated by this ongoing collision, geologists believe that a sticking point in the convergence zone led to a gradual build-up of pressure. This in turn caused a 965-km-long section of plate to subside suddenly, displacing vast amounts of water and producing the massive swells that swept across the Indian Ocean with such devastating results.

Unlike the flows and fluctuations in global climate, which we now understand to be at least partially influenced by human activity, the geological processes that give rise to islands and other major protrusions on the earth's surface remain largely impervious to all the exertions of our species. Along with upwelling of magma, the shifting and shuddering of tectonic plates are evidence that even the ground beneath our feet is in flux. Furthermore, just as human migrations and excursions, the mobility of other living things, and the currents of air and water each constitute different kinds of flow, we might also conceive of these ongoing movements of the earth's crust as a particular kind of flow. Sometimes this flow is gradual, so slow as to be imperceptible, but at other times, as I intimated in Section 1, it manifests itself cataclysmically, in ways that can render our maps obsolete in minutes or seconds.

It may be that for most of us it is only at these occasional or exceptional moments of upheaval that the flow of the ground on which we construct our territories really makes itself felt. However, no less than the flows and circulations that comprise the earth's climate, the flux of plate tectonics is a fully global process in which different parts of the earth's crust work together on the planetary scale. An understanding of this geological volatility of the earth brings another dimension to the sense of territories as constantly in the making, which we have been exploring in various ways throughout this chapter. In a particularly powerful way, this volatility points to the contingency of any territory, and to the possibility for unmaking that is inseparable from the potential of making and remaking. There may be no better illustration of these contingencies than oceanic islands, which are forged from some of our planet's most convulsive processes, and brought to life by some of the most risky and opportunistic migrations ever undertaken.

What does this mean for the plight of islanders like the people of Tuvalu who find themselves in the front line of potentially momentous transformations of global flow? In the following section, we return to the question of human-induced climate change in relation to some of the other active processes and forces we have been examining.

4.3   Dilemmas of climate change

In Section 4.1, we looked at claims that climatic change thousands of years ago triggered the movement of people into the ocean, eventually leading to the settling of islands like Tuvalu. We have also seen that these islands only rose out of the ocean because of dynamic geological processes coupled with dramatic changes in climate and sea level.

Activity 1.8

Take a moment to consider how an understanding of the formation of oceanic islands like Tuvalu makes you feel about the current predicament of the Tuvaluans. Has it changed the way you think about human-induced global climate change and the responses or responsibilities this might entail?

The people of Tuvalu claim that carbon emissions are changing global climate. In particular, they point to the unwillingness of nation states like the USA and Australia to support the Kyoto Protocol, which seeks to reduce these emissions. The idea that the earth's natural greenhouse effect is being enhanced by a build-up in carbon and other greenhouse gases because of non-renewable energy use is fully supported by many environmental campaigners around the world, such as Molly Conisbee and Andrew Simms, the authors of *Environmental Refugees* (2003; see Reading 1B). This notion is also supported by the huge international consortium of climate scientists that comprises the IPCC. Similarly, for Nunn (2003), and many other geographers who have made a study of oceanic islands, the inherent changeability and precariousness of island life is reason not to discount human-induced climate change, but to take it very seriously indeed.

Nonetheless, perhaps unsurprisingly, there are others who see this differently. Some commentators have used the idea of the constant motion of the earth's crust to counter the argument that greenhouse gas emissions are having a significant impact on sea levels. In this regard, US climate negotiator Harlan Watson has noted the particular instability of the Pacific: 'The South Pacific is very volcanically unstable on the sea floor ... so you have some natural subsidence occurring anyway. Islands are appearing and disappearing all the time' (cited in Kriner, 2002, p.2). Other voices in the climate change debate have argued that because global climate fluctuates constantly, current warming is nothing out of the ordinary. Danish statistician Bjorn Lomborg, for example, has suggested that as the planet is still coming out of the Little Ice Age, a gradual warming and attendant rise of sea level is to be expected (Lomborg, 2001, p.263). Similarly, Bill Mitchell of the Australian Tidal Facility claims that there is little evidence in the Pacific of sea level changing more rapidly than that which would be expected from gradual natural warming (Field, 2002).

It would be an oversimplification, however, to suggest that the climate change debate neatly divides itself into two opposing factions. Researchers and campaigners of all persuasions have taken the possibility of human-induced changes into account as well as the many physical variations that are not reducible to human activity, and this leaves room for very different weightings to be applied to the many variables involved.

Thinking through territories and flows does not offer any easy answers to, or any direct route out of, the dilemmas posed by the prospect of a human contribution to global environmental change. Yet it can offer a versatile way to approach any such issue that brings together human and non-human forces. Furthermore, with the kind of issues that present themselves in the contemporary world, the need to address human and non-human processes together seems to be more the rule than the exception.

Summary

- There is evidence that natural fluctuations of climate may have induced the earliest human settlers of oceanic islands to head out into the ocean, and may have put later island territories under severe stress.
- Islands are both created and destroyed by shifts and flows of the earth's crust, forces that are largely beyond human influence.
- The difficulty of disentangling human impacts on global climate from natural fluctuations means that working out the human contribution to these environmental changes is a complex and contested process.
- While territories may appear stable or fixed, our planet is constantly in the making, all the way down to the earth's crust and the molten rock beneath it.

5   Conclusion

The issue of climate change draws attention to the power of human activity to transform the planet in its entirety, and it is brought into sharp focus by the predicament of low-lying islands like Tuvalu. As we have seen in this chapter, the issue of rising sea level and other potential impacts of changing global climate also point to the transformations in the physical world that occur even without human influence. Oceanic islands provide a particularly cogent reminder that the living things with which we share our world, the patterns of the weather, and even the earth beneath our feet, shift and change of their own accord. Faced with a world in which there is instability and movement all around, and deep beneath our feet, we might easily lose our bearings completely. Here, the concepts of territory and flow and a sense of their dynamic interplay are useful, for they help us to 'get a fix' on a world which is always in the making.

Life, weather and geological processes are all dynamic forces that play a part in the forming of islands, and continue to contribute to their ongoing transformation. Similar dynamics are also at work on larger land masses, but because oceanic islands are encircled by sea and often far from other lands, they are especially useful for drawing out the different forces and elements that work together, or sometimes against each other, in the making of the world.

Therefore, when we come to think about the ways in which human activities are transforming islands and the world around them, we must also take into consideration the non-human processes and activities that are inevitably entangled with the things that we do. This chapter has introduced the concept of territory as a way of thinking through the processes by which different elements weave themselves together to form a coherent and integrated whole. Looking at islands as examples of territories, we have seen some of the many ways that human and non-human elements combine forces in the making of places with a recognisable identity – such as Tuvalu – that people identify with and refer to as home.

The chapter also introduced the concept of flow, which offers a way of thinking about how both human and non-human elements circulate through the world, moving within and between territories, in a manner that keeps these territories constantly in touch with the world around them. Territories and flows work together in diverse and dynamic ways to make the world, yet we have seen that they can also interact in unsettling ways to unmake the world. Climate is one such interplay of territory and flow: a vitally important one for human and non-human life. And variations or changes in climate can be both an opportunity and a challenge for human beings and other living things.

The issue of human-induced climate change highlights the flows that connect people's lives on one part of the planet with the lives of others elsewhere, often half the world away. How we respond to the threat of rising sea level and other manifestations of changing climate is not only a matter of acknowledging that there is a serious problem and working out how best to alleviate it; it is a matter of recognising that we are always already entangled in the world – the physical world as much as the social world – and that whatever response we make comes from being caught up in the thick of things.

An appreciation of the dynamic interaction of territories and flows can help to make us aware of the depth of this entanglement. It reminds us that things might have come together differently; the world *could* have been otherwise and, because it is a dynamic planet, the world *will* be otherwise. Considering territories and flows has also shown that there are things that we can influence or redirect, and things that are beyond our influence. There are times when the important or decisive transformations wrought on an island territory are not of human making, as in the case of geological events such as volcanoes or colonisation by biological life. At other moments, it is human activities that have made the crucial difference, such as the discovery and settling of an island or the forming of an independent nation state.

As you will recall from Section 2, writers such as Young (2003) and **Allen (2006)** speak of a form of responsibility that takes account of the way that people's actions in one part of the world can influence the lives of distant others. Because these actions and their impacts are often small, subtle and difficult to track, this sort of shared responsibility can be more complicated than directly attributing guilt or blame **(Allen, 2006)**. This chapter demonstrates that there is an added complication of trying to disentangle the many, small cumulative actions of human beings from the changes wrought by other, non-human forces and processes. This tends to make the apportioning of responsibility even more challenging, as is evidenced in the debates about climate change we encountered in Section 4.3. At the same time, the potentially momentous impact of global environmental change on places like Tuvalu is a compelling reason to not shy away from such challenges.

As we began to see in this chapter, there are options about the way we organise our interactions with the world. International agreements, like the Kyoto Protocol, suggest that major shifts are possible and, in the subsequent chapters of this book, you will encounter other possibilities for reordering the way that certain flows and territories work.

In Chapter 2, the focus is once again on the dynamic interrelationship between territories and flows. However, this time we turn our attention to more recent events, looking closely at flows and formations of territory in which it is human action, or rather the activities of particular groups and collectivities, that is decisive.

References

Allen, J. (2006) 'Claiming connections: a distant world of sweatshops?' in Barnett, C., Robinson, J. and Rose, G. (eds) *A Demanding World*, Milton Keynes, The Open University.

Barnes, D.K.A. (2002) 'Invasions by marine life on plastic debris', *Nature*, vol.416, 25 April, pp.808–9.

Barnett, C. (2006) 'Reaching out: the demands of citizenship in a globalised world' in Barnett, C., Robinson, J. and Rose, G. (eds) *A Demanding World*, Milton Keynes, The Open University.

Batty, H. and Gray, T. (1996) 'Environmental rights and national sovereignty', in Caney, S., George, D. and Jones, P. (eds) *National Rights, International Obligations*, Boulder, CO, Westview Press.

Beck, U. (1992) *Risk Society: Towards a New Modernity*, London, Sage.

Carson, R.L. (1953) *The Sea Around Us*, London, Staples Press.

Colling, A., Dise, N., Francis, P., Harris, N. and Wilson, C. (1997) *The Dynamic Earth*, Milton Keynes, The Open University.

Conisbee, M. and Simms, A. (2003) *Environmental Refugees: The Case for Recognition*, London, New Economics Foundation.

Darwin, C. (1996) *The Origin of Species*, Oxford, Oxford University Press. (First published in 1859.)

Dening, G. (1992) *Mr Bligh's Bad Language: Passion, Power and Theatre on the Bounty*, New York, Cambridge University Press.

Field, M. (2002) 'Global warming not sinking Tuvalu – but maybe its own people are', http://www.tuvaluislands.com/news/archives/2002/2002–03–30.htm (accessed 21 April 2004).

Fischer, S. (2002) *A History of the Pacific Islands*, New York, Palgrove.

Gould, S.J. (1992) *Bully for Brontosaurus: Reflections in Natural History*, New York, W.W. Norton.

Hau'ofa, E. (1993) 'Our sea of islands' in Waddell, E., Naidu, V. and Hau'ofa, E. (eds) *A New Oceania: Rediscovering Our Sea of Islands*, Suva, School of Social and Economic Development and Beake House.

Kriner, S. (2002) 'Tiny Pacific Islands to sue over global warming', www.diasterrelief.org/Disasters/020314Tuvalu (accessed 21 April 2004).

Lewis, D. (1994) *We, the Navigators: The Ancient Art of Landfinding in the Pacific*, Honolulu, University of Hawaii Press.

Lomborg, B. (2001) *The Skeptical Environmentalist: Measuring the Real State of the World*, Cambridge, Cambridge University Press.

Lynas, M. (2003) 'At the end of our weather', *The Observer*, 5 October, Review, pp.1–2.

Nunn, P. (2003) 'Nature–society interactions in the Pacific Islands', *Geografiska Annaler, Series B, Human Geography*, vol.85, no.4, pp.219–29.

Pile, S. (2006) 'A haunted world: the unsettling demands of a globalised past' in Barnett, C., Robinson, J. and Rose, G. (eds) *A Demanding World*, Milton Keynes, The Open University.

Pyne, S. (1997) *Vestal Fire*, Seattle, WA, University of Washington Press.

Quammen, D. (1996) *The Song of the Dodo: Island Biogeography in an Age of Extinctions*, London, Pimlico.

Reuters News Service (2002a) 'Tiny Tuvalu sues United States over rising sea level', http://www.tuvaluislands.com/news/archives/2002/2002–08–29.htm (accessed 21 April 2004).

Reuters News Service (2002b) 'Tuvalu seeks help in US global warming lawsuit', http://www.planetark.com/dailynewsstory.cfm/newsid/17514/story.htm (accessed 21 April 2004).

Rose, G. (2006) 'Envisioning demands: photographs, families and strangers' in Barnett, C., Robinson, J. and Rose, G. (eds) *A Demanding World*, Milton Keynes, The Open University.

Winchester, S. (2004) *Krakatoa: The Day the World Exploded*, London, Penguin.

At the end of our weather

On an epic, sometimes hazardous, personal mission, Mark Lynas travelled the world for three years in search of climate change. In this powerful journal, he describes a planet where global warming is not a distant prospect – it is here and now

It was Christmas time, three years ago. I was with my parents on their small farm in Llangybi, north Wales. As is customary in my family, the slide projector had been set up and complex negotiations over the choice of slides had begun. We settled on Peru, as is also customary, and all sat down to relive memories from 1979, when my father's overseas geological posting took us all to Lima for three years. I was only five back then, but I still remember every moment.

It was probably on my insistence that the slideshow began with my father's photos from Jacabamba, a lonely and remote Andean valley where his expedition had pitched up for a month or so in 1980 to study the rocks. I'm not too interested in rocks: it was the

glaciers that caught my eye – the pristine, shimmering snowfields that topped Jacabamba Valley where the Cordillera Blanca, Peru's highest mountain range, marked the very spine of South America.

The projector whirred and up came my favourite photo. A huge, fan-shaped glacier loomed over a small lake. Icebergs were floating in the slate-grey water, having tumbled from the glacier above. It was spectacular. My father kept up a commentary. He had loved the place and had never forgotten it.

'It might not be the same now,' I cautioned. On a climbing visit to the Alps the previous year, I'd been struck by the obvious rapidity of glacial retreat and become fascinated by global warming, a profound process which our civilisation seemed powerless – or extremely unwilling – to prevent.

My father was unconvinced. 'Perhaps,' he answered, 'but that was a pretty big glacier. There were avalanches coming down all the time.' Once a

calving iceberg had fallen into the lake, causing huge waves that washed away half the expedition's equipment. 'Still,' he mused, 'I wonder what it does look like now. Maybe it has changed.' I looked at the screen and said nothing; I'd just had an idea.

That moment marked the beginning of a three-year journey that would take me across five continents in an often dangerous search for signs of global warming. I was stunned by what I found. The changes were everywhere and people were desperate to talk and to bring attention to their plight in a world that seemed to be unravelling. And, of course, I also retraced my father's steps in Peru, in order to one day come back with my own slides and answer his question.

Tuvalu, South Pacific

I had been in Tuvalu for only two days when the first puddle of water appeared at the side of the small airstrip; more puddles soon joined it. The sea had welled up suddenly through thousands of tiny holes in this atoll's bedrock of coral. People gathered to watch the water flow down paths, around palm trees and into back gardens. Within an hour, it was knee-deep in some places. One of Tuvalu's increasingly regular submergences had begun.

A similar thing occurs most winters in Venice, but Venice has £1.6 billion to spend on a system of protective floodgates. Tuvalu is one of the world's smallest and most obscure nations: 10,000 people, scattered across nine tiny coral atolls. Sea-level rise here is a crisis of national survival: very little of Tuvalu is much more than 20 inches above the Pacific and its coral bedrock is so porous that no amount of coastal protection can save it. According to Professor Patrick Nunn, an ocean geoscientist at the University of the South Pacific in Fiji, atoll nations such as Tuvalu will become

uninhabitable within two or three decades, and may disappear altogether by the end of the century. Pleas by a succession of Tuvalu's Prime Ministers (and those of other atoll nations such as Kiribati and the Maldives) for dramatic cuts in greenhouse-gas emissions have been ignored by other, more powerful states. Tuvaluans will have to move.

The first batch of evacuees, 75 of them, is scheduled to migrate this year to New Zealand, 2,000 miles to the south. But many of the older people say they will refuse to leave. Toaripi Lauti, the first Prime Minister of Tuvalu when it became an independent country (it was a British colony until 1978), said: 'I want my children to be safe. I tell them: you leave so that Tuvaluans will still be living somewhere. But I want to stay on this island. I will go down with Tuvalu.'

Government officials are angry at the international community's lack of response, and particularly with the Bush administration in Washington. Paani Laupepa, a senior official in the environment ministry, told me as we sat on a white-sanded beach: 'We are on the front line of climate change through no fault of our own. The industrialised countries caused the problem, but we are suffering the consequences. America's refusal to sign the Kyoto Protocol will affect the entire security and freedom of future generations of Tuvaluans.'

Tuvalu has recently embarked on legal action to try to win compensation from the countries emitting most greenhouse gases. 'But how do you put a price on a whole nation being relocated?' Laupepa asked. 'How do you value a culture that is being wiped out?'

(Lynas, 2003)

Reading 1B

Molly Conisbee and Andrew Simms, 'Environmental refugees: the case for recognition'

Hostile planet – the forces driving displacement

The Pacific island nation of Tuvalu is a string of nine coral atolls, no more than a few metres above sea level at their highest point. People who have become adept at living in a fragile and changeable environment have inhabited the islands for about 2,000 years. But recent changes to the global climate have seriously undermined their way of life.

In 2000 the floods that Tuvalu has every year lasted, unusually, for five consecutive months. This tiny nation faces huge threats from a range of impacts caused by global warming, from storms and drought to rising sea levels. As a result, its population is faced with the prospect of a phased relocation to neighbouring countries. In March 2002 Tuvalu's President, Koloa Talake, announced that he was considering legal action against the world's worst polluters – the nations most responsible for carbon dioxide emissions – at the International Court of Justice.

Climate change affects both the frequency and the predictability of storms and cyclones. Since the 1970s warmer conditions have resulted in greater incidence of cyclones, especially over the western tropical Pacific. As levels of carbon dioxide increase in the atmosphere it is also anticipated that the intensity of cyclones will increase – with wind speeds potentially 10–20 per cent higher than previously.

Weather-related disasters are making life impossible for many communities. But they are not the only culprit. 'Natural' disasters, together with the effects of resource stripping, have displaced millions. The Oxford University analyst Norman Myers estimates that 25 million people worldwide have been uprooted for environmental reasons – more than the 22 million refugees who have fled from war and other persecutions.

Globally, the problems exemplified by Tuvalu are expected to get worse. According to the World Meteorological Organization, 2001 was the second warmest year on record. Since 1976, the global average temperature has risen at a rate approximately three times faster than the century's average. In 2001, the Intergovernmental Panel on Climate Change (IPCC), the group of scientists that advises international climate negotiations, produced its Third Assessment Report (TAR). It projects that over the period 1990–2100 global average surface temperature will climb at a rate without precedent in the last 10,000 years. The result would be a rise in sea levels of between 9 and 88 cm – a huge threat to island and coastal living across the globe.

Coastal flooding not only erodes landmass. It soaks farmland with salty water, making it impossible to grow crops. It can also affect fresh drinking water supplies. Cities such as Manila, Bangkok, Shanghai, Dhaka and Jakarta are already vulnerable to subsidence. On the Carteret atolls off the coast of Papua New Guinea, rising seas have cut one island in half and increased salt levels in the soil to such an extent that fruit and vegetable crops have been killed off. The atoll has about 1,500 residents – who have been surviving on basic rations of sweet potatoes and rice for the last two years. The Papuan government cannot afford to relocate these communities – and, in any case, where would they relocate them to?

The rise in sea levels is only one of the environmental effects of climate change. The change in sea temperature also damages fragile marine environments such as coral reefs. This has a knock-on effect on marine life, crucial to local ecosystems and livelihoods based on fishing. During the last El Niño of 1997–98, some 90 per cent of live reefs were affected. Drought is another consequence of global warming, potentially affecting millions more. During 1997–98 drought destroyed Fiji's sugar cane crop, costing the government US$18 million.

Overall, according to the International Red Cross and Red Crescent's *World Disasters Report* 2002, in the Oceania region the numbers of those killed by weather-related disasters rose 21 per cent from the 1970s to the 1990s. The numbers of those whose lives were affected rose from 275,000 in the 1970s to 1.2 million in the 1980s to 18 million in the 1990s – a 65-fold increase. These statistics incorporate those affected by events such as cyclones, floods, landslides, droughts and extremes of temperature.

Climate refugees

Despite the predictions, no global assessment of the numbers likely to be displaced by a one-metre rise in sea levels, or even a half-metre rise, has been made. Yet they are likely to prove enormous. Of the world's 19 megacities, 16 are situated on coastlines. All but four are in the developing world. The *World Disasters Report* points out both the human and economic costs involved: 'the most vulnerable areas are found in the tropics, especially the west coast of Africa, south Asia and south-east Asia, and low-lying coral atolls in the Pacific and Indian Oceans. The nations hardest hit will be those least able to afford coastal protection measures and where inhabitants have nowhere else to go.'

A 1998 report by the IPCC summed up some of the regional impacts of climate change. A one-metre rise in sea level would inundate 3 million hectares in Bangladesh, displacing 15–20 million people, it found. Vietnam could lose 500,000 hectares of land in the Red River Delta and another 2 million hectares in the Mekong Delta, displacing roughly 10 million people. About 85 per cent of the Maldives' main island, which contains the capital Male, would be swamped. Most of the Maldives would be turned into sandbars, forcing 300,000 people to flee to India or Sri Lanka. The Maldives, in the words of its president, 'would cease to exist as a nation.'

(Conisbee and Simms, 2003)

Reading 1C

Reuters News Service, 'Tiny Tuvalu sues United States over rising sea level'

29.08.2002

JOHANNESBURG – The United States faces new challenges in the courts over its climate policies despite denying that the world's biggest polluter is responsible for global warming.

The government of the tiny Pacific island state of Tuvalu today said it planned to launch lawsuits within a year against the United States and Australia. Both have rejected the Kyoto protocol on climate change.

Tuvalu, which is only four metres above sea level at its highest point, faces oblivion if the scientists' gloomy scenarios prove right and global warming causes the sea to rise. Tuvalu blames the rising sea level on global warming, caused by polluters.

...

Although the legal threats are small scale, environmentalists say they could be a taste of things to come as victims of rising sea levels and increased droughts and floods go after those they see as responsible – the main polluters.

'Until the United States takes significant action, it is vulnerable to this type of lawsuit,' said Jennifer Morgan of WWF, formerly the World Wildlife Fund, on the sidelines of the World Summit on Sustainable Development.

Washington pulled out of the Kyoto protocol on climate change last year, saying its requirement for developed countries to reduce emissions from sectors like industry, transport and agriculture would hurt its economy.

Despite a voluntary programme to reduce 'energy intensity', and a raft of local initiatives, US emissions continue to rise.

A report released today by US advocacy group the National Environment Trust showed the United States' 288 million population emit the same amount of greenhouse gases as 2.6 billion people living in 151 developing countries.

Looking at emissions state by state, the study found the worst polluter was President George Bush's home state of Texas whose oil-rich 22 million people are responsible for emissions equivalent to those of one billion of the world's poor.

Although lawsuits from the likes of Tuvalu and Boulder, Colorado, are unlikely to give US leaders sleepless nights, they will add to the political pressure on the Bush administration which has come under fire at the World Summit on Sustainable Development.

Bush has declined to join more than 100 world leaders for the finale of the summit, marking 10 years since the first Earth Summit in Rio which spawned global efforts to tackle climate change.

(Reuters News Service, 2002a)

Reading 1D

Reuters News Service, 'Tuvalu seeks help in US global warming lawsuit'

South Africa: August 30, 2002

JOHANNESBURG – The Pacific island of Tuvalu wants to enlist Caribbean and Indian Ocean nations in a planned lawsuit blaming the United States and Australia for global warming that could sink them beneath the waves.

Finance Minister Bikenibeu Paeniu said this week that Tuvalu, a chain of nine coral atolls whose highest point is just four metres (13 feet) above sea level, expects to be ready to launch formal legal action against both within a year.

'We are fighting a giant,' he told Reuters during the Earth Summit in Johannesburg of a plan to take on the United States, the outline of which was unveiled in March.

'It is one of the few options we have.'

He said he was lobbying other low-lying nations at the World Summit on Sustainable Development [to] join it [Tuvalu] in lawsuits.

'In the corridors in this conference there are a number of people who have indicated support,' he said. 'Apart from Pacific islands there are some from the Indian Ocean and the Caribbean.'

Australia and the United States, the biggest world polluter, have rejected the Kyoto pact meant to restrict emissions of gases like carbon dioxide which are blamed for blanketing the planet and driving up temperatures.

Higher temperatures could melt the polar icecaps and raise sea levels worldwide, swamping nations like Tuvalu, which is one of the world's smallest states with about 10,000 inhabitants on an area of 27 square kilometres (10 square miles).

Salt sours farmland

Paeniu said that sea levels had so far not risen around Tuvalu's palm-fringed islands but that storms seemed to be becoming more fierce, spraying damaging sea salt onto farmland.

Tuvalu produces rice, breadfruit, bananas and taro, a type of starch-rich root vegetable. Its people also rely on fishing.

'Just before coming here to South Africa was the first time I was scared. I saw waves coming right over the land,' he said.

'People in some areas were wading up to their thighs.'

'I wouldn't rule out people leaving,' he said. 'But we are not encouraging people to leave because of climate change.'

'It's our land. It's where we live.'

President George W. Bush argued that Kyoto would be too expensive for the U.S. economy and unfair because it excluded developing nations. Australia has also refused to sign up to the pact under which developed states must cut their gas emissions.

Washington says that natural shifts are boosting temperatures and that no amount of restrictions on human use of fossil fuels, like coal, oil or natural gas, could save Tuvalu.

Paeniu said Tuvalu was not targeting nations like the European Union or Japan because they accepted Kyoto.

He said that Tuvalu could not consider following the Dutch example in building dykes around low-lying land to keep out the sea: 'It's one idea,' he said. 'But how would we afford them?'

Reuters News Service (2002b)

US + Australia

Making finance, making worlds

Michael Pryke

Contents

1   Introduction

One of the most frequently repeated claims about globalisation is that there is a marked increase in the reach, intensity and speed of many kinds of flow. In Chapter 1, we encountered a number of forms of flow such as the movements of rock, air, water and life, which have effectively been global for billions of years. Yet we also came across other forms of flow that were clearly set in motion by human beings, such as movements of people, goods or commodities, and ideas. It is these human-produced flows that often attract the most attention in discussions of globalisation, perhaps because their novelty or their rapidly increasing global span renders them so conspicuous.

In this chapter, we focus on a form of human-produced flow that is often taken to be the epitome of globalisation – the movement of finance around the world. As we shall see, these globalised financial flows usually take the form of electronic signals, travelling at the speed of light through the networks of cables that now criss-cross the planet. For many people, the ability of finance to move with apparent ease across great distances, and especially across the borders of national territories, has come to stand for globalisation – and all its attendant risks and opportunities.

From around the globe, the media report stories that link globalisation to various forms of finance: Shanghai shares on a rollercoaster ride; the Brazilian real plummets against the US dollar; deals involving the latest form of global designer finance begin to unravel in New York; and then suddenly the financial foundations of a German multinational shudder. In the UK, it seems obligatory that a financial jingle ends almost every news bulletin: 'In the City the FTSE (Financial Times Stock Exchange) was up 30 at 4980. In New York, the Dow Jones ended the day at 10,547'. Though meaningless to many of us, the noise of finance nevertheless echoes through our everyday lives, whether or not we choose to tune in.

With its emphasis on globalised financial flows, this chapter furthers the discussion of territories and flows begun in Chapter 1. We will be less concerned with the intricacies of global finance, however, and more interested in the deliberate attempts by powerful actors to free financial flows from territorial constraints. At first glance, this idea of freeing finance from the hold of territories might suggest an argument that this sort of globalisation is rendering territory itself redundant. Moreover, this is an argument that is sometimes made about globalisation in general, and globalised financial flows in particular. As discussed in Chapter 1, there are forms of flow that can threaten or damage the integrity of territories and, as we will see in this chapter, there is a very real sense in which the volatility of changing financial flows can indeed prove deeply disruptive of particular territories under certain circumstances. Nonetheless, this is not the same thing as saying that territories have had their day, or that they are no longer relevant or important.

Rather than spelling the end of territory, this chapter shows that territories continue to be active and vital forces in the contemporary globalised world and, in some cases, are even bolstered or reinvigorated by the part they play in the circulation of global finance. In order to understand how this can be so, the chapter explores the ways that the global financial system – viewed as an intricate play of interdependent flows and territories – has evolved over the past few decades. Our point of departure, as in Chapter 1, is a cluster of small islands. This time, the islands are in the Caribbean rather than the Pacific. Small islands, you might be thinking, are an obvious starting point for thinking about global climate change but a rather unlikely site from which to approach transformations in global finance. Yet, as you will see shortly, some islands have come to play an important part in the global financial system. For many people around the world, this only became apparent with the reporting of Hurricane Ivan which struck the Caribbean in September 2004, wreaking destruction on numerous islands, including the Cayman Islands (Figure 2.1 overleaf). The hurricane inflicted severe damage on the Cayman Islands' ability to function as an offshore centre because it destroyed the islands' telecommunications infrastructure – the ability to link into global financial networks.

The Observer reported at the time:

> You probably hadn't realised that the world's fifth-largest finance centre was blown to smithereens last month. Yet discretion is a way of life for Grand Cayman, which ranks behind only New York, London, Tokyo and Hong Kong in the enormity of its bank deposits. This tiny island doesn't like to draw attention to itself – even when Hurricane Ivan comes calling.

(Walsh, 2004)

That a hurricane is capable of delivering such a blow to a group of islands should not be a surprise. What is a surprise is the appearance of the Cayman Islands alongside the likes of New York and London in a roll call of the world's leading financial centres. What are islands associated more with white sands and clear tropical waters doing in the company of places more readily associated with the hustle and bustle of global financial centres?

Figure 2.1   Cayman reaps the whirlwind

The Caymans are only one of a number of offshore financial centres (OFCs) through which a significant proportion of the world's financial flows are channelled. The emergence of the Cayman Islands as a financial centre has not happened by chance; it has come about through the activity of particular groups of people working with an array of materials, including the latest information technologies. As we will see in Section 2, these 'actors' have been able to take advantage of changes in the arrangements of the flows and territories that make up the global financial system in order to transform the national territory that is the Cayman Islands.

There are other indicators of dramatic changes that have taken place in the global finance system over recent decades in Europe. One of these is the Exchange Rate Mechanism (ERM) crisis of 1992. Having delayed entry into the ERM and then come in at what many analysts thought was too high a value, the Pound Sterling found itself under pressure from international speculators, which the UK Government attempted to beat off by using foreign exchange reserves to buy pounds, and so keep its value up. The attempt cost several billion pounds but failed, and consequently Sterling crashed out of the ERM and fell to a lower value.

Global financial interests today contain very real powers that can destabilise major economies like the UK, not to mention less developed economies. You may have read about the importance of the latest communications technologies in facilitating the power and reach of finance, and this chapter emphasises that electronic communications, fibre optic cables, satellites and so on are not only essential to the workings of global finance today, but form one of the material aspects to what might at first seem purely ethereal flows. Figure 2.2 illustrates some of the institutions and technologies which are needed to make virtual money move.

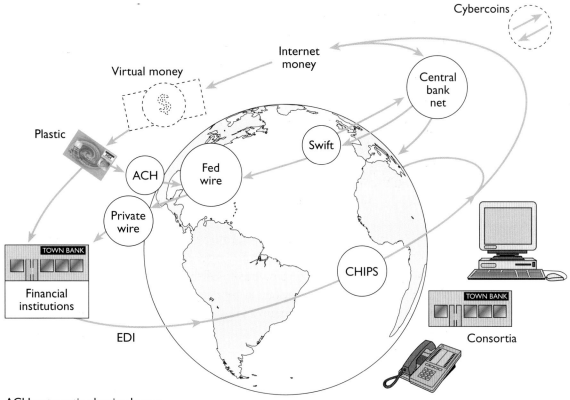

ACH: automatic clearing house
CHIPS: clearing house interbank payments system
EDI: electronic data interchange
Swift: Society for Worldwide Interbank Financial Telecommunications
Fed wire: electronic transfer system connecting Federal Reserve banks and the US Treasury

Figure 2.2   Global money: some of the means by which money is transferred around the globe as swiftly and securely as possible. They range from everyday transactions such as a cash withdrawal made at a cash machine on holiday in a foreign country to 'time sensitive' financial transfers such as those conducted by the US Treasury through Fed Wire in the USA

Source: Solomon, 1997

What is at least of equal importance as communication technologies is the changed regulation of finance. How, after all, did finance gain the upper hand over European states, and what sorts of rules allow for the easy movement of such colossal financial sums? Section 2 discusses the emergence in the mid twentieth century of a system of controls for the flow of finance between territories. It goes on to track the demise of this system and its replacement by an alternative known as 'neo-liberalism', which set in train new interdependencies between financial flows and territories at a global level. In the context of the 'liberalisation' of flows of finance, Section 3 goes on to consider the continued importance of territory, or rather certain specific territories, in the current global financial system. Section 4 looks at both the well-established and well-known financial centres, such as London, and the rise of the newer and less familiar offshore centres, such as the Cayman and British Virgin Islands. In Section 5, a feeling for the particular ways that flows of finance can both settle and quite rapidly unsettle and move on again forms the backdrop to a consideration of the harm that volatile, uneven flows can visit on the places where people live and make their living. This returns us to the issue of the transformation of global financial systems that has occurred in the past, raising the possibility that these systems might once again be subject to dramatic change.

Chapter aims

♦ To show why the money that circulates around the world also needs to fix and settle in particular places.

♦ To show how territories and flows are shaped and reshaped in a financially globalised world.

2   Financial flows, architecture and markets

Finance is today perhaps the exemplar of globalisation as it moves swiftly across borders and around the globe in search of profit. As far as it is legally possible, the owners and managers of finance endlessly search out places and activities in which to put 'their' money in order to seek a higher return than if the money just stayed put. Finance, in other words, needs to flow; it needs motion if it is to multiply. However, if the motion is too rapid, problems may arise. The fast flow of finance in and out of territories may cause crises, panics or a rush on a currency; loss of confidence in the economic system and a country's economic policy may undermine the social stability of territories. Thus, historically, nation states have often sought to control movements of finance, and have sometimes succeeded. There are, though, different visions of freely flowing versus highly territorialised financial systems, and so we need to consider what might be at stake in deciding between these visions and in implementing whichever vision is preferred. In this way, an understanding of how and why different financial systems have been set up in the past sets the stage for thinking critically about the current system.

2.1 Financial flows need an architecture

For more than a century, any discussion of national economic policy has tended to identify tensions between the advantages of free trade and those of state regulation. The tension is even greater when considering finance, where proponents of free flows of investment and profit are opposed by those who prefer state control over capital movements. As this section shows, at the beginning of the twenty-first century, the advocates of free flows of finance seem to be winning the argument, but we should not forget that in the twentieth century the way of organising finance globally changed from free trade to a high degree of state control before swinging back towards free markets.

We might think about efforts to organise territories and flows in particular patterns as an 'architecture'. The use of the term 'architecture' aims simply to convey the sense that the choice between, say, a state- or market-led movement of financial flows and the consequent relationship between territories and flows is not happenstance. Imagination and decisions are involved: people – some sitting in front of screens say in London or Frankfurt; others attending a string of meetings from New York through to Tokyo – have to draw up, agree and implement specific designs for markets. There has to be agreement too about how these markets should be regulated and about who the regulators should be, for example the state or the private sector. (You might like to think about who these people are and whose interests they give voice to when such designs are pieced together.) Thus, no matter whether it is in today's digital finance or in the days when financiers wrote with quills and Genoa was the major centre for international finance, groups of people, somewhere, have to make and agree the rules and regulations, the financial architecture, that will shape the markets and the flows and how these will affect territories. One significant set of decisions was made at a meeting in the USA in the early 1940s.

Shareholders!

2.2 From Bretton Woods to neo-liberalism

In July 1944, finance ministers from the major Western countries met in Bretton Woods, a small town in New Hampshire, USA. Their purpose was to establish an architecture for the post-world war international financial system. This was to be an architecture agreed by state power; private bankers were almost wholly excluded; markets were to be subordinate to states in the new planned and managed international financial system. The two key proponents of the new system, John Maynard Keynes and Harry Dexter White, drew up what is now known as the 'Bretton Woods Agreement', the blueprint for the post-war financial system.

In the opening speech, the US Secretary of the Treasury reminded the representatives of the forty-four countries gathered at the conference exactly why they were meeting:

> All of us have seen great economic tragedy in our time. We saw the worldwide depression of the 1930s. We saw currency disorders develop and spread from land to land, destroying the basis for international trade and international investment and even international faith. In their wake, we saw unemployment and wretchedness – idle tools, wasted wealth. We saw their victims fall prey, in places, to demagogues and dictators. We saw bewilderment and bitterness become the breeders of fascism, and finally, war.
>
> (cited in Panić, 1995, p.39)

Figure 2.3   The Bretton Woods Conference: the hotel where it was held, and, top, John Maynard Keynes and, bottom, Harry Dexter White

Strong words indeed. Clearly, the way that the pre-war system of financial flows was organised left much to be desired. Bretton Woods produced a global financial architecture to help the world recover economically and financially in the aftermath of the Second World War and to prevent the recurrence of the sort of financial disaster that, following the Wall Street crash of 1929, culminated in the depression of the 1930s. As Susan Strange, a leading commentator, remarked, the '1930s Depression convinced Americans and many Europeans that the world market economy could not be left to work by itself. Rules were needed' (Strange, 1994, p.53). In fact, as Strange also points out, Bretton Woods saw for the first time in history governments of the leading economies meeting explicitly to agree a set of rules, an architecture, for collective management (Strange, 1994, p.55). The governments agreed to give stability to the international financial system, in which national economic agendas would be recognised and respected. Finance was to continue to move around the globe, but its movements were to be re-regulated and managed. The negotiated solution, technically known as a system of 'fixed but adjustable exchange rates', lasted until the early 1970s. Two international institutions, the International Monetary Fund (IMF) and the World Bank, have lasted much longer. During this period, international finance flowed within an architecture that saw currencies fixed in terms of the US dollar, with any significant exchange rate disequilibrium between countries made good by the actions of the IMF.

The Bretton Woods system gave national territories scope to establish a set of policies in relation to the international markets, rather than being dominated by such markets. Importantly, national controls over financial inflows and outflows were in place throughout the period that the Agreement stood. This is not to say that flows between countries did not exist; of course they did since it was necessary to fund trade and

Defining the World Bank and the IMF

The World Bank and the IMF are key institutions in the present global financial system, and central to its previous and present architectures. Both institutions date back to the Bretton Woods Agreement. Designed initially to help channel funds for the post-world war reconstruction of Europe, the World Bank today focuses on an agenda to reduce world poverty. The Washington, DC-based Bank now helps to orchestrate macroeconomic policy and debt rescheduling, particularly of developing countries. Not without its critics, the Bank is heavily involved in shaping economic policy at a global level.

The IMF is the central coordinator of the international monetary system. This system exerts strong influence over the flows of international financial payments and exchange rates between countries. Through a mixture of policy advice, agenda-setting and the monitoring of economic and financial developments, at both country specific and global levels, the IMF effectively establishes the strengths and weaknesses of the territories of nation states and therefore influences the pattern of financial flows among them.

some international investment. However, the Bretton Woods Agreement provided a largely state-led regulatory architecture to facilitate the stable passage of financial flows. Crucially, this financial architecture was a vision, or set of ideas and decisions, about how flows might move between territories with the minimum of volatility and risk. The appropriateness of the financial architecture agreed at Bretton Woods was contested at the time of its inception and throughout its relatively short life. The system did not last, and collapsed in the early 1970s. With cracks appearing in the regulatory architecture, finance increasingly escaped regulated territories – at first opportunistically, then by arguing for a new architecture. More and more, commercial banks found ways to circumvent state controls on financial flows. The development of 'Euromarkets', in which dollar deposits and loans were made outside the USA by banks from a variety of countries, is the prime example of such regulatory circumnavigation. The Euromarkets, essentially markets in 'stateless money', grew rapidly from around US$11 billion in 1964 to an estimated US$2.8 trillion at the end of the 1980s, the growth rate accelerating through the 1970s (Martin, 1994).

Defining neo-liberalism

Neo-liberalism is a significant international political project aimed at transforming a host of key agreements or settlements that were established at the end of the Second World War. The liberalisation of finance is part of this project, and is pithily described by a critic as follows:

> The essence of financial liberalisation consists in three sets of measures: first, to open up a country to the free flow of international finance; secondly, to remove controls and restrictions on the functioning of domestic banks and other financial institutions so that they get properly integrated as participants in the world financial markets; and thirdly, to provide autonomy from the government to the central bank so that its supervisory and regulatory role vis-à-vis the banking sector is dissociated from the political process of the country, and hence from _any accountability to the people._

(Patnaik, 1999)

While the detailed reasons behind the collapse of the Bretton Woods system need not concern us, we do need to recognise that the collapse signalled a systemic change in the world of international finance. Most notable is the change in the composition of flows of stateless finance that came with the 'liberalisation of finance' from the 1970s onwards (Hirst and Thompson, 1999, first published 1996), and the impact this had on the interdependencies between flows and territories at a global level. The breakdown of Bretton Woods and the accompanying move from exchange rates fixed by the state to flexible exchange rates also signalled a shift in power from states to markets, and can be viewed as heralding the era of neo-liberalism.

What did this shift in financial architecture signal for the relationship between financial flows and territories? This is a central issue for this chapter and it also raises issues for the world we live in, not least of which is the financial power wielded by certain territories over others in the context of liberalised financial flows. The summary of the arguments for and against financial liberalisation in Sections 2.3 and 2.4 helps to identify some of the key points of contention that surround its very real effects on the interdependencies between territories and flows.

2.3 Liberalising flows: arguments for financial liberalisation

The advocates of financial liberalisation wish to see a world where there are no barriers to the free flow of private finance, whether of short-term portfolio flows (including equities and bank loans) or the longer-term flows of foreign direct investment or FDI (the type of finance mentioned in **Allen, 2006**). There are specific aims to financial liberalisation, they argue. One is to produce a world where there is a greater degree of financial integration and thus, they claim, benefits from access to more and more varied sources of private finance. This is achieved by a marked increase in cross-border flows of finance as investment funds flow to the places where they can be invested most efficiently.

Those who are pro-liberalisation view it as potentially beneficial to less developed countries. Since the cost of important factors of production, such as labour, land and buildings, are lower in the less developed world, investors should, in theory, tend to invest more in poor countries. Such investments would both be economically efficient (since the goods and services would be cheaper and hence in high demand) and tend to reduce the disparities in development which were maintained by controls over capital movement between countries.

As articulated by two staff members of the IMF (Kose and Prasad, 2004), the argument remains that there are real benefits from freer flows of finance. They argue that the flows will tend to be from capital-rich industrial countries, territories where there is an abundance of private finance, to capital-poor developing countries, countries where finance is needed to develop. It is claimed that there will be benefits all round: those in developed countries supplying the financial flows will gain higher returns, while the developing countries now refashioned by financial inflows see economic growth, growing employment and rising living standards.

Moreover, whereas in the past many governments created problems, and even crises, by intervening unwisely in their economies, it is claimed that the rules of financial liberalisation will ensure that countries will subscribe to the ideas and practices of sound economic management, since those rules are monitored and supervised by private financial organisations as well as international institutions like the IMF. Should national economic policy be seen to break the rules, then investors will withdraw their finance from that country. Private finance would, in other words, hightail it for more secure territories.

According to the advocates of liberalisation, the relationship between territories and private financial flows could not be clearer. Play the game and a territory replenished by the goodness of private financial flows will see long-term economic growth and rising living standards; play another game and flows of nutrient-packed private finance will either quickly make their exit or not come visiting at all, with obvious withering consequences.

2.4   Unravelling territories: arguments against financial liberalisation

Critics of financial liberalisation argue that the picture painted by the proponents is far too rosy, since it points to potential benefits to less developed countries, but ignores some of the actual disbenefits – including a strong tendency for capital to flow from less to more developed countries.

This section draws on a critique by Prabhat Patnaik, a Professor of Economics in New Delhi. Patnaik draws our attention to the new interdependencies between different territories that liberalisation produces, and uses the case of financial sector reforms in India to illustrate his argument about the consequences of a country becoming a liquid part of globalised finance. Patnaik stresses that one needs to distinguish between capital inflows in the form of FDI, which benefits the productive capacity of the economy, and short-term flows. The latter he views as 'essentially speculative in nature', and he argues that they damage rather than serve the needs of developing countries, since they expose vulnerable countries 'to the vortex of speculative capital movements', that is, to the flows of short-term finance in search of quick profits (Patnaik, 1999).

For Patnaik, it seems obvious that, on a planet where finance is free to flow, it will head for the highest returns, and/or where the interest rate environment is most assured. Other things being equal, Patnaik says, finance will move to advanced countries. To counter this, developing countries must offer what he calls 'blandishments', such as lower tax rates than those to be found in developed countries. As private finance is moved around the globe searching for the best returns, the process creates a new set of interdependencies between nation states. Each state will try to offer higher returns to private finance than its neighbour in an effort to make itself more attractive. This process brings with it potential social costs. The price of the new interdependencies is often borne by the poor, and arises because reductions in tax mean that less money is available to spend nationally on health and education.

In this new world of flows, governments no longer have the options that existed when capital could be controlled. To raise taxes would mean driving away corporations, for these firms are relatively free to relocate (Allen, 2006). To increase government expenditure and rely on deficit financing would fall foul of the rules laid down by the IMF and would not be looked on favourably by private sector banks and investment houses located in key financial territories such as London, Tokyo and New York. In particular, this type of action would frighten short-term investors, because they would be unsure whether their investments would be safe in a country where the government was pursuing unsound policies.

Nor does a single government have a realistic option of restoring controls on capital movements, as shown by the experience of Malaysia when, in 1998, it reintroduced controls on capital movements into and out of the country. Almost at once, the large US investment bank Morgan Stanley dropped Malaysia from its country coverage, including indices used by institutional investors when deciding where to invest. The International Finance Corporation, an organisation established by the IMF and based in Washington, DC, took the same decision. Absent from such indices, Malaysia found itself effectively 'off the map' of global finance, and inflows of investment dried up. The Malaysian government quickly learned its lesson.

> When Malaysia introduced market-friendly changes to capital controls in February 1999, market analysts anticipated that Malaysia would soon be reinstated in these indices. ... In line with these expectations, on 13th August 1999 Morgan Stanley Capital International announced that it would reinstate Malaysia in its All Country Far-East Ex-Japan Index and Emerging Market Free Index with effect from February 2000. This decision, coupled with the ending of uncertainty about the possible outcome of the lifting of the one-year moratorium on portfolio investment, is likely to boost the recent pick up in fresh portfolio flows to Malaysia.
>
> (Athukorala, 2001, p.271)

Figure 2.4   Where decisions are made: some finance corporation offices in London

Events like those in Malaysia have even encouraged some critics to challenge the claim that neo-liberalism is characterised by the free markets its advocates praise. Economic geographer Ron Martin articulates the central issue when he states that 'financial markets are as much political as economic in character, founded on and shaped by unequal relations of power between lenders and borrowers' (Martin, 1994, p.271). The theory that informs the neo-liberal position, Martin argues, removes itself from what actually takes place in the world. In practice, he asserts, powerful private sector organisations, such as the big investment banks and securities houses, pension funds, mutual funds, multinational corporations, institutions like the IMF and the leading group of capitalist countries operating as G7, G8 or G10, are the financial system's dominant architects. It is these economic actors, rather than the myriad of small, equally powerful, decision makers assumed in neo-liberal theory, that make the markets that move finance from territory to territory (Martin, 1994, p.272). Altogether, it seems unlikely that decisions made within such organisations will be fair to all and exemplify free market competition. Far from 'ending geography', as early commentators on a flow-based world economy expected, Martin concludes that financial globalisation is 'reconfiguring geographies of money, power and dependency' (Martin, 1994, p.274).

2.5   A globalised financial architecture

This section has shown that financial architecture has shifted from a territorially based system under Bretton Woods to one with greater freedom for capital to flow after the 1970s. The new system, part of a *Thatcher + Reagan* self-conscious neo-liberal movement in politics and economics since about 1980, is highly contentious, with powerful supporters, mainly from more prosperous parts of developed economies, and many *Washington consensus* vociferous critics, mainly from less affluent groups and less developed countries. Rather than attempting to resolve the dispute, which is as much a political as an academic task, Sections 3 and 4 move on to examine how the new system works, and show that territory still plays very significant roles. Section 5 returns to assess some of the criticisms.

Summary

- Since 1944, the world's financial architecture has moved from a territorially based organisation formalised at Bretton Woods to a much more freely flowing system in the era of neo-liberalism.

- Advocates of neo-liberalism argue that it is a more efficient way of organising investment, promotes sound economic policy and has the potential to bring development to previously less developed areas.

- Critics of neo-liberalism argue that the new architecture undermines governments' ability to manage local problems, brings uneven benefits to different territories and increases the volatility of the whole system.

one size fit all does not work

3   Making markets in flows: the continuing importance of certain territories

This section discusses the reasons for the lasting, and indeed increased, importance of key financial centres. Central to an understanding of the significance of these territories is the working of today's global financial markets.

A key feature of neo-liberal financial architecture is the dominance of major international financial markets, notably London and New York. These are the places where the leading private financial institutions concentrate and undertake market transactions.

Perhaps we should begin by trying to set out how a market in finance works, what technologies are involved and why specific territories are required. Markets in global finance are not the usual run-of-the-mill markets. They are complex and, in the way they operate today, are arguably distinct from earlier financial markets, notably in the manner in which they rely upon ICTs (information and communication technologies) to assemble, not gold and silver coins, but seemingly unearthly flows of finance – the digitisation into electronic streams of 1s and 0s that facilitate the movement of funds across the world. Indeed, as Saskia Sassen (2004), a leading commentator on these matters, has remarked, global financial markets involve the movement of what seem at first to be dematerialised flows, stripped of any notion of the material and social worlds associated with the workings of so many other markets. What is more, as outlined in Section 2, somewhere in the workings and design of global financial markets and flows lies the potential for making and exerting considerable economic and political power over the territories of nation states around the globe.

Just how dematerialised flows can, often forcefully, transfigure economic landscapes has less to do with alchemy than it has to do with decisions actively made by humans in financial centres. Key to this effect is

Defining financial markets

A central aspect of modern economies is that activities are coordinated by market exchange. Finance and financial markets are central to the operation of this system of exchange; moreover, they have become concentrated in a few particular places. Within global financial market places such as the City of London and New York's Wall Street, financiers, bankers and a host of other financial market traders and dealers make markets in a growing range of increasingly sophisticated forms of global finance.

Global financial markets deal with flows of financial assets and financial information that cross the territorial borders of nation states. Furthermore, these financial markets involve networks formed between hosts of financial organisations, as well as legal and accounting firms, dispersed spatially and temporally yet organised through specific territories, of which the City of London and Wall Street are two key examples. For our purposes, financial markets then are sophisticated combinations of technologies and human organisations located in specific territories.

digitisation; digitisation refers particularly to computer-based technologies (Sassen, 2004, p.227). Three related aspects are central to the impact of digitisation, and each is a reminder of the materiality of finance and the importance of the architecture of financial rules and regulations.

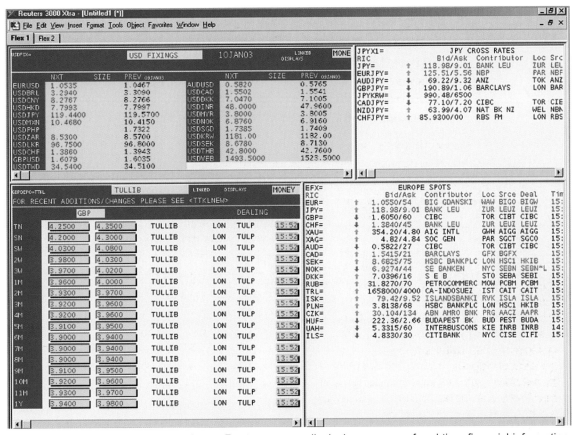

Figure 2.5   Following market action: a Reuters screen displaying a range of real-time financial information

First is the use of sophisticated software. The software facilitates the way financial markets operate; it provides a constant real-time update of markets and prices, and thus allows financial organisations to follow the stories that matter (see Figure 2.5). It also enables a high degree of innovation in the development of financial instruments. Whether these instruments are bonds to enable large quoted companies to raise debt finance or odd-sounding things like derivatives designed to safeguard firms against unexpected rises in interest rates, their design and innovation depends on software. Though complex in design, sophisticated software makes trade in financial products relatively easy and thus in turn enables the growth of such forms of finance.

Second, the application of digital technologies allows the interweaving of financial flows and territories. Digitisation thickens interconnectedness and makes interdependencies between territories and flows almost inevitable. A trader in any one of today's global financial markets sitting at his or her desk in the City of London is able to keep track of the price of, say, corporate bonds or debt in the USA as well as variations in their price relative to movements in the price of similar financial products in Germany, France and Tokyo. There is another equally important enabling part to this point, too; the liberalisation of these markets has more recently allowed the financial web woven by the software applied to financial market innovation and trading to become more intense. Previously separate markets have now broken free of the restraints established by past regulation. These markets surge together, one potentially influencing the performance of the next. Moreover, such intensity is boosted further because of the ways in which sophisticated analytics enable the real-time assessment of the performance of any one of these markets. For instance, graphics displayed on financial screens display a product's price history, for example the price of a US corporation's bond, project future cash flows and prices, and thus help a trader to gauge the advantages or disadvantages of holding rather than selling the product. This real-time trading transmits financial flows of information virtually instantaneously from any number of countries or territories on to screens in the heart of key financial centres.

Third, the form of present-day financial transactions has changed, as Sassen reminds us, 'because finance is particularly about transactions rather than simply flows of money, the technical properties of digital networks assume added meaning. Interconnectivity, simultaneity, decentralised access, all contribute to multiply the number of transactions ... and thereby the number of participants. The overall outcome is a complex architecture of transaction' (2004, p.228).

Altogether, these factors make for a system of financial markets that is markedly different from those of the past. Digitised finance is a special kind of market flow that works in real time and, in turn, this signals an altered relation between territories and flows in general, and specifically between financial centres and other territories.

Yet something rather odd seems to be happening. While digitisation has dispersed financial flows across the globe, affecting the nature of interdependencies between territories, the same process appears to have led to the further concentration of the most significant global financial markets within specific territories. Table 2.1 shows the concentrations of one significant form of global finance – global equities, shown here by the value held in each market.

wealth concentrated in a handful of areas

Table 2.1   The ten biggest stock markets in the world (US$ billions) by market capitalisation

Stock market	Market capitalisation (2001[1])	Percentage of members' capitalisation (2001[1])	Market capitalisation (2000)	Percentage of members' capitalisation (2000)
New York Stock Exchange (NYSE)	11,026.6	41.4	11,534.6	37.1
Nasdaq	2,739.7	10.3	3,597.1	8.8
Tokyo	2,264.5	8.5	3,157.2	7.3
London	2,164.7	8.1	2,612.2	7.0
Euronext[2]	1,843.5	6.9	2,271.7	5.9
Deutsche Borse	1,071.7	4.0	1,270.2	3.4
Toronto	611.5	2.3	766.2	2.0
Italy	527.5	2.0	768.3	1.7
Swiss Exchange	527.3	2.0	792.3	1.7
Hong Kong	506.1	1.9	506.1	1.6
Total for Federation members	26,610.0	87.5	31,125.0	76.4

Compiled from the 2001 Annual Report, p.92, with calculations of percentages added. [1]2001 figures are year-end figures. [2]Euronext includes Brussels, Amsterdam and Paris.

Source: Sassen, 2004, p.234

Equities are financial instruments that form part of global stock markets, a major subset of global financial markets. Together, the stock markets of New York (NYSE and the Nasdaq), Tokyo and London account for around 68 per cent of the world's capitalisation of stock market trade. This is a clear sign of a concentration rather than a dispersal of the power that accompanies financial flows. Table 2.2 (overleaf) is another way of emphasising the same trend towards a concentration of control in stock market activity. London, New York and Tokyo account for in the region of 33 per cent of global institutional equity holdings. The same three territories account for just under 60 per cent of the foreign exchange market, another key global financial market.

Table 2.2   Foreign listings in major stock exchanges

Exchange	Number of foreign listings (2000)	Percentage of foreign listings (2000)	Number of foreign listings (2001[1])	Percentage of foreign listings (2001[1])
Nasdaq	445	11.0	488	10.3
New York Stock Exchange (NYSE)	461	19.2	433	17.5
London	409	17.5	448	18.9
Deutsche Borse	235	23.9	241	24.5
Euronext[2]	–	–	–	–
Swiss Exchange	149	36.2	164	39.4
Tokyo	38	1.8	41	2.0

Compiled from the 2001 Annual Report, p.86, with calculations of percentages added. [1]2001 figures are year-end figures. [2]Euronext includes Brussels, Amsterdam and Paris.

Source: Sassen, 2004, p.235

Why do only a handful of financial centres continue to matter? It seems that the answer lies in the fact that there has to be some place, somewhere, to 'place your bets' (Pryke and Lee, 1995), to meet and discuss market rumour, to assess market confidence, and generally to judge the state of play (Thrift, 1994, pp.333–4). Locations such as London, and exchanges such as New York's Nasdaq, noted in the tables shown earlier, are those places: specific territories where the culture of global finance is most strongly exhibited. The experts and market players form themselves into social networks which work on the basis of trust, interpretive schemes – that is, strategies to make sense of what is going on – and, of course, more information (Thrift, 1994). All these features of current financial flows and financial centres call for more, not fewer, face-to-face meetings; people active in the market and the organisations they work for, together with the institutions regulating their activities, need a physical, material, presence to work through endless, complex financial flows. The more dematerialised and digitised finance becomes – that is the more able it is to flow – the greater the need for territories, but territories of a specific kind. The territories of global finance that we call 'financial centres' act functionally; financial markets require making, and this involves people, organisations such as investment banks and brokers, and technologies and buildings. Yet financial centres have a symbolic role too. Places like the City of London symbolise, and thereby reinforce, the economic power and strength of private finance. Consequently, to be a player of note in the game of global finance still requires the right type of building in the right address from where financial flows can be made sense of and made into markets (see Figures 2.4 and 2.6).

Figure 2.6   What is a territory and what is a flow? The prestigious building of a global investment bank and financial information

Activity 2.1

For another explanation of financial centralisation, turn to Reading 2A by
Saskia Sassen (2004) entitled 'The locational and institutional
embeddedness of electronic markets', which you will find at the end of the
chapter. As you read the extract, make a note of how Sassen highlights
many issues relevant to this chapter.

The issues that Reading 2A (Sassen, 2004) focuses on, which are
relevant to this chapter, include:

- Flows of finance are human produced in conjunction with
  materials such as computers and software, and more.

- Territories and flows are interdependent. Note the way
  technologies help to make the dispersal of global flows
  manageable, yet in the same action pull the control of such flows
  ever more tightly into specific territories such as New York.

- The vast offices crowding the financial centres of such cities as
  London and New York continue to symbolise a demonstrable
  political economic power. It is within such territories that social
  rather than simple technical connectivity thickens into the ability to
  direct flows globally. The regional conduits, such as São Paulo and
  Bombay, are minor nodes when set against the City of London or
  New York. The latter territories are where the authority lies to
  makes sense of global flows.

- The exercise of such economic power involves making decisions
  about where financial products are to flow, for how long, under
  what conditions, and when such flows should reverse their
  movement and return to key financial centres.

- There is a tendency for collaboration between key financial centres
  and 'global elites' to ensure that global flows keep flowing, and this
  in turn preserves concentration and hierarchy.

From Reading 2A, you will have noted how the need for specific
financial territories seems to have increased rather than decreased in
importance. In addition, Sassen (2004) underscores the importance of
territories to the operation of global financial flows, a tendency she
terms 'agglomeration', that is, the clustering together of financial
markets and their participants. Moreover, Sassen comments that, as the
volume of financial flows increases, so the territories from where the
flows are coordinated seem to consolidate. The faster the flows
increase, the more need there is for the breadth and depth of certain
financial centres to make sense of what is going on.

The next section brings together several of these issues and explores what they imply for the making of interdependencies between territories and flows in a world of global finance.

Summary

- Those involved in the financial transaction need sets of rules and regulations, that is, a financial architecture.
- Financial flows need specific territories from which to transact.

[handwritten margin note: Companies based overseas avoid paying tax and therefore make more profit.]

4   Financial flows and the making of financial territories

This section sets out the key reasons behind the emergence of new financial territories – so-called offshore financial centres (OFCs) – and the work needed to transform financial flows into one such territory.

The financial architecture agreed at Bretton Woods aimed to regulate the movement of private financial flows between territories. As we have already seen, the collapse of the system in the 1970s freed global finance to roam through a growing number of territories with new-found intensity. The growth of Euromarkets, noted in Section 2.2, is a good example of this process. Moreover, with the balance of power moving towards markets and away from states from the 1970s onwards, any state attempts to regulate finance in ways viewed unfavourably by private sector interests were met with a simple response: to switch operations to less-regulated territories, such as OFCs (see Figure 2.7 overleaf). It is in this way that a growing number of OFCs became part of the circuits of global finance.

[handwritten margin note: Companies exist primarily to make profit. The services/products they provide are secondary.]

4.1   Islands of finance: offshore financial centres

The attempt to create a liberalised architecture for global finance had the obvious effect of privileging flows over territories. However, it also had the unanticipated side effect of boosting the possibilities for the emergence of new financial territories similar to those that had begun to appear as the Bretton Woods architecture started to crack. These

Figure 2.7   Offshore financial centres and tax havens

Source: Campbell, 2004

latest territories were to be places where the pickings were potentially richer due chiefly to the laxity of regulations. The emergence of OFCs is a clear example of the tension between differently regulated territories and flows. According to the IMF, trying to pin down and control private finance has not been easy:

> The growth of offshore centres can be traced back to the restrictive regulatory regimes in many advanced countries in the 1960s and 1970s. These regimes blocked the flow of capital to and from other countries (excluding trade financing), or imposed restrictions on the interest rates banks could offer, or raised banks' funding costs in domestic markets ... These restrictions, which, in many cases, were intended to provide governments with more control over monetary policy, encouraged a shift in deposits and borrowing to less regulated institutions, including banks in jurisdictions not subject to such restrictions.

> (Darbar et al., 2003, p.32)

Initially, financial institutions sought out territories that had low tax regimes for historic reasons, but more recently territories wishing to become OFCs have deliberately attempted to lower taxation rates and to establish a jurisdiction friendly to private financial flows. The attractiveness of OFCs is primarily their tax advantages, both for rich individuals and for businesses. In addition, these centres offer qualities such as confidentiality and political stability, sheltered from unwelcome regulation. The idea of 'bank secrecy' as we know it today was first legislated for in 1934 when the Swiss Confederation, the home of one of the original OFCs, made it a crime for a bank employee to reveal the name of a bank's clients (a measure not lost on US gangsters who made great use of secrecy laws and offshore accounts to launder mob money). Subsequent OFCs adopted this model to the letter, though most have since been obliged to provide information relevant to criminal investigation. Low direct taxation and discretion maintained their appeal to international finance even when regulations restricting flows were eased, and in many cases abolished, with the end of Bretton Woods.

While the expectation was that financial liberalisation in the 1980s and 1990s would put an end to OFCs, this has not proved to be the case; global finance now firmly incorporates OFCs. Private sector banks, in particular, strategically direct flows to those centres whose qualities, for example of lenient taxation, make them important territories, integral to the map of global finance (as Extract 2.1, from Deutsche Bank, shows). OFCs accounted for around 8 per cent of global financial flows in 2003 (Bank of England Quarterly Bulletin, 2003).

Extract 2.1

'Guiding flows offshore'

An introduction to the offshore group

Our clients consist mainly of financial institutions and corporations ranging from the largest multi-nationals to privately held business, as well as intermediaries such as trust companies, captive insurance managers, advocates, solicitors and accountancy firms and their advisors. Additionally certain services are available to high-net-worth individuals.

At the very outset of a client relationship, we take the time to discuss their needs with them. Only when these have been fully explored and defined do we develop a solution that cuts across business streams and geographic boundaries; a solution that is tailored to suit the individual client, not the individual centre.

Many offshore banking and financial services groups are strongly committed to one particular offshore centre. This narrowly focused 'single solution' approach is rarely ideal for the client. At Deutsche Bank, we take a more flexible approach, offering a full range of services from several centres worldwide, each with their own specialities and strengths.

An introduction to Cayman Islands

A British dependent territory and one of a group of islands in the northern Caribbean, Cayman has grown rapidly from its modest beginnings as an offshore banking centre in the 1970s. It is now among the largest banking centres in the world and the finance industry is by far its main source of income and employment. The Deutsche Bank operation has enjoyed similar growth since its Cayman office opened in 1983; it now numbers a staff of more than 50 professionals who provide a fully comprehensive range of offshore services for international corporate, institutional and private clients, mainly from Japan and the USA.

(Deutsche Bank, 2004)

Table 2.3 presents the ranking of financial centres in terms of how much of their assets are invested in them from abroad. This table does a great deal to put the offshore centres into context because it makes clear that the UK, and in particular London, is the world's major centre for offshore funds; that the USA and Japan are very significant in the field; and that a number of European countries are very active. Among them, Switzerland and Luxembourg stand out as holding surprisingly large amounts of offshore funds. Hong Kong and Singapore, starting as small offshore centres, are now the second and third ranked international financial centres serving Asia.

Table 2.3   International financial centres ranked by banks' external assets, end 2000

	External assets (US$ billions)
UK	2095
Japan	1199
Germany	975
USA	951
Cayman Islands	782
Switzerland	740
France	640
Luxembourg	510
Hong Kong	450
Singapore	424
Netherlands	290
Belgium	285
Bahamas	276

Source: Bank for International Settlements

In among the more established international centres in Table 2.3 are two OFCs from the Caribbean, the Cayman Islands and the Bahamas. OFCs such as these are extreme cases of territories almost wholly reliant on global financial flows. The manner in which global finance dominates offshore territories really hits home if one looks at the scale of international banking activities in proportion to the size of the domestic economy, measured in gross domestic product (GDP). For the Caymans, international banking activity is 518 times greater than the islands' gross domestic product. For the USA, on the other hand, the multiple of GDP is only 0.2 (Dixon, 2001). OFCs it seems are territories made almost wholly of private financial flows. How has this strange situation come about?

4.2 Making finance, making identities

In Chapter 1, we saw how island territories shape themselves by weaving together many different elements. The way that certain islands are able to attract global flows of finance can be seen as a new dimension of this process. Operating as OFCs, islands provide specialised services required by global finance for which small fees are charged. If the flows are of sufficient magnitude, these charges or fees can make a significant contribution to the material wealth of the island in question.

In return, OFCs offer to global finance low and sometimes zero direct taxes and high levels of secrecy, along with an innovative regulatory and legal environment. In working to provide these services, these centres are competing to distinguish themselves. In effect, each OFC is attempting to shape a unique territory out of global financial flows. To illustrate how this process might work let us take the example of the British Virgin Islands.

In the entry to the *Offshore Finance Yearbook*, the British Virgin Islands is described in this way: 'As one of the world's leading offshore corporate domiciles, the British Virgin Islands offers an attractive combination of a safe, politically stable environment, with a legislative framework developed in close consultation with the private sector' (Euromoney, 2002, p.58). The *Offshore Finance Yearbook* goes on to set out what the British Virgin Islands has to offer the world of global finance. At the head of a list offering advantages such as a zero tax rate, no wealth, capital gains or estate taxes for offshore entities (features common to many OFCs), is a feature that may be passed over all too easily. The British Virgin Islands has one of the 'most popular and long-established' International Companies Acts in the

[handwritten margin note: Cayman is don't export much, rely on banking for their economy]

world (Euromoney, 2002, p.58). Enacted in 1984 to enable the territory 'to continue as an offshore financial centre after the termination of the double tax treaty between the US and the BVI [British Virgin Islands]' (Euromoney, 2002, p.58), over 350,000 International Business Companies (IBC) have now been incorporated.

The significance of this single Act should not be lost for it offers a clue as to how the British Virgin Islands 'rewired' itself into the international financial system, and allows a glimpse of the range of influences drawn upon by the islands to help to stabilise the volatile, hyperactive, immaterial flows of global finance. As the social anthropologist Bill Maurer writes in his study of the islands: 'In 1984, the British Virgin Islanders became authors. The Legislative Council enacted what was perhaps the most significant piece of legislation in BVI history' (1997, p.247). The significance lies not only in the effect of this Act on the status of British Virgin Islands as an OFC, which in itself was considerable, but also in terms of the sense of national identity the enactment gave to the islanders. The International Business Companies legislation made it possible to incorporate a new kind of investment vehicle. Before the establishment of the IBC, other jurisdictions marketing themselves to investors as tax havens imposed minimal income tax on investment earnings or else mandated that boards of directors meet once a year on tax-haven soil. Through the IBC vehicle, the British Virgin Islands allowed investors to bypass these constraints. The legislators paid attention to what the offshore investment community wanted, provided it, and rose quickly to prominence as an OFC.

The IBC legislation had other, equally significant, effects on this territory. Chiefly, it enabled the island to rewire its sense of identity; in selling itself into the anonymous flows of global finance, a group of islanders can bolster a relatively stable identity. As Maurer writes:

> While certainly one of the most important pieces of legislation for the economic prosperity for the territory, [the IBC] occupies a place in the national imagination because it is a 'local' law, because 'we' wrote it 'ourselves' and didn't borrow it from anyone, and not necessarily because it had such a huge impact on the economy.
>
> (Maurer, 1997, p.248)

This quote conveys something of the range of influences and non-economic and non-technological work that goes into making a financial territory. Although financial flows may pass everywhere, or so it seems, this does not mean that territories shaped by financial flows are all the same. In the conclusion to his study of British Virgin Islands, Maurer writes:

The production of national difference is not in conflict with globalising tendencies. Rather, the processes of globalisation, including the creation of large-scale legal arenas, capital flows, and migrations, work to foster rather than mute ideas about national uniqueness and national difference ... As it worked toward 'self-rule', the BVI [British Virgin Islands] legislature engaged in a struggle for the authority to constitute a distinct national 'self' that could write laws expressing and regulating its identity. This was a struggle over authorship. The stakes were modern identity and subjecthood. The struggle made a 'history' for the BVI written as the history of 'progress' toward legislative self-determination.

But the kind of national self created through law deeply entrenched continued colonial rule and at the same time fostered the integration of the British Virgin Islands into the world economy. With the authoring of the International Business Companies Ordinance, the BVI named an identity for itself as an author, a modern writer and subject of law, and also as a specialised niche in the world economy, an identity that is marketable. British Virgin Islands' national identity and its identity on the global market are now inseparable, so long as the IBC Ordinance remains in effect and so long as current global conditions and inequalities require the movement of capital across legal regimes.

The BVI's emergence as a tax haven bolstered continued colonial rule around the idea of 'reputation'. To maintain reputability, the BVI has had to assert its 'heritage' of 'law and order'. The national self envisioned in local lawmaking and popular discourse is a 'law and order' self.

(Maurer, 1997, pp.257–8)

Through a mix of financial flows and historical connections, the British Virgin Islands has made an identity that is at once 'distinct' and 'British'. Part of and present in global flows, the islands are dependent on historical colonial interconnections with Britain, made most visible in the British Virgin Islands' introduction of the IBC Ordinance, its trump card in establishing itself as an OFC, a corporate statute which is dependent upon connections to the British common law tradition (Maurer, 1997, p.25).

More broadly, the story of the efforts of British Virgin Islands authorities to make a territory acceptable and attractive to global financial flows reminds us of the importance of history, legal systems, material and cultural practices to processes of constructing a territory in a globalising world. All of these ingredients are to be found when abstract financial flows are unpacked. They are all involved in making flows congeal as well as flow, a point that echoes those made in Section 3 in relation to the lingering importance of key financial centres. The story of the British Virgin Islands also highlights the importance of decisions to the direction that financial flows take and the quality of territories made through them.

In terms of geographies of finance, as Roberts (1994) notes, OFCs have become an essential part of the globalised financial system and speak well to the complex nature of links between territories and flows, since they are 'at once on the margins and at the centre of global capitalism's displacement of crisis' (Roberts, 1994, p.111). Yet we should not read the occasional move to the centre as anything more than a rise up the league tables of global banks' external assets (see Table 2.3); the move is not to the centre of the powerful decision making of global finance. The political economy of global finance remains overwhelmingly under the control of key Western institutions, some of which date back to the Bretton Woods era. The private sector banks headquartered in the symbolic central territories of global finance, and often with branches in many major centres, have more active control of financial flows than any OFC. An important part of the power of such institutions is that they coordinate the movement of finance, an ability out of reach of any OFC.

Clearly, the British Virgin Islands came into existence as a distinct kind of financial territory to facilitate the profitable flow of global finance. Key people on the islands made firm decisions to leap at the opportunity to become a profitable pivot in the movement of finance. However, absent from the discussion so far is any notion of the responsibilities that might attach either to such decisions or to the broader decisions to move global finance around the world generally, or specifically through OFCs where such profits earned can rest safe from fear of taxation. Section 5 will consider this issue in more detail.

Summary

- Offshore financial centres (OFCs) illustrate the complex interdependencies of financial flows and territories.
- Financial flows may evade regulated territories and form new territories such as OFCs.
- The processes involved in making OFCs are not reducible to just one factor such as the enabling abilities of the latest ICTs. Histories, cultures, legal systems, local and international politics all feed the process of making particular financial territories.

5   Making profits, making responsibilities?

This section considers some of the key responsibilities that perhaps should attach to the movement of finance, especially through such territories as OFCs, and the types of decision that might inform a more socially responsible financial architecture.

While most global financial organisations have their main offices in the most powerful centres of global finance, many, particularly banks, have a branch or subsidiary located in an OFC jurisdiction, although such representation may only take the form of a plaque on a wall. The purpose of these branches is to keep the flows of global finance moving. Movement via an OFC keeps deductions in the form of taxes to a minimum. This is a choice that corporations, financial institutions and 'high net worth individuals' make to reduce taxation, as far as legally possible. But are there any wider social costs that potentially result from such decisions, and what type of responsibilities might attach to decisions to make use of tax havens? In a world of increasing globalisation, maybe there is a need to think through some of the wider consequences of funnelling flows of private finance through OFCs.

Activity 2.2

Turn now to Reading 2B by Duncan Campbell (2004) entitled 'Havens that have become a tax on the world's poor', which you will find at the end of the chapter. This is an article from *The Guardian* that not only reports on the quite stunning increase in the number of offshore companies – reportedly now forming at the rate of 150,000 per year – but also points out who pays the burden of tax avoidance. Read the article and note how the wealthy use OFCs to avoid or to lessen their tax bills. In what ways does the issue of 'responsibility' arise in the use of OFCs as a means of avoiding taxation?

[handwritten margin note: nation state no longer control finance]

As Reading 2B certainly makes clear, the issue of tax avoidance raises the question of responsibility. **Barnett et al. (2006)** use the work of Iris Marion Young as a way of reminding us that the borderlines on a map, either marking out political jurisdictions, such as offshore financial centres, or state territories more generally, should not delimit our notion of the idea of responsibility in a globalised world. In the case of finance and tax avoidance, it is helpful to deploy this line of thinking to progress the idea that responsibilities also attach to the movement of finance around the globe. To adopt Young's approach, 'the scope for justice' should follow the flows; the notion of responsibility should not be restricted to a territorially bounded view of finance – after all, global finance now overflows national borders   and thus responsibilities attach broadly to the world-making potential of financial markets. This issue is particularly clear in the case of OFCs. As the author of the report 'Fiscal paradise or tax on development?' writes, tax havens provide the 'secrecy space' where 'anti social and illegal activity' can take place which hits the world's poor hardest of all (Murphy, 2005). There is a real issue here of responsibility – both individual and corporate. As the campaigning group Tax Justice Network spells out:

> The current shape of the globalised economy makes it difficult if not impossible for national tax regimes to collect corporate taxes fairly. Many multinational corporations have structured their affairs in such a way as to avoid taxes in virtually every jurisdiction in which they operate. Some may argue that this demonstrates the innate skills and superior efficiency of these economies. But according to Tax Justice Network the problem of aggressive tax avoidance is a manifestation of systemic failures of global tax policies, leading to market distortions, economic free-riding, slower rates of global growth and widening wealth disparities within and between nation states. The lack of political will to tackle these systemic failures undermines the integrity of tax regimes and opens up possibilities for business to compete on an unethical and harmful basis. ... Businesses which engage in aggressive tax avoidance are failing in their role as corporate citizens and demonstrating a lack of integrity in their dealings with society.
>
> (Misbach et al., 2005)

You may agree with the above words. Alternatively, you may consider an eminent judge's dissenting statement in a tax case dating from 1947 to be a more appropriate view of taxation. Those who favour minimum taxation cite his words with great regularity: 'there is nothing sinister in so arranging one's affairs as to keep taxes as low as possible. Everybody does so, rich or poor; and all do right, for nobody owes any public duty to pay more than the law demands; taxes are enforced exactions, not voluntary contributions' (Judge Learned Hand, 1947).

Yet just how appropriate are the judge's views in our present interconnected, interdependent, globalising world? Is it still appropriate to think territorially, that is, in a bounded nation state sense, about such responsibilities as tax payments when their payment could help to even out a very economically and socially uneven world? Is it

it is irresponsible

responsible of an individual to use offshore tax havens aggressively to avoid taxation when his or her fellow citizens stand to lose out because of this decision? In the light of earlier sections, perhaps we should also ask whether there is scope for rethinking the financial architecture that currently permits the use of OFCs to avoid tax. It may be possible to design a different architecture to divert flows of tax payments to rebuild less developed territories.

The issues raised here cannot be brushed aside easily. After all, substantial sums are involved. In 1998, estimates (and this is all there can be given the elusiveness of offshore business) by Merrill Lynch/ Cap Gemini in their World Wealth Report suggested that the value of assets held by the rich with liquid financial assets of US$1 million or more was US$27.2 trillion in 2002/2003, of which $8.5 trillion (31 per cent) was held offshore. The figure is increasing by an estimated $600 billion per year, making the 2005 figure about $9.7 trillion (Misbach et al., 2005).

Some may argue that a definite responsibility exists to pay taxes demanded of one's nation state because these sums may be used to the benefit of society as a whole. Furthermore, especially for large international corporations, financial gains achieved through a world of entangled flows **(Allen, 2006)** mean that wider responsibilities are owed. According to tax research experts, working with official data such as those from the Bank for International Settlement as well as Forbes and Cap Gemini, the figure of US$255 billion is the annual global tax loss resulting from wealthy individuals holding their assets offshore (Misbach et al., 2005). The present financial architecture helps to produce such tax losses. As the director of the Global Economies Programme at the New Economic Foundation notes:

relationship with states

states are not seeing more multinational companies

> The issues of tax havens and tax competition are symptomatic of a much wider malaise at the heart of the international financial system. This is a critical time for development, and particularly for the achievement of the Millennium Development Goals. If we are serious about reducing poverty, one of the first things we need to tackle is an international financial system run by the rich, for the rich, at the expense of the poor. It is time to rethink what the system is for.
>
> (quoted in Campbell, 2005, p.4)

To ask what the system of financial markets and flows is about and for whom it exists (questions aired in the early discussion of Section 2) is not as idealistic as it may sound. In fact, this is just what governments have been doing for a decade or more. OFCs have been criticised on a number of grounds and by a range of institutions. The earliest and most extensive critique has concerned their usefulness to organised crime and, more recently, terrorism. The US Government took action in the 1980s, first through duress, and then through treaties, to obtain access to information relevant to criminal investigations. In 1989, the G7 group of industrialised countries set up the Financial Action Task Force (FATF) to press all OFCs to cooperate with law enforcement agencies and then to take proactive responsibility to 'know their customers', as the FATF would put it, and to report suspicious transactions. Curiously, this increased regulation seems to have promoted more use of OFCs as their reputation improved.

A more aggressive challenge to OFCs came in 1996 as the OECD launched a campaign against 'harmful tax competition'. Initially, it targeted low tax rates per se as well as other tax arrangements that were classed as damaging. The campaign to shame OFCs ran into two serious problems. First, some of the harmful practices were found in onshore tax arrangements, including those of some OECD members, notably Switzerland. Second, once President George W. Bush took office, the USA changed its position to argue that territories were entitled to set low tax rates, provided they applied to local as well as non-resident businesses. As a result, much of the force went out of the initiative, and it became a largely technical revision of tax laws and regulation in both on- and offshore centres. Some OFCs were able to delay implementation of some provisions by stating that they would only implement them when Switzerland did so, knowing that this was unlikely. Similar problems arose during the European Union's (EU) negotiations over its Savings Tax Directive, which was intended to require EU and associated territories, especially British dependencies, to supply information about EU citizens' interest earnings to their home tax authorities. Again, this had to be modified to give some financial centres the option of applying a withholding tax (a tax on interest taken by the host country and regardless of the account holder's circumstances) rather than supplying the information, since they feared that business would be lost to Switzerland.

The modest results of these attempts to deal with OFCs in isolation, rather than tackling major onshore centres, are a reminder that the problems of tax losses because of international financial flows are a difficulty of a whole system rather than simply of one of its components. But then what does 'a whole system' mean? And how is responsibility distributed within it? **Allen's (2006)** analysis of multinational manufacturing pointed to the way in which global inequalities are the result of a myriad of decisions and actions. The same can be said in the case of finance. Finance and banking is now one of the biggest employers of people in many developed countries. Every day, people sign forms, check accounts, shift an investment from here to there, make small decisions that are part of bigger ones.

In this chapter, we have come across those who design new legislation to entice people to OFCs, those who dream up the new financial packages, and those who participate in the major world financial centres of London, New York and Tokyo. All of them are implicated in 'the system' and, in that sense, responsibility is distributed among them. The same argument that applies to consumers of sweatshop clothes also applies to consumers of finance.

Activity 2.3

You may not work in finance, but there might be other ways in which you are entangled with it. See if you can identify some ways in which you participate in financial systems. Try to think not only about how you are entangled, but whether you have any room for changing how you participate.

Obviously, we cannot provide you with answers, but here are a few hints in relation to the question of how you may be entangled:

1   Do you have bank or building society current accounts? If you used to bank with the Midland Bank or Abbey National Building Society, you will have had the post Bretton Woods era brought to your attention by waking up to find yourself a customer of the Hong Kong and Shanghai or another bank with global intentions – but do you know what that means for the interest you pay or receive?

2   Do you have savings or investments, either directly or through a pension fund or life assurance account? Do you know where or how the interest, dividends or bonuses you receive are earned? Have you thought of adopting an 'ethical investment' position and, if so, what does that mean to you?

3   Do you have debts, whether on credit card, personal loan or mortgage? If you had a mortgage thirty years ago, you might want to reflect on the fact that it was difficult to get, but charged low and sometimes negative interest when inflation was taken into account, whereas in recent years mortgages have been freely available but remorselessly positive with their rates. We might view this as the contrast between Bretton Woods and neo-liberalism writ small.

While it is important to understand the way in which so many of us are implicated in the current financial architecture, and therefore in some measure have responsibility within it, it is also the case that this responsibility is distributed very unequally. One of the strongest themes of this chapter has been that, in the middle of all the flux and flow of globalised finance, there are systematic territorial concentrations of power. The global reach of finance sets up a string of complex interdependencies between territories. Yet the flows and the strengths of territories involved are far from equal. There is clear inequality, for instance, between the economic and financial strengths of global financial markets organised through, say, New York and the financial resources available to Malaysia. There is thus real possibility that massive flows of rather impetuous finance may reshape less economically powerful countries, and not always in ways that such countries would prefer. The process of shaping and reshaping the territories of nation states through financial flows is buttressed, lest we forget, just as much by the actions of international institutions such as the IMF as it is by the equally coercive powers of leading private sector financial organisations such as large investment banks and their influential performance indices, as we saw again in the case of Malaysia in Section 2.3.

There is also a broad global geography here. Many of the major economic powers are beneficiaries of the finance industry – possibly the UK more than any other – and so they tend to be very cautious in considering changes to the system, or even tighter regulation. It remains to be seen whether pressure groups like the Tax Justice Network and Oxfam will be able to enlist sufficient support to move from a radical reappraisal of the consequences of a liberalised financial system towards some form of tighter international regulation. The past changes in financial architecture show that changes can happen, but the alliance that brought about the neo-liberal system of today remains extremely powerful.

Summary

- The movement of finance involves decisions, and with these come responsibilities that draw into critical focus wider social and political interdependencies between global financial flows and territories.
- These responsibilities are dispersed and varied, following the geographies of power within the financial architecture.

6 Conclusion

As the chapter has shown, finances need to flow to make a profit. Yet, for all the speed, scale and global reach that has come to characterise finance on the move, these flows also need to fix and settle. There need to be buildings, there needs to be face-to-face contact, and there is the need to build trust. Moreover, certain territories can adapt themselves specifically to be the places that best fulfil these requirements of finance.

As we saw in Section 2, the past few decades have seen the concentration of financial market making in just a few key territories or financial centres. The continued significance of certain territories, like London and New York, lies in the fact that, although dematerialised and seemingly ethereal, finance needs to settle in particular places where information, expertise and contacts are most concentrated. Those responsible for making markets in finance and for moving finance into and out of a range of territories around the globe are found in such centres. This, then, achieves the first aim of this chapter.

Where finance flows and where it settles are the outcomes of decisions. The map of possible routes and destinations for finance is drawn by a range of decision makers that may be made up of private sector organisations, or states and international institutions, like the IMF, or a combination of these and other groups. No matter who makes the decisions, it is clear that there is a need for sets of rules and regulations, a financial architecture, to ensure that as far as possible flows do not lead to financial crises.

We have also seen that these architectures of territories and flows, though produced through powerful forces, can break down and require rebuilding. The collapse of one such architecture, the Bretton Woods Agreement, saw the liberalisation of finance. This marked a shift from state-organised regulation of financial markets to a market-orchestrated system. In effect, it set finance free to explore the globe, and it occurred at a time of rapid innovation and development of ICTs. The combination of liberalising financial flows and their digitisation through the latest ICTs has led to the intensification of interdependencies between financial flows and economic territories.

Finance can now circulate globally and in a variety of combinations following the liberalisation of financial markets. Rather than finance which is organised to fund trade, as tended to be the case in the Bretton Woods era, finance today can fund itself in speculative explorations around the globe such as short-term portfolio flows and bank lending, as well as provide funds such as FDI in a string of developing countries. Finance now circulates at a global level, but still fixes and settles in territories for short or long periods in an effort to enhance its profitability.

The examples of OFCs and the consequences of financial liberalisation bring to the fore the simple fact that there is no inevitability about the present global financial architecture. Interdependencies between flows and territories made through private financial markets could be otherwise. It is conceivable that wider social and political responsibilities might inform the making of a new financial architecture – one that would allow finance to make the world go round differently.

Chapter 1 showed how some aspects of the world that we tend to experience as stable and unchanging, such as the ground beneath our feet or the broader patterns of climate, turn out to be much more dynamic when viewed in terms of interacting territories and flows. Even nature, it was argued, shifts and flows. In this chapter, we have examined an example of flows set up and set into motion by human actors, flows that are often taken to be the very epitome of the rootless, restless character of life in a globalised world. When viewed in terms of their dynamic relationship with territories, however, these flows revealed strong tendencies to settle down, to fix or entrench themselves in particular places. Chapter 3 looks at some of the ways that nature moves – or is made to move – in the context of the economic or financial systems introduced in this chapter, and it considers the question of what kind of architecture might best regulate the movement and settling of nature in a globalised world.

References

Allen, J. (2006) 'Claiming connections: a distant world of sweatshops' in Barnett, C., Robinson, J. and Rose, G. (eds) *A Demanding World*, Milton Keynes, The Open University.

Athukorala, P. (2001) *Crisis and Recovery in Malaysia: The Role of Capital Controls*, Cheltenham, Edward Elgar Publishing.

Barnett, C., Robinson, J. and Rose, G. (2006) 'Conclusion' in Barnett, C., Robinson, J. and Rose, G. (eds) *A Demanding World*, Milton Keynes, The Open University.

Campbell, D. (2004) 'Havens that have become a tax on the world's poor', *The Guardian*, 21 September, p.14.

Campbell, D. (2005) 'Where the rich stash their cash', *The Observer*, Business Section, 27 March, pp.4–5.

Darbar, S, Johnston, R.B. and Zephrin, M.G. (2003) 'Assessing offshore financial centres: filling the gap in global surveillance', *Finance and Development*, September, pp.32–5.

Deutsche Bank (2004) 'An introduction to the offshore group', http://www.dboffshore.com, (accessed on 7 April 2005).

Dixon, L. (2001) 'Financial flows via offshore financial centres', *Bank of England Financial Stability Review*, June 2001, pp.105–6.

Euromoney (2002) *Offshore Finance Yearbook*, London, Euromoney Books.

Hirst, P. and Thompson, G. (1999) *Globalisation in Question*, Cambridge, Polity Press. (First published in 1996.)

Judge Learned Hand (1947) Commissioner vs Newman, 159 F.2D, 848, 850–1 (CA2).

Kose, M.A. and Prasad, E.S. (2004) 'Liberalising capital account restrictions', *Finance and Development*, September, pp.50–1.

Martin, R. (1994) 'The end of geography?' in Corbridge, S., Martin, R. and Thrift, N. (eds) *Money, Power, Space*, Oxford, Blackwell.

Maurer, B. (1997) *Recharting the Caribbean*, Michigan, Michigan University Press.

Merrill Lynch and Cap Gemini (2004) *World Wealth Report*, New York, NY, Merrill Lynch & Co., Inc., World Financial Centre.

Misbach, A., Gurtner, B. and Christensen, J. (2005) 'The price of offshore', http://www.taxjustice.net (accessed 12 April 2005).

Murphy, R. (2005) 'Fiscal paradise or a tax on development?', http://www.taxjustice.net (accessed 12 April 2005).

Panić, M. (1995) 'The Bretton Woods system: concept and practice' in Mitchie, J. and Grieve Smith, J. (eds) *Managing the Global Economy*, Oxford, Oxford University Press, pp.37–54.

Patnaik, P. (1999) 'The real face of financial liberalisation', *The Hindu*, vol.16, no.4, 13–26 February, reproduced in http://www.geocities.com/Eureka/Concourse/8751/edisi03/glob03.htm (14 January 2005).

Pryke, M. and Lee, R. (1995) 'Place your bets: towards an understanding of globalisation, socio-financial engineering and competition within a financial centre', *Urban Studies*, vol.32, no.2, pp.329 44.

Roberts, S. (1994) 'Fictitious capital, fictitious spaces: the geography of offshore financial flows' in Corbridge, S., Martin, R. and Thrift, N. (eds) *Money, Power, Space*, Oxford, Blackwell.

Sassen, S. (2004) 'The locational and institutional embededdness of electronic markets' in Bevir, M. and Trentmann, F. (eds) *Markets in Historical Context: Ideas and Politics in the Modern World*, Cambridge, Cambridge University Press.

Solomon, E.H. (1997) *Virtual Money*, Oxford, Oxford University Press.

Strange, S. (1994) 'From Bretton Woods to the casino economy' in Corbridge, S., Martin, R. and Thrift, N. (eds) *Money, Power, Space*, Oxford, Blackwell.

Thrift, N. (1994) 'On the social and cultural determinants of international financial centres: the case of the City of London' in Corbridge, S., Martin, R. and Thrift, N. (eds) *Money, Power, Space*, Oxford, Blackwell.

Walsh, C. (2004) 'Cayman reaps the whirlwind', *The Observer*, Business Section, 3 October, p.7.

[handwritten margin notes: "Territories", "flaw", "rules + regulation", "in reality and rendering territories", "meaning?", "flows important to financial mikm but so are territories"]

Reading 2A

Saskia Sassen, 'The locational and institutional embededness of electronic markets'

The continuing utility of spatial agglomeration

The continuing weight of major centres is, in a way, countersensical, as is, for that matter, the existence of an expanding network of financial centres. The rapid development of electronic exchanges, the growing digitization of much financial activity, the fact that finance has become one of the leading sectors in a growing number of countries, and that it is a sector that produces a dematerialized, hybermobile product, all suggest that location should not matter. In fact geographical dispersal would seem to be a good option given the high cost of operating in major financial centres. Further, the last ten years have seen an increased geographic mobility of experts and financial services firms.

There are, in my view, at least three reasons that explain the trend towards consolidation in a few centres rather than massive dispersal.

(a) *The importance of social connectivity and central functions*. First, while the new communications technologies do indeed facilitate geographic dispersal of economic activities without losing system integration, they have also had the effect of strengthening the importance of central coordination and control functions for firms and, even, markets. Indeed for firms in any sector, operating a widely dispersed network of branches and affiliates and operating in multiple markets has made central functions far more complicated. Their execution requires access to top talent, not only inside headquarters but also, more generally, access to innovative milieux – in technology, accounting, legal services, economic forecasting, and all sorts of other, many new, specialized corporate services. Major centres have massive concentrations of state of the art resources that allow them to maximize the benefits of the new communication technologies and to govern the new conditions for operating globally. Even electronic markets such as NASDAQ and E*Trade rely on traders and banks which are located somewhere, with at least some in a major financial centre. The question of risk and how it is handled and perceived is yet another factor which has an impact on how the industry organizes itself, where it locates operations, what markets become integrated into the global capital market, and so on.

One fact that has become increasingly evident is that to maximize the benefits of the new information technologies firms need not only the infrastructure but a complex mix of other resources. In my analysis organizational complexity is a key variable allowing firms to maximize the utility/benefits they can derive from using digital technology. In the case of financial markets we could make a parallel argument. Most of the value added that these technologies can produce for advanced service firms lies in so-called externalities. And this means the material and human resources – state-of-the-art office buildings, top talent, and the social networking infrastructure that maximizes connectivity. Any town can have fibre optic cables, but this is not sufficient.

A second fact that is emerging with greater clarity concerns the meaning of 'information.' There are two types of information. One is the datum, which may be complex yet is standard knowledge: the level at which a stock market closes, a privatization of a public utility, the bankruptcy of a bank. But there is a far more difficult type of 'information', akin to an interpretation/evaluation/judgement. It entails negotiating a series of data and a series of interpretations of a mix of data in the hope of producing a higher order datum. Access to the first kind of information is now global and immediate from just about any place in the highly developed world thanks to the digital revolution. But it is the second type of information that requires a complicated mixture of elements – the social infrastructure for global connectivity – which gives major financial centres a leading edge.

It is possible, in principle, to reproduce the technical infrastructure anywhere. Singapore, for example, has technical connectivity matching Hong Kong's. But does it have Hong Kong's social connectivity? At a higher level of global social connectivity we could probably say the same for Frankfurt and London. When the more complex forms of information needed to execute major international deals cannot be got from existing data bases, no matter what one can pay, then one needs the social information loop and the associated de facto interpretations and inferences that come with bouncing off information among talented, informed people. It is the weight of this input that has given a whole new importance to credit rating agencies, for instance. Part of the rating has to do with interpreting and inferring. When this interpreting becomes 'authoritative' it becomes 'information' available to all. The process of making inferences/ interpretations into 'information' takes quite a mix of talents and resources as well as a professional subculture. In brief, financial centres provide the social connectivity which allows a firm or market to maximize the benefits of its technical connectivity.

(b) *Cross-border mergers and alliances.* Global firms and markets in the financial industry need enormous resources, a trend which is leading to rapid mergers and acquisitions of firms and strategic alliances among markets in different countries. These are happening on a scale and in combinations few would have foreseen as recently as the early 1990s.

There are growing numbers of mergers among respectively financial services firms, accounting firms, law firms, insurance brokers, in brief, firms that need to provide a global service. A similar evolution is also possible for the global telecommunications industry which will have to consolidate in order to offer a state-of-the-art, globe-spanning service to its global clients, among which are the financial firms.

Bloomberg?

I would argue that yet another kind of 'merger' is the consolidation of electronic networks that connect a very select number of markets. There are a number of networks that have been set up in the last few years to connect exchanges. In 1999 NASDAQ, the second largest US stock market after the New York Stock Exchange, set up Nasdaq Japan and in 2000 Nasdaq Canada. This gives investors in Japan and Canada direct access to the market in the US. Europe's more than thirty stock exchanges have been seeking to shape various alliances. Euronext (NEXT) is Europe's largest stock exchange merger, an alliance among the Paris, Amsterdam and Brussels bourses. The Toronto Stock Exchange has joined an alliance with the New York Stock Exchange (NYSE) to create a separate global trading platform. The NYSE is a founding member of a global trading alliance, Global Equity Market (GEM) which includes ten exchanges, among them Tokyo and NEXT. Also small exchanges are merging: in March 2001 the Tallinn Stock Exchange in Estonia and its Helsinki counterpart created an alliance. A novel pattern is hostile takeovers, not of firms, but of exchanges, such as the attempt by the owners of the Stockholm Stock Exchange to buy the London Stock Exchange (for a price of US$3.7 billion).

Merging of bourses but nevertheless bourses still remain important

These developments may well ensure the consolidation of a stratum of select financial centres at the top of the worldwide network of thirty or forty cities through which the global financial industry operates. Taking an indicator such as equities under management shows a similar pattern of spread and simultaneous concentration at the top of the hierarchy. The worldwide distribution of equities under institutional management is spread among a large number of cities which have become integrated into the global equity market along with deregulation of their economies and the whole notion of 'emerging markets' as an attractive investment destination. In 1999, institutional money managers around the world controlled approximately US$14 trillion. Thomson Financials (1999), for instance, has estimated that at the end of 1999, twenty-five cities accounted for about 80 per cent of the world's valuation. These twenty-five cities also accounted for roughly 48 per cent of the total market capitalization of the world which stood at US$24 trillion at the end of 1999. On the other hand, this global market is characterized by a disproportionate concentration in the top six or seven cities. London, New York and Tokyo together accounted for a third of the world's total equities under institutional management in 1999.

These developments make clear a second important trend that in many ways specifies the current global era. These various centres don't just compete with each other: there is collaboration and division of labour. In the international system of the post-war decades, each country's financial centre, in principle, covered the universe of necessary functions to service its national companies and markets. The world of finance was, of course, much simpler than it is today. In the initial stage of deregulation in the 1980s there was a strong tendency to see the relation among the major centres as one of straight competition when it came to international transactions. New York, London and Tokyo, then the major centres in the system, were seen as competing. But in my research in the later 1980s on these three top centres I found clear evidence of a division of labour already then. They remain the major centres in the system today with the addition of Frankfurt and Paris in the 1990s. What we are seeing now is an additional pattern whereby the cooperation or division of functions is somewhat institutionalized: strategic alliances not only between firms across borders but also between markets. There is competition, strategic collaboration and hierarchy.

In brief, the need for enormous resources to handle increasingly global operations, in combination with the growth of central functions described earlier, produces strong tendencies towards concentration and hence hierarchy even as the network of financial centres has expanded.

(c) *De-nationalized elites and agendas.* National attachments and identities are becoming weaker for global firms and their customers. This is particularly strong in the West, but may develop in Asia as well. Deregulation and privatization have weakened the need for national financial centres. The nationality question simply plays differently in these sectors than it did even a decade ago. Global financial products are accessible in national markets and national investors can operate in global markets. For instance, some of the major Brazilian firms now list on the New York Stock Exchange, and by-pass the São Paulo exchange, a new practice which has caused somewhat of an uproar in specialized circles in Brazil. While it is as yet inconceivable in the Asian case, this may well change given the growing number of foreign acquisitions of major firms in several Asian countries. Another indicator of this trend is the fact that the major US and European investment banks have set up specialized offices in London to handle various aspects of their global business. Even French banks have set up some of their global specialized operations in London, inconceivable a decade ago and still not avowed in national rhetoric.

One way of describing this process is as what I call an incipient and highly specialized denationalization of particular institutional arenas. It can be argued that such denationalization is a necessary condition for economic globalization as we know it today. The sophistication of this system lies in the fact that it only needs to involve strategic institutional areas – most national systems can be left basically unaltered. China is a good example. It adopted international accounting rules in 1993, necessary to engage in international transactions. To do so it did not have to change much of its domestic economy. Japanese firms operating overseas adopted such standards long before Japan's government considered requiring them. In this regard the 'wholesale' side of globalization is quite different from the global consumer markets, in which success necessitates altering national tastes at a mass level. This process of denationalization has been strengthened by state policy enabling privatization and foreign acquisition. In some ways one might say that the Asian financial crisis has functioned as a mechanism to denationalize, at least partly, control over key sectors of economies which, while allowing the massive entry of foreign investment, never relinquished that control. Major international business centres produce what we could think of as a new subculture, a move from the 'national' version of international activities to the 'global' version. The long-standing resistance in Europe to M&As, especially hostile takeovers, or to foreign ownership and control in East Asia, signal national business cultures that are somewhat incompatible with the new global economic culture. I would posit that major cities, and the variety of so-called global business meetings (such as those of the World Economic Forum in Davos and other similar occasions), contribute to denationalize corporate elites. Whether this is good or bad is a separate issue; but it is, I would argue, one of the conditions for setting in place the systems and subcultures necessary for a global economic system.

(Sassen, 2004, pp.236–41)

Reading 2B

Havens that have become a tax on the world's poor

Duncan Campbell

Billions of pounds, enough to pay for the entire primary health and education needs of the world's developing countries, are being siphoned off through offshore companies and tax havens, according to a body formed to expose the offenders.

Aid organisations are alarmed that money which should be used for building the infrastructure of the poorest countries is being hidden in havens by corrupt politicians and multinationals exploiting tax loopholes. Offshore companies are being formed at the rate of about 150,000 a year. While in the 70s there were just 25 tax havens, there are at least 63 now, about half of them British protectorates or former colonies. Tax avoidance in

Britain alone is estimated at between £25bn and £85bn.

This month the Tax Justice Network, which was formed last year by tax experts and economists worried about the trend, launched an international secretariat in London. It will work with the UN and other international bodies to reverse the practice of hiding money from governments worldwide.

John Christensen, coordinator of the secretariat,

said: 'Many developing countries are now dominated by elites that are involved in tax havens. Things have actually got worse in the last few years.' As new havens are formed, existing ones offer better deals.

Mr Christensen, a former economic adviser to the Jersey government who has also worked at the then Department of Overseas Development and with Oxfam, said many of the havens were now 'locked in a desperate competition. They like to suggest that they oil the wheels of global capital but there is no case for that. What has happened is that tax havens transfer the burden of tax away from capital and towards labour and the consumer.'

He also believes that the attraction of making money by putting it in offshore havens damaged British industry because money which could have been invested in Britain had been removed from the country.

Kofi Annan, the UN secretary general, has also expressed concern that money which should be spent on developing countries is being moved offshore.

A UN spokesman confirmed yesterday that Mr Annan saw the issue as a priority. 'The secretary general has indicated repeatedly that he believes money should be spent on development rather than going offshore,' he said.

The secretariat believes the UN has a vital role to play in tracking the money. 'The remedies have to be global and the UN is the only body able to do it,' said Mr Christensen. 'The WTO [World Trade Organisation] has failed.'

Tax havens have also attracted the attention of John Kerry, the US Democratic party's presidential candidate, who has indicated that if elected he will pursue the companies that hide their profits abroad. In April, the US general accounting office said 61% of US corporations paid no federal income tax in the late 90s. Tax havens contain only 1.2% of the world's population and 3% of the world's GDP, but 26% of assets and 31% of the profits of US multinationals are held there.

Global phenomena

Almost every part of the world now has access to havens. Europeans can use the old-established ones such as Jersey and Liechtenstein or the newer ones, like Cyprus and Malta; the Asian Pacific has the Pacific islands and Singapore; India and southern Africa have the Seychelles and Mauritius; and North America has the Caribbean islands and Central America.

While a number of havens, such as the Cayman islands and Bermuda, have improved

regulations, the effect of this has been, in the view of Mr Christensen, to legitimise them. 'Merely chasing out the worst havens and setting international standards for the better ones does little to address the real problems,' he said.

The list of political figures who have availed themselves of the system includes Haiti's 'Baby Doc' Duvalier, Zaire's President Mobutu, Sani Abacha, the former president of Nigeria, and Raul Salinas, the brother of the former Mexican president. Mr Abacha, during his period as president, had a standing order to transfer $15m (£8.4m at current exchange rates) a day of stolen funds to his Swiss bank account. Much of this money has been lost forever to the countries concerned although some has been traced; the current president of Nigeria recently visited Jersey to thank the authorities there for tracking down the millions that Mr Abacha had hidden.

In 1999, the Economist estimated that African leaders had $20bn in Swiss bank accounts alone, twice the amount that sub-Saharan Africa spends on servicing debts.

Among the latest countries offering such services is Somalia, which Mr Christensen describes as 'an example of what can happen when the cancer is not cut out'. He believes that the main function of the financial *moneys [shareholders] could* / *not be reinvested* / *in worthwhile* / *projects and* / *schemes is doing* / *indeed* / *to make* / *people extremely rich* / *just a few*

Chapter 2 Making Finance, Making Worlds 103

markets in Somalia will be money laundering.

Tax avoidance also breeds other unethical habits: when Enron was investigated in 2001, it emerged it had 881 offshore subsidiaries, 692 incorporated in the Cayman islands. The change has been assisted by technological change in communication and the liberalisation of the marketplace.

Many major charities are also concerned about the situation. 'The implications of tax avoidance on development are manifold,' said Tim Peat, economic justice campaigner at War on Want. 'While transnational corporations endeavour to hold on to cash by shoring it up in tax havens, millions are lost that could have been used in the fight against poverty.'

'Every time we investigate corruption in the oil industry, we find that looted public money has been laundered through offshore tax havens,' said Gavin Hayman of Global Witness, the international resource watchdog group.

'Billions of dollars pass from public to private hands this way with no comeback. The collateral damage to the licit international system and to international development is truly enormous and the only people who benefit are those who have something bad to hide. Tax havens are the seedy backstreet bars of the financial world, where corporations and multi-millionaires huddle in shadowy corners to pursue their business out of sight of respectable citizens.'

Instability

The latest Oxfam report on tax havens, on which Mr Christensen worked, suggested the amount secreted in tax havens was equivalent to six times the estimated annual cost of universal primary education and almost three times the cost of universal primary health.

He said that offshore centres undermined economies in three ways: the capacity of countries to raise tax revenue was limited, thus restricting a poor country's ability to finance investments in health and education; secondly, the offshore system provided a safe haven for money laundering, illicit arms dealing and diamond trafficking; thirdly, the offshore system contributed to financial instability which led to the crises in the Indonesian and Thai economies in the 90s. His colleague Sony Kapoor, the secretariat's economic adviser, agreed: 'Tax evasion and tax avoidance on a large scale is inhibiting development in poor countries and eroding the existing welfare state in the rich states.'

A variety of international organisations are now attempting to address the problem in differing ways. They include the Organisation for Economic Cooperation and Development, the EU, the UN drugs control programme and the Financial Action Task Force, which was set up by the G7 countries. Charities and churches across Europe, particularly in France, are also becoming more involved.

Richard Murphy, of Tax Research, which works closely with the new organisation, said it was important that the wealthier countries were seen not to be dictating terms to poorer countries.

'You cannot dictate to nation states their level of taxes,' he said, 'but you can require that they only tax what is theirs to tax.'

The notion of tax havens goes back to just after the Napoleonic wars when demobbed officers moved to Jersey, but it was not until the 1960s that the high rates of British taxation acted as a motivation for people to move their money abroad.

Allowing British protectorates or former colonies to set themselves up as tax havens was also an attractive proposition for Britain in that it allowed those places to become self-sufficient. Now the whole process has accelerated to the extent that billions of pounds are being removed from the very countries that need them most.

(Campbell, 2004, p.14)

Bioprospecting and the global entanglement of people, plants and pills

Nick Bingham

Contents

1   Introduction

It is estimated that nearly 100 billion aspirin tablets are taken every year globally. Although we have endeavoured to write this book in such a way that reading it does not cause too many headaches and thus unnecessarily add to that figure, such an enormous number does mean that it is very unlikely that there are many people who have picked up this book who have not had one (and probably fairly recently). At the present time it is probable that it would have been taken as a painkiller, or perhaps in order to thin the blood, but researchers are now telling us that aspirin may be of benefit to everything from diabetes to dementia, cataracts to cancer. No wonder that (despite some significant side effects) it is regularly referred to as a 'miracle' or a 'wonder' drug, and that that 100 billion is expected only to increase in the future.

Have you ever considered, however, the origin of that miracle and wonder, or how there come to be 100 billion tablets available to take, ready and waiting at the local shop, if not in the medicine cabinet at home? Probably not, and fair enough (you are most likely taking it to stop the pain, after all). But, in fact, every time you pop one of those pills, you are participating in long and complex geographies and histories which stretch from plants to pharmaceuticals, and from ancient civilisations to modern medicine. The horticultural writer David Stuart explains:

> Its modern history started on 10 August 1897, when Felix Hoffmann, a chemist working for a German dyestuffs company called Bayer, managed to acetylate the phenol group of a widely prescribed compound called salicylic acid. Hoffmann's new substance was acetylsalicylic acid. He was extremely excited. Salicylic acid produced from natural materials had been known since the 1830s. It was used, at high doses, to treat the pain and swelling in diseases such as arthritis, and to treat fever in illnesses like influenza. It had a bad side effect: acute stomach irritation. It did indeed reduce inflammation, but many sufferers found its effects too extreme to continue. Felix Hoffmann's father had arthritis and also suffered the side effects of salicylic acid. Felix thought that if he could alter the chemistry of the basic salicylic acid by incorporating an acetyl group into the molecule, the new

formula might be less of an irritant. It was. The head of Bayer's pharmacology laboratory, Heinrich Dreser, was impressed. He even tested Hoffmann's new drug on himself. He then demonstrated the anti-inflammatory and pain killing effects of acetylsalicylic acid on animals. The new substance, given the commercial name of aspirin, was soon in use worldwide. Hoffmann's discovery paved the way for the modern pharmaceuticals industry.

Aspirin was only two steps removed from a living plant. The first step was made in 1829, when a pharmacist called Henri Leroux discovered a crystalline compound in the bark of willow trees that he called salicylin. This, he discovered, was the active chemical. A few years later, an Italian chemist called Raffaele Piria split up 'salicylin' to obtain salicylic acid in a pure state. This was much easier to administer than either natural bark extract or salicylin, and could be easily created in the laboratory or the factory. Felix Hoffmann made the third step.

The step before the chemists' first step was made thousands of years earlier. Clay tablets from the Sumerian period in Mesopotamia, one of the earliest of all urban cultures, describe the use of willow leaves to treat rheumatism. The ancient Egyptians also used the willow leaf and bark potions for their painkilling effects. Chinese doctors were using willow by 500 BC. Hippocrates prescribed it for women in painful labour; he also used it for aches and fever. In North America, the black willow (*Salix nigra*), which has a slightly different form of salicylin, was used by native Americans as a remedy for asthma, colds, influenza and indigestion, and as a diaphoretic and sedative.

(Stuart, 2004, pp.62, 64)

Even this fairly lengthy quotation only begins to do justice to the range of characters (both human and nonhuman) that were involved in making aspirin so commonplace today that most of us reading this book have the privilege of assuming both its availability and its efficacy. Stuart's words do give a sense, however, of three things. The first is that the ultimate source of the miracle and wonder of one of our most important pharmaceutical products is to be found not in a laboratory but in a plant. The second is that it took a huge amount of effort (on the part of healers, scientists and corporations, for example)

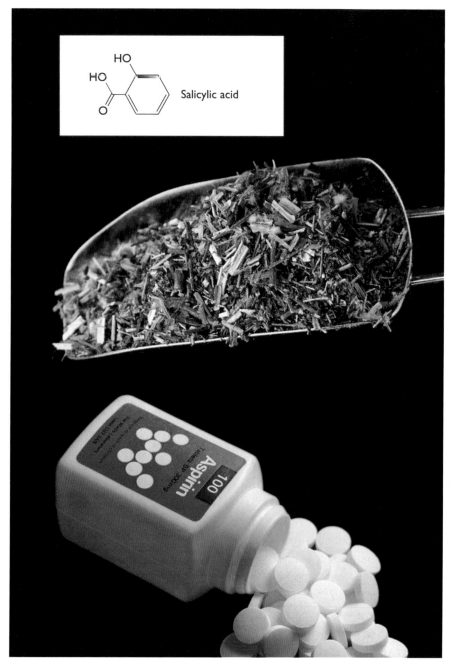

Figure 3.1   Aspects of aspirin

and a wide range of knowledges (from what was inscribed on the Mesopotamian tablets, and information passed down through mainly oral traditions by indigenous Americans, to Western chemical formulae) to 'make' aspirin. And the third is that each of the three big 'steps' that Stuart mentions involved taking what was available and transforming it (from plant to bark extract, bark extract to salicylic acid, salicylic acid to acetylsalicylic acid, and thus to aspirin more or less as we know it) into a form that was both more effective (to obtain pain relief from arthritis takes between 3 and 21 cups of willow bark tea) and more easily distributed (eventually into powder and then tablets).

In what follows, these three points about *plants*, *effort* and *transformation* turn out to be generalisable, both to the main example of the chapter and, more broadly, to the consideration of a globalised world-in-the-making which animates this book. More specifically, in this chapter I shall bring together the messages of Chapters 1 and 2 to explore one way in which people are entangled with the biophysical aspects of the planet in a neo-liberal market system. That entanglement has been given the name of 'bioprospecting' and consideration of it will take us deeper into the world of plants, knowledges and big business that the aspirin example introduced.

This examination will reinforce why understanding the making of our globalised world means appreciating both the long and complex histories and geographies that have got us to where we are, and also what is different and specific about the form those histories and geographies are taking now. This double requirement will shape the structure of the chapter. Section 2 traces the long and globe-spanning entanglement of people and plants I have already touched on with the aspirin example above. Sections 3, 4 and 5 then outline the three developments that make bioprospecting now both different from as well as connected to the global movements of plants that went before. Finally, before a very brief conclusion, I will summarise in Section 6 some of the main challenges these developments pose to our living in a globalised world and some of the alternative responses to those challenges.

> ## Chapter aims
>
> ◆   To consider why bioprospecting is a key contemporary form of entanglement of people and plants in a globalised world.
>
> ◆   To appreciate that the effort required to make pills from plants is an example of the more general work that has to be done to make and remake a globalised world.
>
> ◆   To understand that the key transformations involved in bioprospecting represent a particular interplay of territory and flow, a particular interplay which operates in the making of a globalised world more broadly.

2   People and plants: a globalising relationship

Not being able to move might seem a strange place to start to think about globalisation, but according to the writer Michael Pollan, that is exactly where we need to begin if we want to understand how plants have traversed the planet. For it is immobility (or rather the inability to move of their own accord) which, he argues, is the 'great existential fact of plant life' (Pollan, 2002, p.xviii). It is the source of their greatest weakness – 'Plants can't escape the creatures that prey on them; they also can't change location or extend their range without help' (p.xviii) – but also of their incredible complexity and diversity. For, in the absence of being able to move, plants have had to rely, in evolutionary terms, on different ways of surviving. Most notably, they have exploited their position as 'nature's alchemists', as Pollan puts it, 'transforming water, soil, and sunlight into an array of precious substances, many of them beyond the ability of humans to conceive, much less manufacture' (p.xvii). 'Why would they go to all this trouble?' Pollan asks. 'Why should plants bother to devise the recipes for so many complex molecules and then expend the energy needed to manufacture them?' (p.xviii). The answer is both defence ('[a] great many of the chemicals plants produce are designed, by natural selection, to compel other creatures to leave them alone: deadly poisons, foul flavours, toxins to confound the minds of predators': p. xviii) and attraction ('many other substances plants make have exactly the opposite effect, drawing other creatures to them by stirring and gratifying their desires': p.xviii).

The attraction route has twice paid enormous dividends for plants. First:

> ... about a hundred million years ago plants stumbled on a way — actually a few thousand different ways — of getting animals to carry them, and their genes, here and there. ... This was the evolutionary watershed associated with the advent of the angiosperms, an extraordinary new class of plants that made showy flowers and formed large seeds that other species were intended to disseminate.
>
> (Pollan, 2002, p.xviii)

And then, rather more recently:

> About ten thousand years ago, the world witnessed a second flowering of plant diversity that we would come to call, somewhat self-centredly, 'the invention of agriculture'. A group of angiosperms refined their basic put-the-animals-to-work strategy to take advantage of one particular animal that had evolved not only to move freely around the earth, but to think and trade complicated thoughts. These plants hit on a remarkably clever strategy: getting us to move and think for them. Now came edible grasses (such as wheat and corn) that incited humans to cut down vast forests to make more room for them; flowers whose beauty would transfix whole cultures, plants so compelling and useful and tasty they would inspire human beings to seed, transport, extol, and even write books about them.
>
> (Pollan, 2002, p.xix)

From a human perspective, rather than from a 'plant's eye view of the world' (to use the subtitle of Pollan's book), the entanglement of people and plants tends to look rather different. While the importance of the immobility and diverse biochemistry of plants is also stressed, an ethnobotanist (ethnobotany is the academic discipline dedicated to studying the interactions between people and plants) will tend to be more interested in the different ways in which individuals and groups of people have incorporated plants into their lives: how plants constitute 'the material basis of human culture'. As two ethnobotanists have put it, 'the peoples of the earth have long depended on plants for food, clothing, shelter, transportation, medicine, and ritual' (Balick and Cox, 1996, p.7).

Without plants and the work they do both in regulating the atmosphere to make it bearable and breathable for humans, and (in terms of the flora in our bodies) in simply keeping us alive, we would not be here at all. Ethnobotanists usually focus their attention on the plant use of 'indigenous peoples', defined by Balick and Cox (1996, p.5) as 'peoples who follow traditional, nonindustrial lifestyles in areas they have occupied for generations'. This is because (in the words of Balick and Cox again) 'the relationships between plants and people are often clearer in indigenous societies than our own, since the link between production and consumption is usually more direct' (p.5). However, as the example of aspirin in Section 1 served to illustrate, even if the link between production and consumption is often considerably less direct, it is hardly impossible to recognise the relationships between people and plants in our own lives (something you might like to do for yourselves, and a theme which will be further developed in Chapters 5 and 8).

One indication of the depth of the entanglement of people and plants today is found in the fact that it is now generally accepted that humans have superseded all other mechanisms as the principal global disperser of plants (at least, of vascular plants: that is, those having roots, a stem and leaves). On the geological timescale, it has been two of the world-making mechanisms discussed in Chapter 1 – plate tectonics and climate change – that have been the external factors responsible for the most significant disruptions to plant distributions. The collision of the Australasian and Asian plates in the Miocene, for example, brought together previously separated species in one landmass and provided new pathways for their dispersal. Plants known as 'relict flora', meanwhile, survive in parts of the world where one would not expect them to grow, from a time when the prevailing temperature and rainfall conditions in the region would have been very different (the European White Elm in Western Siberia is one example).

On a timescale over which the Earth can be considered to have been more geologically and climatically stable (since the last Ice Age, say), it would have been the currents of winds and waves or the movements of birds, insects and animals (all harnessed by the angiosperm plants) that would have taken over as the most important facilitators of plant migration. But now it is us. Sometimes this is intentional; at other times it is unintentional (for instance, in addition to the examples of plants 'hitching a ride' provided by Nigel Clark in Chapter 1, more recently the accidental carrying of plants considered 'weeds' across physical or national boundaries has given rise to fears of so-called 'biological invasions'). Whether intentional or unintentional, however, humans are currently the major players in the globalisation of plants.

Activity 3.1

There has been much discussion and debate in the historical and horticultural literatures about whether it is possible to identify patterns in these human-mediated global flows of plants. Take a look at the maps that make up Figure 3.2. They show (simplified) migration routes for a set of well-known plants. See if you can ascertain any general trends or directions to those movements. If you can, consider what major feature of global history over the last few hundred years might be responsible for those commonalities.   Colonialism

There is a lot going on in the maps in Figure 3.2 and, as I mentioned, the question of identifying patterns has been the subject of much controversy, so don't worry if patterns are not immediately obvious. What you might have picked out, however, is that all of the plants originate outside Europe, but Europe is a stage in several of their journeys. Sugar cane, wheat and rubber are all examples of this pattern. This is often interpreted as meaning that the countries of Europe have benefited from the transfer of some of the useful plants of the rest of the world. As to how this might have happened, and why, the Europe-centred empires that were built between the fifteenth and twentieth centuries have emerged here, as elsewhere, as a hugely significant mechanism of globalisation.

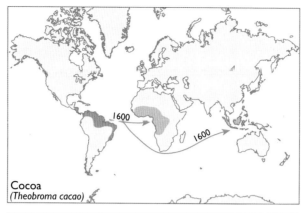

Cocoa
(*Theobroma cacao*)

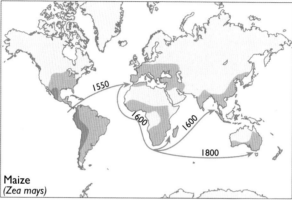

Maize
(*Zea mays*)

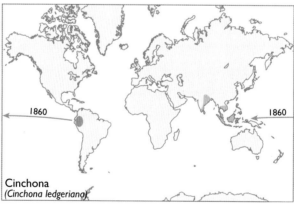

Cinchona
(*Cinchona ledgeriana*)

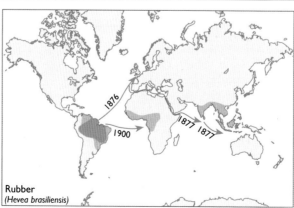

Rubber
(*Hevea brasiliensis*)

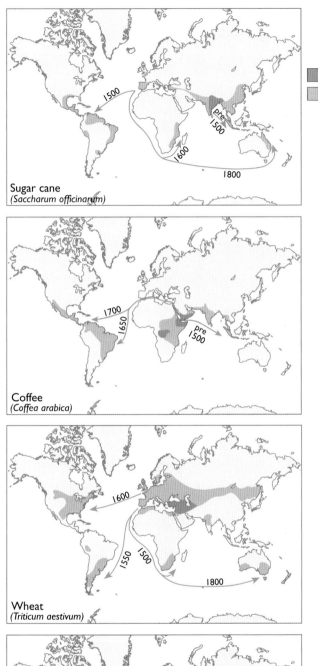

native home
adopted home

Sugar cane
(Saccharum officinarum)

1500
pre 1500
1600
1800

Coffee
(Coffea arabica)

1700
1650
pre 1500

Wheat
(Triticum aestivum)

1600
1550
1500
1800

Potato
(Solanum tuberosum)

1700
1550
1600
1600
1800

Figure 3.2   The migration of some familiar plants
Source: Edlin, 1973

Activity 3.2

To learn more about this relationship between empire and the movement of plants, turn to Reading 3A by Lucile Brockway (1983) entitled 'Plant imperialism', which you will find at the end of the chapter, and Figure 3.5 in this text, which is reproduced from Brockway's article. As you read this extract, pay attention to the importance of territories and flows, and their interaction in the operation of 'plant imperialism'.

As well as now having a much stronger sense of how some of the plants (in particular, cinchona) whose travels are mapped in Figure 3.2 came to cross the globe, you should also have been able to recognise, from what you learned in the previous two chapters, something of how such movements involved the interplay of territories and flows. The smuggling of cinchona seeds out of Peru by Richard Spruce offers a simple example of how flows (of people, of seeds) can cross territories (in this case in the form of a bounded state), something you will be familiar with from the migrations of people, birds, animals and finance covered in Chapters 1 and 2. The place of Kew Gardens at the centre of British imperial botany offers an example, on the other hand, of how territories are in certain situations necessary to bring together and make sense of flows (think of the financial centres in Chapter 2). You might also have spotted an example of how territories are both made and sustained by flows (which again you should remember from the islands of Chapter 1 and the new financial territories of Chapter 2) in Brockway's account in Reading 3A of how the circulation of at least one plant (in the form of quinine) actually expanded and helped to protect the limits of the European empires, especially in the parts of Africa where malaria was endemic.

Defining empire and imperialism

'An empire is a large, composite, multi-ethnic or multinational political unit, usually created by conquest, and divided between a dominant centre and subordinate, sometimes far distant, peripheries.

Imperialism is used to mean the actions and attitudes which create or uphold such big political units – but also less obvious and direct kinds of control or domination by one people or country over another. It may make sense to use terms like cultural or economic imperialism to describe some of these less formal acts of domination: but such labels will always be contentious. Some analysts also use terms like dependency – closely associated with economic underdevelopment – to describe these relationships. And they are clearly bound up with ideas about the newest of all these words: globalization. The 'anti-globalization' protestors who have confronted police forces in numerous world cities over the past few years evidently see globalization and imperialism as just two names for the same thing.'

(Howe, 2002, p.30)

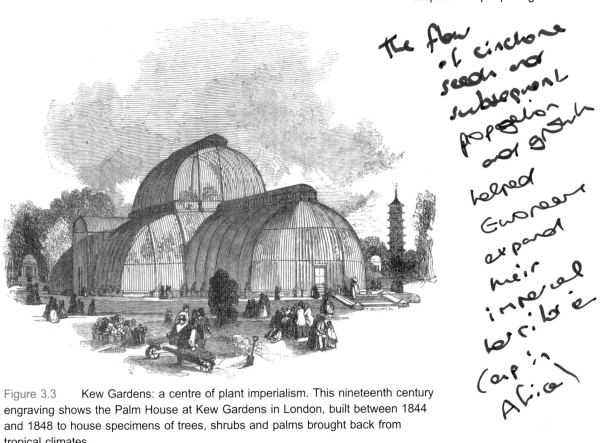

The flow of cinchona seeds and subtropical population and growth helped Europeans expand their imperial territorie (esp in Africa)

Figure 3.3   Kew Gardens: a centre of plant imperialism. This nineteenth century engraving shows the Palm House at Kew Gardens in London, built between 1844 and 1848 to house specimens of trees, shrubs and palms brought back from tropical climates

There was one further interplay of territory and flow at work in the events described in Reading 3A, an interplay which is represented in the form of the Wardian case (see Figure 3.5 overleaf). The invention of what was effectively a portable greenhouse was absolutely critical to the success of plant imperialism in that it allowed living tropical plants to be successfully and reliably transported on long sea voyages for the first time. While the flows (voyages) here are fairly apparent, the role of territory is much less so. There is no reason, though, why, under certain conditions, a plant – just as much as an island, a state or a financial centre – cannot be described as a territory. Think back to the discussion in Chapter 1 of the two ways in which territories are formed.

A new territory

check chapter 1 !

Tab. 292.

ZORN. IC. PL. MED.

Cinchona officinalis. L.

B. Thanner. del.   J.C. Claußner. fc.

Figure 3.4   The cinchona tree: an example of plant imperialism. This botanical illustration was made in 1869

The first way – outlined in relation to Tuvalu – in which territories emerge is as a pattern or 'fabric' in which many different features are bound or woven together: in other words, a set of relationships. This works well when one considers the physical forms, people and other living things that constitute a Pacific island, but could equally be applied to something like a plant (or even, as we shall see, bits of plants) which is also always the outcome of the various flows and components (from sunlight and chlorophyll to water and roots) which they manage to focus. The only difference in formal terms is that a plant is much smaller than an island.

If this seems reasonable (even if a little counter-intuitive at first), consider now the second way in which territories were described in Chapter 1 as being constructed. That had more to do with the ways in which boundaries are drawn: what distinguishes the inside from the outside of a territory (borders were the example used). It is less a completely separate process from the first way of thinking about territories as constructed, and more something extra that is done if it is necessary that the territory in question is to be clearly defined and differentiated from its surroundings. It is this second kind of territory making, with its reliance on cutting away or bounding things from their setting, which I will be concentrating on in this chapter.

When we are dealing with plants, what this bounding action does is to make that entity into a thing which can be moved or transported, and this is where the Wardian case comes in. By allowing the cinchona (as well as other plants) both literally and metaphorically to be uprooted, and cut off from the connections which would normally define its existence, this glass container allowed the plant to be removed from one context and re-placed in another (with all that followed from that). In more general terms, therefore, the Wardian case helps us to visualise how, in order to flow, something often has to be detached from its environment.

Figure 3.5   The Wardian case: a tool of plant imperialism. Nathaniel Ward's sealed case made possible the transfer of plants on long voyages, protecting them from sea spray

This operation – this type of territory making or territorialisation – can be extremely powerful because it lies right at the heart of what the geographer Bronwyn Parry calls the 'social and spatial dynamics' of collection (Parry, 2004, p.14). The 'ability of particular groups to access, acquire, concentrate, and monopolise materials', as Parry characterises the collecting process (Parry, 2004, p.15), places those groups in a very strong position by creating inequalities between the 'haves' and the 'have-nots' with respect to the materials in question.

The same power is also evident today in the practice of bioprospecting. In Sections 3, 4 and 5 I will focus on how three related but distinguishable developments – *economic*, *technical* and *legal* – are all providing new opportunities for the territorialisation of plants (and thus, simultaneously, new possibilities for flow and collection). The point is not that these developments can be reduced to the operation of making territories, but that the deceptively simple act of drawing a boundary, cutting something out from its surroundings, is at play in all of them, and that certain groups are willing to do a lot of work in order to acquire particular botanical materials in this way. If further confirmation were needed of the power that territorialisation can offer, the fact that bioprospecting – and the relationships between plants, the knowledge of indigenous peoples and big business that it involves – is today profoundly politicised (Dutfield, 2004) should be evidence enough. As we shall see, the architectures that organise bioprospecting at a global level are highly contested, usually on the basis that those presently in place will either exacerbate existing inequalities or create new ones. In order to put some flesh on the bones of this analysis, we shall now return to the example of Peru and the way in which the operation of territorialisation, the different kinds of work it involved and the contestation that it provoked all played out on the ground.

Summary

- Both people and plants have put a lot of effort and creativity into their mutual entanglement.
- At the global scale, humans are now the primary agents in the dispersal of plants.
- The process of botanical collection – a practice systematised by empire – is characterised by a territorialisation that turns plant material into things that can flow.

3   Making bioprospecting profitable: territorialisation through commodification

On 20 July 1994, Professor Walter Lewis of Washington University in St Louis, Missouri, in the USA, an authority in the field of medical botany, was awarded, along with a number of colleagues, a substantial grant to undertake research on Peruvian medicinal plant sources of new pharmaceuticals. In doing so, he was participating in 'an historic revival of interest in collecting' (Parry, 2004, p.107). Since the mid 1980s the world has witnessed the most significantly concerted and concentrated accumulation of biological material since that of the age of empire. For example, in the period between 1985 and 1995 – at which this accumulation was probably at its peak – it has been estimated that over 200 different US-based organisations began new biological collection programmes (Parry, 2004). As we shall see over the next three sections, the impetus for all this activity was manifold, but I will begin with the reframing of the place of plants in a globalised world that has taken place over the last two or three decades.

Sustainable development an oxymoron?

To do this means taking a closer look at the notion of biodiversity. You may well be familiar with the term, as it has become a widespread shorthand today for referring to the range of organisms with which we share the planet. That familiarity, however, can make it easy to forget that the term 'biodiversity' is both of relatively recent coinage and defines those organisms in a very particular way.

The ideas about biodiversity developed by biologists and conservationists were taken up by a group of influential economists who sought both to put a monetary value on this 'biodiversity' and to argue that neoliberal capitalism (the very system that was held responsible by many for the coming extinction of species) could also be its saviour. The basic idea of what has been termed 'free market environmentalism' (Eckersley, 1993) is that we could and should 'sell nature to save it' (McAfee, 1994): that, in other words, pricing and privatising nature is the key to protecting it. More than that even, they suggested that by merchandising their previously un- or undervalued (at least in financial terms) biological 'assets', economically poor but biologically wealthy countries (and especially those, often indigenous, groups within such countries, who were actively involved in conserving biodiversity) would be offered a new way of 'developing'.

Via the Brundtland Report (the result of a United Nations commission through which the idea of 'sustainable development' became popular in 1987), these ideas gained both an institutional legitimacy and a much broader audience as they became embedded (much to the disquiet of many of the delegates present) in the United Nations Convention on Biological Diversity – perhaps the most

Defining biodiversity

Biodiversity is simply a contraction of the term 'biological diversity' and is a concept that describes the variation of life on Earth. More specifically, biodiversity can be broken down into genetic diversity (which refers to the variation of genes within a species), species diversity (which refers to the range of different species in a given region) and habitat diversity (which refers to the variety of habitat types within a region). The countries with the greatest amount of biodiversity have been classified as centres of megadiversity (see Figure 3.6 overleaf).

The term biodiversity began to be used in the mid 1980s by a collection of biologists and conservationists (of whom E.O. Wilson is perhaps the most well known) as a way of drawing the attention of policy makers to what they saw as a catastrophic loss of species from the planet, a loss for which the attitudes and activities of the 'developed' world was held largely, if not solely, responsible. This group argued that, with the irreversible disappearance of the organisms whose habitats humans were deeply implicated in the unmaking of, we were waving goodbye to resources of enormous economic value.

Figure 3.6   Global centres of megadiversity: the twelve countries which contain 70 per cent of the world's plant biodiversity

significant global architecture through which bioprospecting is currently organised – in 1992. At this decisive gathering and its subsequent manifestations, the argument was (and is) very much the utilitarian one propounded by the aforementioned alliance of biologists, conservationists, economists and policy makers, that the living nonhumans with which we coexist are best conserved both by and for economic development. Everyone and everything – the biodiversity, the custodians of that biodiversity and the rest of the world – is a winner, or so it was suggested.

If the arrival of 'biodiversity' was the first indication that the collection of plants at a global scale was being made more attractive again, a series of developments within the pharmaceutical industry was giving added impetus to the notion that plants might be profitable. Professor Lewis puts this into some sort of overall context in the introduction to his textbook, *Medical Botany*:

> Plant-based traditional medicine systems continue to play an essential role in health care, with about 80% of the world's inhabitants relying mainly on traditional medicines for their primary health care. Plant products also play an important role in the health care of the remaining 20% who reside in developed countries. About 25% of prescription drugs dispensed from community pharmacies in the United States from 1959 to 1980 contained plant extracts or active principles derived from higher plants. At least

119 chemical substances derived from 90 plant species are important drugs currently in use. Of these 119 drugs 74% were discovered as a result of research directed at the isolation of active compounds from plants used in traditional medicine. Based on 1991 sales, half of the leading pharmaceuticals were either derived from natural products or contained a pharmacophore that was based on natural products. In 1993, 57% of the top 150 brand-name products prescribed contained at least one major active compound, or were derived or patterned after compounds, reflecting biological diversity.

(Lewis, 2003, p.4)

This was new. Since the 1950s, most companies had dedicated the bulk of their research and development efforts to synthetic chemistry: that is to say, the designing of molecules in laboratories with specific disease targets in mind, or screening and modifying existing compounds. But then, in the late 1980s, came a renewed (or in some cases entirely novel) commitment on the part of drugs companies to screening natural specimens and, in some cases, using ethnobotanical leads for bioactive compounds. Part of the reason for this shift can be related to new technical developments and possibilities (which I examine in the next section); part to the slowing of the rate of innovation within the laboratory-driven pharmaceutical industry (there was a sense that all the 'easy' and effective molecules had already been synthesised); and part to a combined excitement and opportunism in the face of the possibility that this increasingly scarce but increasingly valuable thing called biodiversity might 'pay for itself'.

It was in this double context that collection became both fashionable and potentially profitable again, and the funding awarded to Professor Lewis in 1994 became available. The International Cooperative Biodiversity Groups (ICBG) program had its beginnings in a workshop held in Washington, DC in 1991, jointly organised by the US National Institutes of Health (NIH), the National Science Foundation (NSF) and the US Agency for International Development (USAID). This workshop concluded that pharmaceuticals derived from tropical natural products could, under appropriate circumstances, both promote economic growth in developing countries and conserve the biological resources from which these products are derived (Schweitzer et al., 1991), and in 1993 the first request for proposals under the ICBG program banner was sent out.

Table 3.1   Fifty drugs discovered from ethnobotanical leads

Drug	Medical use	Plant species	Family
Ajmaline	Heart arrhythmia	Rauvolfia spp.	Apocynaceae
Asprin	Analgesic, inflammation	Filipendula ulmaria	Rosaceae
Atropine	Ophthalmology	Atropa belladonna	Solanaceae
Benzoin	Oral disinfectant	Styrax tonkinensis	Styracaceae
Caffeine	Stimulant	Camellia sinensis	Theaceae
Camphor	Rheumatic pain	Cinnamomum camphora	Lauraceae
Cascara	Purgative	Rhamnus purshiana	Rhamnaceae
Cocaine	Ophthalmologic anaesthetic	Erythroxylum coca	Erythroxylaceae
Codeine	Analgesic, antitussive	Papaver somniferum	Papaveraceae
Colchicine	Gout	Colchicum autumnale	Liliaceae
Demecolcine	Leukaemia, lymphomata	Colchicum autumnale	Liliaceae
Deserpidine	Hypertension	Rauvolfia canescens	Apocynaceae
Dicoumarol	Thrombosis	Melilotus officinalis	Fabaceae
Digitoxin	Atrial fibrillation	Digitalis purpurea	Scrophulariaceae
Digoxin	Atrial fibrillation	Digitalis purpurea	Scrophulariaceae
Emetine	Amoebic dysentery	Cephaelis ipecachuanha	Rubiaceae
Ephedrine	Bronchodilator	Ephedra sinica	Ephedraceae
Eugenol	Toothache	Syzygium aromaticum	Myrtaceae
Gallotanins	Haemorrhoid suppository	Hamamelis virginiana	Hamamelidaceae
Hyoscyamine	Anticholinergic	Hyoscyamus niger	Solanaceae
Ipecac	Emetic	Cephaelis ipecacuanha	Rubiaceae
Ipratropium	Bronchodilator	Hyoscyamus niger	Solanaceae
Morphine	Analgesic	Papaver somniferum	Papaveraceae
Noscapine	Antitussive	Papaver somniferum	Papaveraceae
Papain	Attenuates mucus	Carica papaya	Caricaceae
Papaverine	Antispasmodic	Papaver somniferum	Papaveraceae
Physostigmine	Glaucoma	Physostigma venenosum	Fabaceae
Picrotoxin	Barbiturate antidote	Anamirta cocculus	Menispermaceae
Pilocarpine	Glaucoma	Pilocarpus jaborandi	Rutaceae
Podophyllotoxin	Condylomata acuminata	Podophyllum peltatum	Berberidaceae
Proscillaridin	Cardiac malfunction	Drimia maritima	Liliaceae
Protoveratrine	Hypertension	Veratrum album	Liliaceae

Drug	Medical use	Plant species	Family
Pseudoephedrine	Rhinitis	*Ephedra sinica*	Ephedraceae
Psoralen	Vitiligo	*Psoralea corylifolia*	Fabaceae
Quinidine	Cardiac arrhythmia	*Cinchona pubescens*	Rubiaceae
Quinine	Malaria prophylaxis	*Cinchona pubescens*	Rubiaceae
Rescinnamine	Hypertension	*Rauvolfia serpentina*	Apocynaceae
Reserpine	Hypertension	*Rauvolfia serpentina*	Apocynaceae
Sennoside A, B	Laxative	*Cassia angustifolia*	Caesalpiniaceae
Scopolamine	Motion sickness	*Datura stramonium*	Solanaceae
Stigmasterol	Steroidal precursor	*Physostigma venenosum*	Fabaceae
Strophanthin	Congestive heart failure	*Strophanthus gratus*	Apocynaceae
Teniposide	Bladder neoplasms	*Podophyllum peltatum*	Berberidaceae
THC	Antiemetic	*Cannabis sativa*	Cannabaceae
Theophylline	Diuretic, asthma	*Camellia sinensis*	Theaceae
Toxiferine	Surgery, relaxant	*Strychnos guianensis*	Loganiaceae
Tubocurarine	Muscle relaxant	*Chondrodendron tomentosum*	Menispermaceae
Vinblastine	Hodgkin's disease	*Catharanthus roseus*	Apocynaceae
Vincristine	Paediatric leukaemia	*Catharanthus roseus*	Apocynaceae
Xanthotoxin	Vitiligo	*Ammi majus*	Apiaceae

Source: Balick and Cox, 1996, pp.34–5

One of the first wave of projects to be funded was that on 'Peruvian medicinal plant sources of new pharmaceuticals' mentioned at the start of this section, on which Professor Lewis was named as principal investigator. The stated purpose of what became known as the ICBG-Peru project was to identify new pharmaceuticals based originally on 'ethnobotanical pre-screening' (that is, the knowledges of local people), while at the same time conserving biodiversity in northern Peru by enhancing growth among the collaborating indigenous group, the Aguaruna (in passing you might like to note the historical irony that the Aguaruna were – as far as anyone can establish – also the group responsible for passing on their knowledge of the properties of cinchona to the Spanish invaders). In terms of its institutional architecture (see Figure 3.7 overleaf), ICBG-Peru was a partnership comprising three universities, a corporate sponsor and an indigenous organisation.

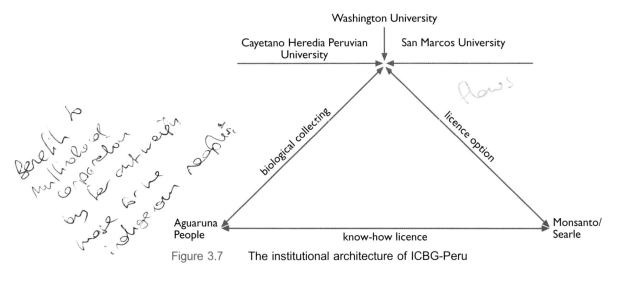

Figure 3.7   The institutional architecture of ICBG-Peru

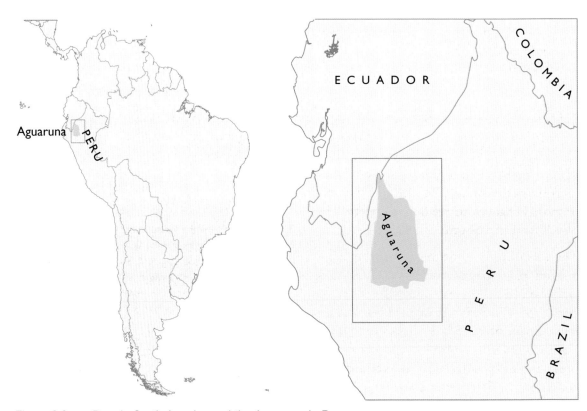

Figure 3.8   Peru in South America and the Aguaruna in Peru

In his book (Lewis, 2003, p.4) and elsewhere, Professor Lewis explicitly positions himself in the long line of explorer-scientists who have scoured a diverse world, learning from local peoples about the useful properties of certain plants. This is what he terms 'assessing the worth to humanity of drugs already known and used' (Lewis, 200, p.4), a story he identifies as beginning with the movement of cinchona–quinine about which you learned in Reading 3A. Nothing could be more 'relevant' today, he argues, than continuing this search.

If Lewis's own words indicate that there are all sorts of continuities between the imperial and modern plant-collecting projects, his next statement reminds us, however, that there is something quite distinct and new about this modern form of global entanglement:

> Before conducting ethnobotanical research, it is essential to obtain agreements among all parties, addressing prior informed consent, confidentiality, ownership of intellectual property and tangible biological materials, collecting area scope, conservation of medicinal plants and habitats, responsibilities of all parties, benefit sharing, compensation due parties at all stages of research, development, and commercialization, and supplier of materials.
>
> (Lewis, 2003, p.4)

This emphasis on good practice, and particularly on building 'benefit sharing' into the enterprise, can – like the idea of selling nature to save it – be traced back to the UN Convention on Biological Diversity (CBD), which in turn reflects some of the thinking in the Brandt Report of 1980 and its proposed changes to relations between 'the North' and 'the South'.

The CBD can be thought of as providing institutional encouragement to the globalisation of biodiversity; it also – in Article 16 – introduced an explicitly new requirement of reciprocity in respect of those same materials in recognition of both prevailing inequalities and the power of collection. In other words, the South will now only continue to provide access to genetic resources if the North provides compensation, technology transfer or other kinds of benefits in exchange. This provision was one of the most significant and contested aspects of the global architecture

Defining North and South

The Brandt Commission, commissioned by the World Bank and named after its Chair, former German Chancellor Willy Brandt, proposed an ambitious series of reforms in relations between developing and developed countries in 1980. Although widely praised at the time, few of the recommendations were implemented, and the report is largely forgotten. However, one aspect of it has been very influential – its ingenious drawing of a line separating the developed 'North' from the less developed 'South'.

In this usage Australia is a part of the North and several Northern Hemisphere countries are part of the South, emphasising that these terms relate primarily to variations in political and economic power.

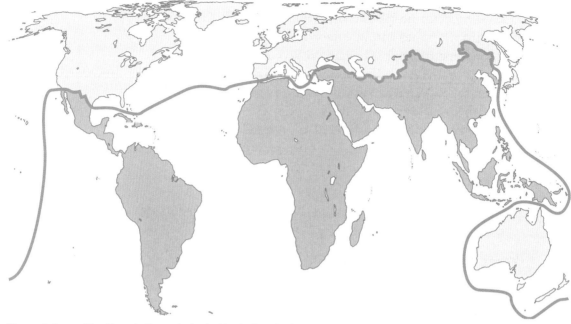

Figure 3.9   The Brandt Commission's North–South divide

that the CBD provided for bioprospecting, both while it was being drafted and in the subsequent meetings where its implementation continues to be negotiated. Although supported by most of the Southern delegations to the 1992 meetings in Rio, many in the North – and especially much of the US-dominated biotechnology lobby – were and remain vehemently opposed to its strictures. The South did not have it all its own way, however, as while nation states do indeed have the rights to determine the terms on which access to what have been designated 'their' biological materials can be granted, the CBD also requires that these resources be made available to outside parties (access, in other words, cannot be 'unreasonably restricted' to use the term of the Convention).

Taken together, then, these three related developments – the transformation of plants into biodiversity, their reappearance on the profit radar of the pharmaceutical companies and the need to provide benefits in return for their acquisition – represent what we might call the global commodification of biological materials. In a postcolonial situation, it is no longer seen as appropriate for the countries of the North just to 'take' the plant resources of the South. However, in a world in which our entanglement with the biophysical world is now bound up with our entanglement with the world of markets, it is possible to find other ways of detaching plants from their environments. For commodities can be defined at their most basic by two features: (1) they can be 'placed in a context in which they have exchange value'; and (2) they can be dissociated from 'producers, former users, or prior context' (Thomas, 1991, p.39). This is almost exactly what the work of treaty building and institution creating, represented by the CBD and ICBG-Peru, has done. Commodification is thus the first form of territorialisation involved in bioprospecting. Making the world's medicinal plants available for commercialisation of course involves all kinds of flows, but – to recapitulate – in order for plants to flow, they must first be made into territories.

flow of knowledge

important.

Summary

- The first set of developments which define bioprospecting involve economic work.

- These economic developments take the form of the invention of biodiversity, the pharmaceutical industry's 'return to nature' and the provision of benefit-sharing regimes to encourage the exchange of biodiversity on a global scale.

- The transformation of biological materials into commodities which these developments together comprise operates through the decontextualising activity that we have identified as a kind of territorialisation.

4   Making bioprospecting practical: territorialisation through technology

On 1 August 2000, Washington University in St Louis made available the following press release.

Biologists find Peruvian plants inhibit growth of TB bacterium

Researchers at Washington University in St. Louis studying medicinal plants from the Peruvian rainforests have come across results that may significantly influence the direction of the fight against tuberculosis (TB) worldwide. Walter H. Lewis, Ph.D., professor of biology at Washington University, and his colleagues examined about 1,250 plant extracts returned from Peru and found that 46 per cent showed an inhibition against *Mycobacterium tuberculosis* (*M. tuberculosis*), the bacterium that causes TB.

The finding is a first step toward developing potential drugs that can combat the disease.

The unexpected results came after months of working in conjunction with the native Aguaruna people of Peru through the International Cooperative Biodiversity Groups Program-Peru or ICBG-Peru, whose primary goals are to identify new pharmaceutical possibilities from medicinal plants and to promote cultural and economic support to the native Indians. Lewis and his team lived among the tribe, collecting plant samples and learning about specific plants the Indians use in herbal medicinal practices. [...]

Through the technique of bio-directed assaying, Lewis and his fellow researchers identified the amount of reactivity present in each of the samples against various diseases – including diarrhoea, leishmania, and certain strains of cancer – but the inhibitions against these paled in comparison to how effective the Peruvian plants proved against TB.

'The results just surprised us. We didn't realize the difference until the final results came in', Lewis says. [...]

The Aguaruna, a tribe of the Jivaro Indians of the Upper Amazon Basin, still rely largely on memorization and the oral passing down of knowledge of their medicinal plants to survive. However, as increasing numbers of younger Aguaruna are exposed to the outside world, many lose interest in learning the practice of herbal medicine. Thus, with fewer numbers of Aguaruna willing to learn all of the medicinal wonders and knowledge of their elders, medicinal plant knowledge could be lost forever as well. Recording this knowledge and documenting it thus becomes as crucial an activity of the Washington University team as discovering new medicinal plant species.

(Washington University, 2000)

The presence of terms such as 'plant extracts' and 'plant samples', or 'technique of bio-directed assaying' and 'amount of reactivity' in this document, gives a strong sense of the second kind of work that characterises modern bioprospecting – that is, the technical work that has to be done before we can find out what the flora of this part of Peru might do for us. In other words, it is all very well making bioprospecting economically viable in theory and even in practice, but for there to be a return on that literal and metaphorical investment in biodiversity – for there to be tangible results such as pills on shelves – something (and probably some things) needs to undergo travel, transformation and testing. And all that necessitates a great deal of technical effort of one kind or another.

Of course this is nothing new. Although it might not immediately strike us as technology in the way in which we usually consider it today, the Wardian case mentioned earlier provides a good illustration of this effort. As you will recall, the case was used to transport samples of plants across the oceans which separated the centres of empire from their peripheries,

Figure 3.10   Professor Lewis with Aguaruna colleagues

allowing a tiny part of South America (for example) to be literally and metaphorically uprooted and brought back to Europe. The technical work that Lewis, his colleagues and others involved in bioprospecting today perform on the plants they find or are led to is at once very similar and utterly different from that of the Wardian case. It is similar because nothing has changed in terms of things having to be bounded and contained if they are to travel (turned into a territory-like form before they can flow). While there is less necessity today to bring back whole plants, the 1250 plant extracts collected by ICBG-Peru all had to be made able to survive their various voyages just as did those collected hundreds of years before. In the case of ICBG-Peru, field samples were collected in two parts: pressed (fixed in alcohol) and dried specimens serving as what are called 'herbarium vouchers' (that is to say, parts of the plant that stand for the whole to facilitate taxonomic identification and classification), and about 0.5 kilograms of fresh plant part dried as quickly as possible in mesh bags. Dried material destined for experimentation was then stored at $-20\,^{\circ}$C at the University of Lima before being powdered and extracted there in 95 per cent ethanol. Two hundred milligrams of each of those extracts were then sent for bio-assaying (a laboratory test used to determine the strength or biological activity of a substance which today involves a whole array of machinery and other technical equipment) at Washington University and at Searle, the commercial partner (Lewis, 1999).

If the techniques (from freeze-drying through air-freight to automated sample screening; see Figures 3.11 and 3.12) available today allow the physical territorialisation of plant material required for travel, transport and testing to proceed much more effectively than (but essentially in the same way as) the Wardian case did, then another set of technical developments has taken the use of medicinal plants into previously uncharted territories. These are related to the processes of 'digitization' that were outlined in the previous chapter and which have served significantly to influence the shape of our globalised world. Biology, just like finance, was transformed by the arrival of computer technologies and the ways of thinking that accompanied them, most notably in the field of genetics. Suddenly, what became valuable about a plant was less the plant itself than the information it contained in the form of its genetic code. These technical developments mean that it is now possible to turn bits of plants – right down to their genetic codes – into territories. Again, the same mechanism which the Wardian case illustrated so well – taking a territory formed by the weaving of flows and then bounding and decontextualising it – lies behind this new move.

Figure 3.11   Herbarium specimen storage facility

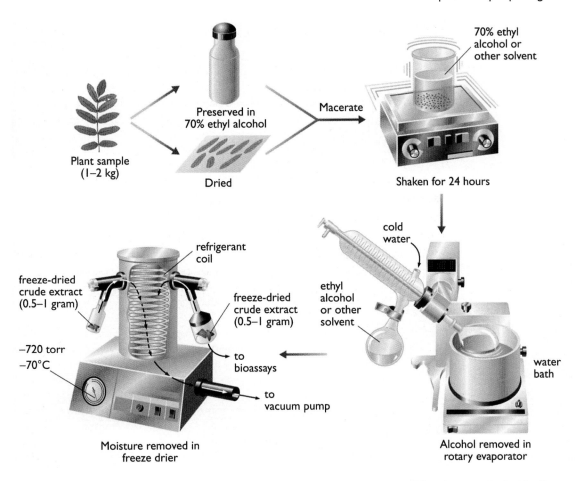

Figure 3.12   Diagram showing the way in which plant samples are prepared for pharmacological testing. (Please note that it is not necessary to understand the detail of this figure, only to appreciate the type and amount of technical work required to make a plant sample ready for pharmacological testing)

However, if we are not careful, it can be all too easy to think that it is the North with all its high-tech tools that is doing all the work here. That is, it is all too easy to forget the practical work done to and with the plants by the Aguaruna. For, as the critical legal theorist Rosemary Coombe has nicely summarised:

> Scientists, social scientists, and policy-makers are increasingly aware that biological diversity is not something 'discovered' in nature, but something that has been cultivated by human beings over extensive periods of time. Nature, in other words, may be one of the biggest human artefacts, in two senses. First the Western world created the concept, which is largely a mythic one, of pristine wilderness to advance its own colonial and imperialist agendas. Second those areas of the world we regard as the most pristine, in fact appear to be the product of complex human landscape management (a term which does an injustice, I believe, to the cosmologies of those

peoples who regard themselves as parts of an ecosystem of interdependence and ongoing responsibility – resource management being an inappropriate industrial term). The world environmental community now understands forests as anthropogenic, habitats as culturally inscribed, and seeds as cultivated, not simply in breeding labs, but in the smallest of farmers' fields.

(Coombe, 2003, pp.1178–9)

As we have been emphasising throughout this book, then, the making of a globalised world involves humans and nonhumans alike, a great deal of effort and a changing and changeable outcome. Coombe's point is particularly appropriate in the case of the Aguaruna given that they live in one of those assumed pristine parts of the world that she mentions and that their culture is characterised by a world view which stresses the intimate connections between humans and nonhumans (which is partly manifested in a tradition of biomedicine that, while generally dismissed as 'unscientific', yielded both the properties of the cinchona tree in the sixteenth century and the clues to a new treatment for tuberculosis much more recently). Gaining any external respect or recognition of all this entanglement and work has been difficult for the Aguaruna. The anthropologist Michael F. Brown (2004) has demonstrated this in his story of how – before the 'jackpot' of economically exploitable biodiversity came along in the 1990s – the Peruvian government was regularly encouraging them to be more 'productive with the lands the state had allocated to them' (Brown, 2004, p.99). This was despite the fact that the Aguaruna's knowledge and use of their environment gave them a better diet and health than that of most other Peruvians.

Summary

- The second set of developments which define bioprospecting involve technical work.

- These technical developments take the form of the creation of robust samples, fast and reliable transport and the digitization of biology.

- The transformation of biological materials into information, which these developments together comprise, represents a second form of the decontextualising activity which we have identified as a kind of territorialisation.

5   Making bioprospecting legal: territorialisation through property

Whereas the previous section began with a press release from Washington University on the success of ICBG-Peru, this section starts with a press release that reflects a very different perspective on the project. Under the title 'Bio-prospectors' hall of shame ... or guess who's coming to pirate your plants?!', the Canadian-based campaigning group now called the ETC (Action Group on Erosion, Technology and Concentration) posted the following on its website in 1994, when the group was known as RAFI (Rural Advancement Foundation International):

> According to the ICBG, intellectual property agreements have been negotiated among participating institutions so that discoveries are equitably shared and accrue to local communities and indigenous peoples involved in the discovery of the natural product. Although 'benefit sharing agreements' are frequently mentioned, the specific terms of benefit sharing are strictly confidential. While the rhetoric is more than a little convincing, the reality is that indigenous communities can expect to gain very little and give up a great deal. By and large, the terms and conditions under which indigenous peoples might benefit financially are controlled by Northern corporations that are free to claim intellectual property on indigenous knowledge and biodiversity. Indigenous communities will find these same intellectual property systems culturally and ethically alien, as well as politically and economically inaccessible.

> Pharmaceutical corporations participating in the ICBG programs have agreed to profit sharing through 'donation' of a percentage of royalties from the sales of products developed through the ICBG program, and inclusion of indigenous or local people as inventors on patents. Sounds good? For indigenous peoples, the dream of windfall profits is illusory.

> Consider the royalty payment scheme negotiated by G.D. Searle and Co. (a subsidiary of Monsanto) and Washington University (St. Louis, Missouri, USA) for collection of Peruvian medicinal plant extracts [...] under the ICBG agreement. RAFI received a copy of the confidential agreement from an anonymous source.

> The royalty sharing agreement [...] is a corporate patent lawyer's dream: It is riddled with loopholes, legal and technical jargon. Enforcement rests entirely with U.S.-based institutions pursuant to United States government laws. For example, the license option agreement states that, 'in the event that the biological activity of an

disputes over notions (handwritten margin note)

active agent was in the public domain or was known or otherwise available to Searle, as evidenced by Searle's written records, prior to Searle's discovery of the biological activity of the active agent in a Plant Extract,' Searle is under no obligation to pay any fee, royalty or other compensation (but Searle retains the right to make, use or sell worldwide the active agent or any derivative)! When all is said and done, if Searle determines that a valuable extract from Peru was 'known or otherwise available to Searle' the company has no obligation to compensate the source country or community. But nothing prevents Searle from commercializing the valuable genetic material.

(RAFI, 1994, pp.6–7)

At the root of RAFI's contestation of the ICBG-Peru bioprospecting project was the question of property. Whose biodiversity was it anyway? Clearly this question raises the issues of power and inequality that are fundamentally entwined with the practice of bioprospecting. It is, however, far from an easy question to answer. In part that is because the whole notion of property is not as simple as it may appear.

Activity 3.3

Consider for a moment what you understand by the word 'property'. Why do you think that thinking of biodiversity as property might involve another example of the process of territorialisation we have been exploring in this chapter?

Perhaps you (like me) would come up with a formulation vaguely along the lines of 'To own something refers to when something is yours, when you can decide what to do with something, and you can stop other people doing things with it'. Certainly this notion of association with ideas of ownership and thus exclusion is central to the way in which we (at least in the West) have traditionally thought about property, whether that property comprises our personal possessions or the natural resources of a state. In this broad reading, the concept of property is used to refer to any system of rules governing people's use of things. These things may be of all different kinds (tangible or intangible, natural or manufactured), but property rules are most often considered necessary where the things in question – particularly things which are scarce relative to the demands that may be put upon them – are likely to provoke conflicts concerning access or control. Property rights, therefore, are very much social rights. They embody the ways in which different societies choose to recognise the claims of certain individuals and groups, but not others, to certain particularly significant and/or potentially limited things.

Ownership relates to territorialisation because the ability to delineate or bound an object is essential to it. Ownership requires that something be cut away from its surroundings, detached from all that has made it, and thus territorialised in the sense of being given a fixed border to whichever regime of access, use and control will apply.

The trouble is that there is more than one regime of access, use and control which might be applied to biodiversity. Much of the politicisation of bioprospecting that was flagged earlier in the chapter has centred around contestations over which (if any) of the three 'species' of property arrangement usually identified – common, collective or private – should apply to global biodiversity.

These contestations came to a head in the negotiations of two global agreements, with the result that there are now two partly complementary, partly contradictory ways in which biodiversity is currently counted as property (both of which are highly controversial). The first sense in which biodiversity is owned is enshrined in the architecture provided by the 1992 Convention on Biological Diversity mentioned in Section 3. In the preamble to the Convention it is clearly stated that 'states have sovereign rights over their own biological resources'. While not an absolute right in the sense that states are above all 'responsible for conserving their biological diversity and for using their biological resources in a sustainable manner', biological materials are here being defined as collective property. The CBD was upholding a fundamental principle of international law dating back to sixteenth-century Europe,

Defining species of property

'In a *common property* arrangement, resources are governed by rules whose point is to make them available for use by all or any members of the society. A tract of common land, for example, may be used by everyone in a community for grazing cattle or gathering food. A public park may be open to all for picnics, sports, or recreation. The aim of any restrictions on use is simply to secure fair access for all and to prevent anyone from using the common resources in a way that would preclude their use by others.'

'*Collective property* is a rather different idea. In a system of collective property, resources are not left open to all-comers. Rather, the community as a whole determines how resources are to be used: these determinations are made on the basis of the social interest through the society's mechanisms of collective decision making [...]'

'*Private property* is an alternative to both collective property and common property. In a private property arrangement, rules of property are organized around the idea that contested resources are to be regarded as separate objects each assigned to the decisional authority of some particular individual (or family or firm). The person to whom a given object is assigned by the principles of private property (for example, the person who found it or made it) has control over the object; it is for her to decide what should be done with it. In exercising this authority she is not understood to be acting as an agent or official of the society. Instead, we say that the resource is her property; it belongs to her; she is its owner; it is as much hers as her arms and legs, kidneys, and corneas.'

(Waldron, 1999, pp.5–6)

according to which independent states have a right to permanent sovereignty over their territories, including the natural resources existing within them. Such a reaffirmation was far from unanimously adopted, however, as a leading commentator in this area explains:

> Preference for 'sovereignty' (accompanied by 'common concern') over the alternative of 'common heritage' followed some difficult negotiations, pitting negotiators representing governments from the industrialized world against those of biodiversity-rich developing countries. Some developing countries felt resentful that influential conservation organizations and developed country governments were expecting them to protect their forests at their expense and forgo the economic benefits from selling timber or converting them to other uses. Realizing the potential economic value of their biogenetic resources and needing to improve their scientific, technological, and financial capacities to exploit them, they asserted their sovereign right to control their resources and access to them ... Adoption of the sovereignty principle in the CBD was a clear victory for the developing country negotiators. Whether or not it was a victory for developing country interests is less obvious though.
>
> (Dutfield, 2004, pp.5–6)

In another profoundly significant international architecture that has come to organise aspects of the practice of bioprospecting, namely the 1994 Agreement on Trade-related Aspects of Intellectual Property Rights (TRIPS), which is administered by the World Trade Organisation (WTO), the model of private property was favoured, specifically patents. Patents are designed to provide inventors with legal rights for a fixed period (usually 20 years) to prevent others from using, selling or importing their inventions. Applications for a patent must satisfy a national patent office that the invention described in the application is new and useful, and that its creation involved an inventive step either beyond the present state of the art or unobvious to a skilled practitioner.

Over time, more and more things have become patentable as business interests (and especially recently the life science firms involved in producing medicines) have successfully argued that patents are essential for their ability to make a return on the high research and development investment required to discover, produce and obtain regulatory approval for new products. Such an extension is reflected in TRIPS.

The idea that plant materials (if not plants themselves) should be privately owned – even in the temporary form offered by patents – has been hugely controversial and often contested. Some object that it is morally inappropriate that the legal–commercial logic of property should be extended to living things in any form. For others, what is

Chapter 3 Bioprospecting   139

inappropriate is the imposition of a Western model of property onto situations involving peoples who might – like the Aguaruna – collectively make sense of the world in very different terms. The anthropologist and activist Darrell Posey usefully summarised some of these sort of objections:

(i) [intellectual property rights, IPRs] are founded upon a conception of individual authorship that does not suit community innovation. Indigenous knowledge may, for example, be attributed to ancestor spirits, vision quests, or lineage groups, but rarely to individuals. [...]

(ii) they are intended to benefit society through the granting of exclusive rights to individuals and juridical persons (i.e. corporate entities). Indigenous peoples and local communities do not usually have a legal personality and cannot easily claim legal rights as a group.

(iii) they cannot easily protect information not resulting from a specific historic act of 'discovery'. Most indigenous knowledge is transgenerational, communally shared, and is usually considered to be in the public domain, and therefore unprotectable.

(iv) they are likely to conflict with customary systems of ownership, tenure, and access.

(v) they help owners to capture the market value of knowledge, but fail to reflect spiritual, aesthetic, or cultural – or even local economic – values [...]

(vi) they are subject to manipulation by economic interests that wield the most political power. So while *sui generis* protection has been obtained for, say, semiconductor chips, indigenous peoples lack the legal means for protecting even their most sacred plants, places, songs, art, or artefacts.

(vii) most IPRs (especially patents) are expensive, complicated, and time-consuming to obtain, and even more difficult to defend.

(Posey, 2002, pp.8, 9)

Activity 3.4

Disputes about whether biological materials should or should not be treated as private property are both extremely important and extremely complicated. To help make sure you have understood the basic positions, make a list summarising the arguments both for and against the practice of treating biological material as private property.

It was in this maelstrom of contestation that the term 'biopiracy' was coined (by Pat Roy Mooney, one of the founders of the RAFI/ETC group) as a way of drawing a direct lineage between bioprospecting projects like ICBG-Peru and the sorts of imperial 'adventures' through which cinchona–quinine was globalised (interestingly, the Director of Kew Gardens in 1999, Peter Crane, said that their nineteenth-century activities would today be seen as 'pure biopiracy'; UNESCO, 2000). As one of the popularisers of the term, the Indian scientist and activist Vandana Shiva, puts it:

> Biopiracy takes place when knowledge from other cultures is taken freely, converted into patented 'intellectual property' with a right to deny people free access to that knowledge and to force them to pay royalties and high prices for seeds and medicines, including the communities from which the biodiversity and knowledge first came.

(Shiva, 2000, p.40)

For commentators like Mooney, Shiva and many others, then, the possibilities for the territorialisation of plant genetic materials offered by (particularly private) property are far from beneficial for all involved (as its proponents would have it), but instead are organised by self-serving global architectures of the powerful which produce ever deeper inequalities between North and South.

Activity 3.5

Turn now to Reading 3B which is taken from Chapter 1 in *Enclosures of the Mind: Intellectual Monopolies. A Resource Kit on Community Knowledge, Biodiversity and Intellectual Property* by RAFI (1996). As you read, pay particular attention to the way in which the territorialisation represented by (intellectual) property is likened to an act of enclosure, and the political significance of this parallel.

Undoubtedly there have been more than a few cases in which the term biopiracy is exactly the right one to describe the way in which plant knowledge has been decontextualised from its social and physical environment. Take, for example, the hoodia case documented by the intellectual property specialist Graham Dutfield:

> Certain groups of San (bush) people (inhabiting the Kalahari desert of Southern Africa), known as Khomani, eat parts of a plant called hoodia as an appetite suppressant. This helps them to endure long hunting trips in areas of the desert where food is scarce. The

practice was noticed by South African soldiers who used the Khomani people as trackers during the 1980s when Namibia was fighting its war for independence. The South African Council for Scientific and Industrial Research (CSIR), a government institution, investigated the plant and patented certain compounds possessing appetite suppressant activity. The CSIR has high hopes that it will form the basis of a successful anti-obesity treatment and will become Africa's first blockbuster drug. [...] The patent specification may well provide the first biochemical description of how the plant produces its commercially promising effect. But the intended use of the plant would hardly be considered as novel by the Khomani, who are not mentioned in the patent. Following an investigation by a South African activist, Rachel Wynberg, and a subsequent newspaper exposé, the CSIR and the two companies involved found themselves criticised by international NGOs [non-governmental organisations]. In 2001, the CSIR responded by initiating a benefit-sharing agreement through which the San people will receive milestone payments and royalties from any drug developed from their knowledge.

(Dutfield, 2004, pp.52–3)

ICBG-Peru, however, does seem to have gone to at least some lengths to distance itself from such practices. In fact, one might argue that it was the very attempt to recognise and reward in various ways the medicinal knowledge of the Aguaruna, and their role in the co-production of the plant landscapes in which Professor Lewis and his colleagues were interested, that attracted the attention of RAFI and led to the subsequent episode of contestation.

The ICBG researchers had initially worked out collaborative agreements with a large and influential federation called the Aguaruna-Huambisa Council. The project promised to employ and train Aguaruna workers, provide financial support for indigenous organisations and – as we have seen – provide royalties should the activities of ICBG-Peru produce marketable pharmaceuticals. As the collecting process got under way, however, relations between the research team and the Aguaruna-Huambisa Council soured, largely over the question of the royalty rates, and in no small part due to the intervention of RAFI in the negotiations. In no doubt admirable attempts to get the Aguaruna a better deal, RAFI (like ICBG-Peru) took the Aguaruna-Huambisa Council as the only true representative of the Aguaruna people and thus – according to the anthropologist Michael F. Brown who spent years with them studying their way of life – 'inadvertently mimicked the actions of colonial powers who assumed that native people were, almost by definition, organised as tribes under the direction of chiefs' (Brown, 2004, p.113). In fact, says Brown, the Aguaruna are members of local and regional indigenous federations that have become strategic points of contact with the Peruvian government and the outside world, federations whose fortunes rise and fall and which are riven by internal conflict (not unlike our own political parties).

At the end of the day, the way in which RAFI threw in its lot with the Aguaruna-Huambisa Council both slowed the resolution of the conflict with ICBG-Peru and probably resulted in a better deal (and the only 'know-how' licence ever operationalised in bioprospecting at the time of writing, 2005) for the multi-ethnic native federation called CONAP (Confederation of Amazonian Nationalities of Peru) with whom ICBG-Peru negotiated a new agreement. It is not difficult, however, to detect in the words of Cesar Sarasara, the president of CONAP, a certain frustration with RAFI's intervention, a frustration which throws up some difficult questions about who knows best, and who should be making the decisions in the profoundly entangled situations which activities like bioprospecting are increasingly creating in a globalised world. 'CONAP', Sarasara said in an interview with Brown in 2001, 'is working to find new formulas for collaborating with industry so that we're not looking in from the outside. We are not waiting for NGOs or the Catholic Church to help us. We're looking for opportunities to exploit the economic value of our resources' (Brown, 2004, p.114).

Summary

- The third set of developments which define bioprospecting involve legal work.

- These legal developments take the form of the international agreements which allow both the national (CBD) and private (TRIPS) ownership of biodiversity: agreements which are worked out in local negotiations.

- The transformation of biological materials into property, which these developments together comprise, offers a third form of the decontextualising activity which is a kind of territorialisation.

6 The challenge of territorialisation in a globalised world

In this final main section, we will take a step back from the detail of the theory and practice of bioprospecting that we have been exploring over the last three sections, in order to reflect on some of the broader issues raised by this particular way of making a globalised world.

One place to start is the last line of the quotation from the political theorist Stephen Howe that formed our working definition of empire and imperialism in Section 2. There he noted that the anti-globalisation protestors of today 'see globalization and imperialism as ... the same thing'. This is a big and significant claim. Have we seen any evidence to support this equation in our study of bioprospecting? In some senses we have seen quite a lot. Certainly the language of 'biopiracy' and 'biocolonialism' that pervades the discourse of those ranged against the collection of biological materials in its current form is designed to evoke the memories and inequalities of the plant imperialism of the nineteenth century as described by Lucile Brockway in Reading 3A. Equally, the many attempts to calculate the benefit that the North has gained from the inequitable patterns of plant genetic material exchange both in the past and in the present echo the arguments about compensation that characterise the aftermath of slavery (see **Lambert, 2006**) as well as other aspects of globalisation.

However, if there are obvious and politically and ethically critical continuities between the (plant) imperialism of the past and the (bioprospecting) globalisation of the present, we have also found it analytically necessary to distinguish between the practices and processes making the world today and those which have brought us here. This is important, too, in terms of bioprospecting as much as it was for climate change and the financial markets that were examined in the previous two chapters. For, as we have seen over the last three sections, new developments are both accelerating and radically altering previous and existing ways of world making. In the case of bioprospecting, Bronwyn Parry (2004) has argued that – taken together – these developments have completely changed the social and spatial dynamics of collecting. This has implications far beyond the gathering and use of biological materials. There are many and diverse areas which are touched by the fact that the forces of commodification, technology and property rights mean that it is now easier to territorialise things (and, thus, allow them to flow) than ever before. From the fate of aboriginal art to the spread of DNA fingerprinting, the possibilities of previously context-specific entities being turned into things that can be packaged, owned and sold (with all the issues of power that these developments raise) is a concern that runs through debates about globalisation, provoking both hopes and fears.

How should we think through these new as well as the old challenges, and act appropriately in the face of them? One intellectual and political approach has been to conceptualise aspects of a globalised world as a commons of shared access and benefit. We have encountered this in preceding sections, most notably from Vandana Shiva (2000) and RAFI (1994) when they bemoan the loss of an apparently once present space of community-based plant genetic exchange and improvement. One problem with this undeniably seductive and important set of ideas (at least in the context of bioprospecting: you might like to compare the situation with that of Antarctica after reading the next chapter) is that, in both international legal theory and practice (as we have also already noted), such a global commons has never really existed.

Rather, although lip service has been paid to the principle by many parties when it has been politically expedient, in international law the nation state has always been sovereign over all the nonhuman entities within its boundaries (a situation, as we noted earlier, which the CBD reaffirmed). If the attempt by the Peruvian and Bolivian governments in the nineteenth century to prevent the removal of cinchona trees from their countries offers an example of this state of affairs in action, their failure illustrates our second point that, in practice, the powerful (whether states, corporations or individuals) have always found ways of justifying their actions (such as smuggling seeds) by arguing for unrestricted flows when it suits, while aggressively protecting their interests by restricting the free circulation of their own goods (think of the politics of quinine stocks again). This flexible logic (which can also work the other way around) leads to the irony described by the sociologists Jack Kloppenburg and Daniel Lee Kleinman in relation to crop resources:

> ... in a world economic system based on private property, each side of the debate wants to define the other side's possessions as common heritage. The advanced industrial nations of the North wish to retain free access to the developing world's storehouse of genetic diversity, while the South would like to have the proprietary varieties of the North's seed industry declared a similarly public good.
>
> (Kloppenburg and Kleinman, 1988, p.188)

No wonder Rosemary Coombe has asked us to think twice when unreflectively singing the praises of the public domain with respect to biological materials, and to ask ourselves how they got to be counted as public in the first place. As she suggests, 'by using the idiom of property, then, many indigenous peoples [like CONAP] may simply be taking the initial and limited step of insisting upon a levelling of the playing field before working out the details of particular contractual arrangements' (Coombe, 1998, p.208).

If the notion of a commons is very useful for thinking about freedoms (of access, use, circulation), it is perhaps – at least in its less qualified versions – not enough on its own to help us fully to get to grips with the issue of responsibilities. And it is responsibilities – as the example of bioprospecting has further confirmed – that living in a globalised world-in-the-making continually throws up: not always, or even usually, strictly speaking personal responsibilities (although they can be), but more often collective responsibilities of the sort that can be implemented through the kind of alternative architectures of which Michael Pryke offered some examples at the end of the previous chapter. So it is with a very brief review of three proposals to regulate bioprospecting a little more responsibly, with a little more attention to the power and inequalities involved in the process of collecting, that I want to close this section.

These three proposals all take seriously the fact that a responsible bioprospecting architecture must be at once responsible to: the different groups of humans involved (and thus especially but not only recognise the world-making work marginalised peoples have done and continue to do); the different kinds of nonhumans involved (and thus especially but not only recognise our profound and multiple entanglement with the planet's biodiversity); and, finally (and perhaps most importantly), the urgency of a situation in which the indigenous peoples, knowledges and languages, and (in consequence) the biological environments of the South, are being unmade and often lost forever at an alarming rate.

Ironically, of course, we have already come across a global architecture that carries a recognition of these three entwined responsibilities at its very centre: the Convention on Biological Diversity. As we have seen, however, having made such a hugely significant step, the CBD proceeded to offer only a single, neo-liberal, 'one size fits all' solution to this problematic. For many this was inappropriate and, even if one restricts oneself to a single instance of bioprospecting (for us the ICBG-Peru project that we have tracked throughout the chapter), it is not difficult to find a whole panoply of suggestions about how the making of the world it represents could be otherwise.

What often distinguishes these alternative architectures (and certainly the three considered here) is a judgement about which part of the territory/flow interplay that characterises bioprospecting offers the most appropriate and effective site of intervention and regulation. For example, having spent an extended period of fieldwork following the encounter between the Aguaruna and the ICBG-Peru project, the anthropologist Shane Greene concluded that a 'territory-based approach' to issues of bioprospecting is necessary if its relationships to traditional knowledges are to be connected to broader struggles in which peoples like the Aguaruna are engaged. For him:

> The concept of territoriality has played a central role in indigenous peoples' struggle for land rights for decades, based on the premise that without a definable and defendable territory indigenousness is undermined and local cultures eroded. In that sense, the material claim to specific geographic territories cannot be separated from what is fundamentally a political and moral claim to self-determination, a concept heavily promoted by indigenous groups themselves and recognised in international treaties like the UN Draft Declaration on the Rights of Indigenous Peoples. Refocusing attention on the more fundamental notion of territoriality might encourage projects dealing with traditional knowledge and bioprospection, like the ICBG, to be phrased in terms of access to territory rather than to knowledge. In this sense the proposal is perhaps more radical rather than less. A strategy of territorial rights explicitly promotes greater autonomy and hence bolsters a politics of self-determination that indigenous peoples are already demanding.
>
> (Greene, 2002, p.245)

For Bronwyn Parry, on the other hand, following the social and spatial dynamics of the ICBG-sponsored collection from the initial act of territorialisation of plants right through the various economic, technical and legal transformations of plant genetic materials that are now possible, led her to conclude that it is too late to worry only about keeping biological things under control and in place. Given that so many flows are already out there, she asks why, despite 'an increasingly baroque regulatory framework, it remains the fact that supplying countries and communities have yet to receive any substantial economic returns from the exploitation of their collected materials' (Parry, 2004, p.254).

In the place of this framework, Parry proposes that we abandon what she argues are now impossible attempts to trace all 'the myriad uses that are made of collected genetic and biochemical materials and information', and concentrate instead on 'working to secure a voluntary, global agreement from the pharmaceutical industry that they will add a sum of between 3 and 5 percent of their profit ratio to all those products that they currently have in the marketplace that are based on collected natural materials' (Parry, 2004, p.261). Such a levy, which Parry suggests should apply also to users of genetic-sequence and indigenous knowledge databases, would remain in place for as long as those products are sold, and be paid directly into a superfund to which countries and communities from the South could apply with proposals for development and conservation projects.

[handwritten margin note: Voluntary? Would not work?]

If Parry's alternative architecture is designed to make us realise the extent to which we are acting after the horse has bolted with regard to the flows of biodiversity that recent developments in the territorialisation of plant materials have facilitated, our final example differs again. Whereas the preceding two proposals are speculative in character, this one is actually in the process of being put into practice at the time of writing. Born of a recognition by the Peruvian government that, as a centre of increasingly valuable megadiversity, the ICBG-Peru project would not be the last time bioprospectors would turn to their country's riches, it takes the form of a legal framework within which future encounters would take place. After an unprecedented level of civil society participation, since 2002, as Graham Dutfield summarises:

> ... those who wish to access such knowledge for scientific, commercial, or industrial application are required to secure the prior informed consent of the holders of the knowledge. For commercial use or industrial application, a (non-exclusive) license is required guaranteeing an access fee plus 0.5 percent of the value of future sales to go to a Fund for the Development of Indigenous Peoples ... With respect to knowledge in the public domain, indigenous peoples will still be able to make an agreement with and request compensation from outside parties. Again 0.5 percent of sales must go to the Fund. A Register of Collective Knowledge will [also] be created for which INDECOPI [the National Institute for the Defence of Competition and Intellectual Property] will take responsibility ... Access to the register will require written consent of the indigenous peoples who own the specific knowledge of interest to those requesting access.

[handwritten margin note: 0.5%!]

> (Dutfield, 2004, p.120)

This legislation represents balance both in how it handles geopolitical realities, and in its emphasis on both the territorialisations and the flows of bioprospecting. It is truly one of a kind at present in offering a fully fledged *sui generis* (that is, self-generated) alternative to WTO structures, and it will be worth your checking, whenever you are reading this, how it has fared in practice.

Summary

- There exist both significant continuities and significant differences between the past process of globalisation we have referred to as plant imperialism and the present practice of bioprospecting.
- Bioprospecting raises a number of issues of what it means to be responsible in a globalised world-in-the-making, including how to be responsible to distant others, how to be responsible to nonhuman others, and how to be urgently responsible.
- There are a number of proposals for responsible architectures with respect to bioprospecting, proposals which differ in part by which aspect of the territory/flow interplay they concentrate on.

7   Conclusion

The title of this book was chosen to signal three things. The first was that the globalised world in which we live is always made, and, further, made out of all sorts of things. The second was that making a globalised world always involves many types of work. And the third was that a globalised world is never finished being made, but is, rather, forever being made, unmade and remade. We have seen elements of all these aspects of a world-in-the-making in this chapter.

In response to the first aim of the chapter, to consider bioprospecting as a key contemporary form of entanglement of people and plants in a globalised world, we have seen how the world is co-constructed from everything from the tiniest bits of plant genetic code to the most vast global treaties. In response to the second aim, to appreciate that the effort required to make pills from plants is an example of the more general work that has to be done to make and remake a globalised world, we have explored how huge amounts of economic, technical and legal work are all required to make possible just this one particular world-making-practice. We have learned how territorialisation of a particular sort allows the world to be arranged and rearranged in ever new and shifting combinations. In other words, and in relation to our third aim, we have understood how the key transformations involved in bioprospecting represent a particular interplay of territory and flow, a particular interplay which operates in the making of a globalised world more broadly. Moreover, in exploring this story I have also emphasised once again that this globalised world, and its architectures of territory and flow, is the product of contested forces and is continually open to challenge and change.

References

Balick, M. and Cox, P. (1996) *Plants, People, and Culture: The Science of Ethnobotany*, New York, Scientific American Press.

Brockway, L. (1983) 'Plant imperialism', *History Today*, vol.33, no.7, pp.31–6.

Brown, M.F. (2004) *Who Owns Native Culture?*, New York, Harvard University Press.

Coombe, R. (1998) 'Reply to "Can culture be copyrighted?"', by Brown, M.F., *Current Anthropology*, vol.39, no.2.

Coombe, R. (2003) 'Fear, hope, and longing for the future of authorship and a revitalised public domain in global regimes of intellectual property', *DePaul Law Review*, vol.52.

Dutfield, G. (2004) *Intellectual Property, Biogenetic Resources and Traditional Knowledge*, London, Earthscan.

Eckersley, R. (1993) 'Free market environmentalism', *Environmental Politics*, vol.2, pp.1–19.

Edlin, H. (1973) *The Atlas of Plant Life*, London, Heinemann.

Greene, S. (2002) 'Intellectual property, resources or territory? Reframing the debate over indigenous rights, traditional knowledge, and pharmaceutical bioprospection' in Bradley, M. and Petro, P. (eds) *Truth Claims: Representation and Human Rights*, New Jersey, Rutgers University Press.

Howe, S. (2002) *Empire: A Very Short Introduction*, Oxford, Oxford University Press.

Kloppenburg, J. and Kleinman, D. (1988) 'Seeds of controversy: national property versus common heritage' in Kloppenburg, J. (ed.) *Seeds and Sovereignty: The Uses and Control of Plant Resources*, Durham, NC, Duke University Press.

Lambert, D. (2006) 'Making the past present: historical wrongs and demands for reparation' in Barnett, C., Robinson, J. and Rose, G. (eds) *A Demanding World*, Milton Keynes, The Open University.

Lewis, W. (1999) 'Peruvian medicinal plant sources of new pharmaceuticals', *Pharmaceutical Biology,* vol.37, pp.69–83.

Lewis, W. (2003) *Medical Botany: Plants Affecting Human Health*, New York, John Wiley.

McAfee, K. (1994) 'Selling nature to save it?', *Society and Space*, vol.17, pp.133–54.

Parry, B. (2004) *Trading the Genome: Investigating the Commodification of Bio-Information*, New York , Columbia University Press.

Pollan, M. (2002) *The Botany of Desire: A Plant's Eye View of the World*, London, Bloomsbury.

Posey, D. (2002) '(Re)discovering the wealth of biodiversity, genetic resources, and the native peoples of Latin America', *Anales Nueva Época*, no.5, pp.1–30.

RAFI (1994) 'Bio-prospectors' hall of shame ... or guess who's coming to pirate your plants?!', www.etcgroup.org/article.asp?newsid=212 (accessed 1 October 2005).

RAFI (1996) *Enclosures of the Mind: Intellectual Monopolies. A Resource Kit on Community Knowledge, Biodiversity and Intellectual Property*, Ottawa, RAFI.

Schweitzer, J. et al. (1991) 'Summary of the workshop on drug development, biological diversity and economic growth', *Journal of the National Cancer Institute*, vol.83.

Shiva, V. (2000) *Tomorrow's Biodiversity*, London, Thames and Hudson.

Stuart, D. (2004) *Dangerous Garden: The Quest for Plants to Change Our Lives*, London, Francis Lincoln.

Thomas, N. (1991) *Entangled Objects: Exchange, Material Culture and Colonialism in the Pacific*, New York, Harvard University Press.

UNESCO (2000) www.unesco.org/courier/2000_05/uk/doss32.htm (accessed 1 October 2005).

Waldron, J. (1999) 'Property law' in Patterson, D. (ed.) *A Companion to Philosophy of Law and Legal Theory*, Oxford, Blackwell.

Washington University (2000) 'Biologists find Peruvian plants inhibit growth of TB bacterium', press release (August), St Louis, MO, Washington University.

World Commission on Environment and Development (1987) *Our Common Future (The Brundtland Report)*, Oxford, Oxford University Press.

Reading 3A

Lucile Brockway, 'Plant imperialism'

'The greatest service which can be rendered to any country is to add a useful plant to its culture', wrote Thomas Jefferson. The movement of plants by human agency has affected the course of history. New staples have prevented famines, as when New World maize and sweet potato were introduced into China in the sixteenth century; they have supported population explosions, as when the Andean white potato spread throughout northern Europe in the eighteenth and nineteenth centuries and fed the workers in the burgeoning industrial cities. New plantation crops have helped to make some nations rich and others poorer, when a local plant-based industry was undermined by a plant transfer.

Seeds have been one of the most precious and easily transported cultural artefacts. They have been exchanged in local and long distance trade, have prompted voyages of discovery, and have been carried thousands of miles by migrating peoples. ...

Natural plant monopolies have been short-lived. Being small and easily concealed, like diamonds or gold, seeds have often been smuggled. Until very recently, plant hunters and their sponsors, whether national governments, botanic gardens, commercial nurseries, or pharmaceutical houses, have treated plants as part of nature's bounty, theirs for the taking. Yet any plant worth taking has already been identified and put to use in a local ecosystem. Modern ethnobotanists are more ready than old-time plant hunters to acknowledge the scientific value of local lore, to consult with local experts, and to make suitable arrangements with local or national institutions. ...

But in the eighteenth and nineteenth centuries botany was an ally of the expanding European empires. Botanists sailed on the great exploratory voyages of Captain Cook and his successors, collecting plants in the name of science and for the benefit of the mother country. ...

'Well-ripened seeds of rarities will always be acceptable. Simply address Hooker at Kew', wrote the Director of Kew Gardens in his annual report of 1851. Under William J. Hooker's direction Kew Gardens became a depôt for the exchange of plants within the Empire, receiving seeds from its collectors, propagating them in Kew greenhouses, and sending those plants with economic possibilities to colonies with suitable climates. Cork oaks were sent to the Punjab, ipecac, mahogany, and papyrus to India, West Indian pineapples to the Straits Settlements, tea plants to Jamaica, an improved strain of tobacco to Natal. Plant transfer is as old as the practice of agriculture, but it had never before been undertaken on such a scale.

Victorian botanists were so imbued with the imperialist ethos of the times that in some instances of plant transfer they failed to respect the rights of independent states with whom their government had diplomatic relations, and they gave little thought to the loss sustained by the country of origin. …

Europeans decided in the nineteenth century that they wanted certain plants native to areas of Latin America which by that time were post-colonial, independent nation states. Europeans could not bring in their armies, or steal plants from each other. Diplomatic pressure was tried, or subterfuge, or both, as in the case of cinchona.

Cinchona's only natural habitat is on the eastern slopes of the Andes, where the bark was collected by forest-dwelling Indians working for absentee land owners. When European observers like the famous naturalist Alexander von Humboldt saw the Indians cutting down whole trees to strip bark, they were convinced that this 'wasteful harvesting practice' would kill the industry. In point of fact, the barkless trunks would have been eaten by insects, whereas in six years new shoots sprouting from the roots were ready for cutting. The cinchona transfer is one of the most intrigue-filled tales in plant history, with both the British and the Dutch trying to get seeds out of the Andean republics, and later vying for control of the Asian-based trade. The Andean republics, newly liberated from Spain and plagued by counter-revolution, were too weak to protect their infant chichona bark industry.

Charles Hasskarl, director of the Dutch Buitenzorg Gardens on Java, penetrated the Caravaya region of Peru and Bolivia in 1854 under an assumed name. Clements Markham, leader of the British expedition in 1860, fled with his seeds from irate local authorities across southern Peru, avoiding the towns, with only a compass to guide him. Richard Spruce, a renowned explorer and botanist who had worked his way up the Amazon headwaters to Ecuador before being hired as a Kew Gardens cinchona collector, set up camp in a remote mountain valley, collected 100,000 dried seeds and grew over 600 cinchona seedlings. He successfully transported them by raft down to the coast, but these endeavours cost him his health and he never walked again. These efforts, however, yielded few living plants, except for Spruce's 'red cinchonas,' which supplied the stock for thousands of cinchona trees planted in the hilly areas of India and Ceylon. Ironically, this 'red bark' of commerce proved to be inferior in quinine content to the Ledger varieties grown by the Dutch on Java from seeds purchased in 1865 from an English trader, whose Aymara servant smuggled them out of Bolivia, was imprisoned for his treason, and died from prison hardships.

In addition to this piece of luck as regards species, the Dutch programme of intensive care of the cinchona trees gave them a further advantage over the British planters, and by the 1890s a cartel of Dutch quinine processors had control of the market. Many British planters in India and Ceylon switched to tea. The market for South American wild bark had already dwindled to near zero, from a high point of nine million kilos of bark in 1881 before plantation bark had come on the market in quantity.

But those who contend that the British cinchona coup turned out to be a costly fiasco miss the point. The British government did not undertake the cinchona transfer for the benefit of planters, but because it wanted to protect the health of its troops and civil administrators in India, where British rule had been severely shaken by the Sepoy Mutiny of 1857. And this was accomplished: British-made quinine and quinidine were reserved for the representatives of the British *raj*, and Britain's grip on India was made more secure by an influx of soldiers and civil servants who no longer feared 'the deadly climate'.

The much-vaunted programme to sell government-made 'totaquine', a less refined and cheaper anti-malarial derived from cinchona bark, 'at every post office in Bengal' was never pursued with vigour and was soon allowed to lapse. European quinine processors made big profits from plantation-grown cinchona bark in South Asia. Quinine became a more and more expensive drug, mostly beyond the purse of the indigenous peoples of malarial areas, but useful to their Western masters, and especially to Western armies. In the First World War the Allies faced a shortage of quinine, since the neutral Netherlands sold bark and quinine to Germany. A representative of Howard & Sons, the British quinine processing firm, negotiated an agreement to pool Allied resources and to get access to the Java bark. He also 'saved' the output of British cinchona estates from going to the India office, hence to the Indian public. In 1942 when the worst combined famine and malaria epidemic hit India and Ceylon, taking over two million lives, the British would not release quinine stockpiled in India to the civilian population. The cinchona plantations of Java were at that time in the hands of the Japanese and constituted one of the great prizes of their conquest of Southeast Asia. The United States, also desperately in need of quinine for its military forces in the South Pacific, instituted a successful crash programme to rehabilitate the wild cinchona of the Andes. In two and a half years 18,000 tons of cinchona bark were harvested for processing in the United States.

Quinine was also essential to the British, French, and Germans in their 'scramble for Africa', where appalling death rates had confined Europeans to the coast until quinine prophylaxis was adopted. It seems no coincidence that the New Imperialism of the late nineteenth century represented a European expansion into parts of the world where malaria was hyper-endemic.

In the post-Second World War era, synthetic drugs largely replaced quinine in the Western world, but there was still a market for the drug. In 1959 a new cartel of Dutch, German, French, and British quinine processing companies was formed to control every aspect of the production and distribution of the world's supply of quinine, with reserved geographic markets for each firm and a uniform system of pricing. The main objective of this cartel was to eliminate competition, both among themselves and from outsiders, in bidding for the huge United States stockpile of bulk quinine, surplus war material then being put on the market. Members of the cartel agreed not to buy quinine from the Bandoeng factory in the Republic of Indonesia, a legacy from Dutch colonial days and the largest non-European processor of cinchona bark. By restricting its market, the cartel also gained access to Javanese cinchona bark which would otherwise have gone to the Bandoeng factory.

(Brockway, 1983, pp.31–2, 34–5)

Reading 3B

RAFI, 'Enclosures of the mind: an introduction to intellectual monopolies'

Overview

A new industrial and agricultural revolution is underway that enables the private sector and transnational corporations to create monopolies over many biological processes and life forms through the use of intellectual property. Intellectual property laws now allow patents on living organisms and can be used to privatize indigenous knowledge. Biodiversity, a diminishing resource, has been adequately managed up to now by many indigenous farming societies and cultures. New life industries that use biotechnology and operate under intellectual property systems are poised to take control of valuable organisms and knowledge systems under international accords such as the Convention on Biological Diversity/ Biodiversity Convention and the General Agreement on Tariffs and Trade (GATT).

The new act of enclosure

For most of history, security and the route to power have been invested in land: land to graze animals, gather food and medicine, collect fuel wood, and build shelters. In virtually every farming society, some portion of the available land is set aside as 'the commons' for the entire community.

Although there may be rules governing access to and use of the commons, often logically linked to seasonal or other biologically-determined factors, they have remained outside of private ownership.

This was the situation in Europe until the agricultural revolution in the late 18th century, when powerful landlords, championing the cause of scientific progress and claiming the need to feed the continent's growing population, persuaded the governments of the day to allow them to buy the commons. What was not for governments to sell became the private property of the already-rich. Within a matter of decades, landlords fenced off the commons in a political coup that became infamous as the Acts of Enclosure.

Europe's farming communities lost much of their most important land. Their access to forages and medicines was curtailed. Millions were driven from their ancestral lands either to labour in the factory towns of the new scientific revolution or to emigrate overseas to the Americas.

...

In the late 20th century, we are now in the midst of a new 'act of enclosure' and on the threshold of another agricultural and industrial revolution. The new revolution combines microbiology (or biotechnology) and micro-electronics (or informatics). The key to this micro-revolution lies in its control of information, especially information in the life sciences. The new act of enclosure is the intellectual property (IP) system that allows today's 'landlords' of technology to expropriate our intellectual commons, which is the knowledge and skills of farming and indigenous peoples both today and back through history.

...

... When the power of computer technologies to manage information is placed at the service of the life-manipulation powers of biotechnology, industry can take charge of the most powerful revolution in human history. When industry is allowed exclusive monopoly control over life information through intellectual property, an 'enclosure of the mind' occurs.

Until recently, this subject was confined to industry boardrooms and to an exclusive circle of trade negotiators. In light of recent international agreements, the new enclosure system has assumed enormous importance for governments and people of the South. Forty percent of the world economy is based upon biological products and processes. The world's poor rely on biodiversity for 85% to 95% of their livelihoods. All this is at stake in the global drive to allow the patenting of living organisms. For farming and other rural communities, the struggle against the new enclosures of the mind is a fight for survival.

...

Enclosing strategies

That biodiversity is declining, that corporations are becoming more concentrated, or even that the South's bioresources are being pirated, is something less than news. That something as esoteric as intellectual property plays a significant role in all this is probably more of a surprise.

Intellectual property encompasses a group of laws that were intended to protect inventors and artists from losing control over their intellectual creations, such as sewing machines, books, or pottery designs. Everyone from Galileo to Pasteur and Picasso has used intellectual property to make sure that others didn't steal their inventions or creations. The theory is that intellectual property laws give inventors and investors confidence that their work will be rewarded and not pirated. Without that assurance, IP supporters argue, inventors wouldn't invent and investors wouldn't put up the research funds they need.

Over time, intellectual property regimes have grown into mechanisms that allow corporations, not individual inventors, to protect markets rather than ideas. Rather than ensuring that inventors have an opportunity for reward, IP provisions now grant exclusive monopolies that are scale-biased to allow major enterprises to trade technologies among themselves and keep smaller enterprises out of the marketplace altogether.

...

Owning intellectual property over living things is not like owning individual cows or fruit trees, a vegetable garden, a rice harvest, or a fish pond. It is a different and more far-reaching form of ownership. The distinction can be likened to the difference between owning a bucket (or lake) full of water, and owning the chemical formula for water. A patent holder for water's chemical formula would have the right not only to decide who could have access to a particular lake, but to any water anywhere, and to the use of the chemical formula for any purpose.

When someone has intellectual property rights over a new wheat variety, for instance, anyone else who grows it must pay a royalty to the intellectual property holder. In fact, it is more and more possible for IP holders to prohibit farmers from saving seed for the next year's planting or to exchange seed with neighbours. Under patent laws, it is also possible to monopolize the parts of a plant or animal such as specific genes or genetic characteristics. If someone is granted a patent on a gene that determines an inherited plant or animal trait, or controls the onset of a human disease, they acquire enormous power in the marketplace because they set the conditions for access and sale of the patented technology. Others must obtain a license from the intellectual property holder to use it.

By legal sleight of hand, the inherited characteristics of living organisms, the building blocks of life itself, are defined as intellectual property. They are protected by monopoly rights and traded as commodities in the global

market place. In recent years, in fact, intellectual property has become a
trade and environment issue in international treaties.

Enclosing global conventions

Until very recently, intellectual property was subject only to national
legislation. In the mid-1990s, however, it became an international
obligation. After eight years of heated negotiation, 1994 saw the conclusion
of the Uruguay Round of the General Agreement on Tariffs and Trade
(GATT) and the creation of the World Trade Organization (WTO) which
came into being in January 1995 to administer the multilateral accord. By
January 1996, the WTO had 115 member states, most of them from the
South.

For the first time in history, the WTO/GATT agreement includes a little-
known section on Trade-Related Aspects of Intellectual Property (TRIPS),
which represents the globalization of the intellectual enclosure system. The
powerful WTO now obligates signatories who don't already have such
legislation to adopt intellectual property laws for plant varieties and
microorganisms. Many have observed that this is an assault on national
sovereignty, in an area historically left to national discretion. Until TRIPS,
all nations were free to determine whether and how they would recognize
intellectual property.

...

The Convention, like the WTO, facilitates the expropriation of biological
resources and knowledge from the South, especially in its articles on
access to genetic resources and technology transfer. It encourages one-to-
one, bilateral arrangements between those (mostly corporations) who want
access to resources and knowledge, and governments which are deemed
to have sovereign control over the resources that corporations may want.
Yet the Convention proposes no binding multilateral parameters or
internationally-accepted code of conduct for such negotiations. Tragically,
while granting sovereignty to governments over the indigenous knowledge
and the resources of rural societies, the Convention fails to spell out any
protection for community innovation systems. Farming communities risk
being played off against one another by corporate bioprospectors and even
by their own governments. Reviewing the Biodiversity Convention, a Ciba-
Geigy (now Novartis) official wrote that the agreement could be interpreted
to do a better job protecting intellectual property than the WTO.

The WTO and the Biodiversity Convention could amount to a pincer
movement, threatening the genius and genetic resources of farming
communities. But the pincer is by no means closed. The Convention is
now engaged in a multi-year process of negotiation over its approach to
indigenous knowledge and intellectual property. The WTO will review its
intellectual property chapter in 1999. No developing country is obliged to

adopt IP legislation consistent with TRIPS until at least the year 2000. 'Least-developed' countries (a term not yet defined by the WTO) have until 2004. There is scope for change and cause for optimism.

So has there been any change?

(RAFI, 1996, pp.2, 3, 6, 7–9)

Chapter 4

The Ice: unstable geographies of Antarctica

Klaus Dodds

Contents

1   Introduction

Imagine we are looking at a globe and our gaze moves southwards towards the icy mass of Antarctica. We could be forgiven for thinking that whatever else has been changing with reference to former states such as the Soviet Union or Yugoslavia, Antarctica remains reassuringly stable. We might also imagine that there would not be much call for anyone to impose political boundaries, let alone fight over who owns a particular piece of ice. Antarctica, many would contend, is hardly equivalent to the territorial struggles embroiling Israel and Palestine, for example.

Consequently, you may be surprised to hear that Antarctica has been the source of considerable contention. Just because the polar continent does not have an indigenous human population, it does not follow that people have not argued over which particular government or agency does – or does not – 'own' Antarctica.

In Chapter 3, we saw that human actors are currently subjecting biological life to a form of territorialisation in order to assert ownership over specific plants or their component parts. As Nick Bingham showed, this kind of territorialisation calls for the establishment of clear-cut boundaries or borders which make it easier for particular actors to identify, claim and control the object in question. Bearing in mind the more familiar usage of the term 'territory', you may have noted that a similar sort of territorialisation has been applied to land.

In this chapter, we take as our point of departure the fact that most of the earth's surface which extends above sea level is divided up into bounded units over which specific states claim jurisdiction or 'sovereignty'. In this regard, Antarctica is something of an exception for, in a number of ways, it has proved resistant to this kind of political territorialisation. Parts of the continent have been temporarily occupied, and some states have even sought to claim Antarctica for themselves. Yet such claims have tended to be highly contested by other states or claimant groups – and continue to be contested. One of the advantages of focusing on this apparent aberration, however, is that we can use it to remind ourselves about everyday or taken-for-granted norms. This chapter suggests that the exceptional nature of Antarctica – or 'the Ice', as polar aficionados sometimes refer to it – can help us understand something fundamental about the nature of our political world.

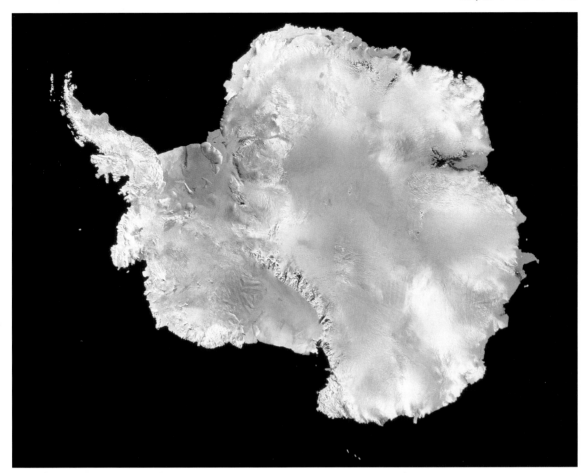

Figure 4.1   Antarctica in the summer season

We will see that the contestation of sovereign claims to Antarctica has led to assertions that the continent should be shared by all. In Chapter 3, the question was raised as to whether global biodiversity should be considered 'common property' and thereby precluded from forms of territorialisation that entail exclusive rights, access or ownership. Similarly, it has been proposed that Antarctica should belong to everyone: the term 'global common' being used to convey this sense of collective ownership.

The very fact that commons can be thought of as 'global' is suggestive of a world that is already politically globalised. And, indeed, the call for Antarctica to be designated as a global common draws attention to the

Defining global common

This is a term used to describe areas of the planet, such as the deep seabed, the earth's atmosphere and Antarctica, where no one state or group of states can lay claim to exclusive ownership. As a consequence, interested parties have sought to devise new mechanisms that encourage communal cooperation and even communal ownership. One example is the creation of an International Seabed Authority for the purpose of considering ownership rights over mineral resources found in the deep seabed.

dominance of the idea and practice of dividing the planet's land area into sovereign states, even as it poses a challenge to this arrangement. In the terms of this book, we would say that the division of the world into states with distinct national territories is the dominant form of political architecture for the contemporary world.

If we start to think about why the Antarctic region does not fit, and has never fitted, comfortably into this dominant political architecture, it soon becomes apparent that there is a lot more at issue than simply drawing lines on a map or establishing and contesting ownership. The very physical conditions of the polar continent pose immense challenges to the 'normal' or taken-for-granted practices of political territorialisation. Antarctica's political instability needs to be addressed in relation to its profound physical instability.

Alongside temperature extremes, processes associated with ice formation and flow contribute to the making of this particular continental territory in ways that call into question the very notion of a 'terra firma', or solid earth. Every winter season (between March and October), temperatures plummet to as low as −80°C, while the region doubles in size as sea ice freezes on to the edges of the polar continent. Moreover, while human-induced climate change may be playing a part in imperilling the ice caps of Antarctica, the continent itself remains volatile and unpredictable. Along with high winds and temperature extremes, shifting ice and episodes of volcanic activity have played havoc with attempts at human settlement and other practices of establishing a political presence. In other words, on the polar continent, the processes of political territorialisation have encountered some fairly intractable forms of flow: flows which have the capacity to perturb and sometimes preclude conventional practices of making and marking territory.

Therefore, the dominant political architecture of a globalised world is not only challenged by the fact that territorial claims in Antarctica encounter resistance from other human actors; it is also the case that the dynamics of the physical environment test and stretch these arrangements. Furthermore, we will find that Antarctica' s apparent exceptionality can turn out to be surprisingly revealing of the limits and tensions in the global political architecture in ways that have a relevance far beyond the polar regions.

Section 2 takes a closer look at the ideas and practices of sovereignty and the political architecture that supports the global system of sovereign states. In Section 3, we begin to build up a picture of the southern polar region, to get a feeling for the way that the continent and its surrounding oceans present a real challenge to these practices of sovereignty.

Sections 4 and 5 then proceed to explore the way that different claimants to Antarctica have sought to come to terms both with competing claimants and with the extreme physical conditions of the continent. An international community of states has developed a series of novel sovereignty practices to deal with these issues, and yet controversy over who is to govern the continent and who is to have access to its resources has continued.

Finally, having the considered alternative possibilities for governing Antarctica that are now on the agenda, in Section 6 we return to confront the issue of the physical volatility of the continent, and begin to ponder the broader implications of this for global political architectures.

Chapter aims

- To explore the ways in which the apparently exceptional case of Antarctica helps us to understand how we manage our dynamic and unpredictable planet.

- To consider how the planet calls into question the work done by human actors to produce and claim particular territories.

2   State sovereignty and political architecture

Antarctica, as we have noted, is in some ways an exception from the dominant forms of political territorialisation in the contemporary world. In order to understand this apparent aberration and what it means, a sense is needed of what has come to be considered normal: an appreciation, that is, of the division of the world into discrete political units, and the system or framework that organises the relationship between these units.

2.1   Introducing sovereignty

The key to making sense of politics in a globalised world is the notion of sovereignty. From the viewpoint of this book, sovereignty can be seen as a mechanism for regulating both territories and flows. If a state enjoys sovereignty over a particular territory, then it also has the potential to regulate at least some of the flows arriving in and departing from that space. For those living in Europe and North America, this framework is part of a taken-for-granted world. For example, when wishing to travel, Europeans and North Americans simply turn up at the station, the airport or seaport with luggage and a passport. The latter is the most important document to carry and not only confirms legal nationality but also enables the crossing of other national boundaries. Without it, passengers would be turned back by their own authorities and refused permission to travel. As a certain number of European Union (EU) states begin to call into question the permanence of national borders, it is instructive to recall that early twentieth-century travellers crossed European borders with the minimum of official documentation (Agnew, 2001, p.7). The passport stabilises a particular political architecture: national borders have to be respected and documents are needed to cross territories.

In this regard, as John Torpey (2000) has noted, the passport is an apparently mundane yet powerful illustration of sovereignty. If sovereignty can be defined in legal terms as a mechanism for creating legal obligations and commitments, it is for our purposes a set of practices which not only regulate movement across defined territories but also determine activities within a particular territorial jurisdiction. The effectiveness of these practices depends upon other parties recognising the authority of a sovereign state. As a UK passport holder, my ability to travel requires other countries to recognise the validity of my travel documents. If they fail to do so, my capacity to cross borders is highly circumscribed. For those people without valid passports or visas, the only option available is some form of 'illegal' entry, and many states, including the UK, are currently putting a huge amount of effort into trying to deter such movements through enhanced security at border crossings and along borderlines.

Defining sovereignty

This term is used to describe the legal and political circumstances enabling a state to claim exclusive jurisdiction over a particular physical territory. Since the seventeenth century, this idea of exclusive territorial control has gradually become hegemonic – that is to say, dominant as an idea and as a practice – as exclusive authority over every part of the earth's terrestrial surface has been claimed by individual states. Antarctica is the sole exception.

Activity 4.1

Think about whether you have ever been somewhere that requires a visa in order to secure entry. When I wanted to travel to China in April 2000, for example, I had to apply in person to the Chinese Embassy in London for a visa prior to travel. When I arrived at London Heathrow airport, I (like everyone else) had to negotiate a series of procedures such as passport control and baggage security. This process was repeated at Beijing airport where my passport and visa were inspected. In both places, my movement was strictly controlled and directed. You may have experienced something similar.

India

Considering the procedures at airports and other border posts reminds us of the extent to which our movements are monitored and controlled. There is a great deal of work involved in ensuring that such structures of control and surveillance materialise – customs officials have to be trained, baggage checking machines and security cameras have to be installed and airlines have to collaborate with national regulatory authorities. Yet what happens in the case of Antarctica? Do you need a visa to travel there? And once you arrive – are there any passport offices or border controls?

The short answer to the question about whether a visa is needed for travelling to Antarctica is no. Likewise, there are no passport offices or border posts in the Antarctic region. If you needed a visa to travel to Antarctica, it would imply that some country or other enjoyed exclusive control of the polar continent and was thus in a position to regulate flows of people and issue visas. With my UK passport, I can fly to the far south of Argentina or Chile and then take a ship on to Antarctica. Officials at the national airport in Buenos Aires or Santiago issue the standard entry stamp for incoming visitors to Argentina or Chile but not for Antarctica. Alternatively, I can travel by ship or plane from other so-called 'gateway' countries such as Australia, New Zealand and South Africa.

2.2 Reciprocal and shared sovereignty

As the ideas and practices associated with sovereignty have become more widespread, so states and their governments have had to learn to cooperate. Sovereignty, in other words, requires governments to work with one another in the making and unmaking of territories and flows. Despite a great deal of interstate warfare, such as the two world wars, the twentieth century witnessed important developments regarding interstate cooperation. The creation of the United Nations (UN) in

1945 is one significant example of the way that states sought to create a charter for the purpose of guiding world affairs and for securing reciprocal sovereignty. If a state claims sovereignty for itself, it must also, at the same time, recognise the territories of other states. This is a crucial element of international affairs because, without such mutual recognition, sovereignty would be a hollow concept; if no one takes your claims seriously regarding self-rule, then the implications could be very serious indeed. For instance, what is to stop another country from simply invading an unrecognised neighbour?

As a community of sovereign states, the UN attempts to guide rather than regulate behaviour. This is an important point because if sovereign states exercise control over their particular territories then no other body should have any determining role; there is no 'world government' which states can turn to in order to enforce sovereignty. Instead, the principle of sovereignty, as we have already noted, relies on states respecting one another's territory. What happens, however, when the behaviour of one state has serious implications for another neighbouring state? The first three chapters in this book have shown how activities, ranging from human-induced environmental change to offshore financial investment and bioprospecting, can and do have consequences for a wider community of states. In each of these cases, flows pass through or over territorial borders. We have already encountered a number of ways in which states and other actors, in order to help regulate such flows, have sought to develop cooperative structures of governance – or what we have referred to in Chapters 2 and 3 as 'architectures'. The questions of how and by whom Antarctica is to be governed present us with an early example of the demand for a cooperative architecture.

As the previous chapter emphasized, a great deal of work is involved in the creation and maintenance of territories, and this is also the case with regard to cooperative structures of governance. When two or more states are involved, the mechanisms for securing agreement and shared sovereignty inevitably become more complicated as a greater number of parties have to agree to a set of common rules and principles. Transnational cooperation, in order to be successful, is usually strongly rules-based (Ruggie, 1993, p.151). If states are inclined to relinquish or even restrain their sovereign authority, this will usually occur against a backdrop of an agreed set of rules governing individual and collective behaviour, which is important for four reasons. First, it defines particular communities and legitimates dominion. Second, it enables cooperation and shared sovereignty to occur because all parties believe that they are subject to the same rules and caveats; it helps, so

it is believed, to create a culture of trust and mutual recognition.
Third, it enables parties to identify any member who does not respect
or follow the rules; a failure to obey the rules may mean that the other
parties seek to expel a particular state from a shared sovereignty
agreement. As we will see in Section 5, the creation and maintenance
of such agreements is difficult, time consuming and occasionally highly
controversial. Fourth, it also identifies parties who are not party to
such agreements and sharing. In the case of Antarctica, the decision by
some states to declare the polar continent a common heritage was
taken in part as an act of defiance against those who had made
decisions affecting its status, a point we return to in Section 6.2.

Summary

- Sovereignty is a mechanism for regulating territories and flows.
- Ideas and practices associated with sovereignty shape the architecture of international politics.
- Sovereignty gains its effectiveness from being reciprocal.
- To regulate flows that pass across a number of political territories, states may attempt to set up structures of cooperative governance, or shared sovereignty.

3   Unstable geographies: the Antarctic environment as a challenge to sovereignty

Thus far, we have examined some of the ways that principles of
sovereignty operate. We have seen that sovereignty over any particular
political territory only makes sense if it is part of a broader system in
which each state affords due recognition to other states. This system is
now almost fully globalised, Antarctica being the major exception. This
section will consider the features and conditions of the continent,
providing the background as to why it has presented a particular
challenge to the conventions of state sovereignty.

It is hardly surprising that Antarctica is often referred to as an extreme
environment. The work that is carried out by human actors on the
continent remains seasonally dependent but, regardless of season,

human beings occupy less than 0.01 per cent of its surface area. During the winter season, for instance, residents at the US-administered South Pole station are effectively trapped. No aircraft landings can be attempted during this period because it would be too dangerous, and emergency supplies have occasionally had to be parachuted from a passing plane. In one remarkable example, in 1999, medical equipment was dropped at the South Pole station so that a female resident (who was a qualified doctor) could carry out an operation on herself to remove a suspected malignant chest lump.

When it comes to mapping Antarctica, the continent is usually portrayed in its summer season guise (see Figure 4.2). The vast expanses of additional sea ice, so prevalent in the winter season, are frequently omitted. As a consequence, the Antarctic tends to appear more stable in shape and size than is actually the case.

More than 99 per cent of the Antarctic landmass is permanently covered with ice, and the few remaining areas, such as the Dry Valleys on the South Pacific side of the continent, are composed of exposed rock. The sheer scale and dynamism of the ice-filled continent is something to marvel at. Antarctica occupies 10 per cent of the earth's surface and is as large as Europe and North America combined. As the travel writer Sarah Wheeler reflects:

> Like glutinous white icing flowing off a wedding cake, the layer of ice on the surface of Antarctica is slowly but persistently rolling towards the coast, forcing its way between mountains, turning itself into glaciers split by crevasses and inching its way into a floating ice shelf or collapsing into the Southern Ocean. One of them, the Ross Ice Shelf, is larger than France.
>
> (Wheeler, 1997 pp.6–7)

Antarctica is commonly divided into two geological constituents – East Antarctica and West Antarctica. The Transantarctic Mountains bisect these two geologically complex zones, and a network of additional mountains (some of them volcanic) punctuates the continent. Some of the surrounding islands, such as Deception Island off the Antarctic Peninsula, are also volcanically active. Beyond the coastal fringes of the continent, the immense polar plateau helps to ensure that the Antarctic is the highest, windiest, driest and of course coldest continent in the world; it is a continent of superlatives. At the centre of the Antarctic lies the South Pole, and even the pole's position is unstable, varying with the axis of the earth's rotation. Furthermore, the history of human contact is extremely recent – 1800s onwards – compared with the five other continents.

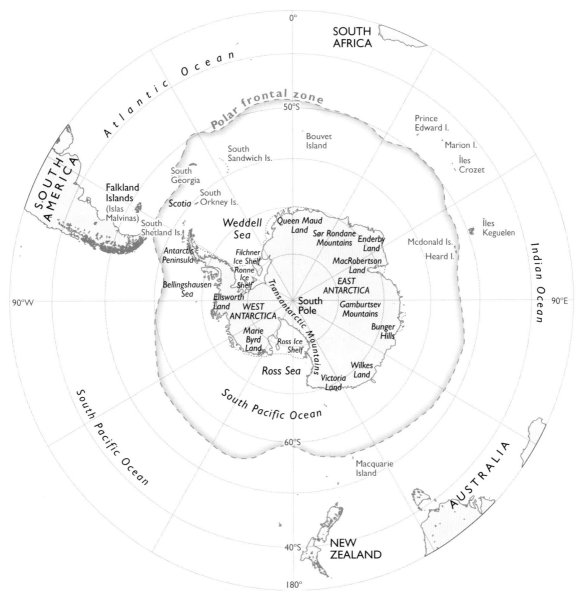

Figure 4.2   The physical contours of Antarctica, the surrounding Southern Ocean and the polar frontal zone in the summer season

Antarctic Environments and Resources: A Geographical Perspective by J.D. Hansom and J.E. Gordon, Pearson Education Limited, Copyright © Addison Wesley Longman Limited 1998.

While human beings are not indigenous to Antarctica and the Southern Ocean, the same cannot be said for penguins, whales, fish and birds such as the wandering albatross. Along with shifts and movements in the non-living environment, the existence of wildlife has also complicated subsequent endeavours to manage the southern continent – politically and ecologically.

How has Antarctica's instability as a physical entity impacted on its definition as a political entity? The state-based notion of sovereignty starts with the assumption that one has to define a particular territory in order to exercise authority and management. However, if drawing lines on a map appears comparatively simple, the nature of Antarctica frequently defies such tidy definition. The physical and biological territories of Antarctica shift with the seasons, and the continent undergoes immense seasonal changes which, furthermore, vary from year to year.

While many of the boundaries that define national territories are strictly human-made, there are many other cases where the borderline takes advantage of natural features, such as the coast of an island or the river between the USA and Mexico (see Chapter 1, Section 2.2). Such features may change, nevertheless, as the physical world shifts and transforms, with Antarctica offering an extreme and thus particularly problematic instance of this. The tendency to include the Southern Ocean as part of the Antarctic region adds to the quandary. This ocean abuts the southerly edges of the Atlantic, Indian and Pacific Oceans – raising the question of where it begins and ends. Environmental geographers contend that the polar frontal zone can help define Antarctica (see Figure 4.2). Here the cold and dense waters of the Southern Ocean meet and sink beneath the warmer and less dense fringes of the Atlantic, Indian and Pacific Oceans. Yet as a zone rather than a boundary, the Southern Ocean defies exact geographical delineation, being highly dynamic and varying from year to year. I have made four visits to Antarctica by sea, and certainly felt that sense of transition as we crossed the Drake Passage. Each time I tried to guess when I might see the first substantial iceberg, but there is no pronounced boundary, and each voyage was slightly different in terms of iceberg encounters.

We shall see in Section 5.2 that this definitional dilemma has had, and continues to have, serious implications for the management of the polar continent, and for the relationship between territories and flows of people, ice and ideas.

As Section 4 will discuss further, the ways in which the Antarctic has been claimed and occupied by states need to be understood before we can consider how states have sought to manage the polar continent. European subjects began to settle other so-called 'empty spaces' such as the Americas from the sixteenth century and Australia from the eighteenth century. These acts of colonisation were crucial in terms of developing the necessary conditions for establishing sovereignty –

apparently unchallenged control of particular parcels of territory. When later applied to Antarctica in the twentieth century, this particular notion of sovereignty was the one that prevailed. A great deal of emphasis was placed on 'effective occupation', the idea that possession was related to a demonstrable occupying presence. Nonetheless, ideas relating to authority and control are far from fixed, and Antarctica provides an invaluable reminder that our conceptions of sovereignty have changed over time.

Summary

- Flows of ice, sea and living creatures ensure that the territory of Antarctica is dynamic, unpredictable and difficult to define.

- Antarctica presents a challenge to prevailing conceptions of a sovereign territory.

4   Claiming Antarctica

A great deal of effort goes into the making of territories and the demarcation of their boundaries – the processes we have termed 'territorialisation' – as you have seen in the case of oceanic islands, financial centres and plant products. In this section, we begin with one of the most familiar forms of territorialisation – the making and the demarcating of the nation state – viewed through the strange and distorting lens of Antarctica.

4.1   Marking territory: ceremonies of possession

In her fascinating study of the European conquest of the Americas (between the 1490s and 1640s), Patricia Seed demonstrates how the ceremonies of possession varied greatly among the Dutch, English, French, Portuguese and Spanish colonialists (1995, pp.2–3). Despite their differences, work had to be carried out in order to 'root' claims to ownership, and for the subsequent exercise of sovereignty. Flags were planted, crosses mounted, maps drawn, speeches delivered and fences erected. These performances, in order to be effective, depended upon audience. When the Spanish first landed in the Americas, their ceremonies of possession were seeking to convince the Spanish crown, international competitors such as the Portuguese and the subjugated local populations that they were intent on developing sovereign authority over a particular territory.

From the fifteenth-century English point of view, the Spanish ceremonies of possession (especially the accompanying speech of possession called the Requirement) made little sense because they failed to take into account the need to demonstrate active usage of the claimed territory in question. For the English colonist in the Americas, the most important element in establishing sovereign authority was not a grandiose speech of intention. Instead, emphasis was placed on occupation, habitation and planting. The construction of a house, the erection of a fence and the cultivation of a garden were taken to be the most appropriate indicators of long-term settlement. Using and occupying land, in other words, counted for more in the English colonial imagination than in the Spanish. Elsewhere, in places as diverse as Australia and the Falkland Islands, the English colonialists cultivated gardens and carried out detailed descriptions of the land (Seed, 1995, p.17). Over time, a consensus emerged about the way that unoccupied territory should be claimed and administered.

When the British first pressed a claim to Antarctica in 1908, they were the first state to undertake such an act of possession. Antarctica, however, presented a dilemma. How could the traditional indicators of ownership such as the erection of houses or fences apply to this continent? Moreover, there was no chance of making fields to cultivate, and the types of formal gardening favoured by English-speaking colonists in the temperate and tropical world were impossible. Lack of soil and the unrelenting winds ruled out the planting of trees and hedges.

If it was impossible to carry out gardening or fence erection then the completion of basic surveys was judged to be a satisfactory alternative, especially if the territory was not inhabited by an indigenous population (see Figure 4.3). Surveys not only provided a detailed description of the territory in question, they also reminded other parties that the occupants were serious in purpose. But even basic surveying was a formidable task. Well into the twentieth century, surveyors working in the Antarctic had a hard time meeting the normal criteria relating to maps and survey production because of consistently inclement weather.

Figure 4.3   Surveyor, British expedition to Antarctica, 1911

As a consequence of the challenges posed by the Antarctic environment, ceremonies of possession (and accompanying standards of surveying) were altered to reflect the prevailing geographical conditions. While due emphasis was still given to occupation, different indicators were used to demonstrate sovereign intent. Though the act of naming had been important in the establishing of British colonial authority in the seventeenth century, it was even more pivotal in the case of Antarctica. Naming helped to consolidate ownership because it alleviated the problem posed by an absence of permanent and widespread settlement and cultivation. The political map of Antarctica, as a consequence, bears witness to the naming practices of English/ British claimants and other interested parties. Look at any map of the Antarctic and you will see how names commemorate places and people –the South Shetland Islands are named in memory of the Shetland Islands off Scotland's eastern coast, and the Ross Sea is named after the nineteenth-century explorer James Clark Ross. However, bear in mind that maps of Antarctica made by different countries may include alternative names with different points of reference.

In this way, simple but often demanding actions, such as carrying out a survey, establishing a name, erecting a flag and constructing a base camp, became important elements in the early occupation of Antarctica (see Figure 4.4 overleaf).

Figure 4.4   British expedition to Antarctica, 1911

This work helped to establish claims to sovereign authority. Names helped to stabilise a territory and assured the visitor of a mapped location. As Seed (1995) notes with reference to the conquest of the Americas, this need not mean that other parties accepted those claims. For one thing, there were significant differences between claimants with regard to ceremonies of possession and displays of sovereignty. Argentina and Chile, for example, believe that their claims to polar territory are stronger than those of any other claimants because of the fact that they are geographically closer to Antarctica. For the UK, geographical proximity has not been a strong claim, given that London lies over 16,000 km from the South Pole. Consequently, important issues remain to be settled.

4.2 Maintaining sovereignty

If claiming a particular territory involves a great deal of work, maintaining a presence is no less strenuous. One not only has to administer the territory but also to attempt to control and regulate flows. The territorial claims pressed by countries such as the UK, Australia and New Zealand in Antarctica were to be expanded upon by countries such as France (1924), and challenged by others such as the USA (see Figure 4.5 overleaf). Extensive surveying and mapping by the USA in the 1930s and 1940s worried earlier claimant parties precisely because the latter were unable to regulate the movement of US personnel in Antarctica. The problem was how to get others to take seriously particular claims to Antarctic territory.

Establishing a sovereign presence on 'the Ice' has inevitably been precarious given the nature of the polar environment. Without an established domestic citizenry, claimant states devised procedures, institutions and ceremonies in order to regulate the behaviour of their own few citizens and the occasional visitors. Bureaucracy was not being established just for its own sake, however. By the 1930s, international law placed great emphasis on 'effective occupation' in places that were described as 'terra nullius' – belonging to no one. Effective occupation was not the same as settlement: it did not require a permanent and viable population, or the trappings of permanence such as fencing or cultivation, but it did require some sort of official presence. The creation of base camps and scientific stations emerged as the main evidence of effective occupation, along with the appointment of postmasters, Justices of the Peace and civilian administrators. Fixing a presence (and recording and mapping that presence) on the Ice was part and parcel of administration and occupation.

[handwritten margin note: naming helped to stabilise a territory give it an identity and an association with a particular nation state]

Figure 4.5   Territorial claims made on Antarctica since the beginning of the twentieth century

Antarctic Environments and Resources: A Geographical Perspective by J.D. Hansom and J.E. Gordon,
Pearson Education Limited, Copyright © Addison Wesley Longman Limited 1998.

Regulating activities was another element of sovereign control. The British claim to the Antarctic in 1908 (and refined in 1917) depended initially on their regulation of two types of movements – people and whales. The Norwegians had set up a whaling station on South Georgia, and the British recognised that whaling was emerging as the most lucrative activity in the South Atlantic region. The industrial processing of these large mammals helped to establish a market for commodities such as whale oil, which was used for domestic lighting and heating. Fearing that other states might gain a foothold in South Georgia and surrounding islands such as South Orkneys, the British declared that a vast area of the Antarctic Peninsula and accompanying sub-Antarctic islands was now under the administrative control of the Colonial Office in London. The justification for this territorial claim was that past British explorers such as James Cook had helped to discover and explore the region. No objection was raised by other states, including Norway, and henceforth all whaling activity was regulated by the British through the introduction of licensing. Norwegian, Argentine and Chilean companies all purchased licences from the British and thus the latter's effective sovereignty was recognised.

While the British and their allies enjoyed some international recognition vis-à-vis their territorial claims, other states such as the USA refused to accept their legitimacy. As a major sponsor of polar expeditions, successive US administrations from the 1920s to the 1950s encouraged explorers such as Richard Byrd and Lincoln Ellsworth to make further discoveries in the interior of the continent – facilitated by the use of aircraft. In this way, the aeroplane replaced the dog sled and US aviators (despite the official policy of non-recognition of all claims to Antarctica) were instructed to drop hundreds of mini US flags out of the aircraft window. Any passer-by on the polar interior below would then have to appreciate (whether they liked it or not) the substantial achievements of US discovery and exploration. The USA was not the only state to use flags to signify its territorial presence; the 1938–39 Nazi German expedition to Neu Schwabenland deposited a great number of Swastikas on the polar ice to help establish a German presence in Antarctica.

Such flag dropping activities may seem silly, but their significance can be understood within a context of sovereignty as a performance. All interested parties confronted a dilemma: how to establish a permanent presence in a continent as large and forbidding as Antarctica. Settling the polar continent was out of the question, so it was hoped that flags might serve as a visual reminder to others that these countries intended to assert their authority over the continent.

Nevertheless, the nature of the Antarctic nullified even this strategy; the flags were soon buried under ice or scattered by the winds. In this way, the Antarctic environment itself helped to shape both reception and long-term recognition. When the UK launched a determined attempt to colonise the Antarctic Peninsula and surrounding sub-Antarctic islands during 1943–44, its personnel planted signs declaring that these territories were now part of 'Crown Lands' and that the act of trespassing was not going to be tolerated. Within a season, the wooden signs were destroyed by the unrelenting winds, and the flags fluttering on poles close to the newly constructed stations were ripped beyond recognition.

The proliferation of exploratory and scientific activities needs to be viewed in the context of this determination of claimant states to continue their occupation of Antarctica. After the Second World War, new waves of investment helped to establish scientific activity as the principal rationale for continued activity in Antarctica. The UK, for instance, created and funded a Falkland Islands Dependencies Survey (FIDS) from the mid 1940s as part of its attempt to map, survey and occupy its territorial stake. The FIDS had no mandate to carry out research outside the boundaries of the Falkland Islands Dependencies – which included the Antarctic Peninsula. Likewise, counter-claimants Argentina and Chile concentrated their political and scientific energies on their own territorial sectors. As the UK mapping and surveying of Antarctica improved, so interest grew in its perceived resource wealth. Geological research helped to propagate a view of the polar continent as a treasure house of minerals such as uranium and coal.

The 'ground rules' relating to Antarctic sovereignty were changing again, as the physical nature of the continent impelled parties to adapt their ideas concerning occupation, recognition and legitimacy.

4.3   International Geophysical Year: from sovereignty games to global science

The political situation of Antarctica in the 1940s and 1950s illustrates only too well how much hard work was involved in establishing territories, creating boundaries and regulating movement. Despite the inherent difficulties, both Argentina and Chile considered the Antarctic Peninsula to be part of their national territory. Yet this kind of territorial claim was to be challenged by a new way of looking at Antarctica which emphasised the continent's implication in the wider political and geophysical contours of the planet. In effect, it called into question attempts to demarcate Antarctica as anyone's 'national territory'.

Securing any kind of consensus on Antarctica's territorial status was still problematic. During the Antarctic summer season, it was common practice for rival scientific parties (and their accompanying logistical supporters) to spend a great deal of time consolidating particular territorial claims at the expense of other parties (see Figure 4.6). The Antarctic Peninsula was particularly vulnerable to what were euphemistically called 'sovereignty games', as rival parties sought to destroy or diminish any signs of alien occupation or evidence of trespass. Such activities were, of course, highly seasonal. With the onset of the Antarctic winter, all parties were forced to concentrate on survival and sovereignty games were frozen for at least six months.

Figure 4.6   Flag waving ceremony organised by the British, Australian and New Zealand expedition to Antarctica, January 1931

The personnel operating in the Antarctic Peninsula endured a schizophrenic existence – were they scientists, administrators or occupiers? Were they operating in the Falkland Islands Dependencies, the Argentine Antarctic Territory or the Chilean Antarctic Territory? The 'Antarctic problem' was to enter a new phase in the post-war years, largely as a result of the attention brought to the continent by the Antarctic programme of the International Geophysical Year (IGY) of 1957–58. First proposed in 1950 in the wake of the second International Polar Year in 1932, the IGY was to entail twelve months of scientific study devoted to generating new data. Once adopted by the International Council of Scientific Unions in 1953, the programme expanded in scope and attention to encompass three main areas – Antarctica, the ocean depths and outer space. Twelve parties (Argentina, Australia, Belgium, Chile, France, Japan, New Zealand, Norway, South Africa, the UK, the USSR and the USA) participated in the 1957–58 IGY. Many scientific stations were set up, and many new techniques for gathering data were tested and developed. Moreover, as it turned out, the IGY ushered in an extraordinary change of attitude – Antarctica was no longer considered a strange place on the margins of the world. Instead, the polar continent was conceptualised as an essential element in the earth's geophysical condition and, as such, warranted careful study.

Activity 4.2

Now turn to Reading 4A by Laurence Gould (1958) entitled 'The polar regions in their relation to human affairs', which you will find at the end of the chapter. Laurence Gould was a geologist who played an important part in the surveying of Antarctica on the 1928–30 US expedition under Richard Byrd. He went on to become the first director of the US Antarctica programme. It is interesting to note the extent to which thinking about life in a global – or globalising world – is already present in Gould's account of the IGY in 1958 (considering that the idea of globalisation really only took hold in the social sciences during the 1980s). As you are reading, jot down any points that Gould makes which remind you in some way of themes or ideas we have looked at in the first half of this book.

From Reading 4A, you may have noticed Gould's reference to jet transportation with its 'increased speed and global flights'. We might see this as a kind of precursor to today's global interconnectivity which forms the background to Chapter 2, for example.

Perhaps you also made note of Gould's point that all the geophysical sciences (or earth sciences, as we referred to them in Chapter 1) are 'global in character'. By this he means that the processes being studied are themselves fully global, in the sense that what is happening in one part of the world has implications for the rest of the planet. This is reminiscent of the arguments made about active earth processes in Chapter 1, Section 4.2.

Gould goes on to make the point that climatic systems, or the
circulation of the atmosphere, link distant places across the planet's
surface – and he even raises the possibility that melting ice in one part
of the world could, through rising sea level, affect low-lying areas
throughout the world. In a more general way, the connection Gould
draws between progress and the question of 'man's eventual survival
on this planet' (or as we would now say, *human* survival) seems to
further hint at the kind of global environmental changes that you will
be familiar with from Chapter 1.

As Gould's account suggests, the IGY represented a major step in
thinking about the earth as a single, dynamic and interconnected
system. It was no accident that the IGY also looked outwards to the
solar system, for new ways of thinking about the earth as a whole
were bound up with an interest in comparing it with other whole
planets (Pyne, 2003, p.108). Data gathered in Antarctica turned out to
be vital to understanding earth processes in numerous ways but, as
Gould notes, the role of the ice-bound continent was particularly
important in making sense of the dynamics of global climate. Not only
is the integrated view of land, sea and ice pioneered in the IGY era
still pivotal to contemporary climate change research, but the role of
Antarctica – especially the effect on global sea level of the breaking up
of its ice sheets – remains a cornerstone of concern over changing
climate.

Possibly what is most fascinating and most momentous about the IGY
is not simply this new conception of the geophysical integration of the
planet, but the way that this was closely bound up with a new sense of
'geopolitical' integration. Gould's point about the geophysical sciences
being global also conveys a sense that global collaboration was the only
real way to go about doing such science. Moreover, if the scientific
data of Antarctica were turning out to be of much greater value to
humankind than its mineral riches or its marine life, as Gould
suggested, then something other than the previously existing national
scramble for territorial control of the continent seemed to be called
for. As Gould (1958, p.8) puts it, 'Since the geophysicist is inevitably a
truly international scientist, the IGY may turn out to be a brilliant new
approach toward international understanding and organization'.

Reading 4A may have reminded you of the different sorts of
architecture that were discussed in Chapters 2 and 3, and earlier in this
chapter. As you will recall, architecture is the term we have been using

to refer to different ways of organising territories and flows. Gould's account of the IGY seems to be suggesting, in the terms of this book, that a new understanding of global physical flows, in which Antarctica played a crucial role, is prompting the call for a new international architecture for governing the polar region.

As it turned out, moves towards the establishment of a new post-IGY architecture or framework were initiated by the USA in 1958–59, which convened a series of diplomatic discussions with the intention of developing a new political consensus. It was reasoned that if participants could agree to a 'sovereignty freeze' – a suspension of territorial claims and counter-claims – it might be possible to create a new modus operandi for Antarctica. This immediately raised questions. Australia had misgivings about the Soviet Union, for instance, but the latter had to be included to ensure legitimacy and effectiveness. With important implications for future discussions, attempts to raise the question of Antarctica in the UN in 1956 and 1958 by post-colonial states such as India were unsuccessful, as Gould noted. If a framework were to be established, it was assumed that the twelve IGY parties – given their practical involvement in Antarctica – were to be the key players. Seven claimant states – Argentina, Australia, Chile, France, New Zealand, Norway and the UK – and five non-claimant states – Belgium, Japan, South Africa, the USA and the USSR – became the self-appointed guardians of the polar continent.

Summary

- The physical conditions of Antarctica proved problematic to colonial traditions of making and marking political territory.
- Naming, mapping, surveying and establishing bases emerged as key markers of political territory.
- The IGY's focus on scientific research offered an alternative to the contest between states for sovereign rights over Antarctica.
- The IGY established Antarctica as a vital part of an integrated geophysical view of the planet, which also had important geopolitical implications.

Geopolitical

5   Sharing sovereignty: the Antarctic Treaty

In the absence of any existing, workable model of sovereign authority, all the interested parties had to accept that no one state was going to enjoy exclusive sovereignty over Antarctica. This section explores how a particular agreement called the 1959 Antarctic Treaty helped to construct a novel form of shared sovereignty – what we are terming a new architecture – for governing the polar continent.

Given the present tendency to view the world's geography in terms of states and bounded territories, the evolution of the Antarctic Treaty provides evidence of charting how states work together to manage a region in which ownership is disputed. Two elements will be elaborated further. First, we will look at how the Antarctic Treaty led to the development of an international regime. Second, we will consider how a strictly bounded view of Antarctica was perturbed by physical or biological flows.

5.1   Negotiating the Antarctic Treaty

Prior to 1959, a great deal of emphasis was given to sovereign expressions such as expeditions in the Antarctic and their accompanying work-based performances. After 1959, those claims (and counter-claims) were treated rather differently as greater emphasis was given to science and scientific activity rather than simply pressing a claim to a particular part of the polar continent. This sort of transformation helps us to understand not only how ideas and practices related to sovereignty can change but also how recognition by other parties is highly significant. By the time the IGY polar participants, led by the USA, gathered in Washington, DC to discuss the future of Antarctica in October 1959, a great deal of political and scientific intrigue had occurred. Despite fundamental disagreements over the status of territorial claims to Antarctica, all the interested parties agreed that there was real danger of conflict in the absence of an agreement to regulate present and future behaviour. The prevailing context of the Cold War between the USA and the Soviet Union was never absent from the diplomatic radar screen. Both superpowers were deeply embroiled in a geopolitical game of spying, surveillance and submarine patrols that extended to the Arctic Ocean, so there was no reason to believe that the Antarctic would be immune to such manoeuvres. Others, such as the UK, had an added incentive to seek a modus operandi for the Antarctic because of mounting costs in administering and policing the remains of an imperial portfolio.

Precious funds were being devoured by the FIDS, and the Royal Navy was forced to deploy ships and personnel to patrol the extreme limits of the South Atlantic empire. By way of contrast, rival claimants such as Argentina and Chile could afford to devote resources to protect their interest in a region which lay less than 1000 km south of their metropolitan territories.

Activity 4.3

Consider the following quote from Brian Roberts, the British Foreign Office's chief polar advisor, who attended the 1959 Washington, DC Conference. What does it tell us about political rivalries in Antarctica?

The Americans were in a stronger position than ourselves to convene a conference. We need a lasting settlement with the Argentines and Chileans if we want the Treaty to be as comprehensive as possible. There are, of course, also all the expected difficulties with the Argentines and Chileans, both of whom are constantly raising the question of sovereignty. This is not what we came here to discuss. Their attitude is purely political and national and they are still being quite unhelpful in seeking solutions which recognise that others also have Antarctic interests. This Treaty holds out the possibility of ending our quarrel about the Antarctic, there is no hope at all of ending the Falkland Islands dispute [a territory disputed with Argentina and lying outside the proposed Treaty area] within a measurable time.

I think it represents an important milestone in Antarctic affairs. But it is only a beginning.

(quoted in Scott Polar Research Institute Archives, MS 1308/9: BJ)

Brian Roberts's comments about the Washington Conference tell us something important about territories and the practices associated with sovereignty. National rivalries were well entrenched and some states still found it hard to think of Antarctica in terms other than those of national territory. Despite this persistence of the idea of territorial exclusivity, political leaders were being asked to forgo their own particular interests in favour of a broader agreement which recognised the rights of all parties. Consequently, the Antarctic Treaty negotiators had to find a formula that allowed all parties to acknowledge a new international regime. The solution lay with a clever diplomatic fudge on the one hand, and new forms of cooperative behaviour engendered by recent scientific endeavour on the other.

Some of the main provisions of the 1959 Antarctic Treaty

Article I: Antarctica shall be used for peaceful purposes only

Article II: There should be freedom to conduct scientific investigations in Antarctica ...

Article IV: Sovereignty claims are considered suspended

Article V: No nuclear explosions shall be carried out in Antarctica

Article VI: The Treaty area is defined as the area south of 60 degrees South

Article VII: A right to inspection is established throughout Antarctica ...

Article XII: Modification is possible of the Treaty (only after 30 years from the date of entry into force)

Article XIII: The Treaty is open to accession by any member of the United Nations

(Natural Environment Research Council British Antarctic Survey, 2004)

Article IV of the 1959 Antarctic Treaty stipulates that all territorial claims are considered 'suspended for the duration of the Treaty', which came into force in 1961. Thus, the status of claims and rights in the region (including possible claims by major non-claimants such as the USA and the Soviet Union) were suspended. All interested parties recognised that this was probably the only option in terms of resolving the deep disagreements between claimant states such as Argentina, Australia and France (who were initially hostile to Article IV) and those who refused to negotiate a Treaty without the guarantee to suspend sovereign claims (as embodied by Article IV).

In order to facilitate a spirit of cooperative behaviour on and off the Antarctic continent, considerable attention was paid to the role that scientific investigation should perform. The 1957–58 IGY had demonstrated that states and their respective scientific parties could collaborate with one another. That due prominence should be given to the peaceful use of Antarctica and scientific investigation is stipulated in Articles I and II of the Treaty. In a direct acknowledgement of the dangerous politics of the Cold War, Article V of the Treaty prohibits all forms of nuclear testing, storage and dumping in the Antarctic region, and further prohibits all forms of military activity. This was particularly significant for Southern Hemisphere states, such as Australia and South Africa, which feared that the nuclear testing superpowers, including the UK, might be tempted to carry out nuclear weapons testing in an uninhabited continent. (While Antarctica was secured as the world's first nuclear-free zone, at various times between the 1950s and 1990s nations which were signatories to the Treaty took advantage of the supposedly empty spaces of Nevada, Siberia, southern Australia and a number of islands in the Pacific Ocean as nuclear weapons testing sites.) In order to foster an atmosphere of trust, it was also agreed that signatories to the Treaty had the right to inspect one another's scientific bases in order to ensure that the provisions of the Treaty were being respected.

The Antarctic Treaty was signed on 1 December 1959, and US President J.F. Kennedy subsequently described its ratification eighteen months later as a 'positive step in the direction of worldwide peace' (cited in Chaturvedi, 1990, p.53). The Treaty provided the foundation for an international regime or architecture which has framed the governance of Antarctica for over forty years.

Therefore, science and scientific research became the new sovereign currency as all signatories agreed that flag waving and base construction (simply to secure effective occupation) were moribund in Antarctica. Arguably, then, the Antarctic Treaty helped to create a new form of sovereignty: a political architecture in which multiple states collaborated in the governance of a single territory. However, this meant that states persisted as the primary political actors. Furthermore, this was not just any states, but those states that had previously been prominent in the drive to assert their own interests in Antarctica, including those that had been most active in claiming exclusive rights over sections of the continent. As we will see, this persistence of pre-existing forms of power and influence would eventually raise important questions about the future governance of the continent.

5.2   The Antarctic Treaty as an international regime

According to most commentators, the 1959 Antarctic Treaty has proven to be a remarkably durable and effective legal instrument. It is not difficult to see why such an assessment might have gained considerable favour. The Treaty provided a 'road map' for resolving the immediate tensions surrounding the 'Antarctic problem'. All signatories agreed that, for the duration of the Treaty, the arguments over sovereignty claims would be put to one side. This did not mean that anyone was expected (or would ever agree) to relinquish existing or future claim attempts. Scientific endeavour (supported by a Scientific Committee on Antarctic Research) was secured as the primary incentive for polar occupation. Military conflict has been absent from the continent and this must be considered illustrative of how at least one particular flow (that is, troops and armaments) was prevented from entering a particular territory. Yet Antarctica remains a contested global common, and the ending of the Cold War has not changed that position.

The Antarctic Treaty was designed to provide a mechanism for cooperation, and sought to do so by creating a series of norms, practices and processes for regulating (or, more accurately, guiding) behaviour in the Antarctic region. Taken together these elements are said to constitute an international regime.

Defining international regime

International regimes refer to agreements that participating parties (usually states but also others such as non-governmental organisations) have created for the purpose of facilitating cooperation over issues that are not easily dealt with on a one-to-one basis. This might include, for example, the regulation of living resources, such as fish, which migrate over sizeable regions such as the Southern Ocean. It also might involve factors such as pollution control or scientific exchange. Regimes, in order to be both effective and legitimate, depend on all parties 'signing up' to a series of rules and regulations. An international regime is another version of what we refer to in this book as an 'architecture'.

The intention of such a regime is to foster cooperation and a general spirit of good will. In the context of a highly disputed region, such as Antarctica, this is understandable. Nonetheless, the very nature of the polar continent made such a system all the more desirable. Given the enormous challenges of Antarctica (in terms of its scale, physical conditions and lack of habitation), no one country – even with the resources of the USA – was in a position to monitor closely the behaviour of other parties. Inevitably, all parties had to trust one another and hope that the rules of the Antarctic Treaty were being respected, with scientific activity providing a benchmark for judging the activities of all concerned.

The area of application of the Antarctic Treaty was declared to be all territory (including ice shelves) and seas below 60° South. While there were disagreements at the time of the Treaty negotiations over the delimitation of the area of application, 60° South was chosen because it encapsulated the entire polar continent and thus provided a convenient territorial reference point. One of the ways that the dominance of thinking and acting in terms of sovereign political territories persisted was in the assumption that there had to be a clear boundary line; no one suggested in 1959 that the northern fringes of the Antarctic region should be conceived in terms of a zone of transition or frontier region. In the process, Antarctica was remade and re-imagined as a singular political unit.

However, the political boundary of 60° South bore no resemblance to the biogeographical boundaries of the Antarctic and the Southern

Ocean. For example, as noted earlier, many biologists and environmental geographers would point to the highly significant zone of polar convergence where the cold waters surrounding the Antarctic confront the warmer waters of the Atlantic, Indian and Pacific Oceans. Islands, such as South Georgia, Prince Edward and Heard, lie close to this highly dynamic boundary and their coastal waters support a rich abundance of marine life, including a variety of fish such as the Patagonian Toothfish. While the Antarctic Treaty provided a stable territorial definition for political and legal management, it was unable to offer a suitable reference point for subsequent fisheries management in the Southern Ocean. The incorporation into the Treaty of the Convention for the Conservation of Antarctic Marine Living Resources (CCAMLR) in 1981 recognised that the area of management should be extended north of 60° South. In this way, the flow of biological life served to problematise the notion that a unit of political governance or administration was best suited by a hard, inflexible boundary.

5.3   The persistence of sovereignty

One of the most significant outcomes of the IGY, as Section 4 suggested, was a new move towards thinking of the earth as a single, dynamic and interconnected physical system. And yet, the Antarctic Treaty System (ATS) – the mechanisms and procedures through which the Treaty is put into practice – which emerged in the aftermath of IGY continued to push for the establishment of a clear boundary for Antarctica. Despite the achievements of the IGY, it seems that important aspects of the making and marking of sovereign political territories have persisted into the era of shared sovereignty. Moreover, it is not simply the case that the work of forging sovereign territories simply shifted from the level of individual state claims to the level of a larger, collectively governed continent. Rather, within the framework of the ATS and the international regime it put in place, there is evidence that claimant states carried on with their individual endeavours to carve out a slice of Antarctica for themselves.

Maintaining or fixing a territorial presence on the Ice has continued to be a priority for most of the claimant states. Argentina, for example, took the extraordinary step of flying pregnant women to Antarctica in the late 1970s in order that they could give birth in what was viewed as the most southerly portion of the Argentine Republic. Why did Argentina carry out such activities? The then military regime in Argentina was determined not only to remind the wider world of its sovereign claims to Antarctica but also eager to impress its own citizens with an illustration of territorialising bravado.

While this may be an extreme case, other claimant parties have found their own ways to remind domestic citizens and international onlookers of the validity of their various territorial ambitions – including more map making and the issuing of special postage stamps. Even the scientific activities of the participant states in the ATS are a far cry from the globally-oriented vision of science imagined by Gould (1958) and other key figures in the IGY. In order to secure the coveted Consultative Status in the ATS, which confers full voting rights at Treaty meetings, the parties in question must demonstrate to existing members that they have carried out 'substantial scientific research'. The Treaty does not define what such a term might mean but it was generally understood to imply that an applicant should have either established a permanent scientific presence on the Ice or carried out a significant body of polar research. Such a criterion, with associated costs in terms of time and finance, was designed to restrict membership.

One unintended consequence of such a ruling has been to concentrate research stations in areas of relative accessibility such as the Antarctic Peninsula and the South Shetland Islands. The Antarctic Treaty has therefore narrowed the geographical distribution of scientific endeavour. As we will see in Section 6, new members have been admitted to the ATS, but these new states – including China, Brazil, Poland and South Korea – have joined Chile, the UK and Argentina in focusing their energies on the Antarctic Peninsula region. Accordingly, in spite of the intentions of the post-IGY agreements, nation state politics has not become subservient to science, but rather has continued to be of significant influence on scientific activity. Indeed, there is a strong sense in which research stations retain the status of colonies.

Meanwhile, the vast majority of Antarctica's land surface remains largely untroubled by the movement of scientists and support personnel. The inverse, however, does not hold. The movement of the land continues to trouble its human occupants, with the flow of ice and episodic volcanic activity ensuring that some research stations were never going to be permanent presences on the Ice. The British, Argentines and Chileans all had to evacuate their bases on Deception Island because of a volcanic eruption in the late 1960s. In another case, an Argentine station in the Antarctic Peninsula was consumed by fire, lit by a base commander who had been driven insane by the claustrophobia of station life. As the US explorer Richard Byrd noted in his book, *Alone* (1939), the Antarctic could be intensely unsettling and unpredictable and at the same time lonely and claustrophobic. Human beings and Antarctica itself could both behave unpredictably.

While claimant states persist in pursuing dreams of exclusive sovereign control, flows of water, ice, biological life and the earth itself, along with other challenges of the Antarctic environment, continue to undermine the work of sovereign political territorialisation. And, on a different scale, these same forces also present difficulties for the attempt to demarcate the space of a larger, shared sovereignty of the ATS, in spite of the fact that international regimes are created precisely to deal with such demands.

In this section, we have seen that the sharing of sovereignty put in place by the Antarctic Treaty, despite the 'globalising' intentions of the IGY and the explicit suspension of sovereignty claims of Article IV, has allowed for the persistence of practices of claiming sovereignty. Territorialising 'performances', such as the creation of an Argentine Antarctic citizenry and the maintenance of scientific stations, remind us that states also have to legitimise their membership of international regimes to domestic audiences.

In this way, the ATS and the international regime it put in place enable a select group of states to pursue their individual interests in the region. Or at least this is how it has come to appear for those parties who

Figure 4.7   Traces of human activity in the Antarctic. The aeroplane and whaling boat are on Deception Island. The shipwreck is off the Antarctic peninsula

have kept an eye on developments in Antarctica without attaining ATS member status. In Section 6, we will see how the restricted membership of the ATS, and the possibility that non-admission to this 'club' might also mean exclusion from any share in the bounty of the polar region, is increasingly bringing the current regime or architecture into question.

Summary

- The 1959 Antarctic Treaty put in place an architecture in which sovereignty was shared by select nations with pre-existing interests in the region.
- In its capacity as an international regime, the Antarctic Treaty was intended to facilitate cooperation between different actors.
- International regimes have particular relevance where flows problematise sovereign forms of political territorialisation.
- Despite the supposed ascendance of scientific activity as a unifying practice with a 'globalised' agenda, the work of sovereign political territorialisation in Antarctica has persisted.

6 Contesting Antarctica

While arrangements for the governance of Antarctica were being orchestrated by a select few, other states (especially the majority of those states that came to be known as the 'developing world') simply did not have the wherewithal to respond, let alone contest the legitimacy of such activities. By the 1980s, this state of affairs had evolved, with Antarctica becoming a highly politicised territory involving new parties, such as new states and non-governmental organisations (NGOs). In this section, we see how and why a number of these parties have expressed resentment at their exclusion from the restricted membership of the ATS, and how proposals have arisen for a more inclusive architecture. We return to the notion of Antarctica as a global common and address the possibility of giving this notion recognition in international law. We also revisit a question that refuses to go away: the question, that is, of how any political architecture could ever be flexible enough to take account of the inherently dynamic qualities of an environment such as that of Antarctica.

6.1 Cracks in the Antarctic Treaty

The creators of the international regime governing the Antarctic have had to be flexible in the face of policy challenges and competitive forces. This is not something unique to the Antarctic experience. All forms of shared sovereignty agreements have to consider the twin pressures of effectiveness and recognition. In other words, does the international regime in question work, and do the member parties as well as others recognise its legitimacy (and therefore right) to operate in a particular geographical region? On both grounds, the ATS has been called into question, and as such it highlights the fragility of cooperative arrangements among sovereign states.

As you will recall from Section 4.3, twelve countries set themselves up as the guardians and managers of Antarctica under the auspices of the 1959 Antarctic Treaty. Political decision making and the export of academic knowledge lay in the hands of this elite group; other parties, whether state or non-state, were at best peripheral and at worst irrelevant. This meant that political life, in the early years of the Treaty, was relatively simple. Prevailing tensions could be kept within a small club-like environment, and largely free from international opprobrium. Claimant and non-claimant states could grumble at one another in the secret biannual (and then annual) meetings of the ATS. Physical access to the Antarctic was impossible without the assistance of specialised shipping (and, later, restricted air travel) and this in turn greatly restricted access. The entry into force of the Treaty in 1961 also helped to forestall earlier attempts by India in 1956 and 1958 to raise the issue of control and management of Antarctica in the UN.

Those earlier attempts by India to involve the UN in the management of Antarctica are interesting precisely because they questioned the right of a select number of states to decide the future of the world's only uninhabited (in human terms at least) continent. The then Indian Prime Minister, Jawaharlal Nehru, explained his country's concern in the following terms:

> We are not challenging anybody's right there [in Antarctica]. But it has become important that the matter be considered by the United Nations. The fact that Antarctica contains many very important minerals – especially atomic energy minerals – is one reason why this area is attractive to various countries. We thought it would be desirable to have a discussion about this in the United Nations.

(cited in Dey, 1992, p.173)

The twelve parties attached to the IGY and the subsequent Washington Conference did not share this desire for UN involvement. They were collectively fearful that the UN might interfere with their plans to create an international regime with limited membership and, moreover, upset the delicate sovereignty negotiations that led to Article IV. After repeated reassurances that Antarctica would not be used for nuclear testing or exploited for its minerals, the Indian Government shelved its objections to the initiation and development of the ATS as an international regime.

At least with regard to membership, the ATS did reveal itself to be relatively flexible. By 2005, membership had expanded to 46 state parties, although this still included only one representative from the African continent and none from the Middle East. Nevertheless, certain vital restrictions remained in place from the formative years of the Antarctic Treaty. In order to secure the coveted Consultative Status, applicants still had to demonstrate that they had carried out 'substantial scientific research' – a demand that continued to discriminate against states without the available economic or scientific resources. Furthermore, only states were eligible for membership. Non-governmental organisations, even those with demonstrable polar scientific research behind them, such as Greenpeace, were excluded. Discontent over these restrictions, especially among excluded parties, has increasingly fuelled questions and doubts about the legitimacy of the ATS.

One area of continuing contention has been the resource issue. Despite the early assurances to the Indian Government about non-exploitation of minerals, and in spite of Gould's (1958) claim about the ascendance of the value of scientific data over more material resources, interest in the possibility of utilising the resources of the continent and its surrounding oceans has persisted. Indeed, much of the ongoing scientific investigation of the continent has contributed directly or indirectly to the knowledge of potentially exploitable resources. By the 1980s, the constant resurfacing of the issue of the exploitation of Antarctic mineral resources had provoked a damaging schism. After six years of negotiation, the proposed Convention for the Regulation of Antarctic Mineral Resource Activities (CRAMRA) still caused great unease. Some Treaty parties, such as Australia and France, publicly rejected the notion that mining should ever occur in Antarctica. This was also the position held, and loudly proclaimed, by environmental organisations – most notably Greenpeace.

The resource exploitation issue highlighted, in a particularly acute way, the difference between a regime that was international (in the sense of pertaining to a number of nations) and one that might be fully global. There were cracks in the Antarctic Treaty, in other words, and they were growing more pronounced.

6.2   Antarctica as common heritage of humankind?

Arguably, we have reached a point where the notion of Antarctica as part of the integrated geophysical system of the planet reconnects with the sense of a fully geopolitically integrated world. That is, the ideal behind the 1957–58 IGY, when a scientific understanding of the physical interconnectedness and unity of the globe sought to inspire a social or political sense of 'globality', seemed to be back on the agenda in the debates of the 1980s, this time with a much more inclusive sense of a politically globalised world. The consensus regarding the legitimacy of the ATS had begun to wane as developing world parties posed an apparently simple question in the UN in the early 1980s: Who owns Antarctica? If sovereignty was contested, then perhaps Antarctica could be designated as the common heritage of humankind.

Post-colonial states, such as Malaysia, charged the ATS parties with being colonialists who were seeking to 'rob' the developing world of their share of Antarctic resources. Inspired by ocean developments and, specifically, the 1982 Law of the Sea Convention, which declared the deep seabed a common heritage, Malaysia and other developing states, in 1982–83, demanded a debate on Antarctica as a terra communis – a communal land. Effectively, these states were attesting to the way that power – the capacity to act or assert oneself – had been transmitted through time. Much of the early advantage of the colonial nations, that is to say the inequality in power between colonisers and those who were colonised, could still be discerned in the way that current arrangements disadvantaged developing states. The alternative – Antarctica legally instated as common

Defining common heritage of humankind

The notion of 'common heritage of humankind', popularised in the late 1960s, can be applied to the regulation of things or resources that are found in particular national territories, such as the biological life we read about in Chapter 3. In practice, however, the concept has tended to be applied in order to give a legal framework to the idea of global commons – which is to say those areas beyond the jurisdiction of individual states. This includes the moon and outer space, the deep seabed and, potentially, Antarctica. In the 1960s and 1970s, developing states, especially, were growing anxious that technologically advanced states, such as the USA and Japan, might exploit these potentially valuable regions and, in so doing, exclude others from any potential gains. The UN agreed to create an International Seabed Authority to help regulate access to and exploitation rights of the deep seabed. The USA has refused to accept the provisions of this particular convention because it feels that it places unfair burdens on the more developed states.

heritage of all humankind – presented a challenge to both individual sovereign claims (such as the British claim of 1908) and the shared sovereignty implicit within the international regime of the ATS. If Antarctica were a communal space, then developing effective occupation would become less significant; there would be no need to assert a presence because all parties would have a stake in the territory regardless of their levels of activity. This would clearly represent a fundamental change in power relations.

Activity 4.4

Read the following two extracts from a representative of Antigua (a non-signatory of the 1959 Antarctic Treaty) and the former Director of the British Antarctic Survey. The UK was an original signatory to the Treaty and the first claimant state. What are the main claims made by the authors, and what do these claims say about relations of power with regard to Antarctica?

Lloyd Jacobs, Antigua representative speaking at the UN General Assembly in 1984 (on BBC Radio 4, 'The World Today', broadcast on 9 January 1985):

> To add to all of this, the world has vastly changed since the Antarctic Treaty was signed in 1959. There are now 169 member-states of the United Nations, most of which are developing countries. In 1959, they had neither the opportunity nor the sovereign competence to participate in Antarctica. It is not only unfair, it is unjust to suggest that we should abide by decisions made without our involvement. Indeed, we warned the world that if the status quo in Antarctica is maintained and further institutionalised a confrontation is bound to develop between the consultative parties and the rest of the world.

Sir Vivian Fuchs, Former Director of the British Antarctic Survey speaking in 1984 (on BBC Radio 4, 'The World Today', broadcast on 9 January 1985):

> To expect 150, or whatever it is, nations to be able to agree, sensibly, *colonial attitude* on what you do in a region where they do not understand the conditions – very few of them, that is – doesn't seem to me very sensible. The Treaty itself is one course open to any nation to join. The original signatories were twelve, and today there is a total of 32 nations who have adhered to the Treaty. So it's only up to the others, if they have got an interest, to say they will sign on.

Jacobs (1985) seems to be raising some unsettling issues in his discussion of Antarctica. He reminds us that political decisions affecting Antarctica were made at a time when many states were simply not able to participate. Antigua did not formally exist until 1981, and is a former British colony. As a representative of a recently decolonised territory, Jacobs is asking whether such a position is just. If the political status quo remains, then he foresees the possibility of Antarctica becoming a major issue between the developed and developing worlds. In other words, Antarctica should be conceived of as a communal space and as an opportunity to reflect upon inequalities of power – past and present.

Yet Fuchs (1985) favours the continuation of the ATS, and hence the political status quo. As an original member and claimant state, the UK has no incentive to agree to the proposition that Antarctica is a common heritage of humankind. Fuchs, like many others, believes that new parties such as Antigua would simply have to 'sign up' to the ATS and accept its modus operandi. This would mean, for example, acknowledging the primacy of scientific activity and the continued value of Article IV in terms of managing sovereignty disputes within Antarctica. This also implies giving consent to the distribution of power that inheres in this particular system.

6.3   Political architectures for a dynamic planet

The collective legitimacy of the ATS and the dominant geographical conception of Antarctica have been called into question. If Jacobs's (1985) arguments had prevailed, the political territory of Antarctica would have been made in a rather different manner. The ATS continued to be challenged in the UN General Assembly throughout the 1980s, but there was effectively a deadlock. Significantly, the political and moral authority of the ATS was only restored when the Protocol on Environmental Protection was adopted in 1991, which confirmed that mining was prohibited in the Antarctic Treaty region, and the ATS parties agreed to be more forthcoming about their activities vis-à-vis the UN and other interested parties. Consequently, at the time of writing, the Treaty and the ATS – rather than the legal framework of the common heritage of humankind – remain the primary mechanisms for the governance of Antarctica.

However, it is unlikely that the call for a more inclusive framework or architecture for governing Antarctica has been silenced for long. Gould's (1958) statements about the centrality of Antarctica to global climate, and its possible significance in sea-level rise and other global environmental change, now look more relevant than ever. This drives home the idea that Antarctica itself, as a physical territory, is volatile and shifting. More than this, it reminds us that the polar continent, however its territory is politically demarcated, is deeply entangled in dynamic and changeable flows which encompass the planet in its entirety. The climatic changes brought about by non-renewable energy use throughout the rest of the world could impact dramatically upon Antarctica, and the changes that result could impact just as dramatically back on the rest of world.

As geographers Sarah Shafer and Alexander Murphy warn us: 'The warmer, more crowded, more connected but more diverse world of the twenty-first century will necessarily require that we reach beyond the map of states to consider the underlying geographical complexities of the planet' (1998, p.271). What they seem to be suggesting is that the dominant political architecture of national territories and sovereign states may not be sophisticated enough to deal with the liveliness and interconnectedness of the earth itself – especially at a time when human-induced changes may be adding to the planet's inherent volatility.

We can pause at this point and review where this chapter has taken us. We have seen that attempts by a few nation states to assert exclusive political control over sections of the territory of Antarctica have been contested, in different ways, by other actors who have felt themselves to be excluded. The capacity of just a handful of nations to act out their needs and desires in the polar continent, and to perform expressions of political assertiveness, has been held up to scrutiny, not just by other nation states but also by NGOs such as environmental groups. In this way, the power of these few states to claim state sovereignty over Antarctica has been challenged, and the architectures they have set up in order to share and coordinate this power have been brought into question. Alternative architectures, such as the framework that would administer and govern Antarctica as a common heritage of all humankind and not just of the members of certain nation states historically associated with the continent, have been proposed and are still clearly on the agenda.

Yet even if the Antarctic were to be successfully incorporated in a new political architecture, one that dispersed the responsibility for the region and access to whatever resources it offers evenly among all human parties throughout the world, something still seems amiss. As Stephen Pyne has noted, there is an air of fantasy about any attempt, however fairly distributed, to govern or regulate what goes on in Antarctica (Pyne, 2003, p.377). Besides, it would seem that the

Figure 4.8   Scenes from the Antarctic Peninsula

designation of Antarctica as the 'property' of all humankind still leaves intact the assumption that the polar continent can be identified and marked out as a single, bounded territory. Again and again, throughout this chapter, we have seen that there are physical processes at work in Antarctica and its surrounding seas that defy all such human efforts at boundary marking and regulation, forces with a capacity to exert themselves in ways that constantly overwhelm or undermine the exertions of human actors. This too is a kind of power on the part of the land – a capacity to act or exert in ways that make a difference.

Ultimately, Antarctica raises issues that go beyond any architectures that have a remit merely to regulate or govern, whether this is in the interests of all of humankind or restricted groups. The southern polar region, in a particularly assertive way, reminds us that there are flows and territorialisations of the earth itself that have an awesome power of their own. How to take account of such forces – with their capacity to cross over and shake up any form of human political territorialisation of the planet – is an immense challenge. Something of this challenge already seems to be anticipated by Gould (1958), writing in the wake of the 1957–58 IGY. Nevertheless, perhaps it is only with the growing awareness of the possibility of global environmental change over recent decades that the need for global political architectures which encompass both human and large-scale physical forces has begun to be more widely acknowledged.

Summary

- The governance of Antarctica by a handful of states under the remit of the Antarctic Treaty has been contested by other states and NGOs.
- The contestation of the governance of Antarctica has led to proposals that Antarctica be considered the common heritage of all humankind.
- Even if responsibility for and access to Antarctica were to be extended to all of humankind, the dynamic character of physical flows and territories would still present challenges to the political architecture.

7   Conclusion

In this chapter, we have seen that a great deal of work has been done by human actors to produce and claim the territory of Antarctica. Moreover, we have looked at the ways that the polar continent itself calls into question these human actions or performances. Life in the earth's 'deep freeze' remains precarious. The Ice has swallowed up stations, and scientists continue to lose their lives on the continent and at sea; ships occasionally founder and symbols of sovereignty such as the ubiquitous national flags are soon devoured by the unrelenting winds. As you will recall, over 99 per cent of the polar continent remains devoid of any evidence of human inhabitation.

In many ways, the physical conditions of Antarctica make it an exceptional continent but, as the chapter has suggested, an understanding of the way that political relations have been acted out or performed under the extraordinary conditions of the polar continent can reveal a great deal of the taken-for-granted assumptions about political territorialisation. In particular, we have seen just how persistent notions of sovereignty can be, even under the most unfavourable conditions.

In another, quite different sense, the Antarctic is turning out to be much less marginal to global politics than we might have imagined. By virtue of its extreme physical conditions, the southern polar region may now be seen as a kind of test case for dealing with the kind of issues raised by a dynamic and unpredictable planet. While Antarctica may present some extreme examples of physical flow and territorial instability, there is also a strong sense in which every region of the planet has its own dynamic environmental conditions: whether it is the geological restlessness of oceanic islands, the threat of tropical cyclones or the mobilities of plants and other forms of life. Although Antarctica may appear to have a special significance, given the dangers posed to global sea level by its massive and volatile stores of ice, it is also well accepted now that every part of the earth's surface is linked by flows and connections to other parts of the planet.

There is an important sense that the way in which human political actors are being compelled to consider the dynamics of the Antarctic environment is of relevance far beyond the continent itself. The issue of developing political architectures that have the capacity to deal with shifting physical flows and territorial instability is not only one that applies to the relatively uninhabited regions of the planet; it has implications for all of us, wherever we live.

Possibly surprisingly, at first thought, many scientists, explorers and others who have spent time in Antarctica have grown to feel a deep emotional attachment to the place, for all its tribulations and dangers. For some people at least, the ongoing attempt to rethink and rework the territoriality of the continent has meant something much more than the manoeuvrings of powerful political actors. In Chapter 5, we take up this question of emotional entanglements with place, in a context that, for most of us, may seem a little more familiar.

References

Agnew, J. (2001) *Reinventing Geopolitics*, Heidelberg, University of Heidelberg, Hettner Lectures, no.4.

Byrd, R. (1939) *Alone*, New York, G.P. Putnam.

Chaturvedi, S. (1990) *Dawning of Antarctica: A Geopolitical Analysis*, New Delhi, Segment Books.

Dey, A. (1992) 'India in Antarctica: perspectives, programmes and achievements', *International Studies*, vol.29, pp.173–85.

Fuchs, V. (1985) 'The World Today', BBC Radio 4, broadcast 9 January 1985.

Gould, L.M. (1958) *The Polar Regions in Their Relation to Human Affairs*, New York, The American Geographical Society.

Jacobs, L. (1985) 'The World Today', BBC Radio 4, broadcast 9 January 1985.

Natural Environment Research Council British Antarctic Survey (2004) The Antarctic Treaty, www.antarctica.ac.uk/About_Antarctica/ Treaty/treaty.html (accessed 15 September 2005).

Pyne, S. (2003) *The Ice*, London, Weidenfeld & Nicolson.

Ruggie, J. (1993) 'Territoriality and beyond', *International Organisation*, vol.47, pp. 139–74.

Scott Polar Research Institute Archives, MS 1308/9: BJ.

Seed, P. (1995) *Ceremonies of Possession in Europe's Conquest of the New World 1492–1640*, Cambridge, Cambridge University Press.

Shafer, S. and Murphy, A. (1998) 'The territorial strategies of IGOs: implications for environment and development', *Global Governance*, vol.4, pp.257–74.

Torpey, J. (2000) *The Invention of the Passport*, Cambridge, Cambridge University Press.

Wheeler, S. (1997) *Terra Incognita*, London, Vintage.

Laurence Gould, 'The polar regions in their relation to human affairs'

Antarctica in the IGY

I come toward the end of this address and conclude with what seems to me the most important role Antarctica has ever played in human affairs and one which I trust it will play for a long time. I refer to the International Geophysical Year. As you may know, the overall International Geophysical Year program blankets the earth with several thousand stations manned by scientists from sixty-six different nations. The program includes the study of the shape and structure of the earth, more precise measurements of longitude and latitude, the study of the earth's heat and water budget (meteorology, oceanography, glaciology), and the physics and chemistry of the upper air, even to outer space.

This is the most comprehensive scientific program ever undertaken by man. It is the first attempt at a total study of his environment. Every one of the geophysical sciences is global in character, by which I mean that data collected in any one part of the earth have relevance throughout the rest. None can be fully explored or understood on a provincial basis. Antarctica as the earth's last great empty quarter was destined to play a major role in such a universal program. No field of geophysics can be understood or complete without specific data available only from this vast continent and its surrounding oceans.

The geophysical sciences touch all of man's major activities. Such fields as agriculture, transportation, and communication of all sorts are inseparably involved in them. Indeed, human progress from a long-range point of view and man's eventual survival on this planet depend upon an increasingly better knowledge of his environment.

I shall not take your time to go into details about the various aspects of the IGY program in Antarctica. There are a few special high spots, however, that I think would interest you particularly. I suppose of all aspects of man's environment the one that touches everyone most is meteorology, the study of the earth's weather. Blanketing our earth in a closed system is the atmosphere that provides us with life-giving oxygen and water and also protects us from the lethal rays of the sun. Surprisingly little is known about the exchange of the air masses between the polar regions and the tropics. The vast Antarctic ice cap, which is large enough to cover the

United States and Europe combined, has long been suspected of having a profound effect on weather and climate. The air over Antarctica today may be over Chile tomorrow. Certainly the hub of the atmospheric circulation of the Southern Hemisphere is located on Antarctica and just as certainly it is the world's greatest factory for cold weather.

We are now achieving coordinated observations from many stations in and around Antarctica which may provide a major breakthrough in our understanding of the role played in weather and climate by this vast, ice-covered continent. I predict that this role will be so important that it will dramatize the urgency of providing the continuous flow of data necessary for the construction of world-wide weather maps through the maintenance of Antarctic weather stations. Such maps are becoming indispensable with man's increased speed and global flights, which are surely coming with jet transportation.

To the casual observer the vast Antarctic ice cap itself may appear to be of only technical or scientific interest; this is not true. Inasmuch as nearly ninety per cent of all of the land ice in the world lies in Antarctica, changes in the volume and thickness of the ice are matters of universal concern. The return of only a few feet of thickness of ice to the oceans by melting would have serious effects in many places. If all of the ice melted into the sea, its level would rise perhaps two or three hundred feet, submerging all of the world's densely populated coastal lowlands and all of its seaports. Great changes in the volume of Antarctic ice have taken place in the past and may recur. That such changes may not happen with catastrophic suddenness does not mean that they are not of practical concern to man if he expects the earth to support his progeny for thousands of years.

Borings are being made into the Antarctic ice right now which will be studied in great detail. They may reveal layers that will show us the succession of stages involved in the formation of the ice. They may give us much more accurate clues to climate of the past centuries than are to be derived in any other way. Similar observations might be made about the peculiar importance of cosmic rays, ionospheric physics, aurora and airglow, geomagnetism, and seismology in Antarctica. There is not time to give you details about these.

Currently the IGY program in Antarctica is implemented by forty-eight stations established by twelve countries. The United States has six major scientific stations in addition to its great central logistic naval facility at McMurdo Sound. One of these stations at Cape Hallett is operated jointly with New Zealand.

The establishment of two of the stations warrants particular mention here. They are the Amundsen-Scott Station at the South Pole and Byrd Station, which lies six hundred and forty-seven miles southwest of Little America. The successful establishment of these two stations by Operation

Deepfreeze II under Admiral Dufek's command was one of the great logistic achievements in the long history of polar exploration.

The establishment of the South Pole Station was accomplished by air dropping materials from the great Air Force Globemasters. Some eight hundred tons of materials were dropped for the establishment of the station, including a 14,000-pound tractor. Only the personnel and limited amounts of equipment were flown in and landed by ski-equipped planes.

The techniques used in establishing Byrd Station were equally impressive. Globemaster air drops were also important here, but the main mission was carried out by great tractor train operations, which included crossing a dangerously crevassed area more than seven miles in width. It took five weeks for the special Army Transportation Corps teamed with Navy personnel to 'bridge' this crevassed zone and establish a well-marked route.

Of the other nations in the Antarctic operations, the Soviet Union has the most ambitious program next to ours. Their main base at Mirny is the largest and best-equipped station in Antarctica. On December 16, 1957, they established a second major base at the South Geomagnetic Pole and they still hope to establish a station at the so-called 'pole of inaccessibility' or the geographic center of the continent, approximately four hundred miles from the South Pole at longitude 63° E. In addition to these main stations, the Soviets have established a minor one called Oasis in the Bunger Hills midway between Mirny and our American base, Wilkes, on the Knox Coast.

The United Kingdom has a total of sixteen stations, eleven of which lie within the Falkland Islands Dependencies on or near Palmer Peninsula. They were established before the IGY, but have been enlarged to include its program. The main new IGY base was established by the Royal Society near the head of Weddell Sea.

Argentina operates ten stations, six of which are on the Palmer Peninsula. It has a major base at the head of Weddell Sea, which was established in 1955. Australia established its major station at 60° 30' S., 62° 54' E. in 1954 and named it for the most distinguished Antarctic explorer, Sir Douglas Mawson. This was later enlarged to include the IGY program and early in 1957 an auxiliary station was established some three hundred miles west of Mawson. Belgium has recently established a station at Breid Bay, 70° 30' S. and 23° 00' E.

Chile's six long-time meteorological stations in the Palmer Peninsula area are carrying on IGY programs, as are her three sub-Antarctic stations. France established a main station on the coast of Adélie Land and a small auxiliary one three hundred miles inland. In January, 1957, Japan established Showa Station at 69° 02' S., 39° 36' E. In addition to the station cooperatively maintained with the United States, New Zealand has a major base, Scott Station, located on Pram Point about two miles from the United States' installation at McMurdo Sound.

In January, 1957, Norway established its IGY station at 70° 30' S., 2° 32' W. This is really a re-establishment of the international station which had operated there in 1948–1950. The Union of South Africa reactivated its station on Marion Island in 1955–1956 as a part of the IGY.

Naturally as the IGY draws toward its close on December 31, 1958, those of us who have been involved in the program are concerned about its continuation. We are sure now as I speak that there will be such continuity. It is apparent to anyone that the value of scientific data being gathered by IGY is cumulative. The longer continuous observations can be maintained, the greater is the value to any part of our accumulated knowledge, as well as to the whole. Dr. Harry Wexler, who is chief of the research activities of the United States Weather Bureau, estimates that a ten-year minimum of continuous observations is necessary to get a comprehensive understanding of Antarctic weather and climate and the effect it has throughout the rest of the world.

I believe that the major exports of Antarctica are scientific data. Certainly that is true now and I think it will be true for a long time and I think these data may turn out to be of vastly more value to all mankind than all of the mineral riches of the continent and the life of the seas that surround it.

On September 9, 1957, an *ad hoc* committee on post-IGY activities in Antarctica met in Stockholm. There were representatives from Argentina, Chile, France, Great Britain, Norway, Japan, the Soviet Union, and the United States. This committee recommended to its parent ICSU (International Council of Scientific Unions) that plans should be carried out for a continuing cooperative scientific program in Antarctica. Toward this end ICSU invited participating nations to name representatives for the creation of a Special Committee on Antarctic Research (SCAR). This committee is meeting on February 3–6 in The Hague. As the United States representative I shall be flying over there to participate in what to me is an important historic activity. I am sure that the result will be the recommendation of a program that will not only continue IGY scientific activities, but will also embrace other important scientific aspects of Antarctic research as well. For instance, as a geologist I must insist that geology shall be a part of all programs at all stations where geological phenomena are accessible. Furthermore, it is of fundamental importance that a coordinated, comprehensive mapping program be carried out. Maps and charts are indispensable tools to almost all of the other scientific activities in Antarctica.

The United States and Antarctica in the future

Of course, no account of Antarctica would be complete without some further comment about the future political attitude of the United States.

You will have noted that Britain, Argentina, and Chile claim the most attractive part of Antarctica, Palmer Peninsula. This is part of Antarctica which we believe was discovered by an American. The United States could review Secretary Hull's proposal to invoke the Monroe Doctrine to include all lands to the South Pole, but I doubt if such a proposal would be acceptable to any of the present claimant nations.

Shall the United States officially declare its sovereignty over the unclaimed section between longitudes 90° W. and 150° W.? To limit our authority by the 90th meridian, the boundary of Chilean claims, might be interpreted by the British as an endorsement of the Chilean position, but to extend it beyond to the 80th meridian, where Britain ends her claim would be viewed by Chile as sheer trespass and would undoubtedly bring forth vigorous protest.

Probably all of the present claimant nations in Antarctica tacitly accept the United States' right to the area between longitudes 90° W. and 150° W., that is, Marie Byrd Land and Ellsworth Land. That is, however, the most inaccessible part of Antarctica. Repeated attempts made by our ships to penetrate the dense pack ice that hugs the coast of Marie Byrd Land have resulted in only one ship being partially successful and that apparently was due to the fact that it was a freakishly warm summer.

Currently our only access to Marie Byrd Land is by land over the Ross Dependency, an area claimed by New Zealand. Furthermore, the only known land area on rock which could be used as a base for an air strip is also in the Ross Dependency, near our McMurdo Sound naval installation. We know from recent surveys that this area near Marble Point could be used for the establishment of a permanent year-round landing strip.

A joint claim by the United States and New Zealand would have merit and might be advantageous to both. Antarctic exploration is costly, and New Zealand, with a population about equal to my own state of Minnesota, does not have the resources to build and maintain far-flung Antarctic bases. I should guess that New Zealand is currently making a greater per capita investment in Antarctica than is any other nation. A further suggestion is that Australia, New Zealand, and the United States join in a common claim that would include almost two-thirds of the continent.

I have but recently received a letter from Sir Douglas Mawson, commenting upon the question of claims and I am sure he would not mind if I quoted a paragraph from his letter:

'I am still sorry that America has not laid territorial claim to the big unclaimed central Pacific sector. There would be no difficulty with New Zealand, I am sure, having it extended into the Ross Ice Shelf. No doubt also territorial adjustments could be made elsewhere. What seems to me important in such a move is that the Antarctica ice continent if tied up to a limited number of sovereignties of good repute and mutual regard could then be administered on good lines conjointly for the benefit of all and especially of the inhabitants (penguins, birds, seals, etc.). If every nation had a hand in it, some of the life there may soon become extinct.'

Hindsight is inevitably clearer than any other kind of sight. The United States, at the time of Hughes' historic policy, could probably have claimed without much, if any, protest more than half the continent, on the basis of the discoveries of Palmer and Burdick, and more especially on what has only recently been recognized as the brilliant achievements of Wilkes in 1839–1840. Such a claim now would certainly produce 'comment,' to say the least.

The Soviet Union has made it clear that she will not recognize any realignment of claims to which she is not a party, though she has made no Antarctic claims herself. Whether the Russians would accept any of the approaches suggested above is an open question. It might, indeed, stimulate them to make claims based on von Bellingshausen's supposed discoveries.

Nehru of India proposed that the whole matter of Antarctic claims be discussed by the United Nations General Assembly. It has not yet gotten on the agenda. In the long run it is difficult to see how face-saving, especially important to the nations with overlapping claims, can be accomplished other than by some form of international jurisdiction.

Those of us who have been deeply involved in the International Geophysical Year fervently hope that the experiences of cooperation there will point the way toward a satisfactory solution. Since the geophysicist is inevitably a truly international scientist, the IGY may turn out to be a brilliant new approach toward international understanding and organization. The current Antarctic operations have been marked by the friendliest kind of cooperation from all of the nations involved. The work has proceeded without even a discussion of political claims. The location of the various bases was agreed upon at an international conference in Paris in July, 1955. The principal criterion was provision for the best scientific coverage. Our own American stations are located in areas currently claimed by Great Britain, Australia, New Zealand, Argentina, and in the still unclaimed sector between 90° W. and 150° W., and our South Pole Station occupies territory common to all claimants. Great Britain, France, Argentina, Chile, and Norway have their bases on land claimed by the respective nations, but the Russians are located within the sector claimed by Australia.

We do believe that precedents are important in the evolution of civilization. The successful cooperation of IGY in Antarctica and the expectation of a continuing international cooperative program in that vast continent may provide a pattern that will move over into other areas and result in further working together of all nations.

(Gould, 1958)

Chapter 5

Of trees and trails: place in a globalised world

Owain Jones

Contents

1   Introduction

Thomas Hardy's novel *Under the Greenwood Tree* opens with this paragraph:

> To dwellers in a wood, almost every species of tree has its voice as well as its feature. At the passing of the breeze, the fir-trees sob and moan no less distinctly than they rock; the holly whistles as it battles with itself; the ash hisses amid its quiverings; the beech rustles while its flat boughs rise and fall. And winter, which modifies the note of such trees as shed their leaves, does not destroy its individuality.
>
> (Hardy, 1998, p.7)

As in Hardy's other novels, these opening lines demonstrate his commitment to setting the dramas of people's lives in their local landscape. He sought to explore the everyday entanglements of lives lived within families, communities, nature and place, and also within the wider context of power relations, changing economies and shifting social conventions. The passage also acknowledges that when close attention is paid, the life of non-human things, like different trees and the sounds they make, can play an important part in landscapes, places and lives.

So far this book has shown how the spacing of the world can be viewed as the outcome of flows and territories in complex, worked interaction. Quite often the views in the preceding chapters have been panoramic, taking in vast spaces, histories and movements – from the settlement of the Pacific over thousands of years to struggles over the control of Antarctica over the last century. We have seen how different territories jostle and compete as they assert themselves in the world, and appreciated the challenges posed by flows that pass over or through many different territories. In response to the tensions and uncertainties that arise out of this interplay of territories and flows, we examined the way powerful human actors representing their territories have collaborated with representatives of other territories in order to sort out new ways of organising the things they felt to be important.

Yet very few people have such capacities to act in the world. Most ordinary people simply lack the resources or the opportunities to make broad, overarching decisions about territories and flows at international or global levels. In this chapter and the ones that follow, our perspective takes a turn away from the panoramic scope to the detail of the everyday, and our emphasis shifts from performances of the most powerful actors towards more dispersed and day-to-day activities.

It is a subtle shift, however, rather than a total turnaround, for what happens locally, or 'on the ground', as we will see in Sections 3 and 4, is inseparable from more far-reaching processes and events.

How do ordinary people make their way, and make their worlds, in the middle of the bewildering pulse of interconnections that is life in a globalised world? This chapter looks at a way of making sense of the uncertainties of the world, which may be as old as humanity itself – that is, ideas and practices of *place*. From home, village, city, county to nation, people have built, cared for and defended certain kinds of spaces to which they feel an attachment, a sense of belonging or identification. In social science terminology, as in everyday language, 'place' is the term used for these meaning-invested spaces.

Defining place

While place has often been conceptualised as some kind of definable, bounded space, geographers have been keen to show how the spatial characteristics of place are highly nuanced. There are multiple kinds of places which overlap and blur into each other, and places are always interconnected with the wider world in many ways. In spite of this interconnection, or rather because of it, every place is particular; it has its own unique pattern or weave of elements. More than simply a particular section or portion of space, in the eyes of social scientists, artists, writers and many ordinary people, place tends to be associated with feeling, emotion or affect. Places both persist through time and change over time, so may be better thought of as processes rather than as static.

In the terminology of this book, places are a form of territory. Not only does each and every place bring together a distinct and unique combination of elements, or capture and weave together different flows, but place is also the locus of a particular form of making territory that we are terming 'affective territorialisation'. By this we refer to the way in which a territory functions as a workable entity, and moreover how it comes to be imbued with meaning or emotional resonance by the human actors who associate with it in some way. Emotion or affect may be difficult to pin down, to locate on a map, but they may nonetheless add an important dimension to the making of territories. They can make a difference not just for the ability of human beings to act in certain ways, but also with regard to their willingness or desire to act.

As you may have guessed from the opening passage from Hardy (1998), this chapter takes trees as its point of departure for thinking about the ways that affective territorialisation is practised or performed. While trees obviously have a life of their own, it is unlikely to come as a surprise that they can play a big part in the making of the places in which human beings dwell or pass through, and can be a focus of strong human emotional attachment.

Activity 5.1

Turn now to Reading 5A by Stephanie Kaza (1996) entitled 'The attentive heart: conversations with trees', which you will find at the end of the chapter. As you read, write down a list of short points about why you think we have chosen trees as an example to work through in this chapter. Keep in mind the themes of the book so far.

If you wrote down some things about trees being beautiful, useful, resilient, an important part of ecological systems, part of the 'integrity' of places, causes for joy or other human emotions, then you are on your way towards engaging with the themes of this chapter. You might also have noted from Reading 5A the way that trees get caught up in the 'competing territorial interests' that, as we have seen, are so often a part of human social and political life. Moreover, trees play an integral part in another kind of making and remaking of territories, a dynamic, ecological process, which, as Kaza puts it 'happens independently of any human goals and desires'. Trees coming together over time into a 'web of complexity', you may have noticed, resonates with the idea of territories that we have been exploring throughout this book – as a weave or tangle of different things. And you might also have picked up on the idea of an energy flow that 'babbles' through groups of trees, and the suggestion that trees have a sort of 'intelligence' of their own, a point that rather intriguingly hints at a kind of information flow running through the living, non-human world in a way that might remind you of the human-produced flows of information discussed in Chapter 2.

Trees, of course are quite literally 'rooted in place', and not surprisingly they often come to stand for permanence and stability. However, Kaza makes the point clearly that trees are always tied up with the dynamics of place. Furthermore, as we will see in Section 3.3, even the 'rootedness' of trees needs qualifying. Some trees have travelled great distances to arrive at the places they now stand and, in various ways, have connections with other places far beyond their immediate vicinity. Plant life, as we saw in Chapter 3, has a capacity to flow, whether under its own impetus or with human assistance, and in this chapter we will explore some of the implications of this mobility as it plays out in a single place.

The place in question is a village in the southwest of England called Camerton. Camerton sits atop a coalfield, and its history has become closely tied to the unearthing of this mineral resource and the ebb and

Figure 5.1   Three UK 'veteran' trees: a common yew and two oaks

flow of the industry based upon it. Against the backcloth of some rather profound transformations in industrial economies over time – a story that many people who have lived through these changes know only too well – another story emerges that is probably less familiar and perhaps a little surprising. It is a tale of trees coming and going, and of the creation of a nature trail winding its way across the earthworks that are residues of the mining excavations. The revaluation of its mining past by the people of Camerton, and their growing affection for trees that have taken root in the spoils of this past, makes for a rather special and unique narrative. Nevertheless, in its very uniqueness, Camerton is also rather ordinary. For every place, including the place in which you were born or grew up, is a confluence of things, processes and events – with an identity of its own. And in this way, the story of Camerton, and the way its people have responded to their entanglement in a wider world, is a story with at least some relevance to every other place.

We begin, in Section 2, by looking in more depth at the role of trees in the experience of place, and at some of the ways in which human emotion or affect becomes enmeshed with the non-human world. Then, in Section 3, we delve into the case study of Camerton, looking first at the setting up of its nature reserve and heritage trail, and going on to explore some of the geological, biological and social processes that have come together to shape the town and its surrounds. Section 4 considers the conflicts that have arisen out of plans to redevelop the former mining landscape. It focuses on the ways that emotional attachments to place are forged and expressed, and examines what happens when different perspectives on the integrity or character of place come into collision. Then, in Section 5, we ease out of Camerton and address some of the more general issues arising out of practices of 'affective territorialisation', with regard to different motives for action and differing capacities to act.

Chapter aims

- ◆ To show how the making of places matters in a globalised world.

- ◆ To look at the ways in which the emotional attachment of people to the places in which they live can play a part in the making of territories.

- ◆ To explore the sort of everyday involvement in territories and flows which is found in ordinary places.

2   Trees and place

In the making of the wooded place on the Olympic Peninsula, as Kaza (1996) described it in Reading 5A, different kinds of processes came together. Some of these processes were initiated by humans; others were the work of non-humans — the earth and weather. Generalising, we can say that as humans become ever more significant actors on the global stage, the making and remaking of the world increasingly involves both human and non-human forces. While we can imagine an entirely non-human planet prior to the emergence of our species, it is important to remember that all human activity relies on energies and materials made available through the dynamics of the non-human world. Humans, in other words, act in the world by tapping into pre-existing flows and by taking advantage of prior territorialisations. Yet as Kaza (1996) points out so eloquently, it is not simply a matter of human processes and human-produced things coming after the non-human; non-human forces and processes are quite capable of reasserting themselves as soon as humans relax their grip on things, if not sooner. Having read about the formidable non-human forces of Antarctica in Chapter 4, this will be of no surprise!

Activity 5.2

Now read Richard Mabey's quotation below about the riverside fig trees of Sheffield, in northern England. Jot down your answers to the following questions, briefly.

1   What do you think this piece is saying about the relationship between human and non-human processes?

2   How might we read this story in terms of flows and territories (or territorialisations)?

3   What implications might we draw from this example for thinking about a sense of place?

> Naturalisation ... in both the human and natural worlds, involves the slow absorption of a newcomer, which becomes part of the host community without abandoning its essential identity. It also suggests, I think, a certain fittingness, something which goes with the grain and texture of what is already there. It is Thames Valley gravel pits and buddleia on building sites. One of the most fascinating examples of this in modern England has been the colonising of the River Don in Sheffield by feral fig trees. They are not only striking to look at, but stuck amongst the decaying steelworks have a poignant sense of history and place about them. Their story is a remarkable one of

harmonious naturalisation. It seems as if they grew from seeds carried downstream in human sewage (and maybe in waste from food factories), and have the steel industry to thank for their successful establishment in the 1920s. River water was used for cooling purposes in the factories, and the outfall kept the water in the river at a steady temperature of 20 degrees C – warm enough to germinate those seeds of this Mediterranean species when they fetched up on muddy shores. But when stricter controls were introduced on effluent quality, and, later, local steel manufacture went into decline, the river's temperature returned to normal and no new trees were able to sprout.

Local people have become proud of these trees, and have fought successfully to save many of them in the face of tidy-minded officials and developers. As one has said, 'they are as much a part of Sheffield's history as the old steam-hammers and Bessemer converters' – a strange but heartening destiny for a species that began its journey, as did the first Neolithic settlers and landscape-shapers of our islands, in the eastern Mediterranean.

(Mabey, 1993, pp.26–7)

By 'naturalisation', Mabey (1993) refers to processes by which anyone or anything, human or non-human, settles into a community or place. Or, as we might say, how something or someone new becomes woven into an existing territory. However, as Mabey himself suggests, both humans and non-humans can 'naturalise', and this is a term about which we might want to be cautious. There are other aspects of Mabey's (1993) account with which you might also take issue: for example, is it always necessary that newcomers get absorbed slowly? For our purposes, the point Mabey does make clearly and helpfully is that non-human processes – goings on in the world that are not set up or directed by human agency – do not necessarily come before human action. In this case, we see that trees, with an agency partly or largely of their own, take advantage of industrial processes to settle into the Don riverside.

In our terms, this suggests that non-human forces – the forces of life in this instance – can be capable of working with (or tapping into) the flows and territorialisations made available by human activity. You may also have noted that the figs in question are a Mediterranean species, so there are also human-assisted journeys or flows that have brought them to their resting place in Sheffield.

One of the interesting things that comes out of Mabey's (1993) account is the attachment that local people now feel for the fig trees – in spite of the fact that they are relatively recent arrivals. The fig trees

Figure 5.2   Fig trees on the River Don

have become part of the local sense of place but, in the process, we can glimpse the strange and haphazard way in which things can gather together in the making of a place. We also start to get a sense of how the elements that make up a place may well have ties or connections with distant places.

The way that trees move, both of their own accord and by human-assisted means, recalls the account of plants on the move from Chapter 3. It is also important to bear in mind that trees and other plant and animal species are constantly, if gradually, on the move in response to geological and climatic changes. Momentously, for our narrative in this chapter, new forests spread north across Europe some 10,000 years ago following the retreating ice sheets of the last ice age. There are still other flows to consider, some of which are anticipated in Reading 5A: the flow of sap and the extrusion of growth; the take up of nutrients and water from the soil; the exchange of carbon dioxide and oxygen; seasonal changes; movement in the wind; torrents of autumn leaves; the distribution of pollen by wind and insects.

Of course, once a tree is seeded or planted and becomes established, it is not easily moved. It is important to note that all of this focus on movement and flow is not to deny tree characteristics of solidity, rootedness and, if not permanence, then endurance in place over sometimes very long periods of time. For Fraser Harrison (1991), it is this relationship with the passing of time in particular that can lend trees such an iconic significance in experiences of place. Talking about the huge old trees in his local landscape Harrison muses, 'to stand beneath one of these maimed colossi is to be overwhelmed by its powerful, resonant presence' (1991, p.135). These oak trees are 'the living tissue of time,' and in this way they offer points of reference by which we can locate ourselves in time and place (Harrison, 1991, p.135). The oak tree in the churchyard which Harrison describes is part of a nexus of human and non-human processes through which 'the continuities of time and place are made visible, immediate and above all, tangible' (Harrison, 1991, p.139). This kind of understanding of trees has led to campaigns such as the Veteran Trees Initiative, which claims that '[t]heir biological, historical and cultural importance is slowly being recognised, together with their aesthetic appeal and the unique contribution they make to the landscape' (English Nature, 2000, p.1).

Trees, then, in a very physical sense, are often focal points in that confluence and gathering together of diverse elements that we refer to as places. Nonetheless, there is more to place than just things coming together; place also has an affective dimension, an added dimension of meaning or emotion, for which trees can also play a vital part. Affect, or emotion, in this way, can intervene crucially in the negotiations between territory and flow, as we will shortly see in Sections 4.4 and 5. Already we have found that while trees may stand for continuity and passing of time, they can also be an object of attachment when their presence is relatively recent. So too we have had hints that trees are not only affirmed and appreciated; in Reading 5A they also threatened security by impeding coastal surveillance and, as Mabey (1993) noted, some trees could be assailed by 'tidy-minded officials and developers'. These are the kind of tensions and complexities that we explore in Section 3 through the example of Camerton and its nature trail.

Summary

- Trees can be significant actors in the making of places.
- Trees, although fixed and rooted in one sense, can, in other senses, be seen in terms of movements and flows.
- Trees can become the focus of a range of emotional or affective attachments.

3   Camerton Local Nature Reserve and Heritage Trail

3.1   The story of Camerton and its batches

Let's now take a visit to the Camerton Local Nature Reserve and Heritage Trail (LNR/HT), a 1.4-hectare site in the village of Camerton in the county of Bath and Northeast Somerset. The first part of the LNR/HT is next to the road and consists of an open, grassy area which is fenced and gated. Then, through woodland which starts at the far end of the open area, a path leads away on a circular route that takes you up a gradual incline – a long, gently curving, rising ridge – and then down a series of steep, winding steps to a strip of level woodland, which runs parallel and below the ridge (see Figure 5.3). Now heading back towards the road, the path turns up another flight of steep steps to meet itself on the ridge again and then back to the gate.

In effect, you are walking up the ridge of an elongated hill, down its steep abrupt end, turning back along the bottom of the flank of the hill and then climbing steeply to rejoin the path along the ridge. Apart from the initial space, the hill is entirely wooded with a mixture of deciduous and coniferous trees, which have played important roles in the story of this place. The LNR/HT has gone through a number of changes and has had to be defended by a campaign of conservation. It was designated as a local nature reserve in 1997 because it fulfils the criteria of a space open to the public that has significant local ecological interest.

The LNR/HT is a Heritage Trail because it commemorates the local coal mining industry, which was such a feature of this area's past. There is an information point near the gate that has displays and often leaflets to pick up and read as you walk around. There are benches and markers along the path corresponding to information in the leaflet.

Figure 5.3   Inside the Camerton LNR/HT looking up to the ridge

The leaflet tells the story of the Camerton mine and the mining history of the wider area. There is also a large statue of a miner (see Figure 5.4) near the information point. The LNR/HT hill is one of two large spoil heaps (known locally as 'batches') which were thrown

Figure 5.4   The statue of a miner near the entrance to the LNR/HT site

up during almost two centuries of mining at Camerton (see Figure 5.5). There are many such other 'hills' in this part of Somerset.

Figure 5.5   The Camerton batches: the old batch, which is the site of LNR/HT, is on the left; the new, steeper batch is on the right

The old batch and the later batch, with some overlap in time, were generated by the Camerton coal mine as it operated from the 1780s until 1950. Camerton was one of the most north-westerly of the seventy or so pits that formed the Somerset coalfield. The LNR/HT occupies the old pithead area, where the shaft and winding gear were sited (see Figure 5.6), and the older batch spread out from the shaft. Day after day, coal and spoil was extracted from the coal seams below ground and separated out. The coal was taken away first by canal and then by rail (both now dismantled), and the spoil tipped in an ever growing mound along the bottom of the north flank of the Cam Valley. The old pit became problematic, and a new pit was sunk and became operational in 1800 and a second batch formed. Both shafts were used to draw coal throughout the nineteenth century, growing their twin batches. The old pit was closed for coal winding in 1898 while extraction continued in the new pit (see Figure 5.7).

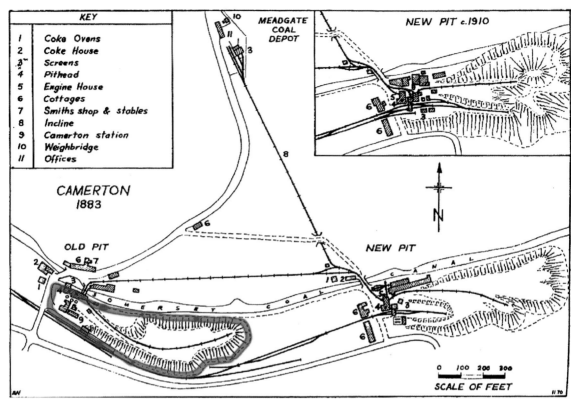

Figure 5.6   Camerton pit in 1883, showing both batches, and the new pit in 1910. The area of the present LNR/HT is outlined in red

Figure 5.7   Camerton pit in the 1930s

3.2   Earth on the move

In Chapter 1, Nigel Clark argued that we should see the earth being on the move as a consequence of non-human geological processes. In Camerton, the distinctive 'hills' have been thrown up by centuries of mining which have left the earth beneath honeycombed with shafts and tunnels. At the height of the Somerset coalfield's activity, it was said to be possible to walk between the towns and villages below ground along the interconnected workings. While this strange underground geography is now sealed off, derelict and flooded, with only odd clues remaining on the surface, such as the remains of airshaft tops in the middle of fields, the spoil heaps remain as prominent reminders of the past.

Not only have these now green hills become part of the local landscape and culture, but the processes which shaped these hills in differing ways have become part of the new landscape. As discussed in Section 3.1, the first part of the path of the LNR/HT follows the ridge of the old batch. Looking back at the map in Figure 5.6 will tell you why. The LNR/HT was the path of the rail track along which wagons of spoil were pulled by horse, and then tipped to let the spoil tumble down the steep flanks of the growing batch (which the flights of steps now descend and climb). As the tip grew, the track was extended. Thus, the very geography of the LNR/HT as it is today, its topography and the layout of its paths, is dependent upon the arrangements by which the spoil was removed from the pithead and tipped more than a century ago.

Around the turn of the twentieth century, the new pit installed a McLean tipper which allowed the spoil to be tipped in a much steeper pile on top of the lower, older tippings of the new batch (see Figure 5.8 overleaf). This gave the new batch its dramatic form, along with the other newer batches in the area, and a steepness which makes walking on it much more difficult. At one time, the new batch attracted interest as the possible site for a dry ski slope.

Activity 5.3

Where do stories begin and where do they go? Thus far we have focused on one small part of the story of Camerton LNR/HT: the throwing up of the spoil heaps and the mark they left on the present geography. Yet where does this story really start? And, thinking about interconnections between places, and about the future, how can you connect this place with the things going on in other parts of the world that we have already discussed in this book?

Figure 5.8   (Left) The McLean tipper allowed the new batch to rise more steeply than the old batch. (Right) The 'fresh' spoil heaps and the progress of the planted trees and self-seeded vegetation on the lower fringes of the new batch

It is difficult to say when any story starts or ends. In a way you could make the claim that any story, and any place as a process, can be traced back, and back again. Often what we consider to be a specific story, say of a life, of an empire's rise and fall, or of a place such as Camerton, is just an episode, or chapter, which is always dependent on what came before. We could argue that the story of the Camerton batches started with the Industrial Revolution, as did so many other stories, or episodes. However, was that the real start? What about the scientific discoveries which came before and ushered in the Industrial Revolution in the first place? We could also claim that the story goes back much further still to the time when the coal in the ground was formed out of swampy tropical forests in the upper carboniferous era. These were the forests that subsequently fell, rotted, became buried in the earth and turned to coal over millions of years. With a nice twist, we are talking of trees again, or giant tree-like ferns. The mining museum at Radstock, three miles from Camerton, has a collection of spectacular fossils of ferns and insects from this time, which were found in the shale of the spoil heaps of the mines. Going back again, how did these tropical forests come to be there to make the coal? They were there because the climate was different then, and because it was so long ago that the land itself was in a different position on the earth's surface. As we saw in Chapter 1, to know the story of a place and how it has become what it is, we need to think about all sorts of flows and movements, some working over very long periods of time.

How can we connect Camerton's story to distant places and their past, present and future? One way could be to note that the coal that Camerton and the other British pits produced helped to fuel the Industrial Revolution and the expansion of the British Empire, and thus reshaped the entire world. Alternatively, it could be said that Camerton has played its small part in the extraction and burning of coal and the release of carbon dioxide into the atmosphere, thereby contributing to the threat of global warming. All that carbon dioxide taken out of the atmosphere by the trees of the ancient forests and locked into the earth as coal has now been released back into the atmosphere, and is therefore directly linked to global warming, sea-level changes and the fates of the Pacific Islands, Antarctica and the world as a whole.

3.3   Trees on the move

What of the trees which are now growing, it could be said, on the ghostly remains of their ancient cousins in Camerton? The batches in the past were planted with certain trees and then colonised by others which have self-seeded. The first thing we might note is that for these trees to colonise and transform such a seemingly unpromising environment as the bare spoil tips (as shown in Figure 5.8) is a creative act in itself. The story of how this has come about takes a number of twists and turns, makes many connections to the wider world, and suggests that there may be an element of chance, or contingency, in the way the place has developed to its present state.

As Figure 5.8 shows, the fresh spoil heaps were bare piles of rubbly shale and limestone. In the first decades of the twentieth century, the old batch was planted with a mix of conifers – Douglas fir, Corsican and Scots pines and larches. There are varying explanations as to why the trees were planted. Some accounts suggest that the owners of the mines, landowners who followed the fashion of digging pits once the lucrative presence of coal had been discovered, planted them for landscaping purposes or to help stabilise the tips. Others suggest that the trees were intended as a home-grown source of the wooden pit props needed for underground work. These were relatively small, difficult mines and we are told that 'the cost of timber was sometimes as much as the selling price of the coal' (Williams, 1976). The later planting may also have been part of the national reforestation programme instigated by the newly formed Forestry Commission to recover timber reserves after the First

World War. The tree species are listed as exemplary for planting on gravelly and disturbed ground in *Webster's Practical Forestry* (Webster, 1919), a book very much concerned with post-war reforestation.

We can consider the story of one of the tree types planted on the batches: the Douglas fir. This coniferous, evergreen tree was named after the Scottish biologist David Douglas: one of the most famous and successful of the nineteenth-century plant hunters. Douglas was sent on expeditions to North America by the then Horticultural Society of London (now the RHS) in the 1820s and 1830s, and he collected over 800 plant types, 249 of which were new species. Douglas is celebrated for his contribution to British forestry because he introduced some of the most successful commercial species to the UK, including Douglas fir and Sitka spruce, which were subsequently extensively planted for timber production. The new forests formed of 'Douglas's trees', according to the Forestry Commission, 'have arguably had the single greatest impact on the rural landscape of Britain in the last 200 years' (2005). Douglas fir old growth forests (that is, established by their own agency rather than planted by humans) were, and are, extensive in the west of North America. Although named after the Scottish bioprospector, they had been known by other names and used by aboriginal North Americans in many ways for centuries, if not millennia.

Why then was a mix of trees planted on the Camerton batches? The Corsican pine, as its name implies, comes originally from the Mediterranean. According to Webster, it is undoubtedly 'one of the best all-round conifers that has found its way into the British Isles,' producing 'strong, tough, elastic, very resinous and easily worked timber' (1919, p.60). It sounds good for pit props. The Scots pine was often planted as a nurse tree, as it could 'grow and flourish almost anywhere – on pure gravel' (Webster, 1919, p.70) and withstand severe, cold and windy conditions. The Douglas fir, although an excellent timber producer, was not so hardy and needed to be protected from wind, usually by being planted with other hardier trees (Edlin, 1948, p.15). These differing tree types were brought to the batches because of their specific capacities and qualities, which were deployed, or enrolled, by those planning the plantations. The planting of these trees on the batches is, in this way, an example of one of the chief ways in which species have been 'on the move', in the sense of being collected, transported, bred and then planted by people seeking commercial and perhaps aesthetic benefits of one kind or another.

These trees, then, like the earth movements behind the formation of the batches, reach out to distant locations. The Camerton trail, in one sense, follows a narrow and circumscribed path, the path that was once the track for tipping. Nevertheless, in another sense, this trail has no real beginning or end; it connects up with other trails that weave their way across a globalised world. When we look at the blend of ingredients that makes Camerton the place it is, there is much which seems the result of chance and little, if anything, that seems inevitable or predestined. This place, in other words, has no single or fixed origin, and its development cannot be said to follow a path that is in any way laid out in advance.

While we may speak of the uniqueness of Camerton, and the contingencies of its making, it is no less important to be mindful that the stretched out spatial and temporal relations that link this place to other places also imply shared dynamics, or common experiences. Places may have their own particular character, but there are also deep-seated structural changes – whether in the physical world or the social world – that can impact on many different places in broadly similar ways. Profound transformations in the UK economy, shifts shared with many other early industrialising centres or regions, have impacted dramatically on Camerton and its neighbouring towns. In the light of these changes, the batches of Camerton, and similarly-planted humped 'hills' of the nearby towns of Radstock and Midsomer Norton on the same coalfield, have come to tell of a lost industrial past (see Figure 5.9).

Figure 5.9   Other batches planted with conifers are prominent landscape features of the Somerset coalfield

By the first decades of the twentieth century, many of the Somerset collieries were in terminal decline. Camerton pit changed ownership in 1911, and was eventually taken into state ownership when the entire UK coal industry was nationalised in 1947. Working continued for a few years but 'the last coal was wound on the 14 April, 1950' (Macmillen, 1990, p.34) and, after a brief period of salvage work, the colliery was closed. The pithead structures were dismantled, the shafts capped off and the branch railway fell into disuse and decay before being removed. The site then went into a 30-year period of economic dormancy.

Of course, in the decades both prior to and after closure, the trees kept growing. The timescale and speed of their growth is captured in the following accounts by local residents, as recorded in interviews by the author in 1998.

> I should think they [the conifers] were planted about, I should say, 70, 80 years ago because when I was a kiddie – those trees on that batch – well I can remember some of them being planted, but some were about 2 feet high so they had been in probably three or four year by then … Oh we always played on there, it was our only means of playing … Well the trees then were about 6 feet high [and by the time the mine closed] oh they were good trees then … very strong trees.

A younger resident told of her post-Second World War childhood memories of the batch: 'All I can remember is tall conifers and where everything was so dense that there was hardly any undergrowth there and there were lots of tracks because us kids used to play there in gangs.' Or, as another of the townsfolk reminisced: 'Oh it used to be our play area.' This resident also told how, for some years, when the trees were still quite small 'everyone got their Christmas tree off the batch', and that people used to pick coal off the tips to use at home.

The steady growth of the trees is evident in the above quotes, and it can be seen that the batches were becoming playgrounds for local children and providers of 'unofficial' benefits for the local community. In other words, an emotional ecology of place was developing through engagement and memory. This is captured in a poem written by the younger resident quoted above, which contains the following lines: 'The batch I think was my main joy … The earth was there to play with. The trees were there to climb.'

The everyday entanglements of this ecology of place are also reflected in material traces in the landscape. The only remaining building from the Camerton pit works, a prefabricated canteen, is now a house. Old railway sleepers are used for fence posts, and remains of the old rail tracks themselves can still be found in the woods (see Figure 5.10). Yet, as in Reading 5A, the growth of the woods slowly overwhelms the physical traces of the old mine works which are not actively maintained.

Figure 5.10   Material traces of the mining past in the local landscape: an old railway sleeper reused as a fence post, the old mine canteen which is now a house, and a section of the old railway track in the mine sidings now lying in the leaf litter of the LNR/HT

Other parts of the site were also reverting to nature. The old pithead site, next to the village road, became overgrown with bramble, and the steeper slopes of new batch, which had not been planted with conifers, were slowly colonised by wild trees and other plants.

This gradual transformation of the site is evident in local history accounts of the landscape. Soon after closure, Camerton was said to be 'still a little gaunt with the relics of its colliery, and with the great pyramids of spoil which blotch the hillside' (Little, 1969, p.23). Nonetheless, by 1969 it was noted that since the closure of the mines 'the process of reversion to rural countryside had gone on apace' and the large spoil heaps at Camerton were 'now becoming overgrown' (Buchanan and Cossons, 1969, pp.96, 97).

Along with the growing conifers, other wild trees were moving in of their own accord and finding places to seed, become established and grow. Together with the conifers, they were gradually turning this industrial wasteland into woodland.

Summary

- The Camerton LNR/HT is situated on a spoil heap thrown up by centuries of mining.
- The Camerton former mining landscape embodies active and flowing earth processes which link it to distant times and spaces.
- The trees on the Camerton batches embody connections across time and space.
- The Camerton batch trees have an agency of their own. They have slowly transformed the site and become a focus of the local community.

4   Place in contention: politics and culture at Camerton

We have seen that Camerton is a place formed from a gathering of many elements from near and far, and that even its 'nature' is far from pure or original. In fact, most of the nature in Camerton's 'nature reserve' has arrived in the aftermath of human activity. What we are also beginning to appreciate in the cases of Mabey's (1993) Sheffield figs, Kaza's Washington State regrowth forest (Reading 5A) and the wooded batches of Camerton is that a relatively recent establishment of 'nature' is no impediment to emotional attachment for some people. This suggests that affective territorialisation, the forging of close emotional bonds to a place or other form of territory, is itself a practice, a kind of work in progress. And, as we will shortly see, this means that there is room for different experiences and interpretations. In this section, we pick up and follow through the Camerton residents' relationship to their mining heritage and to their trees, and look at some of the ways that affective territorialisation manifests itself as a flexible, but also contested, practice.

4.1   Mining heritages

As the trees quietly flourished in Camerton, the social, political and economic contexts around them changed. The village, which had been a place of heavy industry and industrial working class life, was reverting back to the more traditional form of an English rural village. The parish council sought to enter the Council for the Protection of Rural England's Best Kept Village competition, and it saw the abandoned overgrown pithead area as a problem. Consequently, it approached the National Coal Board (NCB) in 1980 to ask permission to clear the area and open it up as a public space. However, at this time other eyes were also on the site.

After the decline of the UK coal mining industry, there was a period of spoil heap removal for safety, environmental, regeneration and development purposes. Specialist companies were recycling spoil heaps and making the cleared land available for industrial development. One company, which had been involved in clearing tips in South Wales, proposed to clear the old batch in Camerton and began discussions with the NCB. The chair of the Camerton Heritage Committee (which was eventually formed by the parish council in 1989 to manage the site once it was acquired) recounts in his interview with the author that at this point a public meeting was held about the batches and 'that's when all hell was let loose'. Another resident recalls that 'there was quite an uproar ... the batch as such had to remain, locals didn't want it disturbed or anything like that, no way'.

This seems to be an important moment, and it is worth pausing here and taking stock. The outburst of local opinion suggests, perhaps to the surprise of developers and their allies, that the batches had by now become key elements in the local sense of place. The batches and the trees upon them, in other words, were physical presences to which emotions and memories had attached, and around which place identity and community action had formed.

A key aspect of this growing local attachment to Camerton's former mining landscape was a re-evaluation of the mining industry itself. The last decades of the twentieth century saw a burgeoning sentiment for, and interest in, the history of past mining communities along with the topography they shaped – with its traces of lost canals, disused branch railways and abandoned pitheads. Radstock museum focuses extensively on mining history and has an old coal winding wheel on prominent display, together with a re-creation of a working coalface. It also has a lively local history group which publishes a newsletter containing old photographs and oral accounts of the mining days.

These mines, like most others, were dangerous places to work, and accidents and deaths were common (these are now recorded in the Radstock museum, in a way similar to roll-calls of the dead from the world wars). The history of the coalfield tells of numerous local strikes and disputes about pay and working conditions. John Skinner, who was rector of Camerton, kept a journal of his daily life that was eventually published, and this is now considered to be of considerable literary and historical interest.

Activity 5.4

Turn now to Reading 5B by John Skinner (1984) entitled 'Journal of a Somerset rector 1803–1834' and Reading 5C by Virginia Woolf (1925) entitled 'The common reader', both of which you will find at the end of the chapter. Reading 5C is from an essay by Woolf on Skinner and his journals. Woolf's commentary starts with a reference to an earlier rector, then goes on to give a sketch of Skinner himself and of some of the political and cultural background to the mine and local community. She describes how Skinner, despairing of his own surroundings, retreated further into Camerton's pre-industrial past (as he imagined it), back to the ancient Britons, Roman invasion and the legends of King Arthur.

1   As you are reading, take note of the conditions of mining life that are being described. Do you think this is what the present-day residents of Camerton wish to commemorate?

2   What do you think Woolf is trying to tell us about the imagining of place?

3   How might this imagining of place relate to the contemporary revaluing of Camerton's mining heritage?

Woolf's account of Reverend Skinner's reveries in Reading 5C offers an example of the sort of construction of place that seeks a purer, simpler or more noble alternative to the present in a glorified past. This idea of a past untarnished by the perceived complications of the present is a very common component of thinking about place, especially during times of noticeable change or uncertainty. This raises the question of whether Camerton's current residents are now beginning to imagine the era of mining as a glorious past, in much the same way as the nineteenth-century rector imagined a mythical and pre-industrial past. Certainly, the Reverend Skinner's journals, with their vivid reportage of poverty and hardship, offer a harsh corrective to such yearnings. Nevertheless, there is also evidence that the contemporary townsfolk of Camerton do not shy away from the grimmer aspects of their mining heritage. Take a look at Figure 5.11, which shows the image that adorns the Guss & Crook pub in neighbouring Timsbury.

The guss and crook is the harness that was used by miners to drag the underground coal trucks, through the lower workings. This device became so notorious that a Royal Commission sat in 1928 to consider its continued use in the Somerset coalfield, but miners were not keen to present evidence about 'inhumane conditions' to the Commission because they feared that the loss of this manual means of hauling coal underground would mark the end of the relatively small mines. The guss and crook became a badge of honour, and boys sent down the mine 'came of age' when they were presented with one.

Indeed, the hardship endured down the mines was described as 'absolute slavery' as late as 1930 by Green (2003) in his memoirs of visiting Camerton: an assessment of mining history that is difficult to evade. Therefore, while it is often the case that histories of place are re-imagined in gilded tones in the present day, it is also true that affective territorialisation, as it is expressed in the imagining of place, can be flexible enough to accommodate the rough with the smooth, the grim and the glorious. This also seems to be the case for the people of past centuries, which may explain how mining communities managed to recast the notorious guss and crook as something worthy of ceremony. Similarly, we should not forget the rather inauspicious origin of the batches – as worthless debris discarded in the pursuit of a resource with 'real' value. It is ironic that with all the pitheads and railways dismantled, the shafts capped and the mined coal long burned, the most obvious remains of the mining industry is its waste products.

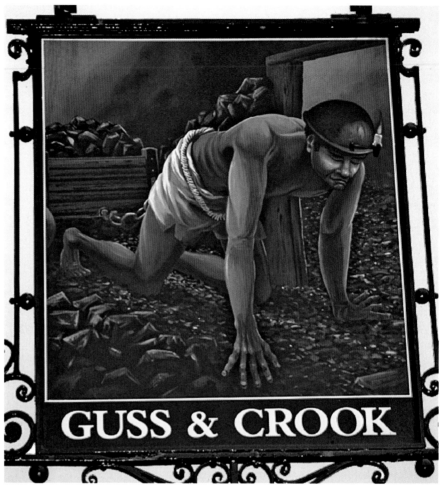

Figure 5.11   The guss and crook device for hauling coal underground, now remembered and depicted by a pub name and sign

4.2   Nature and environment

As Camerton's industrial heritage takes on new values, so the batches gain prominence as the most visible legacy of this rich and variegated past. Yet the tree-covered batches have also become valued for their aesthetic qualities. Part of the scattered village of Camerton is situated on the far side of the valley and looks across and down on to the old mine site, which had acquired the affectionate nickname, 'Little Switzerland'. One elderly resident spoke of her appreciation of this view:

> I used to have to struggle up there [to the other side of the valley] early in the morning to wait for the bus and sometimes it was misty and, you know [it was like] those lovely old Japanese prints, and you'd see these little pointed things with the mist rolling

around − [it was] quite like that sometimes in the mornings ... In a snowstorm or anything like that, you come down the hill and those conifers were gorgeous.

(Interview with author, 1998)

Beyond simply being scenic, however, the batches have been drawn into a set of related concerns about the environment, nature conservation and access to the countryside, all of which developed so markedly in the latter decades of the twentieth century. The environmental and open spaces non-governmental organisation (NGO), the Open Spaces Society, became involved in the campaign to save the batch (Lutley, 1992), and local concern about the threat to the batch combined concern for nature conservation with sentiment for industrial heritage. In many ways, trees and tree felling had become politically contentious issues as demonstrated by the many direct action tree protests which took place in the 1990s. One resident commented:

There has been a new awareness over the last twenty to twenty-five years or so about trees. You hear so much about trees being felled, a lot abroad − the hardwoods where all the forests are brought down, well of course that is sacrilege ... As I already mentioned, through the Dutch elm, there are a lot less trees now − around here.

(Interview with author, 1998)

Dutch elm disease killed tens of thousands of mature elms in the UK in the 1970s, and continues to prevent these trees growing to the spectacular size they once used to reach. This area of Somerset was particularly badly hit because it had a high number of large elms which died.

In the efforts to protect the batches in Camerton from clearance, nature conservation and the trees became a central focus. One of the major weapons used by local activists was to persuade the local authority to issue tree preservation orders for significant trees on both batches. Other actors were enrolled to assess the wider nature conservation value of the site. In 1985, ACCES, the then county council's community works programme scheme, conducted an ecological survey. The report listed:

Beech saplings dotted under the coniferous canopy and one dense thicket of ash saplings on the north slope, and examples of English oak, turkey oak, holm oak, wild cherry, silver birch, English elm, wych elm, Norway maple, sycamore, yew, rowan, holly, hawthorn, blackthorn, pussy-willow, elder, hazel, privet, gelder-rose and wayfaring trees.

(ACCES, 1985, p.2)

A proposed management plan for the old batch was set out, stating that the batches were 'a particularly interesting woodland as an example of what can develop on a sterile coal tip, given time and lack of harmful interference. Part of its function, indeed, could be a demonstration of such reclamation' (ACCES, 1985, p.5).

Beech trees, which had self-seeded in the railway sidings on the edge of the site while the mine was still working, were now spectacular 150-year-old giants featured in the Camerton Heritage Trail information sheet. The trees, both planted and wild, not only played a key part in the production of this place but were enrolled in the fight to save it. The ACCES report recommended that the batch 'be maintained and enhanced as a developing woodland ... and work should be undertaken to create certain features (paths, glades, etc.) which encourage the public to appreciate it as such, but which do not detract from its wildness' (ACCES, 1985, p.4).

After protracted negotiations about the acquisition of the pithead and the conservation of the batches, the NCB agreed that the site should be transferred to the community. The local authority undertook to conduct the legal transactions with the proviso that the parish council took full responsibility for the site thereafter. Negotiations were again protracted (partly due to the 1984 miners' strike which preoccupied the NCB), and the site was finally transferred to the ownership of the parish council in 1987. This may seem to be a happy ending, but the twists and turns of the story do not end here. Subsequently, the management of the site erupted into controversy as the trees, which were the object of emotional attachment, were once again threatened.

4.3   Natives and aliens

From the outset, the Camerton Heritage Committee took the decision to treat the whole site as an opportunity for public access, commemoration of the mining industry and ecological enhancement. The trees, however, were both providential and problematic in these respects, and they continued to be central figures in the story.

Potentially, the committee could attract funding in the form of woodland grants and grants from other sources that supported nature conservation and public access to open space. The problem was that, according to the local authority woodland officer, the conifers made for a 'fairly user unfriendly site which was very dark' (interview with author, 1998). The conifers (see Figure 5.12) had been planted in quite a dense pattern and had 'not been managed as a forest for some generations – if ever – which has meant the original planted trees have grown very closely, very tall, with restricted girth' (ACCES, 1985, p.3).

The trees were also thought to be 'nearing 100 years of age and consequently at the end of their natural life span' (Camerton Heritage Committee, 1993, p.1). In response to this, a scheme devised by the county council woodland officer was drawn up to replace the old conifer trees on the old batch with broadleaf species over a ten-year plus period using funding from the Forestry Commission. The intention was to sell timber from the old trees to help offset the cost of redeveloping the site into an Industrial Heritage and Public Open Space/Amenity area (Camerton Heritage Committee, 1993, p.1).

By the time the Heritage Committee was digesting this report, the Forestry Commission's broadleaves regeneration policy (begun in 1985) was well established. This was a response to years of criticism of conifers and the conifer plantations of the Forestry Commission (including those of Douglas's trees). For example, Massingham, a noted writer and campaigner for 'traditional' rural landscapes, penned an essay entitled 'The curse of the conifer' (1988). These anti-conifer campaigns depicted plantations as ugly, ecologically poor, and sinister reflections of anti-British and anti-democratic ideologies (they were often compared to the totalitarianism of Soviet Russia). The campaigns also played heavily on the distinction between 'native' and 'alien' species, celebrating 'native' broadleaves and decrying the 'alien conifer'.

Figure 5.12   Some of the remaining conifers on Camerton old batch

The generally accepted definition of a 'native tree' in Britain is one that colonised the British Isles before they were separated from mainland Europe by rising sea levels at the end of the last ice age. We have already referred to the forests that spread north across Europe with the retreating of the ice

Defining native and alien species

A native species is one which is considered to belong naturally to a given region or country, on account of it being self-established, whereas an alien species is one that has been introduced by human agency, or has taken advantage of human activities to introduce itself.

sheets: some of these trees established themselves in (what became) the British Isles while they were still connected to the rest of Europe. The receding ice that made way for the forests also caused large sea-level rises as water locked up in the ice sheets melted and rushed down to the sea. Therefore, the native trees of Britain, by this definition, were determined by an interaction of the speed of spreading forest 'racing' against the speed of the rising sea levels that cut the British Isles off. Some trees must have 'just made it' while others would have been 'just too late'.

According to this definition, there are some 33 native tree types in Britain, many of which have accrued much cultural meaning. A case in point is the oak, of which Simon Schama has noted, 'Ancient Britons were thought to have worshipped them; righteous outlaws are sheltered by them; kings on the run hide in them; hearts of oak go to sea and win empires' (2000, p.341). In an era of escalating environmental consciousness, native trees are often presented as ecologically rich and inherently in harmony with their surroundings. Famously, the oak has relationships with over 500 insect species (Miles, 1999), thus being a key species in woodland and field ecological systems and food chains.

Do we need to think further about this firm and distantly set demarcation of native from alien? Clearly, when the bulk of the UK land mass was covered in ice sheets, there were few trees or plants of any description. If you go back far enough, all trees, and in fact just about everything and everyone, are alien. You could even question whether the land itself is native. As we saw in Chapter 1, the earth's crust is itself mobile over geological time spans. By tracking these movements, earth scientists have worked out that parts of 'Britain' were once positioned on the equator, thus raising the question of what it is, precisely, that species are native to.

Arguably, a case can be made that the so-called native trees are of importance because they have, over a long period, become enmeshed in complex sets of cultural and ecological relations. Yet other trees such as the sweet-chestnut and the sycamore, which came to the UK's shores in Roman times, have also become part of 'British' ecology and culture. More recent arrivals have also become established in local landscapes, like the fig trees encountered in Section 2 and the London plane tree, a hybrid between the oriental plane and the US plane, which was first planted in England in about 1680 (Mabey, 1997). Owing to its tolerance of urban conditions, the London plane has become one of the UK's most widespread, useful and spectacular city trees.

Seen in this way, the simple dichotomy between alien and native becomes problematic. Trees, people and just about anything else you care to think about – even the land masses themselves – can all be seen as wanderers of the earth. In differing combinations and over different times, and travelling at very different speeds and for different reasons, they settle for a while and form the associations we are calling territories. And then, perhaps, they move on. To return to Camerton, it is worth noting that, beneath the 'native' soil, the coal seams on which an industry was based were themselves composed of trees which would now be considered alien species.

Consequently, we need to ask better questions of someone or something rather than simply 'Are they native or alien?' and 'Do they belong?' The questions, perhaps, should be 'Can they belong?' and 'On what terms?' – with the fundamental proviso that we also keep questioning what belonging means. In the light of the understanding of flows that we have been developing throughout this book, we might also question the designation of a species as alien simply on the grounds that human activity has played a part in its introduction. If the world consists of all manner of flows and forms of mobility, then why should the species whose passage is assisted by humans be classified as fundamentally different from those carried by wind, ocean currents or animal fur? The seeds themselves, after all, are indifferent to the means of transport.

4.4   Conflicting emotions

The Forestry Commission's 1985 'Broadleaves Policy' was an attempt to reconfigure state forestry functions and public opinion of them. By the time the management plan at Camerton was under way, funding was being exclusively given to the (re)planting of broadleaf woodlands. As the chair of the Heritage Committee summed up: 'we clear felled [the first area of conifers] and replaced with broadleaf because that was the Forestry Commission's edict' (interview with author, 1998) (see Figure 5.13 overleaf).

However, once the felling of the conifers was under way, there was an extremely adverse reaction to the scheme within the village. One of the contractors said that 'the moment we actually started work on the site we were accused of being "the massacrers – the butchers"'. The couple running the post office opposite the entrance to the site gave the contractors 'an earful' every time they went into the shop, although they 'tried and tried' to explain the logic of the felling and the management plans being followed. Another public meeting was held,

Figure 5.13   The old batch with conifers clear felled and replaced by broadleaf saplings

in which the county council woodland officer was asked by the Heritage Committee to explain what was happening and he recalls that 'people's opinions were very strong, and their emotions were running very high ... Their main objection seemed to be the fact that we were ... cutting down all the conifers and replacing with predominantly hardwoods.' The chair added that 'it caused a tremendous amount of feeling [with] the Parish Council who were the saviours [having saved the batch from clearance] being the demons ... Everyone nearly lynched the Parish Council Chairman'. One objector remarked, 'I know they may say that they are not native, but the conifers were very dramatic' (interview with author, 1998). Another, stressing the habitat-making capacities of the trees, recounted:

> I got in a bit of a tizzy because we got some goldcrests over there and they were nesting at the time, they build their nests in conifers, in the little niches and crannies, so I went over and asked the chap very nicely to stop, and I showed him the pictures of the bird he was destroying and they laid it off for a few months. They downed tools that day.

(Interview with author, 1998)

While yet another exclaimed: 'I really fought, oh I was spiteful about it. I fought here there and everywhere, wrote to anyone I could. Lots of [other] people grumbled, quite a few people didn't want them to go' (interview with author, 1998).

The professionals, then, were seeing the former mining landscape of Camerton from one perspective, a view built around ideas of ecological and landscape integrity, and of grants and national forestry policy edicts. After the regeneration plan was abandoned, one contractor concluded:

> The site is kind of a hybrid monster as far as I can tell – that's my own feeling about it – the hybrid monster which people seem happy to visit and [there is a] let sleeping dogs lie attitude about it now. ... Camerton is more of a slog with the added hassle of the local opposition.
>
> (Interview with author, 1998)

Many local people viewed the landscape in rather different terms. Their emotional and aesthetic sensibilities deviated markedly from the anti-conifer, pro-native hardwood sentiments which informed the policy of felling alien trees. For them, it was more a matter of an affective attachment to these particular trees and this particular topography. Their emotional investment seemed to be in the mix of present and remembered elements that had come together to make this place distinctive – rather than any clear-cut set of principles about what belonged. The contractor quoted above summed it up like this:

> With Camerton it's that emotional aspect which has caused difficulties on that site ... I would call it almost like a memorial garden because those conifers there represent the flowers on a grave of something that is no longer. ... When you are dealing with a coal batch, and when you are dealing with a place which has all that history attached to it, you are dealing with a lot of emotional issues besides that of just purely the trees.
>
> (Interview with author, 1998)

It could be argued that in beginning to clear fell the conifers, the contractors and the Heritage Committee ran headlong into an example of topophilia and the emotional response which can occur when places, and markers of place, are threatened.

Defining topophilia

The term 'topophilia' was coined by geographer Yi-Fu Tuan in reference to 'the affective bond between people and place' (1974, p.4). Tuan suggested that the bond between people and place varies according to individuals and cultures but is, nonetheless, an innate characteristic of human beings. It bears some similarity with E.O. Wilson's (1986) idea of 'biophilia', which suggests that humans are 'hard wired' to form affective bonds with elements of nature, though Tuan was careful to say that there was not a simple one-way flow between a given environment and people who then responded to it. Rather, the bonds of topophilia would emerge out of the complex interplay between the physical world and people, and would be mediated through actions, memories and imaginations. In this regard, the notion of topophilia is an important aspect of what is termed 'affective territorialisation' in this chapter, though we are cautious about claims for the innateness or inevitability of such sentiments.

Figure 5.14   A drawing of one of the massive beeches on the Camerton site from the LNR/HT information leaflet

Source: CHT, 1998

Camerton's trees provide a physical presence threading through time around which topophilia could coalesce. The LNR/HT information leaflet emphasises how one massive beech tree connects past and present (see Figure 5.14): 'The magnificent Beech Tree you can see here is at least 150 years old and would have been a fine young sapling when the nearby Old Pit Colliery was in full production'. As one resident reminisced about this tree: 'yes the one the children have got the swing on, I mean he is ever so old, he was that size when I was a little girl' (Camerton Heritage Committee, 1998). The LNR/HT leaflet mentions how young lovers like to carve their names in its bark and, indeed, close inspection of the tree reveals all manner of messages. These traces of past lives have a kind of archaeology, as older inscriptions have distorted, expanded and faded as the tree has grown (see Figure 5.15).

Figure 5.15   Names carved into the bark of the beech tree on the Camerton site

Summary

- Re-evaluation of the often hard and dangerous mining life and its unwanted by-products reveals the flexibility of affective territorialisation.

- Growing environmental sensibilities and appreciation of the countryside have provided new incentives for managing the Camerton batches and their tree cover.

- The distinction between native and alien species has been used as a justification to clear introduced or alien tree species from the Camerton LNR/HT. This distinction, however, is brought into question by an understanding of the dynamic interplay of territories and flows with regard to both landform and life.

- Angry reactions to the management of the LNR/HT, which discriminates against alien trees, offer further evidence of the flexibility of affective territorialisation. These reactions are suggestive of a valuing of the familiar in the landscape that might be termed 'topophilia'.

5   Affective territorialisation and the power of place

The rather poignant statement of one resident of Camerton might give us a clue as to how the depth and power of attachment to place works: 'any time I hear any [chain] sawing now I wonder what's going on' (interview with author). It is likely that for this resident, as for many other people, the whine of the chainsaw stands for something more than just trees being felled. It evokes change to the familiar and the loved. Cultural geographer David Sibley suggests that 'familiarity and predictability are important for many people. There is a common desire to live in a place which is stable and orderly' (1999, p.115). This is not to say that many people do not welcome and enjoy change and dynamism within place, but this change and dynamism has to operate within a delicate relationship of the stable and the familiar. There is nothing like large, apparently permanent, physical presences to lend an air of stability to a place. Trees are an obvious example; there are many others, both human-produced and formed by non-human forces. From monuments to mountains, imposing physical objects help to give a place its local distinctiveness and identity, and in this way become totems for emotional attachment.

It is often only when the familiar seems to be challenged that stronger emotions are stirred. Such threats are usually, but not always accurately, perceived as coming from 'outside' a place or community. We have seen, for instance, that the decline of mining and the resultant upheavals in the local economy and way of life came about largely as a result of structural forces of economic change over which local people had little control (though it is worth keeping in mind that the initial development of mining may well have also been experienced by many people as a similarly disturbing and imposed transformation). Articulating a sense of place is one way of responding to such changes, changes that in the contemporary world increasingly seem to arrive from elsewhere on the globe.

Activity 5.5

Now turn to the reproduction of Common Ground's poster *Rules for Local Distinctiveness* in Figure 5.16. Common Ground is a UK-based environment and arts organisation which campaigns for the preservation of place, that is to say it is interested in the kind of issues that the people of Camerton have faced but in the wider context of places all over the UK. Take a look at each of the squares in Figure 5.16.

1. From what or whom do you think Common Ground wants its readers to defend local places?

2. Do you think Common Ground wants the places in question to remain exactly as they are?

3. How is Common Ground drawing its audience to its cause – and what does it want people to do about the threat to place?

Turn now to Figure 5.16 overleaf before reading on.

It seems, from the evidence at hand, that Common Ground is resisting the processes of standardisation and homogenisation that are linked to corporate interests. Although globalisation is not explicitly referred to in Figure 5.16, it seems to suggest powerful economic or cultural forces that have a capacity to impact at once on a great many places. While there is a strong sense of wishing to preserve a whole range of things, there are also a number of clues to indicate that Common Ground does not simply want places to remain static or unchanging. As you may have noted, the reader is called on to be active, to do work and to 'change things for the better', rather than to 'fossilize' places. As well as responding to powerful outside forces, we are further implored to 'respond to the local and the vernacular'. You may also have detected a pervading current of emotional appeal from the poster: the images and words refer to things that are beautiful, tasty, fun, fascinating, lively and exuberant.

The message Common Ground seems to be conveying here is that marshalling the materials and meanings that define a particular place is not simply spontaneous; it is a kind of work, a process requiring people's active intervention, effort and organisation. Clearly, the emotional charge associated with places, especially when they are cared for or loved, can be a very important impetus to act in the name of place. Affective territorialisation, in this sense, is one of the ways that local people or communities can muster extremely strong resistance on the home front in response to forces and processes, which may otherwise seem beyond their control.

For good reason, Common Ground keeps its message fairly simple and direct. At this stage in the chapter, however, you may have some queries or questions of your own. Did you stop to wonder, for example, where all these 'local' things in Figure 5.16 come from, what trails or journeys they had taken prior to settling down in a particular place? And perhaps you also pondered whether it is only valuable, attractive or interesting things that make places unique.

What makes the Camerton case so revealing is that local people acted in defence of elements of place that were not illustrious, or not deeply rooted: mounds made of waste, trees that had clearly come from somewhere else. These examples provide a counterweight to the idea that what is most distinctive, or most worthy of preservation, in any place are those things that are most natural, or original or have been present for the longest time.

The idea that what is original, what was there from the beginning, is that which belongs is very common in thinking about place or territory in general; it is reflected in the shared derivation of the terms 'nature', 'native' and 'nation' from the Latin *natio* meaning 'birth'. We have already seen this logic at work in the distinction between native and alien species of trees. Nonetheless, a similar logic can be applied to just about any element of place, be it people, ways of making a living, language or elements of the built environment. Moreover, the result can be highly exclusionary. In Chapter 3, we encountered modes of territorialisation that sought exclusive ownership or control. There are many cases where affective territorialisation can also take this form, such as when people, plants or animals which are considered alien to

COMMON GROUND
RULES for
LOCAL DISTINCTIVENESS

A

Acklam Russet
Aldenham Blenheim
Aldwick Beauty
Alfriston
Alton
Ascot
Ashdown Seedling
Ashmead's Kernel
Autumn Pearmain

AYRSHIRE

ABBOTS BROMLEY
HORN DANCE

BAKEWELL PUDDING

Beck Bourne Brook Burn

BARNS

THE BURRY MAN

BRICKS

Accrington Bloods

London Stock

Nettlebed
Purple Headers

Reading Greys

Staffordshire Blues

CHaNGE
things for the
BETTER
Not for the **!!!**
SAKE OF IT

CORNISH PASTIE

LET THE **CHARACTER**
of the people and place
express itself. **KILL**
corporate identity before
it kills our high streets.
Give local shops precedence.

CAMBERWELL BEAUTY

CARDIFF ARMS PARK

DEVONSHIRE
CREAM TEAS

LOCAL **DIALECT**
should be
spoken. **heard**
AND S E E N

DORSET HEATH

E

ELEPHANT & CASTLE

F

FUGGLE

TAKE THE PLACE'S
FINGERPRINT
FORGET words
such as RESOURCE. SITE
CUSTOMERS and THE PUBLIC
Abstractions lead us astray
THINK & talk about places & people

FAIR ISLE SWEATERS

FRENCH
LIEUTENANT'S
WOMAN

BELTED GALLOWAY

GABLE ENDS

H

DON'T FOSSILIZE PLACES
HISTORY
is a continuing process, not
just the past. Celebrate time,
place and the seasons with
★ ★ ★ ★ ★ ★ ★
FESTIVALS & FEASTS

THOMAS HARDY

WORK FOR LOCAL
IDENTITY
▶OPPOSE◀ MONOCULTURE IN OUR FIELDS.
parks, gardens and buildings.
Resist formulae and automatic
ordering from pattern books
which homogenise and deplete

J

JET

JELLIED EELS

JET ISON YOUR CAR
whenever
you can and
go by public
transport. PLACES ARE FOR PEOPLE
AND NATURE NOT CARS. Cars can
detach us from places and
unwittingly allow their destruction.

ROMNEY'S
KENDAL
MINT CAKE

KAOLIN

L

BUY things that are
LOCALLY
DISTINCTIVE
and locally made-such
as food and souvenirs
RESIST THE THINGS THAT
CAN BE FOUND ANYWHERE

LANCASHIRE LAD

Figure 5.16   *Common Ground's* poster Rules for Local Distinctiveness

Topophilia comfort family friendly

the identity of a place attract negative emotional associations and are vigorously resisted and excluded. In this sense, some geographers and other social scientists have been wary of the notion of topophilia, pointing out that it can just as well draw its strength from hostility to 'outsiders' or the wider world as it can be a source of an empowering and generous love of place.

Another aspect of affective territorialisation that can pit the local against the outside world in an exclusive way is the resistance to the local siting of activities or facilities deemed undesirable. Such 'intrusive' presences as power plants, prisons or refugee centres can trigger emotionally charged campaigns for exclusion that have been termed NIMBYism (NIMBY stands for Not In My Back Yard). This is a rather pejorative term, in that it is usually applied to those people or communities that protect their local environment at the expense of other places, that is to say, by opposing a development locally and not caring whether, or actually hoping that, it gets located elsewhere.

We need to be wary, then, in any emotional call to action in the interest of place about what it might entail for other places, and just how selective or exclusionary this call is. Furthermore, keep in mind, as the case study of Camerton drives home, that those things which may now be valued often have past histories involving hardship and suffering or a previous existence as something denigrated and undesired. Besides, as the story of Camerton's trees demonstrates, places always change, and perhaps need to change in order to keep healthy. As a footnote to the Camerton story, such change is not always pleasant or easy to endure. On one of the other nearby planted batches, where no management at all has occurred, the conifers, as predicted in the report for Camerton, are reaching the end of their lifespan. These conifers are crowded and thin in trunk girth, and many have fallen or lean at odd angles (see Figure 5.17). The lesson seems to be that, sometimes, even the whine and bite of the chainsaw may be needed to look after the things we love.

Figure 5.17   Planted conifers leaning and falling

let them fall! they rot break down and from humous

Summary

- Mobilisations of affective territorialisations have a tendency to arise when there are perceived threats to the familiar.

- Affective territorialisation is one of the ways in which local people or communities can muster extremely strong resistance to forces and processes that may otherwise seem beyond their control.

- Affective territorialisation can run the risk of becoming exclusionary and unwelcoming to 'outsiders' and to change in general, especially when its motivating force is a fidelity to what is considered original or natural, and this may result in lack of care for other places.

6   Conclusion

In this chapter, we have seen that the making of place still matters, even in a globalised world. We have looked closely at a case study, the village of Camerton in Somerset, where local people have come together in order to defend aspects of the landscape that are important to them. Their emotional or affective attachment to the traces of the mining industry in the landscape around them and to the trees that have established themselves on the waste heaps or batches around the mines has played a vital part in this defence of place. Accordingly, we have examined how ordinary people, working on the ground, on a day-to-day basis, can actively intervene in the flows and territorialisations which have shaped and continue to shape their local area. In fact, whether or not they choose to work with or manage these dynamic processes, they are inevitably caught up in processes that connect the place they live to other places distant in time or space.

Like the Pacific islands considered in Chapter 1, the place now known as Camerton has been formed from a series of flows which have come together at different times and for differing durations, and have coalesced into territories which become places – people's homes. These territories are never fixed or finished, but continue to be sustained and remade by throughputs of flows. The way in which places emerge from a confluence of shifting elements means that all places are likely to have interesting stories behind them, a present which is in many ways shaped by that past, and futures which might turn out to be as intriguing as the past. The Camerton LNR/HT now seems well established, and is fiercely guarded, but its path through time to the present has not always been secure. In the future, it can be expected that the LNR/HT will continue to be remade as further unexpected twists and turns occur in its story.

Crucially, if places are made then they could have been made differently, and they can always be remade – or even unmade. Human forces do not make places alone, they work on and with, and sometimes against, non-human forces, from the ebb and flow of living things to shifting climate and the instabilities of the earth. Keeping this in mind can make a difference to our relationship with places and to how we experience identity and belonging; it encourages us to sever our sense of place from any sense of a fixed, immutable past. If there is anything 'natural' about the places in which we live, the things with which we cohabit and our attachment to them, our reference point must be to a nature that is dynamic, mobile and mixed up, rather than to one which is stable, pure and in any way anchoring.

Recognising that places are contingent and ever changing can encourage a sense of place that is accepting of, or at least open-minded towards, new arrivals or novel arrangements of already present things. However, as we have seen in Camerton, people can also become deeply attached to, and fervently defensive of, things that have arrived relatively recently. What we have called 'affective territorialisation', then, is a powerful force, one that can be built around arrangements of things that are both old and new, a force capable of embracing and making a place for 'outsiders' but, equally, capable of excluding strangers and novelty. Thus, the defence of place, along with its active reworking or reinvention, is one of the most potentially powerful ways in which people can respond to wider forces, and especially to the volatilities and uncertainties that come with being part of a globalised world. Yet, at the same time, as demonstrated by the example of Camerton with its anciently laid down coal deposits and its distantly sourced trees, every place is itself the outcome of wider world flows.

By the same token that the elements of place gather from near and far, so too can these elements, once settled and seemingly grounded in a particular place, head off on new wanderings. Even those of us who love and deeply care for a certain place are often willing and capable of heading somewhere else. In this chapter we have explored processes of affective territorialisation, which are forged from an overlap between a sense of identity and belonging, and the inhabiting of a specific site or location. What happens to such affections or attachments when 'local people' leave their home turf, when they take off and go somewhere else? This is a question that we turn to in the next chapter.

References

ACCES (1985) *Camerton Old Colliery: Management Scheme for Wooded Batch and Pithead Area*, Bristol, ACCES.

Buchanan, A. and Cossons, N. (1969) *Industrial Archaeology of the Bristol Region*, Newton Abbot, David & Charles.

Camerton Heritage Committee (1993) *Camerton Heritage Project*, Camerton, Camerton Heritage Committee.

Camerton Heritage Committee (1998) Camerton Heritage Trail Information Leaflet (available at Camerton LNR/HT and from Camerton Parish Council, Somerset).

Edlin, H.L. (1948) *Forestry and Woodland Life*, London, Batsford.

English Nature (2000) *Veteran Trees Management Handbook*, http://www.english-nature.org/pubs/handbooks (accessed 8 October 2005).

Forestry Commission (1985) *Broadleaved Woodland Grant Scheme* (revised November 1985), Edinburgh, Forestry Commission.

Forestry Commission (2005) http://www.forestry.gov.uk/HCOU-40FP34 (accessed October 2005).

Green, E.K.M. (2003) Somerset Coal Mines, Lower Writhlington Colliery, Bath (available from Radstock Museum, Bath and Northeast Somerset).

Hardy, T. (1998, first published 1872) *Under the Greenwood Tree,* London, Penguin Books.

Harrison, F. (1991) *The Living Landscape*, London, Mandarin Paperbacks.

Kaza, S. (1996) *The Attentive Heart: Conversations with Trees*, Boston, Shambhala.

Little, B. (1969) *Portrait of Somerset*, London, Robert Hale.

Lutley, W. (1992) *Making Space: Protecting and Creating Open Space for Local Communalities*, Henley-on-Thames, Open Spaces Society.

Mabey, R. (1993) 'Nature and change: the two faces of naturalisation' in Clifford, S. and King, A. (eds) *Local Distinctiveness: Place, Particularity and Identity*, London, Common Ground.

Mabey, R. (1997) *Flora Britannica*, London, Chatto & Windus.

Macmillen, N. (1990) *Coal from Camerton*, Bath, Avon Industrial Buildings Trust.

Massingham, H.J. (1988) 'The curse of the conifer' in Abelson, E. (ed.) *A Mirror of England: An Anthology of the Writings of H.J. Massingham (1888–1952)*, Bideford, Green Books.

Miles, A. (1999) *Silva: The Tree in Britain*, London, Ebury.

Schama, S. (2000) *A History of Britain*, London, BBC Worldwide.

Sibley, D. (1999) 'Creating geographies of difference' in Massey, D., Allen, J., and Sarre, P. (eds) *Human Geography Today*, Cambridge, Polity Press.

Skinner, J. (1984) *Journal of a Somerset Rector 1803–1834*, Coombs, H. and Coombs, P. (eds), Oxford, Oxford University Press.

Tuan, Y.-F. (1974) *Topophilia: A Study of Environmental Perception, Attitudes and Values*, Englewood Cliffs, NJ, Prentice-Hall.

Webster, A.D. (1919) *Webster's Practical Forestry*, London, William Rider.

Williams, W.J. (1976) *Coal Mining in Bishop Sutton, North Somerset, c.1799–1929*.

Wilson, E.O. (1986) *Biophilia: The Human Bond with Other Species*, Harvard, Harvard University Press.

Woolf, V. (1925) *The Common Reader*, New York, Harcourt Brace Jovanovich.

Reading 5A

Stephanie Kaza, 'The attentive heart: conversations with trees'

A multitude of voices

Once there was a clear, unobstructed view from the ridge above Port Townsend, Washington, across the strait to Vancouver Island. For a time this view was used for strategic defense. It was a functional view, a necessary view – far more important than a merely scenic view. The trees were clipped purposefully to monitor the potential for danger at sea. The northern conifer forest of Douglas fir, cedar, spruce, and hemlock was pruned so that unpredictable neighbors could be watched across the forty-eighth parallel. To guarantee ownership of place, gun emplacements were constructed in the wilderness.

Perched on the northeasternmost tip of the Olympic Peninsula, Fort Worden was assigned the task of protecting the sovereign borders of the American nation state. The boundary between Canada and the United States was declared to be halfway across Juan de Fuca Strait. Any party crossing that invisible line could be perceived as enemy, particularly if it represented competing territorial interests. The fort was built in the midst of a two-thousand-mile conifer forest that filled the peninsula to the brim, pouring down the steep slope of the Olympic Mountains to the Quilault and Quillayut rivers and out to the broad beaches of the Pacific. In the wet interior of the peninsula, the temperate rainforest dripped with moss and ferns, and trees grew to swollen dimensions in the absence of interference.

The officers' quarters for the fort stood on the flat plateau above the harbor. A long row of large white houses faced onto the open green, across from military headquarters. From this platform the men were dispatched to seaworthy patrol boats or ridgetop lookouts. Each concrete bunker held food and bedding provisions, water, and ample ammunition for a crude defense of an immeasurable treasure. The simple box fortifications were partially buried in the hills to minimize their presence while still permitting the protrusion of black cannon barrels. The forest was cut back to enhance the strategic view. This view was maintained throughout World War I to guard against invasion by the Japanese. When the war was over, the concrete bunkers finally gave in to the trees that had been trying to grow back the whole time.

Now the forest has thoroughly infiltrated the barricades in a miscellaneous, unstrategic takeover. Sapling alders and wild rose brambles cluster in the sunlight. Their gay, dappled shadows cover the once barren ground; their leaning forms soften the edges of the eroding concrete bunkers. A small crowd of gangly Douglas firs poke through the broken barricades, filling in the gaps left by the military. To a casual observer this might appear to be an average forest. But actually it is a forest coming back, just beginning to be a forest again. Without a war to hold things up, the trees are growing over everything. Leave a spot bare in the northwest forest and moss will cover it over. Leave the soil undisturbed and the seed bank will sprout into full form. Leave the trees alone and they will obscure functional views, inviting a wild thicket of lush growth to take over.

The trees grow like weeds in a lot left untended. They form a blanket of wildness on the land, springing up in the absence of attention. No one has landscaped this arrangement. It is apparently random, chaotic in pattern and shape. Every fern, every alder, every rose tangle is just finding its own way through the competition for space. Some are doing well; others will never make it past the seedling or sapling stage. This is a forest in transition – a bunch of new ideas trying to gain their footing. It is all quite temporary, but left alone long enough, the blanket will persist.

In a bramble of young firs, alders, and thimbleberry lies a half-buried concrete step on the lip of the hill, a fading foothold in the shifting forest. I perch on the step, looking for signs of the former fort. The step doesn't lead anywhere anymore. Ferns have covered over the patch, blocking access to the steep hillside. The forest is rebounding with a ferocious resilience, doing its best to heal the trauma. The bramble of plants has taken back the integrity of the place. Like a single tree with a multitude of voices, the grove of young alders speaks a blessing of peace over the former war zone.

Twenty or thirty years after the war, I imagine this tip of land showed only the rudimentary beginnings of a forest – a few fallen logs, random Douglas fir cones blown in from neighboring trees, and a dusting of countless invisible pollen grains and fern spores. A few ground squirrels and Steller's jays gossiped in the open spaces, dropping madrone berries and rose hips. Underneath the surface of the soil, pale fungal threads digested old logs, preparing the ground for future growth of young tree roots.

The red alders probably moved in first, perhaps after a brush fire that would have cleared any remaining vegetation. Taking well to open areas, the alders thrived in the sunlight and enriched the soil for those to follow. In a complex arrangement of friendliness, the alders grew thickened root nodules to host bacteria capable of processing nitrogen gas into ammonia. The trees then converted this ammonia to amino acids, which formed the protein building blocks for cell growth. The return of the forest began in this cellular act of interpretation, a marriage of producers at the ground level.

In the heat and exposure of the cleared area, Douglas fir cones cracked open, sometimes with the help of mice and chipmunks. When the winter rains came, the seeds germinated, forming sprays of young needles no more than an inch high. The seedlings grew quickly to five- and ten-foot saplings, soaking up the luxury of unblocked sunlight. From a distance they resembled a neglected lot of Christmas trees too scrappy to sell.

In another fifty years the forest will change shape and dimension, growing from youth to early maturity. I lean against a small tree, envisioning the Douglas firs overtaking the alders, squeezing out the sun below their full branches. The alders will die back, falling onto the forest floor, turning over their stored nitrogen to feed the firs. The fungal associates will weave their way into the conifer roots, crisscrossing the soil with a tapestry of mycelia, spewing millions of powdery spores from their fruiting bodies. Warblers, kestrels, and sharp-shinned hawks will lace the airways with flight, while nuthatches, brown creepers, and woodpeckers spiral the trunks as they forage.

In two hundred years, the time of ten human generations, the largest Douglas firs will be rich producers of strong, fine-grained heartwood, dwarfing the old bunkers of the earlier warfare state. Fallen trees will support dense colonies of bark beetles, ants, and centipedes, and fungi will flourish in the rotting logs. Hemlock seedlings will use the soft soil and moisture stored in crumbling nurse logs to gain an advantage over other young trees. Mosses and liverworts will blanket the ground, soaking up the surface runoff like a decorative sponge.

Three hundred years later all traces of war defense will be completely gone, broken down by the steady drip of winter rain over the landscape. Hemlocks, western red cedars, and spruce will stand in the understory shade below the remaining Douglas firs. Craggy and broken-topped, uneven with jagged branches, the firs will tower over the forest. By the random events of history these firs will have become an ancient old-growth forest, and the memory of a clearing will have been replaced by a web of complexity.

In the first stages of reclamation all this is possible. The order of simplification is easily replaced by the chaos of complexity. Time and a good seed bank are the main requirements. Living systems have a proclivity for the unruly; time naturally generates relationship. To allow this forest, this multitude of voices, to take the first step toward recovery is to begin the process of healing. This seems like a joyful thing to me. As a witness to this healing I feel the wilderness affirmed; I hear the highly cultivated life force speaking powerfully on the landscape.

The voice of a forest is an elusive thing. It sings in the sweet warbles of purple finches and Swainson's thrushes. It rustles in the leaves dancing in the afternoon sunlight. It buzzes in the slim sounds of crickets and mosquitoes. It creaks in the sway of tree trunks rubbing against each other. I wonder when a tree gains its voice. How old must it be to speak from its position in the forest? Are the young ones part of the multitude or do only the grand sages claim a voice? The conversation of a forest is a babble of energy flow, an explosion of growing, a richness of intelligence in tree form.

What does this forest have to say? Perhaps its story is just the simplicity of being here. Day after day, year after year, branches growing, trunks expanding – just rising up into being. In the convenience of being ignored, this forest is becoming something unplanned and undesigned, unexpected and unnecessary. In simply following the natural order, Douglas firs, red alders, wild rose, and thimbleberry have co-created a testimony to the miracle of regeneration.

Though it happens independently of any human goals and desires, I feel a need to be part of this re-arising. People need this blanket of green wildness to walk into and remember complexity. This spontaneous becoming is reassuring witness to the power of life. I want to feel certain that the forest will come back no matter how hard it is beaten down.

But is it possible that a forest can be too traumatized to recover? This belief in the possibility of resilience may be a beautiful illusion, based on evolutionary memory rather than present reality. Severe burns, erosion, and climate change can easily reduce the chances for restoration. Yet in our minds we depend on this thing we know about trees – that they will grow over everything. But what if the cumulative and synergistic damage of soil, air, and water challenge this resiliency beyond its capacity? Individual trees may grow back, but the system may be crippled. Many forests have suffered extreme damage in the wake of territorial disputes. So easily the human order displaces the wildness to serve the dictates of conflict.

A healthy forest is rich with structural complexity in the form of tangles, cracks, cavities, and diverse surfaces supporting other organisms. A microspot may be a perching ledge for a butterfly, a nest site for a junco, a crawl space for a centipede. A simplified forest has fewer resting spots, fewer safe places for small creatures. A forest retarded in recovery stays simple, restricted from reaching its full capacity to support life.

In the desire to aid a broken forest, people plant trees – sometimes as an investment in the future, sometimes as a hopeful peace offering. Inevitably the human order makes its own statement, designing its own forests. In some cases, despite the deep and heartfelt need for healing, the trees come out in rows, like soldiers lined up on parade. Tree planting is not a wild activity; it will not necessarily generate randomness. And wild is random, not ordered by any human mind or idea of pattern. There are too many forces at work on every seed and sapling to predict the shape of a forest. It is ungraspable by the solitary human mind.

As I sit here in this recovering forest, I know I could never have planned the fabulous display of intricate shadows dancing on these leaves. I could not predict that just at this time of day the light would be so splendid on the trunks of the alders. I'm not sure it's possible to create the multitude of forest voices just by planting a few trees. With even the greatest of efforts, the human order cannot duplicate a forest's complex attributes.

In this small haven on the top of the bluff, the forest's voice is growing back and speaking from the land. It is blessed with neglect and the kindness of the Pacific maritime climate. The memory of war is being obliterated by random acts of beauty, noticed or not. By mutual preference for peace, the people and the forest have accommodated each other's growing habits. The national state has been at peace long enough to allow the forest to grow back in some places. How long will it take for it to grow back in our minds?

(Kaza, 1996, pp.239–47)

Reading 5B

John Skinner, 'Journal of a Somerset rector 1803–1834'

1803

July

Another stranger from Ireland a little before this, named Culling Macnab, who also worked in the coal pits, being much intoxicated on Saturday night was drowned by falling into the Canal, and afterwards a collier of the name of Cook killed by some loose earth at the bottom of the pit falling upon him, his two sons who were working close by providentially escaped, and endeavoured to dig away the earth from their father, but could not do it in time to save his life, but were near enough to hear him exclaim, 'My poor lads, it will soon be over with me.'

Aaron Horler, another collier, was killed in a very extraordinary manner. He had been drinking at the public house, whence, after behaving in a violent manner by dancing on the tables and stools, etc., and insulting some of his associates there assembled, he walked to the Lower Pit and, it is supposed, endeavoured to slide down the rope (by which the coal is hauled) to the bottom; but going too quick, not being able to retain his hold, he fell down many fathoms and was dashed to pieces, his hands being much burnt by the velocity with which the rope passed through them before he let go his hold. A person going down the pit about ten o'clock to feed the asses kept under-ground was presented with this horrid spectacle on his descent, and was so much frightened as not to recover himself for some time.

[...]

1805

September 18

A little boy of the name of Cottle, son of the Schoolmistress, was killed in the coal pit by some loose ground falling upon him. He was only eight years old, and had worked a year.

Surely the parents and the proprietors of the works are to blame for permitting such little boys to work, who cannot possibly take care of themselves and must be ignorant of the dangers they are exposed to; but what is not sacrificed to the shrine of covetousness?

[...]

1806

January 9

A man of the name of William Bowler was drowned in the brook. The accident was occasioned so far as I could learn from intoxication. At his funeral I took the opportunity to address the people assembled in Church before we went to the grave, and as they seemed very attentive I hope my admonitions were not thrown away.

William Britain, another collier, was killed in the coal pits by a shocking accident. He was riding in a small cart underground drawn by an ass, which vehicle is usually employed to convey the coal from different parts where it is dug to the large store below the mouth of the pit, but was then empty. As the ass was going along at a brisk pace he did not observe he was come to a spot where the roof of the passage was much lower than it was before, and, neglecting to stoop his head, his back was bent double by the sudden violence of the shock and his spine snapped. The poor fellow was drawn up and lived some hours, but his extremities were quite paralysed. He was son to poor old Britain who occasionally works for me. The brother who is left will be of little comfort to him, as he is a sad fellow, indeed quite a savage.

March 22

James Edwards, whose business it was to see the coal brought to land at The Old Pit, in reaching over too far in order to stay the basket which was coming up, fell to the bottom and was dashed to pieces. Horrid to say, his last word was an oath when he found himself going. He left a widow and four children at Cridlingcot.

[...]

1823

Friday, January 3

The frost having broken up, I was occupied in my study. In the evening one of the colliers, A. Garratt, came to say his brother had broken his back in the coal works. I immediately went to his house in Wick Lane, and found him lying in a most deplorable state, the spine having been put out below the shoulder by a mass of coal falling upon him. This is the third instance within these last two years of the same accidents having occurred. I found three or four of the Methodists assembled round the bed exhorting the poor creature to repentance, as they informed him his time was but short, and he must make the best use of it. What with his bodily pains and his mental fears, the sufferings of the man were almost beyond bearing.

[...]

1830

Sunday, April 18

As I heard during the morning that the colliers had it in contemplation to strike work on account of their wages being about to be lowered, I spoke to one of the colliers, and said if they had any just ground for complaint how much better it would be to send two or three whom they might depend on to state their grievances, and if there was any foundation for them I had no doubt but they would be attended to; but if they struck work it would only be taking bread out of their own mouths and the mouths of their families. The man said he thought with me on the subject, and that they would get no good by opposition. It is now six or seven years ago that there was a combination among the colliers, and the Camerton people struck with the rest and did not work for several days. I then went to them and gave them the same advice, which they would not listen to then, but afterwards told me they wished they had done so, as they were influenced by other people, having nothing really to complain of themselves.

I called at the Manor House. Mrs. Jarrett entered into a long account of the intended opposition of the colliers to their employers. She said it was only for the matter of about £80 that they made all this fuss, for it would not be more if the person who rose the steam was continued instead of dispensed with, and that this was the reason they felt dissatisfied; that the Proprietors of the Works knew nothing about the management of them themselves; that she had desired that things might go on as heretofore till the meeting of the Coal Proprietors, and would pay out of her own pocket the wages of the steam man. I had never understood that there had been any dispute about the steam man, but only heard they objected to a diminution of their wages. What authority Mrs. Jarrett had to interfere with the management of the works is another question. She has only a free share; but this politic lady has one thing which gives her the fullest power over the men, and which, if the Proprietors ever come to open contest with her, they find to their cost, renders her power absolute. She has authority over the residences of all the colliers, who are only weekly tenants, and may be dismissed ad libitum.

(Skinner, 1984, pp.12–13, 25, 29, 229, 406–7)

Reading 5C

Virginia Woolf, 'The common reader'

The Rev. John Skinner

A whole world separates Woodforde, who was born in 1740 and died in 1803, from Skinner, who was born in 1772 and died in 1839.

For the few years that separated the two parsons are those momentous years that separate the eighteenth century from the nineteenth. Camerton, it is true, lying in the heart of Somersetshire, was a village of the greatest antiquity; nevertheless, before five pages of the diary are turned we read of coal-works, and how there was a great shouting at the coal-works because a fresh vein of coal had been discovered, and the proprietors had given money to the workmen to celebrate an event which promised such prosperity to the village. Then, though the country gentlemen seemed set as firmly in their seats as ever, it happened that the manor house at Camerton, with all the rights and duties pertaining to it, was in the hands of the Jarretts, whose fortune was derived from the Jamaica trade. This novelty, this incursion of an element quite unknown to Woodforde in his day, had its disturbing influence no doubt upon the character of Skinner himself. Irritable, nervous, apprehensive, he seems to embody, even before the age itself had come into existence, all the strife and unrest of our distracted times. He stands, dressed in the prosaic and unbecoming stocks and pantaloons of the early nineteenth century, at the parting of the ways. Behind him lay order and discipline and all the virtues of the heroic past, but directly he left his study he was faced with drunkenness and immorality; with indiscipline and irreligion; with Methodism and Roman Catholicism; with the Reform Bill and the Catholic Emancipation Act, with a mob clamouring for freedom, with the overthrow of all that was decent and established and right. Tormented and querulous, at the same time conscientious and able, he stands at the parting of the ways, unwilling to yield an inch, unable to concede a point, harsh, peremptory, apprehensive, and without hope.

[...]

Perhaps the village of Camerton in the year 1822, with its coal-miners and the disturbance they brought, was no fair sample of English village life. Certainly it is difficult, as one follows the Rector on his daily rounds, to indulge in pleasant dreams about the quaintness and amenity of old English rural life. ... Wherever one turned there was suffering, wherever one looked one found cruelty behind that suffering. Mr. and Mrs. Hicks, for example, the Overseers, let an infirm pauper lie for ten days in the Poor House without care, 'so that maggots had bred in his flesh and eaten great holes in his body.' His only attendant was an old woman, who was so failing that she was unable to lift him. Happily the pauper died. Happily poor Garratt, the miner, died too. For to add to the evils of drink and poverty and the cholera there was constant peril from the mine itself. Accidents were common and the means of treating them elementary. A fall of coal had broken Garratt's back, but he lingered on, though exposed to the crude methods of country surgeons, from January to November, when at last death released him. Both the stern Rector and the flippant Lady of the Manor, to do them justice, were ready with their half-crowns, with their soups and their medicines, and visited sick-beds without fail. But even allowing for the natural asperity of Mr. Skinner's temper, it would need a very rosy pen and a very kindly eye to make a smiling picture of life in the village of Camerton a century ago. Half-crowns and soup went a very little way to remedy matters; sermons and denunciations made them perhaps even worse.

The Rector found refuge from Camerton neither in dissipation like some of his neighbours, nor in sport like others. ... No, the only refuge from Camerton lay in Camulodunum. The more he thought of it the more certain he became that he had the singular good fortune to live on the identical spot where lived the father of Caractacus, where Ostorius established his colony, where Arthur had fought the traitor Modred, where Alfred very nearly came in his misfortunes. Camerton was undoubtedly the Camulodunum of Tacitus. Shut up in his study alone with his documents, copying, comparing, proving indefatigably, he was safe, at rest, even happy.

(Woolf, 1925, pp.4–7)

Chapter 6

Community, cloth and other travelling objects

Giles Mohan

Contents

1   Introduction

In Chapter 5, we engaged with the issue of the affective dimension of territory. We explored how people in a local place developed attachments to it, to the point of defending it against certain kinds of change even though they knew that the place had changed before and, indeed, that many of the ingredients of the place they valued so highly had arrived there from somewhere else. In this chapter, we continue to explore this theme of attachment to place but through a very different, and longer and more complex, history. For one of the most obvious characteristics of a globalised world is that people migrate, often over long distances. In the midst of such global flows, what happens to the form of territory which is created through attachment to place? Are we to become free-floating, uprooted from any grounded attachment? Is it possible somehow to feel both global and local at the same time? These are some of the most pressing questions posed by globalisation. We explore in this chapter one way in which a group of people has addressed this issue.

Examining the issue of attachment to territories in this way allows us to take our thinking about territories a little further. For, as we shall see, people's attachments are often both to a particular community and to a particular place. Both of these are forms of territorialisation. There is, nonetheless, a long tradition of assuming that the two go together. The term 'local community' is one indicator of this. In the case of migrant groups, though, the two territorialisations of community and place become dislocated from each other – they no longer have the same geographies. Analytical and political challenges are posed as to how to respond to this disjuncture.

The very fact of this dislocation of community and place, and the work that is put in to build something new, emphasises that though these attachments may run very deep, they are not somehow 'given' or predestined. They are made; they are ways in which we organise the world. This chapter explores a history in which the architecture of attachments has been persistently challenged and persistently reorganised.

Activity 6.1

In September 2004 in Denmark, a taxi driver from Copenhagen was elected king. Electing a king is strange because royalty generally inherits or marries into its position. Yet this Danish king is a Ghanaian migrant who was installed as the chief of the Akan people in Denmark. Extract 6.1 is an account of the ceremony from a Danish website. Read through it and look at Figure 6.1. Think about the following questions:

1 Where do the Akan people come from?

2 What kind of a ceremony do you think the inauguration was?

3 What social significance does the event have?

4 What cultural practices and objects are in evidence?

Extract 6.1

The 'coronation' of the local Akan kings and chiefs is an annual event – surprisingly also in Scandinavia. The Akan people are the largest ethnic group in Ghana and their history and rich cultural traditions go as far back as anyone can remember. Keeping traditions alive and passing it on to the next generation is actually one of the main reasons that the ceremony is carried out among the Akans now living in Denmark. The cultural festival marks a new year and maybe a new king, but first of all it is a social and cultural event bringing people together to have fun. It is an occasion where ancestors are honoured and history is explained to the children.

Traditionally in Ghana the royal titles are inherited, but in Denmark the king is democratically elected as chairman for the Akan community. The current king who goes under the name Nana Kwasi Agyemang I, is popular and it was no surprise that he was re-elected this year. The Queen is known as Nana Akua Amoatemaa I and also has several official tasks. The Ghanaian Ambassador attended the event together with representatives from other Ghanaian groups all dressed up in their best. The festival was complete with African food, music, speeches, libation and traditional dances. Highlights of the day were the staged 'kidnapping' of the king and the following outdoor parade, which made many by passers stop and stare.

The Akans consist of several ethnic groups which all speak Twi or Fante. They also have common traditions and culture, among them the importance of sacred stools representing the kings and chiefs. When a king and queen (Akanhene and Akanhemmaa) are elected, they are said to be enstooled. The stool represents their power and draws historic lines back to the ancestors. The hand-woven kente material is another important cultural symbol and nearly everybody wears something of kente on a special occasion like this.

Figure 6.1   The inauguration of the Danish Akan king, Nana Kwasi Agyemang I

The Akanhene does not sit on his chair for the rest of the year. A lot of practical tasks come with the honour – and then there are the realities of European daily life: This king who is also an educated electronic technician, has a day job driving a taxi in Copenhagen.

(Crawfurd, 2004)

The most striking thing about the Akan king's inauguration is that this migrant group has organised a ceremony that is taken from another geographical context altogether. In a sense, it has travelled with them. Indeed, Extract 6.1 mentions that the Danish onlookers stopped and stared at what was an unusual cultural event for them. However, if you were in central Ghana, where the Akan people come from, such an event would seem very ordinary. The Akan are described as an ethnic group, which is a distinct community with its own traditions that is located within a larger national community. The presence of the Ghanaian Ambassador and other Ghanaian groups at the inauguration suggests that this is an important event for the nation's migrants. In terms of attachments to territory, it would seem that there is no tension between being Akan and also being Ghanaian.

The Ambassador's presence, and the fact that somebody recorded the event on a website, also indicates that this was a formal ceremony. People dressed up, and speeches and presentations were made. Ceremonies are about marking things that are important to a particular group. Think about your own experience. Weddings, graduations and birthday celebrations are all ceremonies which affirm that something socially important is taking place. While some ceremonies are very serious, many, including this inauguration, are also gatherings for singing, dancing, eating and generally having fun. Extract 6.1 mentions that such events are necessary for keeping traditions alive and passing them on to each generation. This suggests that migrants are keen to connect back to a particular place. Yet what marks these important attachments to community and place? Extract 6.1 mentions a number of cultural practices and objects – dances, food, language, libations, music, cloth and stools – which mark the Akan as distinct. These cultural phenomena symbolise what it means to belong to this group, and tie it to a particular place even when it is no longer physically located there.

The fact that this ceremony required lots of planning and did not just 'happen' means that decisions were made and organisation was required in order to mark and maintain identification with a particular territory. This indicates that when people move they do not necessarily shed their attachments to the place they leave, but may maintain them at a distance. This chapter addresses the question of how people can maintain attachment to somewhere they do not inhabit. In the brief example we have just looked at, specific objects or materials were deployed in mediating this affective attachment. In particular, Figure 6.1 shows a number of people wearing a cloth called kente (pronounced ken-teh), which is, as we will see later, the sacred cloth of the Akan people. Through this chapter we will analyse kente cloth as a means by which people are affectively attached to their community and place. Nevertheless, this cloth is only one type of object that connects people and we will look at other objects which contribute to these attachments in addressing how flows of objects can be used to make transnational communities.

The chapter is structured around the two key movements of gathering together and dispersing. First, we extend Chapter 5's analysis of how people develop attachments to place and what this contributes to the making of territories; second, we explore how such attachments are maintained and mediated when people move, that is, when community and place become dislocated. We begin, in Section 2, by picking up the discussion from Chapter 5 about how people develop affective ties to communities in place. Even though our focus is on transnational communities and attachments at a distance, this assumes that attachments to place exist in the first place. Therefore, our first task is to understand these place-based, community-making processes.

Whereas for the village of Camerton the settlings of the flows of things were seemingly arbitrary – some even blowing on the wind – we will be looking here at the purposive way in which people make territory. We do this through two related examples – the Asante people, who are the major group within the larger Akan 'nation', and Ghana at the time of its independence in the late 1950s. This involves powerful decisions about what defines those inside the territory, what makes them different from others and how these differences are made meaningful. In doing this, we also develop material from Chapter 4 about how territories are marked and identified symbolically. Yet rather than the making and marking of claims on an 'empty' space like Antarctica, we look at how political leaders of already established nation states have to work to make an affective link between the people and their land. These understandings of community are premised on relatively stable and settled populations that are in some sense 'contained' by their regions. Nonetheless, as we have seen, many people are mobile and defy such a straightforward association with a particular place. In Section 3, we look at how those place-based attachments are reworked from afar, and the role that objects play in maintaining these attachments.

Chapter aims

- To analyse how people on the move can maintain attachment to somewhere they do not inhabit.

- To appreciate how flows of objects can be used to evoke these attachments within dispersed transnational communities.

2   The making of territory

If people feel attached to somewhere they do not inhabit, we need to think first about how territorial attachments are made in situ. In other words, before we look at how people move yet retain attachments to these territories, we need to ask how people actively make territories and become attached to them. By proceeding in this way, we can consolidate Chapters 4 and 5 and build upon them in a number of ways.

In Chapter 5, Owain Jones showed how attachment to place could be generated through the settling of non-human things such as trees. Once the trees were settled in Camerton, people grew attached to them. There was a moment when these attachments were used to argue against external intervention by other people, be they people moving in or attempts to redevelop the area. This perceived threat to the community was based on the idea that it would upset the delicate balance between people and place. So, despite acknowledging that territories are formed out of many flows and are, therefore, inherently dynamic, this attempt to defend place in Camerton was based on a sense of coherence which fixed people to place once and for all. What this showed in Chapter 5, and which we develop here, is that the settling of flows and their formation into a recognisable territorial community is an active, and sometimes intentional, process. Decisions may be made, even if not always consciously, about what it means to be of that place and what cultural characteristics define 'the people'.

Prior to the discussion of affective territories in Chapter 5, in Chapter 4 Klaus Dodds examined how sovereign claims involve symbolically demarcating territory. He described how different scientific, military and diplomatic expeditions tried, often in vain, to mark parts of Antarctica with fences and flags. These were physical markers on the shifting ground which attempted to pinpoint, and thereby make real, the claims of different sovereign states. However, many of the things that mark territories are not so literal. They can, as the Danish king showed, be anything from cultural habits to physical objects, which the bearers invest with meaning and which are a kind of badge of allegiance. The Akan ceremony in Extract 6.1 evoked the distant territory of Ghana by using familiar objects as symbols of that territory.

This section develops the insights from previous chapters by seeing the making of territory as an intentional act and not as something that just happens. Nevertheless, this settling of multiple flows into relatively stable territories is still also contingent; things could have been otherwise. Any decision, as we shall see, to demarcate and bound is simply one permutation in a range of possibilities. Moreover, people do not simply sit in one community, but coexist in several, each bound by its own logic. In this chapter, we shall examine a case, raised by the example of the Danish king, in which people belong to a more localised territory as well as to a national one. While each territory is stabilised by its own logic and values – languages, customs and material cultures – the territories are not necessarily mutually exclusive even if tensions can exist between them.

2.1   Territorial attachment

Even though the Danish Akan king was physically present in one place, he was attached to a number of communities simultaneously, each of which had distinctive cultural and political markers. He was the figurehead for the Akan people, but he was also very much celebrating the shared Ghanaian-ness of the migrant community. Nonetheless, he lived and worked in Denmark and presumably spoke Danish in order to interact with customers.

In Chapter 1, Nigel Clark described territory as a set of relationships that binds physical forms, people and other living things together, 'a sense of territory as a kind of pattern or fabric in which many different things are bound together' (Section 2.2). This image of a weaving together of people and things is very powerful but, as Chapter 1 went on to show, such settling of multiple flows is not random; it often requires decisions to be made and work to be done. In Chapter 5, Owain Jones showed that attachment to a particular place is mediated through culture. This tells us that even affective attachment is not an automatic process, but that it is bound up in a whole set of social, economic and political actions and decisions. How are such decisions made and what effects do they have on the way in which territories are made and imagined? Let's return to the Akan people and their attachments to this region of Ghana as described in Section 1.

Although the Danish king was described as Akan, the Akan are, in fact, made up of various groups who share a common language called Twi (pronounced ch'wee). One of the most important of these groups is the Asante. Geographically, the Asante today occupy the southern-central part of modern Ghana. However, their origins date back over 300 years. The Asante territory of the eighteenth and nineteenth centuries has been described as an empire which was well organised and politically sophisticated with tributary relations with neighbouring areas. The empire was centred on the city of Kumasi where the overall ruler – the Asantehene – still has his palace. Figure 6.2 shows two Asantehenes who ruled 80 years apart. Thus, the Asante were culturally and politically distinct, and they had a regional base, but what affective attachments maintained this coherence? What held the weave of culture and place together?

The story of the Asante people starts in the late seventeenth century with an event where a Golden Stool (a kind of chair) was said to come down from heaven and come to rest on the knees of King Osei Tutu, the Asantehene. According to an account collected over 200 years later

Figure 6.2　　Asantehene – the king of the Asante people

by Captain Rattray, a British anthropologist and administrator, the presiding priest 'told Osei Tutu that this stool contained the sunsum (soul or spirit) of the Asante nation, and that their power, their health, their bravery, their welfare were all in this stool' (Rattray, 1923, p.289). The stool story ties the Asante people to a distinct place because Kumasi means 'under the kuma tree', which is where the King and his entourage were gathered when the stool descended. Figure 6.3 shows Kumasi at the centre of the Ashanti region. This creation story has powerful mythical qualities and is told to legitimise the settling of a people in a place. The right of the Asante to dwell in this place is bolstered by these miraculous events, their very magic setting them beyond explanation and, therefore, contestation. Many territorial attachments are based on similar stories of tradition. Patron saints, ancient kings and magical locations all figure highly in the collective memory of societies laying claim to particular places.

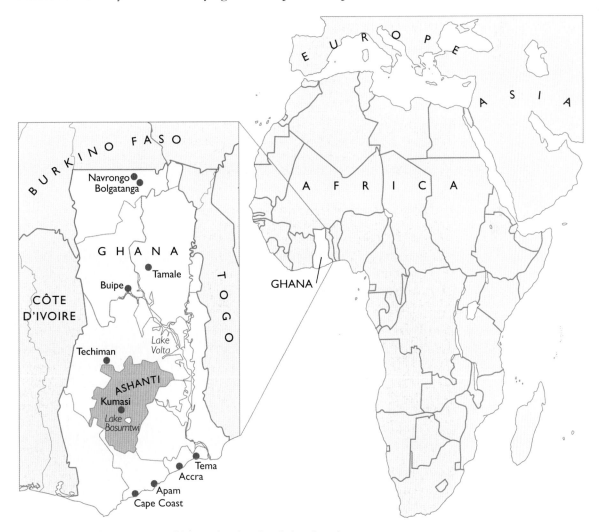

Figure 6.3   Contemporary Ghana showing the Ashanti region

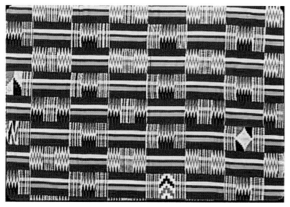

Figure 6.4   Kente cloth, *Oyokoman* design

Kente cloth is, as we have seen, a key part of Asante royal regalia. The role of kente in Asante identity and unity is captured in the Twi word *agyapadie*. According to Rattray, this comes from *adie-pe-agya*, meaning 'something sought after (by the ancestors) and then put aside (for safekeeping)', indicating that sacred objects such as kente cloth are a symbolic link between past and present and affirm the identity of the Asante people (1927, p.331). In this way, kente embodies the soul of the group and expresses continuity with the past. Again, this is a way of capturing collective identity and settling it as a tradition, which marks the Asante as distinctive and special. The cloth's colours are extremely vibrant and the many designs are complex, each giving a distinct moral message reflected in an accompanying proverb (see Figure 6.4).

The *Oyokoman* design in Figure 6.4 refers to the Oyoko clan, from which the Asantehene is drawn. It is one of the oldest and most complex patterns and is incorporated into other designs. The origins of the cloth are described by Ofori-Ansa:

> Oyokoman literally means 'There is fire (crisis) in the Oyoko nation'. The cloth was designed in honor of the Royal Oyoko family from which Asante Kings and Queenmothers [are] selected. It also documents the civil crisis that occurred within the Oyoko family after the death of Osei Tutu in 1731. Green and yellow represent the two branches of the Oyoko family and the red between them symbolizes 'fire' – the civil crisis. In the past, only members of the Royal Family could wear this design. The various versions of the design symbolize ROYALTY, NOBILITY, HONOR, NEED FOR UNITY IN DIVERSITY, RECONCILIATION AND A REMINDER OF THE ADVERSE EFFECTS OF INTERNAL CONFLICTS.
>
> (Ofori-Ansa, 1993, p.21, original capitalisation)

The colours of red, green and gold have been very important in pan-African movements and were to form the base colours for Ghana's flag.

We see that the Asante have an array of distinct cultural practices through which to mark and symbolise their territorial attachment. However, these cultural practices do not exist in isolation but are bound up in complex political structures. The Asante have a hierarchical leadership structure, political institutions designated for different functions and ceremonial rituals. Kente cloth embodies all of these important cultural and political functions, but what does it tell us about territory and attachment?

It is important to note one thing, which will be significant in this chapter: in principle, there are two kinds of territory at issue here. In the general sense in which we are using it, a coherent community is itself a territory – it is a dense weave of social relations. Nevertheless, in the case of the Asante, this community was also related to a particular place – an area of land – which is the more everyday meaning of the term 'territory'. The precise interplay between these two different kinds of territory will develop as the theme of this chapter. The Asante community was place-based and, indeed, that is how we very often implicitly imagine communities. In Section 3 we shall go on to explore what happens when these two kinds of attachment – of community and of place – are ruptured.

The distinctiveness of any community is based on shared values, practices, and the symbols by which the community identifies itself and recognises others as 'belonging'. This dynamic of sameness is evident in the Asante in such things as the shared stories about the group's origins that constitute its 'traditions'; the values given to the objects like kente cloth; and the language they share. It is a form of territorialisation. Moreover, part of recognising those with whom you share a sense of belonging may be in acknowledging that you are different from other communities. This is at the heart of Anthony Cohen's argument where he writes ' "Community" thus seems to imply simultaneously both similarity and difference. The word expresses a relational idea; the opposition of one community to others or to other social entities' (Cohen, 1985, p.12). According to this relational idea of communities, 'us' know themselves by celebrating their unique characteristics in relation to a number of 'thems'.

Activity 6.2

1   How are you the same or different? Do you feel a sense of attachment to a particular community?

2   Is this attachment founded on a sense of shared beliefs or practices, and are these different from those of another group? If so, how do you mark your distinctiveness?

The answers to these questions will be as varied as you, the readers, are. Rather than attempting an answer, we will look at Stuart Hall's view of Englishness. He sees Englishness as having developed through interactions with many others:

> To be English is to know yourself in relation to the French, and the hot-blooded Mediterraneans, and the passionate, traumatized Russian soul. You go round the entire globe: when you know what everybody else is, then you are what they are not.
>
> (Hall, 1991, pp.20–1)

Consequently, communities may be produced through the relational dynamic of sameness and difference, which is marked to a large extent by the cultural practices and objects that both define groups and differentiate them. Furthermore, this differentiation may be about drawing symbolic boundaries around communities. As Anthony Cohen goes on to observe:

> By definition, the boundary marks the beginning and end of a community. But why is such marking necessary? The simple answer is that the boundary encapsulates the identity of the community and, like the identity of the individual, is called into being by the exigencies of social interaction. Boundaries are marked because communities interact in some way or other with entities from which they are, or wish to be, distinguished.
>
> (Cohen, 1985, p.12)

Therefore, in cases where the making of territory is about settling flows and both binding and making boundaries between people, things and places, decisions have to be made about how to define inside and outside. For the people of Camerton in Chapter 5, the threat of encroachment galvanised them into defending place by arguing for what was unique within that place: the affective attachments between the people and the land. The trees not only made the landscape but also acted as visible symbols of the attachment between people and the landscape, making the people appear as the natural or rightful inhabitants. By this means, the people attempted to create a tangible sense of 'insider-ness' with which to repel – or at least dissuade – outsiders.

In the case of Camerton, we were dealing with local people engaged in defining their local place in a particular situation. In the case of the Asante, what is at issue is an ethnic grouping with its own internal social structures and political relations. The need here was to define a political territory in order to govern. There were, moreover, issues of power involved. It was the leaders of the Asante who both needed, and had the capacity to define, the Asante community.

For the nineteenth-century Asante leaders seeking to consolidate their empire, making boundaries was important in order to govern, because it helped stabilise the attachments among the people and between them and their region. In order for these polities to 'work', the people who are being governed need to have some belief in the authority and legitimacy of the political system. The first stage of this is to develop a sense – something deeply cultural and emotional – of attachment to an identifiable culture and place. As a result, political leaders can enhance their ability to rule by invoking 'traditions'. The creation stories of the Asante empire, the regalia and the rituals are ways of emphasising the Asante's cultural coherence and their 'right' to be located where they were and to have control over that region. The golden stool and the other cultural objects provide powerful symbols of unity, which Osei Tutu and subsequent Asantehenes used to explain and justify their incorporation – not always willingly – of neighbouring clans into a greater Asante empire. Tradition and attachment to culture and place conceal a centralised authority structure, which was necessary in order to bind and stabilise the territory.

Attachment to territory, whether that territory be community, place or nation state, can be a powerful political weapon. In addition, this interpretation of territory functions as a powerful political ideology aimed at securing authority; it also implies a rather narrow form of place attachment based on unchanging or primordial belonging. It is very easy to imagine that certain people or things are 'naturally' associated with particular places or communities. And from this it is also often further imagined that affection for such places is somehow 'natural'. Yet people and things are constantly on the move (we saw in Chapter 5 the arbitrariness of the definition of the 'native' British tree); this is even more so now in our globalised world. Moreover, again as we saw in Chapter 5, a love of place (topophilia), while very common, does not depend on rootedness and is not inevitable. The love of those trees in Camerton was 'made': by childhood memories, by exchanging stories, by cultural practices of a wider sort and of course by campaigning. With the Asante, the political leaders (actively and much more purposefully compared with Camerton residents) deployed a range of things, from magical stories to kente cloth, to weave a coherence among those they governed.

2.2   Imagining the nation

Today, however, the Asante are part of a different territory – that of the nation state of Ghana, which has been independent since 1957. The lines drawn by the colonial powers, in Ghana's case Britain, left new distinctions between inside and outside. New attachments have to be forged by the leaders of the newly independent state – both between what were once different communities and within a newly demarcated place.

Figure 6.5 shows one of the most popular kente designs. One of its names is *Fathia Fata Nkrumah* (Kojo Arthur and Rowe, 2003), which means 'Fathia deserves' or 'befits Nkrumah', and it commemorates the marriage between Ghana's first independence leader, Kwame Nkrumah, to his Egyptian bride, Fathia. In 1966, when Nkrumah was overthrown in a coup d'état, the cloth reverted to its original name of *Obaakofo mmu oman*, meaning 'one person does not rule the nation', which was a metaphorical comment on Nkrumah's increasingly centralised rule. Yet, after decades of further misrule, Nkrumah's legacy was re-evaluated and most people now again refer to the design as *Fathia Fata Nkrumah*.

Figure 6.5   Kente cloth, *Fathia Fata Nkrumah* design

In terms of territorial attachment, the *Fathia Fata Nkrumah* cloth highlights that not only can a symbolic object such as kente cloth produced by one community – the Asante – be used to represent a larger community – the Ghanaian state – but also that its meaning changes over time. It shows that the relationship between places, communities and symbolic objects is not static and embedded in some unchanging tradition, but can be a dynamic marker of association and attachment. In this section, we examine in more detail how these dynamic symbols change and how attachments can be formed to more than one territory.

Nation states are larger social entities than ethnic groups but they too involve bringing individuals and groups together (**Barnett et al., 2006**). Again, this bringing together may rely on a dynamic of sameness and difference. However, as people and groups become part of this larger territorial community they do not necessarily shed existing attachments. They may maintain multiple attachments which can pull against each other or reinforce one another.

A key difference between nation states and smaller and more intimate communities is size: face-to-face contact between members of the community becomes impossible. As a result, the symbolisation of community becomes even more important in giving a sense of shared destiny and identity. If you meet other people regularly, you get to know them and can develop a relationship. Over time, you can become embedded in this face-to-face community with all the benefits and drawbacks it brings. People know you and may feel a sense of responsibility for your well-being (though equally they may know your business too well!). As the scale of territory increases, such intimate interactions become less and less easy. This means that symbolic attachments become crucial in creating a sense of national community. Benedict Anderson has described this as a kind of 'imagining' (**Silverstone, 2006**). By this he meant that 'it is imagined because the members of even the smallest nation will never know most of their fellow members, meet them, or even hear them, yet in the minds of each lives the image of communion' (Anderson, 1983, p.15). This process of community making or 'communion' relies on certain cultural technologies and objects. Anderson focused on printing, newspapers and literacy as an important means by which people communicated and began to imagine themselves belonging to a national community. Nevertheless, other forms of cultural communication are available, one of which – as we have already begun to see – is cloth.

The problem of territorial attachment faces all nation states (**Barnett et al., 2006**). Nonetheless, it was more acute for countries like Ghana, which were created by colonial forces. In practice, people do not belong only to one community, even though some community membership, such as that of a state, has more serious implications for one's well-being than other memberships, such as that of a golf club. Consequently, Asante people did not stop being Asante once Ghana came into being in 1957 just as I, for example, see myself as 'from' Sheffield in South Yorkshire as well as being British. A problem for most political leaders is how to manage the relationship between the national community and its constituent communities; how to create a sense of attachment to the territory of the nation state among members of the communities that comprise it. Only if this attachment is formed will it be possible to govern more effectively, while neither eroding nor being captured by these more localised communal structures.

When nation states come into existence, they have to build this internal legitimacy by getting people to feel a sense of attachment. State-building is not an inevitable process; it requires struggles and decisions about what unites the population, where its borders are and, hence, who is included. For new nation states emerging from colonial rule, this necessary project was founded on territories handed down by the colonial authorities, and this created a unique set of problems for post-colonial leaders.

Defining the post-colonial as a historical phase

We are using post-colonial in a sequential historical sense here to mean after the colonial period: that is, after formal colonial rule ended and countries were given independence. Colonialism implied formal settlement in order to rule (this is in contrast to imperialism, which can involve external control without a physical presence – see Chapter 3). Post-colonialism was meant to imply that, in theory, these states were sovereign entities that could control their own political affairs free from outside interference. However, some scholars, activists and political leaders have argued that this sovereignty is very much in theory only because foreign powers continue to exert significant and deleterious influence over domestic economic and political matters. These critics prefer to think not in terms of the post-colonial but rather in terms of the neo-imperial because new forms of imperialism continue despite the ending of colonialism.

Prior to colonialism there were many groupings, like the Asante, existing in particular regions. The colonial legacy was to disrupt this pattern of attachments in a number of ways. First, the colonialists applied the model of their own nation states and drew sharp lines; the pre-colonial regions were not the clearly bounded spaces we see on maps today, though they still possessed their own coherence – what we have termed 'territory'. Second, when they drew the lines, the colonialists rarely accounted for the geography of the existing communities; they were more concerned with grabbing land and the resources they believed were contained within it (note the similarities with the early claims on Antarctica in Chapter 4). This process of drawing lines was often done for expedient reasons – where a river flowed; along a straight line linking two towns; by apportioning lands ceded by other colonial powers. The problem for those building a post-colonial national territory was that some groups were bundled together with those that they hardly mixed with, while others were split in two, forced to straddle a newly created international border.

Figure 6.6 shows Kwame Nkrumah in a full kente cloth in 1957 when Ghana formally shed colonial rule and entered the world system of sovereign nation states. Why in the birth of a multicultural nation state did its new leader opt for the symbol – kente cloth – of a particular ethnic community? The answer is that in many respects the 'idea' of the more localised community became the model for the national one. As Keller notes, 'we always come back to the local community as the foundation of more distant, complex, and abstract forms of collective association: attachment, as sense of belonging, and a deep, personalized, holistic focus' (2003, p.48). By wearing kente cloth, Nkrumah was projecting the idea that post-colonial Ghana had long-standing traditions based on complex and robust political institutions and, therefore, was fit to determine its own destiny free from the divisive paternalism of empire. This embodying of the nation in a cloth is

Figure 6.6   Kwame Nkrumah

something that Ghanaian leaders still do today, and most high-profile visitors to Ghana are given some kente or clothing incorporating the cloth as seen in Figure 6.7.

For Nkrumah, who was trying to fashion a modern nation state, this ethnicisation of national politics was a real problem. The Asante had both violently opposed British colonial rule and yet been incorporated into the structures of colonial governance. As such they had a powerful and rebellious relationship with the colonial state. Cocoa production and gold mining, two of Ghana's main export earners, also take place mainly in the Asante region. Nkrumah knew he could not ignore the Asante, but he had to contain their assertiveness. In addition to policies of regional devolution and the by passing of chiefs through new tiers of village governance, Nkrumah sought to project an image of a multi-ethnic state comprised of many local communities coexisting in harmony: that is, a state in which people had attachments to both their ethnic territory and their national one. This meant Nkrumah could not wear only kente as his symbol of the idealised political community at official engagements, such as his inauguration,

Figure 6.7   President Rawlings and President Clinton with their wives

but had to appeal to and placate other ethnic constituencies. There were potential contests here. As a result he also wore the 'traditional' clothes from other parts of Ghana, most usually the *Fugu*, a baggy smock from the north of the country.

Summary

- The construction of territories through attachment is an active process. The leaders of the Asante in pre-colonial days worked to construct territories of both community and place, and the two mapped onto each other.
- Colonialism disrupted the Asante settlement of territories. New attachments to new territories were constructed by post-colonial leaders.
- In both of the above cases, human-made objects were used as bearers and embodiments of these attachments.
- Territorial attachments are rarely exclusive. People may belong to a range of communities and places.

Symbols of nationhood

3   Transnational attachments

So far we have examined how people may become attached to particular places and how these attachments may be mediated by material culture. However, not only are places shaped by the many flows that cross-cut them (as we saw in Chapter 5), but also people can move out of place and settle elsewhere. As Brah (1996, p.182) observes, 'diasporic journeys are essentially about settling down, about putting roots "elsewhere"'. In this section, we examine in more depth the kinds of long-distance territorial attachments that we saw with the Danish Akan king in Section 1. Once such territories have been woven together, they may maintain a place in people's consciousness even after those people have moved away. In a sense, this is a reverse of the situation in Section 2. There, territories were formed from the settling, bounding and making meaningful of multiple flows. Yet when some of the people who have constituted that territorial coherence move away geographically, the territory does not fall apart, but the people may take some of that territorial integrity or identity with them. This makes for a tension between changes brought about by mobility on the one hand, and a feeling of being rooted or settled born out of attachment to territory on the other. Let's start by looking at Ghanaians on the move.

3.1   The African neo-diaspora: the routes of Ghanaian migration

In Section 1, we discovered that there was a big enough Akan community in Denmark for their own organisations and celebrations to exist in their 'new' country. The migrants we will be focusing on in this section have – like those in Denmark – left Ghana relatively recently. They have been termed the 'neo-diaspora' (Koser, 2003). Diaspora usually refers to the scattering, total or partial, of a particular group, especially where displacement is forced due to ethnic or racial persecution of one group by another. These 'victim' diasporas have included Jews, Armenians and African slaves. The term 'neo-diaspora' indicates that the recent dispersals were the result of grinding hardship, even if they were not all absolutely forced. Crucially, the routes taken by migrants are not random, but build on older trajectories (**Murji, 2006**). The temporal stability and spatial extension of the migrant communities range from cases where people disperse and are only weakly embedded in their new locations to full-blown transnational communities which are strongly embedded in at least two countries and the connections between them are long-lived. In the case of Ghana, we are looking at well-established transnational communities; nonetheless, just because they are 'embedded' in a number of places does not mean they are static and unchanging.

International movements out of West Africa began in the mid seventeenth century at the start of the Atlantic slave trade, which saw an estimated ten million Africans taken from their homes and transported to what was then called the 'New World'. This traumatic period in world history set in train the first large-scale movements of Africans beyond the continent (**Lambert, 2006**). Colonisation of West Africa was quite piecemeal but was relatively stabilised by the end of the nineteenth century. During the colonial period, a few Ghanaians came to the UK because it was regarded as the 'motherland'. These migrants were elites who came for education, often returning to Ghana to become leading political figures. After independence, members of the British Commonwealth were, for a while, given privileged entry rights to the UK. Again this was taken advantage of largely by an elite who came to be trained in administration.

From the mid to late 1960s, many African countries began to slide into economic hardship and political uncertainty. The resulting post-1970 'neo-diaspora' is different from either the slave diasporas or the elite movements associated with colonialism (Koser, 2003). The key differences are the motivations for moving, which affect the desire for return and the internal membership of diasporas, and increase the range of destination countries.

In Ghana, the 1970s was a period of economic mismanagement and worsening terms of trade, which saw the economy go into free fall. The state sought to avert a crisis by borrowing money to expand state employment, but this pushed the country into deep debt. As economic opportunities shrank and welfare support dwindled, many Ghanaians chose to emigrate to Western Europe, North America and to their neighbour Nigeria, which was going through a (short-lived) oil boom. In the 1980s, as a way out of this crisis, the Ghanaian Government turned to the World Bank and the International Monetary Fund for financial support. However, the money the country received was conditional on cutting state expenditure, and this saw the beleaguered health and education sectors cut back, further encouraging professionals to migrate (see Chapter 2 for further discussions on neo-liberalism).

While the data are sketchy, it seems clear that outwards migration from Ghana increased in the 1970s and 1980s, but declined in the 1990s as the economic situation improved. Over time, the make-up of the migrant population has changed. Earlier migrants were largely male, and educated elites, but now there is a roughly equal proportion of men and women as well as unskilled or semi-skilled migrants. One of the key patterns is the high number of professionals who leave Ghana. For example, in 2003 over 1220 nurses and 166 doctors left the country (Twum-Baah, 2004). Moreover, in the earlier periods most elites returned to work in Ghana for the good of the nation; now migrants are more likely to stay until retirement or to settle overseas on a permanent basis.

Another feature is that the colonial ties have weakened, with migration to a wider range of countries occurring. The choice of destination country has varied according to economic opportunities and immigration legislation, as well as according to whether English is widely spoken there. The key destinations now for the Ghanaian neo-diaspora are the UK, Germany, the Netherlands, Canada and the USA, and recently Australia and Japan. There are now sizeable Ghanaian communities in Miami, Chicago, New York, Amsterdam, Toronto and London. As we will see in the rest of this chapter, these are connected to one another in various ways, creating a 'multi-local' community which is also connected to Ghana.

Activity 6.3

Within these broad patterns of movement I want to pick up on one person called Esther. The preceding account of Ghanaian migration suggested that it was in keeping with the experiences of migrants from other African countries. The brief outline dealt in aggregate trends and was essentially a 'big picture' of the how and why of people's movements. There are many advantages to these broad-brush accounts, but they obscure the finer detail and people's individual experiences. As a result, they run the risk of missing an understanding of people as thinking and feeling human beings.

It is a real challenge to social scientists to make the connections between these large trends and individual life experiences. One way is to conduct more personalised research into what motivates people and how they perceive various situations. In 2003, this is what a colleague, Dr Leroi Henry, and I did among some Ghanaian migrants in Milton Keynes in the UK, where The Open University is headquartered. We wanted to find out about why people left Ghana, what routes they took in getting to Milton Keynes and what attachments they maintained with people in the multi-local networks just described, as well as with those 'at home' in Ghana. We began by contacting a Ghanaian Association in Milton Keynes and we interviewed its chairman. Through him, we were given other people to contact and from there developed our own local network of people willing to be interviewed. We undertook quite long interviews, lasting anywhere from forty minutes to over two hours. In total, we spoke to a dozen Ghanaians, and assembled detailed accounts of their journeys and attachments. Given that everybody we spoke to is unique, there is no 'typical' experience, but Esther's story flags up a number of issues regarding this way of being 'elsewhere' while maintaining active attachments to a far-flung territory. You will see how she started doing various jobs but has settled into running her own shop, shown in Figure 6.8, that sells mainly Ghanaian food items, which local Ghanaian migrants, among others, purchase. As you read about Esther's experiences, think about two issues:

1   How does her story reflect the wider migration trends I have described?

2   How do she and other migrants 'reconnect' with the places they no longer inhabit?

Leroi:	Why did you come to the UK? Do you have family here or friends?
Esther:	Yes my mum was here. My mum came to this country in the '60s. So, I came and stayed with her, but now she has gone back home for good. She doesn't like the cold weather. When you are growing old every Ghanaian will tell you as soon as they are getting to a certain age they do not want to stay here, they want to go home.
Leroi:	So when you came to Britain, you came to London?
Esther:	Yes I stayed in London for about a year. A year turned into two years and then we moved down here (Milton Keynes). When I became pregnant with Jessica I started working from home, dressmaking to bring some income in to support Isaac carrying on working in London Transport.
Leroi:	You said that you used to have a stall in the market, is that right?
Esther:	Oh yes, I have been everywhere in Milton Keynes you know. After the kids grew up, I decided it is better to work in the market to see if I can start my own business; I felt I want to be my own boss. I started selling the African batik and toiletries, things like that.
Leroi:	Do you sell dresses as well?

Esther:	Not the cloth, no if someone want me to make it I do it, but I sell the materials. It's the English wax but I do order the batik from Ghana already made and then I sell them as well.
Leroi:	So, when did you decide to open a shop?
Esther:	That was after when I was working with Milton Keynes hospital and as much as I loved the nursing job there is a lot of bitchiness going on within the nursing community. Excuse me to say this, but if you are black they treat you like you are a nobody, even though you work with all your heart. They will make your life difficult and it got to a point that I could not take it.
	So I decided I have to go into business again because there is now a lot of black people have moved down to the area. I know most of them used to travel to London to buy their food. I decide to go to London and buy the food and, you know, sell it. I started from home by telling people 'Oh today I am going to the fish market do you want some? Oh yeah. OK. Come on bring some money and I will buy it for you, but you have to pick it up now, as soon as I arrive'. That is how I started and I realised that there was a demand for it. So I thought well, there is a demand here, so let me start something. I started and it got so good, it's picking up, it's really great.
Leroi:	And who are your customers?
Esther:	It's mixed that is why I have named it multi-cultural, because I have English people coming in, I have got the West Indians coming, I've got the Somalis coming, you know. I get the Africans, the Ghanaians coming, the Nigerians.
Leroi:	And what sort of people use the takeaway?
Esther:	They are English people and the Africans. The Ghanaians, they started tasting it and they love it, especially the fried fish.
Leroi:	Is it families that come in for the food?
Esther:	Yes, it's families but mainly the bachelors, the bachelors they don't like cooking. You know, most Ghanaian men can't cook. Most of them cannot cook, because that's the culture, you know and man is not supposed to be going in the kitchen so when they travel its difficult for them so that is where I come in.
Leroi:	Do most Ghanaian people in Milton Keynes support family in Ghana?

Esther: Yes. I would like to come back so we decide to build a house. It's in a very quiet area. They call us foreigners, because we've been abroad. That place is purposely for those who are coming from America and things like that.

Leroi: And are you a member of the local Ghanaian association?

Esther: Oh yes, from day one. It's a very good idea because we help each other, look after each other's interests if need be.

Leroi: And which type of people in the Milton Keynes community join the association?

Esther: So far as you are a Ghanaian you know it doesn't matter whether you come from the North or you are a Ga or Asante. There is no segregation in it, every Ghanaian can join, which is good.

Leroi: Is it different from the situation in London?

Esther: Yeah, the clans. The London one is always like the Ga Association, the Ewe Association, but not in Milton Keynes it doesn't matter whether you are Asante, we are all one. I love it that way.

(Henry, 2003)

Figure 6.8   Esther's shop in Milton Keynes

The broad-brush account of Ghanaian migrants given above showed that people move for different reasons and that their routes are numerous. Esther followed her mother to England, and Esther and her husband's move to Milton Keynes was encouraged by the local authority, which was seeking to relocate families from the crowded parts of London to this purpose-built new town. Both Esther and her husband have taken a range of jobs, including periods in the public sector. Esther talked movingly about the racism she faced in the health service: a case where relational community boundaries were largely negative and impermeable. Her mother has returned to Ghana, and Esther has built a house in Ghana for herself and her mother, and also plans to return when she gets older. So, the attachments to 'home' that Esther maintains are strong, even though those left behind in Ghana are a little unsure about the migrants.

The means of reconnecting with the place in which Esther no longer lives are numerous. First, there are material goods which are exchanged, such as cloth, clothing and food. These more everyday items, their meaning and use tell us quite a different story of attachment to place than the power-filled and ceremonial use of objects discussed in Section 2. Esther has done very well from importing foodstuffs, cloth and other goods that her Ghanaian acquaintances demanded. Second, there are more formal connections, such as the Ghanaian association Esther mentions towards the end of the dialogue. These are organisations that engage in the types of public events we saw in Denmark, but which also offer more general social support. Esther goes on to discuss the relationship between the 'national' community and more particular ethnic communities, suggesting that people can belong to both. She spoke quite warmly of how people in Milton Keynes interacted on the basis of being Ghanaian as opposed to the more ethnic and clan-based groups in London, only 80 km down the motorway. This suggests that these community identities, these territorialisations, which are carried from 'home', are fluid; they change depending on the nature of the place in which people currently live. In other words, there is a dynamic reworking of the relationship between place and attachment within transnational communities.

3.2   Embedded cosmopolitanism and multiple attachments

Esther's story gives a picture of a diffuse network spread across the globe, but also still attached to people and places in Ghana. This is a community that has a sense of shared values but is not bound in the way that we saw in the case of the nation state. The Ghanaian transnational community is multi-local in that migrants have settled in a number of new places, but have some sense of attachment to one another and to their Ghanaian home. Within this multi-local community, objects and organisations help to bring people together and to maintain these attachments to far-off places.

Transnational communities unsettle the neat attachments between a people or community and 'their' place, whether that is an ethnic region or a nation state. Their sense of community comes from shared origins in a place, however distant or imagined, but they are spread across the world in a kind of network. To negotiate their globalised world, they form multiple attachments – to those places where they currently live, and to family, friends and compatriots both in the original home and in other places in the diaspora. Yet these attachments are not inevitable or essential. Just because people are in some senses 'the same' does not mean a sense of community automatically arises. Rather, as we have seen, territorial attachments have to be actively made and maintained, and this is where objects function so powerfully. We can characterise this negotiation of the global and local as 'embedded cosmopolitanism' (Erskine, 2000).

Activity 6.4

What is cosmopolitanism? Take a few minutes to note down what you think 'cosmopolitan' means.

You may have jotted down words like 'well-travelled' and 'multicultural', or more subjective terms such as 'colourful' and 'sophisticated'. The term cosmopolitan often evokes a place that is 'worldly' in the sense that there is a mixing of different cultures. It is a territory where multiple flows of people, ideas and goods from very different sources come together to create a vibrant lifestyle. A cosmopolitan person is one who enjoys this lifestyle and is adept at noticing, and negotiating between, all these different cultures. In everyday thinking, cosmopolitans are often assumed to be well-educated and mobile. Cosmopolitanism can suggest that people are not stuck in one place and that national identification may become less important as people and cultures mix. Taken to its logical extreme, all cultures become so blurred and mixed together that we have one kaleidoscopic 'world culture', which makes government oriented around discrete national communities increasingly meaningless. The territorialisations of both place and culture are lost.

Certainly, the migrants we have met so far, like Esther, are mobile and they mix with their 'host' culture and with those of other migrants. Recall how Esther's shop, for example, was frequented by Somalians, Nigerians and British people. There is a borrowing and blending of cultures, but there is also a sense of quite specific attachment to distinct communities, whether the migrants are Akans or Ghanaians. It is this sense of being global, mobile and culturally open, yet still attached to particular communities, that makes up embedded cosmopolitanism.

Embedded cosmopolitanism

> offers an alternative to a strictly state-centric or spatially bounded interpretation of the morally constitutive community by combining an account of the moral agent as embedded in particular ties and loyalties with a powerful critique of the communitarian penchant for invoking associations with borders, set territories and given memberships.
>
> (Erskine, 2000, p.575)

This quotation is saying that there is, in embedded cosmopolitanism, an alternative to the simple mapping of communities on to single places, and this alternative includes a sense of attachment to community and place but recognises that these are neither exclusive nor fixed. It is one way of linking local and global in the context of global flows without becoming entirely free-floating.

We saw how Esther had moved a number of times and maintained attachments – ties and loyalties – to complex webs of family and country folk. There is, then, a dynamic process in which identity is not fixed but 'constantly (re)worked, not in a freewheeling manner but through simultaneous embeddedness in more than one society' (Yeoh et al., 2003, p.213). As people move to new places, they do not drop or forget past ties but rework them in the context of the new places they find themselves in. This process is fluid, but it is not 'freewheeling' and the ways these attachments are reworked is through people, objects and organisations.

Defining the post-colonial as a critical attitude

The first defining box on post-colonialism discussed it as a historical moment, but added that some see the effects of colonialism as lingering in many ways. Such thinking informs post-colonialism as a critical attitude, which examines the long-term impacts of colonial contact on both the coloniser and the colonised. One ongoing impact of colonialism is of course on migrations, where cultural contact continues as people from former colonies migrate to the former colonial 'motherland'. These movements of people also involve flows of ideas, goods and cultural practices. Note, too, how this clearly emphasises that while the nation state may be *politically* bounded, in many other ways it is open.

Embedded cosmopolitanism is, then, one approach to an alternative territorialisation in response to the flows of globalisation. It is not, however, without its problems. For instance, the mixing of communities is not always positive or benign; it can be difficult. We saw Esther's changing relationship to the ethnic groups in London and how she found Milton Keynes a refreshing release from the 'clans' in London. She also talked about the racism she experienced in the UK, and how it forced her out of nursing. We mentioned in Section 2 that community can imply closure. In this case, the migrant was made to feel uncomfortable and 'outside' on the basis of skin colour. Hostility by one group towards another can make the persecuted community in turn 'close ranks' as a form of protection. Indeed, attachment to somewhere else becomes more important to people in precarious 'out of place' situations, and things like food and clothing are one way of reconnecting with these distant, but secure and familiar places.

Embedded cosmopolitanism, then, is a creative response to the tension between mobility and place attachment: a way of recombining territory and flow. Nonetheless, it is not possible to generalise as to whether or not this way of negotiating the globalised world is empowering. Racism and various forms of hostility to outsiders can add an important dynamic to community formation and attachment. This has been called 'double consciousness', a term developed by the African American intellectual W.E.B. Du Bois (1903) at the turn of the twentieth century. By this, Du Bois meant that Africans displaced by slavery share an 'origin' of being from Africa and, more importantly, of having black skin. They are also different from the powerfully placed white people in the areas in which they currently live, often experiencing outright hostility. Hence, they have a double consciousness of being in the West, but never really feeling part of it. Even though Du Bois was writing around 100 years ago, his idea of a 'double' attachment is useful in examining the senses of attachment that recent migrants feel. Recall Esther's discussion of her obligations to those in Ghana, of still feeling part of UK society and at the same time of experiencing racism. Esther's 'bi-nationalism' – belonging to both 'here' and 'there' simultaneously – suggests a complex geography of attachment.

We can now return to our second major aim for this chapter – within transnational communities what role do objects play in constituting and mediating these attachments? In Esther's case, we saw how the *exchange* of objects – food, clothes, etc. – functioned as a reconnecting link. She also showed how *organisations* brought people together and worked to attach people out of place to a distant place. The rest of the chapter considers how objects flow through these two, interrelated dynamics of exchange and organisation.

3.3 Attachments through exchange

In Section 3.1, we saw how Esther opened a small shop in Milton Keynes after she realised that demand existed for foodstuffs and cloth. This is common among migrants, and you may have seen or you may shop in, or be part of, such ventures. These shops often become the local hubs for a whole range of services that links migrants to others in the diaspora as well as providing an affective attachment to 'home'. Here is a description of the Gold Coast Marketing Store in Atlanta, USA (the Gold Coast was the colonial name for Ghana):

> This store is oriented towards immigrants from Africa and the Caribbean. Originally, the Gold Coast Marketing Store sold Afro-Caribbean foodstuffs. Later, its owners began to promote African tourism and started offering their customers electronic message services ... The Gold Coast Marketing Store has become an information center where flyers announcing births, deaths, marriages, and the latest news from Ghana are exchanged by Ghanaians ... The owners have managed to eliminate brokers by going to Africa and buying these items directly.
>
> (Arthur, 2000, pp.105–6)

In the quotation, Arthur (2000) describes how the trading of imported goods serves quite specific national and regional markets. These flows of objects carry affective attachments to home and the familiar. Out of the exchange of goods, the Gold Coast Marketing Store grew into providing a range of services through which migrants actively connect with those living a long way away. Some of these connections may be financial transfers, but what is striking here is the importance of social news and contacts around births, deaths and marriages. It is through these everyday interactions that a sense of community emerges.

One important commodity that flows through these communities is cloth. As we have seen, kente was originally a ceremonial cloth denoting status and power, and when away from Ghana migrant

Ghanaians maintain its ceremonial value. Moreover, in their changed circumstances the migrants rework kente's ritual importance. For example, strips of kente cloth with the word 'usher' woven into them are worn by male and female ushers in a largely Ghanaian Baptist church in north London. Or again, on arrival at the airport in Ghana for the first time, second generation Ghanaians are handed a kente strip woven with the word *Akwaaba* ('Twi for 'welcome'). The symbolic use of kente has widened, but it is still used at important social events which link migrants with others or with those at home.

With the development of technology, kente is now mass-produced, making it much cheaper and more widely available. The designs have also been used in and on a wide range of objects. As Ross observes:

> Over the past forty years (kente) cloth has been transformed into hats, ties, bags, shoes, and many other accessories, including jewellery, worn and used on both sides of the Atlantic. Individual kente strips have found a permanent home in the United States and are especially popular when worn as a 'stole' or applied to academic and liturgical robes. Kente patterns have also developed a life of their own and have been appropriated as surface designs for everything from Band-Aids and balloons to greeting cards and book covers. Appearing in contexts both sacred and profane, kente has come to evoke and to celebrate a shared cultural heritage, bridging two continents.
>
> (Ross, 1998, p.19)

Ross is describing the move away from a strictly royal and region-based use of kente. Having once symbolised Akan authority, as discussed in Section 2.1, its first transformation as we have seen was to embody the Ghanaian nation state. Now kente symbolises many communities and places, and its association with authority has waned. The tight attachment between place, community and symbolism has been loosened and multiplied. This change is seen by some, seeking to re-establish the tight attachments between territory and symbol, as a challenge. For example, Mr Prempeh, Executive President of a non-governmental organisation (NGO), was reported in 2004 as seeking to discourage the use of kente cloth as a decorative material:

> The rate at which some Ghanaians are using kente as table spreads and for decoration of coffins and in some cases corpses is a great source of worry ... It can lead to the erosion of confidence in the kente as a unique cloth that portrays the culture of Ghanaians ... It is not only socially wrong but also morally unacceptable for anyone

to use the cherished kente cloth for decorative purposes instead of appearing in it at public functions, festivals and national ceremonies.

(www.ghana.co.uk/news/content.asp?articleID=7071)

Here, reinstating the sacred and ritualistic use of kente is seen as a means of reversing the dissolution of an essential 'Ghanaian-ness'. This suggests an anxiety about the ways in which globalisation – in the sense of a world of flows – has challenged the settled connections not only between people and places, but also between a people and its symbolic objects.

3.4   Attachments through organisation

When you were introduced to Esther in Section 3.1, we found that both the exchange of goods and the formation of associations mediated her attachments to places left behind. As Arthur (2000) observes of African migrants in the USA:

> Immigrants have always established such associations in host countries *to forge closer ties among themselves, with the members of the host society, and with their places of birth.* The African immigrant associations are the building blocks for the creation of African cultural communities in the United States.

(Arthur, 2000, p.71, emphasis added)

In this section, we look in more detail at these collective forms of attachment and the role that different objects play.

3.4.1 Virtual attachments: meeting in cyberspace

The question of symbolic attachment to distant places is similar, in many ways, to that in Anderson's (1983) 'imagined communities' that we discussed in Section 2.2 because, even more than in any nation state, transnational communities exist in dispersed spaces where people cannot know one another intimately. The result is that people tend to rely on symbolic ties to promote a sense of community since they can rarely interact face-to-face with other members.

Nevertheless, these dispersed transnational networks can 'meet' and stay attached to home and others in the diaspora through electronic communication. The double attachments, to a place away from home and to home itself, can be reconciled by connecting through 'virtual' means (**Silverstone, 2006**) like international magazines and websites. For Ghanaians there are a number of international websites. Ghanaweb International (www.ghanaweb.com) is a news and discussion website, which links to Ghanaian communities across the globe. It carries political news from Ghana as well as news from the diaspora, and community announcements. There are also chat rooms where debate ranges from the politics of dual citizenship to the role of chiefs in the diaspora. As you track through some of these links on the website, you arrive at more 'local' hubs in cities such as Miami, London or Sydney. One small 'local' hub is the Association of Ghanaians in Milton Keynes, to which Esther belongs. Its website (www.agmk.co.uk) has links to other Ghanaian associations around the world and also records events taking place in Milton Keynes, such as the Ambassador's visit or a family barbecue.

The Ghana National Council of Metropolitan Chicago has a larger website. Here is an extract from its home page:

> The bedrock of America is its diversity. It has diverse cultures and traditions. Within this diversity are the Ghanaian cultures and traditions which are diverse.

> There is the need to create an organization that would unite these different cultures and traditions that make up the Ghanaian community.

> Welcome to the Ghana National Council of Metropolitan Chicago!!

> The main objective of our organization is to create unity within the Ghanaian community in Metropolitan Chicago, to help develop the various communities around us and to foster relationship with all cultures within the Chicago Metropolitan area and the world at large for that matter through various activities.

> (Ghana National Council of Metropolitan Chicago, 2005)

The Ghana National Council of Metropolitan Chicago website affirms the opportunities that the USA offers, and this resonates with the multiculturalism of Ghana that Nkrumah, among others, was so keen to promote. There is an embedded cosmopolitanism at work here: the Ghana National Council is showing that both integration into the USA and maintaining a sense of one's own Ghanaian cultural identity are important. Within the Council are twelve affiliate organisations in the Chicago region. One of these is the Asanteman Association, meaning people from Asante. When you click onto its web link (ghananationalcouncil.org/asanteman.htm), you are given a mini-history which talks of chiefs, tradition and kente. As in the Danish event with which we started in Section 1, the mini-history works as a reaffirmation of cultural origins being important for people who are away from home and where subsequent generations may lose a sense of identity and attachment. In fact, here there is more than a doubling of consciousness, rather there are multiple attachments – to the place where you live, to fellow nationals in that place and around the world, and to the ethnic group and home country. These different attachments are not switched on and off, but coexist in a complex sense of being part of a transnational community.

3.4.2 Ceremonial attachments: spectacles and events

Virtual attachments are important and made much easier with the rapid developments in technology. However, they serve quite a selective community in so far as they rely on people having access to the technology and being competent and confident in using it. My own family is spread across the globe. My father is from India and we have relatives there and some in Canada and the USA. On my mother's side, family members have emigrated to Spain and Canada. We do not email regularly, but we email each other photographs of weddings, new babies, etc. At family gatherings, my brother and I would chat about the latest news from California or Bombay and my mother became frustrated that she was not part of 'the loop'. Then we gave her an old computer so that she could be part of this family communicative community. Yet, despite access to the technology, my mother still feels uncertain about using it as a means of staying in touch. Thus, these virtual communities are only open to those with access who are comfortable with the technology. In a poor country like Ghana, this means that relatively few people can be part of the virtual community.

Connection flows

Moreover, in Section 1, the inauguration of the Danish Akan king showed that community also needs to be formed through face-to-face interaction. Transnational communities do not arise, as if by nature, simply because people have some ethnic or national cultural characteristics that supposedly unite them. Rather, community has to be worked at. Between late July and mid August 2004, overseas Ghanaians organised a series of transatlantic social events. Starting with Ghanafest 2004 in Chicago on 31 July, it went to New York on 7 August for the 'Mother of all Picnics', before hitting London on 14 August for the 'Meet Me There' party. As the New York organisers stated:

> It is so much fun to travel and show some love and support to our brothers and sisters in other cities. It brings all of us closer and exhibiting our culture for the rest of the world to see.
>
> (GhanaHomePage, 2004a)

The aim of the social events was to celebrate being Ghanaian and to project a positive, and potentially lucrative, image of Ghanaian culture to a global audience. One of the key sponsors was Ghanaweb International, the internet site discussed in Section 3.4.1. The Chicago event was opened by a procession of chiefs, as shown in Figure 6.9, and a delegation from Ghana. There were stalls from ethnic community organisations and Ghanaian businesses, and presentation ceremonies to honour recently deceased association members and to reward outstanding achievements among the Ghanaian diasporic community.

Figure 6.9   The Chicago Ghanafest 2004

All of the three events in Chicago, New York and London were about gathering face-to-face for fun. People made new connections and reaffirmed old ones. There were dancing and football competitions, fashion shows and food stalls. People also did business, and the reports of the events were studded with the names of business sponsors as well as with the political connections of the VIPs.

Amid all this noise and action were various displays of kente cloth. All the website reports mention stalls selling cloth, and fashion shows saw parades of women in the latest clothes designs:

Chicago

Festival goers were treated to seemingly endless caches of African fabrics like kente cloth custom-made into sashes, hats, head-wraps, shawls and coats for men and women.

(GhanaHomePage, 2004b)

New York

This event was well packed and it was an event where many Ghanaians show their latest Ghanaian fashion wear; hats, bandanas, T. Shirts, Fugus, and lot more to catch the eye.

(GhanaHomePage, 2004a)

London

Many Ghanaian entrepreneurs bought stands to exhibit the Ghanaian culture in clothing and art.

(GhanaHomePage, 2004c)

These descriptions show how the symbol of Akan community and national belonging, that is, kente, becomes reworked in the new situations that people find themselves in. During the parade of chiefs that opened the Chicago event, kente was used in its original ceremonial manner; it conveyed the gravity and importance of these leaders and affirmed their status as key players in the diasporic community. Yet the use of kente in things such as bandannas shows other influences, such as hip-hop culture. Such uses symbolise an attachment to Ghana but one that is in relation to the other communities that these migrants encounter. The territory of community is itself becoming more open and mixed.

wide application of kente not altogether approved however

3.4.3 Material attachments: developing home

These different examples of kente's use show how the flow of cultural objects can mediate attachment to a place where one no longer lives. Food, cloth and newspapers, to name but a few, can also do this. We have also seen that organisations and communal events are important for maintaining these attachments, and that cultural objects play important roles in ceremonies and fashions at these events. The very idea of a diasporic community suggests that people left their home country for reasons of economic or political hardship and, for this reason, many are still very much involved in events back home. This can be at the family level through actions like sending money or building a house. For example, in the case of Esther discussed earlier, Esther recently set up a money transfer agency in her shop, which is a way of sending money outside of the banking system. These are very concrete attachments that people have to places in which they no longer live.

This flow of capital echoes Chapter 2 where we saw how money – which is often thought of as endlessly flowing – nonetheless creates territories. Indeed, Chapter 2 showed that money requires these territories for its continued circulation. In sending flows of money back to people in distant territories, the migrants, who are themselves a flow of sorts, seek to secure the ongoing survival of these territories. Consequently, there is a circularity between the constitution of territory and of flow. For economic or political reasons, migrants leave a territory they are attached to, but they may maintain symbolic and material attachments to that territory. This, in turn, may help to maintain the very existence of that territory. Therefore, rather than undermining territories, migrants can help them to keep going.

Some of the financial flows back home to Ghana are remittances to family members. Such flows are huge, outstripping foreign direct investment for every year of the 1990s (Akyeampong, 2000). Recent Bank of Ghana data showed that between 2000 and 2002 the volume of remittances passing though it rose from $400 million to $1.3 billion (Addison, 2004). Given that this is only one bank and that these statistics ignore money wired to individuals, and gifts, the total figure will be much larger than this.

Furthermore, not all of these material flows take place within the family. Some can be for the territory itself rather than for particular individuals within it. Back at the Chicago Ghanafest in 2004, the former Consul General of Ghana in Toronto appealed to Ghanaians in the diaspora 'to do their part in national development efforts' (GhanaHomePage, 2004b). Within transnational communities, the relatively affluent migrants support specific development projects in their 'home' areas. These projects range from supplying hospitals with equipment, through sending money to the ancestral home town's development committee, and even to financing vehicles for the fire service. Such flows of support are important not only to affirm attachment to 'home', but also to secure the longer-term well-being of that territory.

One vehicle for this financial flow is the organisations of school alumni, made up of ex-students who mobilise to 'repay' the school for their start in life:

Otumfuo Education Fund, UK to assist in rehabilitation of library

Nana Otuo Acheampong, Chairman of the UK branch of the Otumfuo Education Fund, ... delivered a goodwill message from members of the UK branch of the Education Fund, and old Students of Dwamena Akenten Secondary School (DASS), resident in the UK, at the 40th Anniversary of the school. Nana Acheampong, who is also an old boy of DASS, and publisher of the Ghana Review Magazine, said the UK branch last year committed 100 million cedis into rehabilitating some of the infrastructure of the library.

...

Nana Acheampong had earlier made a personal pledge of 11 million cedis in support of development of the school.

(GhanaHomePage, 2004d)

Bonwire supports EU project

Bonwire citizens resident in Holland have contributed 2,200 euros (¢20million) towards a ¢2.4billion school complex funded by the European Union for the community.

...

The contribution is in response to an appeal by the Queenmother, Nana Nyarko Fremponaa to citizens resident abroad to help the community.

(GhanaHomePage, 2004e)

These appeals from the 'home' community and the support from overseas migrant networks illustrated in the above quotations show how material attachments are actively made.

Summary

- International migration destabilises the neat mapping of the territories of community and place onto each other.
- The mobility of international migration involves settling 'elsewhere', but it does not necessarily mean that pre-existing attachments are forgotten. Rather, they may be reworked in the new circumstances.
- Human-made objects – or artefacts – are one powerful medium through which pre-existing attachments are reworked.
- The meaning of objects – like one's membership of community – is not fixed but continually reinterpreted and contested.
- Embedded cosmopolitanism is one possible way of remixing territories and flows in response to the challenges of globalisation.

4   Conclusion

The legacy of colonialism and the international migrations that are part and parcel of the current form of globalisation pose challenges to what was once assumed to be a predetermined or essential association between community and place. Attachments to both community and place have been challenged, as has the relation between them; new attachments have had to be forged. The history examined in this chapter allowed us to explore who makes these territories of attachment, and how. These actors were not the 'big powers' of global institutions or dominant nation states; we looked at territory making by Asante leaders, by leaders of newly decolonised states and by migrants themselves.

In the case of our central focus – the migrants themselves – we have explored one kind of response to the challenge of globalisation: embedded cosmopolitanism. In embedded cosmopolitanism, people, although on the move (flowing between places), nonetheless maintain attachments to community and place but in new and less rigid forms.

We began by looking at how territory involves the active and intentional settling of flows and the symbolic marking of these spaces. This highlighted the fact that attachments to territories do not simply exist as if predestined, but they have to be worked at by humans. Ceremonies and stories are some of the ways in which this tying together of people and places occurs. And, in all of this, non-human objects may be important symbols, giving people a sense of belonging and also of difference from others. Yet the meaning of these symbols is not made once and for all; it is constantly reinterpreted.

The attachments of people to territory are even more important when people move en masse, and so we examined how flows of objects can be used in the making of transnational communities. The objects can serve to create attachments to places in which people no longer live. These objects can give a sense of continuity and security in a world of uncertainty and, sometimes, hostility. In this particular history, objects were exchanged, either commercially or otherwise, and served as symbolic markers in ritual, ceremonial and everyday gatherings. The networked migrant communities are attached to other communities and to their original homes; they share something that gives them meaning and support in their new places of residence. Flows of money and support to distant lands also help to maintain these same lands. The flow of people away and the return flows they initiate can be vital in securing the well-being of the people and places left behind. For now, such arrangements are the way in which these migrants are negotiating the global and the local, and mediating between territories and flows.

References

Addison, E.K.Y. (2004) *The Macroeconomic Impact of Remittances*, presentation by the Director of Research, Bank of Ghana, at the conference on migration and development, Accra, September 2004, available at http://www.bog.gov.gh/ (accessed 8 November 2005).

Akyeampong, E. (2000) 'Africans in the diaspora: the diaspora and Africa', *African Affairs*, vol.99, pp.183–215.

Anderson, B. (1983) *Imagined Communities: Reflections on the Origins and Spread of Nationalism*, London, Verso.

Arthur, J. (2000) *Invisible Sojourners: African Immigrant Diaspora in the United States*, Westport, CT, Praeger.

Barnett, C., Robinson, J. and Rose, G. (eds) (2006) *A Demanding World*, Milton Keynes, The Open University.

Brah, A. (1996) *Cartographies of Diaspora: Contesting Identities*, London, Routledge.

Cohen, A. (1985) *The Symbolic Construction of Community*, London, Routledge.

Crawfurd, J. (2004) 'The Akan king in Denmark', http://crawfurd.dk/africa/akanfestival04.htm (accessed 11 October 2005).

Du Bois, W.E.B. (1903) *The Souls of Black Folk: Essays and Sketches*, Chicago, A.C. McClurg.

Erskine, T. (2000) 'Embedded cosmopolitanism and the case of war: restraint, discrimination and overlapping communities', *Global Society*, vol.14, no.4, pp.569–90.

Ghana National Council of Metropolitan Chicago (2005) 'Ghana National Council of Metropolitan Chicago', http://www.ghananationalcouncil.org/index.htm (accessed 11 October 2005).

GhanaHomePage (2004a) 'New York picnic: big crowd, great fun', http://www.ghanaweb.com/GhanaHomePage/diaspora/artikel.php?ID=63655 (accessed 11 October 2005).

GhanaHomePage (2004b) 'GhanaFest2004 – great display of Ghanaian culture', www.ghanaweb.com/GhanaHomePage/diaspora/artikel.php?ID=63327 (accessed 11 October 2005).

GhanaHomePage (2004c) 'Over 3000 at 1st UK "Meet me there"', www.ghanaweb.com/GhanaHomePage/AKOTO/Meetmethere04.pdf (accessed 11 October 2005).

GhanaHomePage (2004d) 'Otumfuo Education Fund, UK to assist in rehabilitation of library', www.ghanaweb.com/GhanaHomePage/diaspora/artikel.php?ID=68936 (accessed 11 October 2005).

GhanaHomePage (2004e) 'Bonwire supports EU projects', www.ghanaweb.com/GhanaHomePage/diaspora/artikel.php?ID=34001 (accessed 11 October 2005).

Hall, S. (1991) 'The local and the global: globalization and ethnicity' in King, A. (ed.) *Culture, Globalization and the World System*, London, Macmillan, pp.19–39.

Henry, L. (2003) Interview with Esther Fiscian by Dr Leroi Henry, 27 February 2003, as part of a project 'Transnational Networks in African Development', funded by The Open University Research Development Fund.

Keller, S. (2003) *Community: Pursuing the Dream, Living the Reality*, Princeton, NJ, Princeton University Press.

Kojo Arthur, G.F. and Rowe, R. (2003) 'Akan kente cloths and motifs', http://www.marshall.edu/akanart/kentecloth_samples.html (accessed 11 October 2005).

Koser, K. (2003) 'New African diasporas: an introduction' in Koser, K. (ed.) *New African Diasporas*, New York, Routledge, pp.1–16.

Lambert, D. (2006) 'Making the past present: historical wrongs and demands for reparation' in Barnett, C., Robinson, J. and Rose, G. (eds) *A Demanding World*, Milton Keynes, The Open University.

Murji, K. (2006) 'A place in the world: geographies of belonging' in Barnett, C., Robinson, J. and Rose, G. (eds) *A Demanding World*, Milton Keynes, The Open University.

Ofori-Ansa, K. (1993) *Kente is More than a Cloth*, Maryland, MD, Sankofa Publications.

Rattray, R. (1923) *Asante*, Oxford, Clarendon Press.

Rattray, R. (1927) *Religion and Art in Asante*, Oxford, Clarendon Press.

Ross, D. (1998) *Wrapped in Pride: Ghanaian Kente and African Identity*, UCLA Fowler Museum of Cultural History Textile Series, no.2, Los Angeles, CA, UCLA.

Silverstone, R. (2006) 'Media and communication in a globalised world' in Barnett, C., Robinson, J. and Rose, G. (eds) *A Demanding World*, Milton Keynes, The Open University.

Twum-Baah, K. (2004) 'Volume and characteristics of international Ghanaian migration', presented at 'Migration and Development' conference held in Accra, 18–20 July.

Yeoh, B., Willis, K. and Fakhri, S. (2003) 'Transnationalism and its edges', *Ethnic and Racial Studies*, vol.26, no.2, pp.207–17.

Chapter 7

Geographies of solidarities

Doreen Massey

Contents

1   Introduction

In earlier chapters of this book, we have encountered some of the powerful forces of globalisation: the finance sector spans the planet, establishing its bases, influencing the fortunes of places everywhere; multinational companies commercialise the natural world; nation states wrestle over the troublesome territory of Antarctica. All of them are organising this world through particular architectures of territory and flow. They are indeed powerful forces, and it is these forces that are often implicitly being referred to when we talk of the world as being 'globalised'.

Yet these major forces are by no means the whole story. Chapters 5 and 6 turned to some less obviously dominating forces: they explored how people may build affective relations with particular places; how post-colonial nations struggle to form and maintain identities within boundaries not of their making; how diasporic groups forge new connections and sustain and rework inherited attachments. All these, too, are integral to the making of a globalised world. It has been a central theme through this book that the world is constantly and inevitably being made. However, it is made through small things as well as big ones: through every action and inaction, through our interactions with other humans and, as we have seen, with and within the non-human world too.

Sometimes (in fact most often), such world making is a process of adaptation, of getting by and making do, without addressing the wider parameters. At other times, there are challenges – people who say 'no'; individuals, groups and campaigns working explicitly for change – people who do not accept that the way things are done is the way they *should* be done. These people challenge the currently dominant architecture of territory and flow – the so-called 'normal' running of the world. The campaigns and arguments that we shall explore in this chapter involve people taking a stand, coming to a position on an issue, and we shall explore the inevitable difficulty and complexity of this.

This chapter begins to look centrally at some of the challenges to the making of a globalised world (Chapter 8 will explore others). There is a whole variety of such activities and with very varying politics, but this chapter concentrates on just a few issues and campaigns, and on ones concerned primarily with working for greater equality. Here we look at attempts to address inequality between places (Section 3), at the campaigns of those who protest against the current form of globalisation altogether (Section 4) and at attempts to link up local struggles in different parts of the world (Section 5). One of the problems that all such campaigns face is how to establish solidarity between different places and different struggles. A common theme is that the local issues which the campaigns address, though they are far apart in physical geographical terms and may occur in places that are very different and unequal in prosperity and access to resources, are in one way or another connected. This connection may vary in its nature. To illustrate, there may be a connection between different parts of the world (different local places within the global) because the flows between places themselves produce the problem; or it may be that the issues faced in different local places – even though they are far apart – seem to be quite similar; or again it may be that local campaigns are connected as a result of the fact that they face a common enemy. These are just examples. There are also, for instance, 'solidarity campaigns' with a whole host of places and peoples (for example, Cuba, Palestine) that arise where there may be no 'connection' in the obvious sense, but nonetheless there are forms of identification or support or fellow feeling **(Robinson, 2006)**.

Such issues and campaigns integrally raise questions of *territory* and *flow*. Locality and global interconnectedness are often part of the very politics, even the focus, of the struggle; they may be precisely what are contested – their rethinking may be a crucial aspect of political organising. These issues and campaigns arise out of a profound questioning, even a rejection, of the way in which the globalised world is currently organised (that is, the current architecture of territory and flow), and a desire to see it organised differently. This may involve working to change particular, presently unequal, connections; it may mean challenging the territories of the powerful; or it may mean questioning the whole current form of globalisation. Whatever the particular issue, such campaigns raise questions about what alternative architectures might be aimed for. We shall pick up on the emerging complexities of territory and flow developed in previous chapters and see again how both of them need to be understood as always in process. What is added in this chapter is an examination of how these concepts can be important in the world of campaigning politics.

Chapter aims

- To explore what kinds of popular solidarities can be developed to contest the way the globalised world is currently being made.

- To show how territory and flow are integral to the 'alternative' politics we analyse, and to explore some alternative architectures that might be built.

2 Another world is possible

2.1 An eruption of discontent

It is difficult to know where to start an introduction to the eruptions of protest that have spread around the world in the face of what has come to be called 'neo-liberal globalisation' (see Chapter 2). Yet perhaps this is in tune with the protesters' point: they do not want to be homogenised, organised or pinned down into tidy categories that would never hold anyway. So, in the spirit of this, let us jump right in and go straight to a particular local struggle (or maybe we ought to call it a local/global struggle).

Activity 7.1

I would like you to turn to Reading 7A from Notes from Nowhere/Katharine Ainger (2003) entitled 'We are everywhere: the irresistible rise of global anticapitalism', which you will find at the end of the chapter.

I found myself both loving this piece and arguing with it all at the same time. If you too found yourself saying, 'Yes, but ...', note down the points you might have raised with Stanis Kaka if you had been talking with him yourself.

No I agreed with everything he said.

Why was the third conference of Peoples' Global Action (PGA) held in Cochabamba, Bolivia anyway? Cochabamba in the previous year (2000) had been the site of a confrontation that had spread hope around hundreds of local struggles like the one in Papua New Guinea (see Shultz, 2003). In the middle of the 1990s, the World Bank had

Figure 7.1   Making links, expanding the imagination

offered Bolivia a loan of $14 million so that it could expand its water services. It was much needed money in one of the poorest countries in Latin America. However, as a condition of this loan, the World Bank demanded that the publicly owned water system of Cochabamba, Bolivia's third largest city, be privatised. The Bolivian Government complied and a company largely owned by a major US corporation took over not only the urban water system but the surrounding rural irrigation system and local wells. It was not long before bills for water were raised, other charges instituted and a local resistance took form. The resistance group was called La Coordinadora, and for months it organised protests, blockades, strikes and refusals to pay bills. Negotiations were instituted and reneged upon. There was violence and serious confrontation with heavily armed police forces (see Figures 7.2 and 7.3). A state of emergency was declared. Through email despatches, news went around the world, and some sympathetic actions were initiated. In the end, the water system contract was cancelled.

> Depending on who you ask, the resistance began 510 years ago when the indigenous of the Américas fought Columbus, or 700 years ago when Robin Hood rode through the forests of England to protect the rights of commoners, or a little over 100 years ago when slavery was abolished throughout the Américas, or 150 years ago when working people became an

Figure 7.2   Citizens resist the clampdown, Cochabamba, Bolivia

international revolutionary movement, or 50 years ago when colonized countries gained their independence, or 30 years ago when populations across Africa, Asia, and Latin America started rioting over the price of bread as the International Monetary Fund (IMF) began restructuring their economies.

Or perhaps it was in 1988 when the IMF and World Bank were almost run out of Berlin by 75,000 protestors, or 1999 when the

Figure 7.3   Stand-off during the water wars, Cochabamba, Bolivia

same number disrupted the World Trade Organization (WTO)
meeting in Seattle ... For those who like their history neat, 1994
emerges as a landmark year as resistance to capitalism snowballed.

(Notes from Nowhere, 2003, pp.21–2)

1 January 1994 was when the resistance group the Zapatistas burst
upon the international scene in Chiapas, southern Mexico. Timed to
coincide with the launch of the North American Free Trade Agreement
(NAFTA), one of its central aims was to resist the privatisation of land
which that treaty might bring in its wake as a result of constitutional
changes. Article 27 of the Mexican Constitution was both hugely
symbolic and utterly material in forming the basis for the organisation
of much of the social and economic life of poorer Mexicans. In the
early 1990s, about half of Mexico's land surface was owned communally
and organised into local *ejidos* (communal landholdings), and about
twenty million people lived on such land. Moreover, the guarantee
of that communal ownership lay in Article 27 – which was now being
modified – and Article 27 had been one of the central gains of the

peasant army which formed one element in the Mexican revolution of 1910–17, and whose leader was Emiliano Zapata; hence the Zapatistas.

Yet the Zapatistas of 1994 were interested in more than this. Everyone, they said, was a Zapatista; everyone who opposed the imposition of 'free' trade, the privatisation of everything and the rule by multinational corporations. The Zapatistas spoke to the world through the internet, they spoke of dreams, they communicated in poetry and they invented new forms of organising. For many across the world, the Zapatistas became a symbol of the hope that change might be possible. '*Ya basta!*' was one of their cries: 'Enough'.

Their cry resonated among local campaigns around the world. In 1996 and 1997, thousands gathered in the Chiapaneco rainforests for international '*Encuentros* (meetings, encounters) against Neo-liberalism and for Humanity'. In 1998 in Spain, from another *Encuentro*, emerged PGA. A network of campaigns had been born. The history since then is as difficult to describe as is the beginning. These campaigns are part of what has been called new social movements.

There have been protests at a whole variety of so-called 'summit' meetings: of the World Bank, the World Trade Organisation (WTO), the International Monetary Fund (IMF). There have been 'parallel summits' where explicitly alternative agendas have been discussed. There are social fora: foci for discussion among the wide variety of campaigns attached to this amorphous movement. Social fora emerged from the belief that protest was not enough. In Porto Alegre in Brazil in 2001, the first World Social Forum was organised. This was a convergence point for groups and movements opposed to global neo-liberalism and intent on thinking through the outlines of possible alternatives. World Social Fora came to be held on an annual basis, attracting tens of thousands of people, and they have proliferated to regional level (for instance the European Social Forum) and local level. These are just some of the ways in which a multitude of local campaigns now finds itself woven into global networks.

The concerns are just as multiple as the campaigns: privatisation, logging, the patenting of knowledge, the patenting of seeds, the lack of economic democracy, the rights of indigenous people, the arms trade, the overwhelming of cities by cars, and so on. And the means are often inventive: there is Guerrilla Gardening, Culture Jamming and Tactical Frivolity. Guerrilla gardeners may be anti-car activists planting flowers in car parks, or South Asian peasants digging vegetable crops into a squatted golf course; culture jammers may spray-paint advertisements with alternative messages; Tactical Frivolity emphasises the ability of humour and playfulness to subvert more obvious and heavy forms of power. The most famous images from Seattle in 1999 were probably those of the endangered turtles marching with threatened shipbuilding workers. There have been arguments about tactics, about democracy and openness, about the use of violence. Moreover, it is important to stress, these arguments continue. There is music, there is dressing up, there is recognition of the power of laughter.

There have been many criticisms made of these exuberant challenges, and we shall look at a number of them as we go along. However, one is of particular relevance to the argument of this book; it is the criticism which adopts a strategic attitude of dismissal. 'For heaven's sake,' declare the spokespeople of the powers that be (such as the multinational corporations and powerful states discussed in earlier chapters), 'don't these people live in the real world? Don't they understand that globalisation is the inevitable result of market forces in a changing economy, and of inexorable developments in technology? Be realistic.'

It is important to be clear about what this response is arguing: not merely that the forces at work are so big and powerful that it will be difficult to change them (which is undoubtedly the case and which the protesters recognise), but that they are *inevitable* – that they are outside the realm of human intervention.

In turn, the response of the protesters has been to contest precisely this: to argue that neither market forces nor technology are forces beyond human intervention, that both are indeed products of human practices and negotiations. The argument is that those aspects of the world against which the protests have been mounted have been *made* by human agency, and thus that they can be made differently. It has been the insistence on this argument that has made so important the popular slogan: Another world is possible.

2.2 Local versus global?

Another set of arguments in and against these protests and campaigns revolves around the term 'globalisation'. In the early days, these social movements often characterised themselves, and were characterised in

Defining new social movements

The term 'new social movements' has quite a history. It refers to campaigns (movements) that grew up from the second half of the twentieth century onwards and which saw themselves as very different from (and sometimes opposed to) the older forms of class and trades union struggle. The feminist, anti-racist and civil rights campaigns were such social movements. The new social movements of today include a huge range of struggles around a host of particular issues. These new movements mark their differences from the old forms through their less hierarchical (more 'horizontal') forms of organising; through their emphasis on bringing in a wider range of different groups; through the kinds of campaigning and direct action that they favour; and through the range of things that they open up to political questioning.

the media, as being 'against globalisation'. It was a problematical identity. For one thing, it laid the movements open to easy attack and this was one reason their detractors used it. How can you possibly argue against the increasing interconnectedness of the world?, came the challenge. And look, you are wearing Nike, you are using the internet, you yourselves are a global movement. In the course of their activities, in the protests, through the proposition of alternatives and in their own emphasis on making global links, the language of the protests evolved as part of the struggles themselves. It began to be more clearly argued that it is not 'the global' in itself that the movements are against, but this particular organisation of global interconnections and disconnections (often encapsulated as neo-liberal globalisation). It is not globalisation they are opposed to but this particular *form* of globalisation: 'Another globalisation is possible'. It is not, in other words, simply that we live 'in a globalised world' but that we live in a world that is globalised *in a particular way*.

Other names and slogans were adopted and experimented with: globalisation from below, the Global Justice Movement. The 1999 J18 event in the City of London was called the Carnival against Capital (J18 stands for June 18); the collection of writings edited by Notes from Nowhere (2003) speaks of 'global anticapitalism'. There was, in other words, a shift away from attacking a certain kind of spatial level (the global) to challenging an economic system (capitalism) and the structural inequalities of power, resources and access which hold together the dominant – and particular – form of 'globalisation'. What was at issue was this *particular* architecture of territory and flow.

Yet there was also something else going on within this political argument. The criticism that 'you're just anti-global' was also meant to imply that 'you're all just localist' (implication: little localists). This is the kind of accusation that carries a huge burden of resonances: 'you can't think big, you can't face up to how to organise the world economy ..., you're all just concerned with your own little territories'.

Although, as we have seen, this is by no means an entirely fair accusation, it does bring to the surface some difficult issues:

1   One of the ways in which people most directly experience 'the globalised world' is through the impact it has on their daily lives; though this impact can be enriching, it can also be disruptive. There are, for instance, constant complaints about the invasion and dislocation of local places by the 'external forces' of globalisation. It is the kind of feeling that does in fact encourage a defence of existing local places against 'the outside'.

flows
into local
territories

Activity 7.2

Read the last paragraph again, and reformulate this feeling in terms of the concepts of territory and flow. Then draw on what we have learned so far about territories and flows in order to refute this criticism. (You will find hints towards an answer in the rest of the section.)

2   There is a frequent complaint that 'places are becoming all the same'; they are losing their uniqueness and being denuded of the particularity of their meaning by global forces of homogenisation. How often we hear the complaint that, 'All high streets are the same now', for instance (you might want to take a look back at one of the squares under 'C' on the Common Ground *Local Distinctiveness* poster in Chapter 5, Figure 5.16). Such changes are an assault on the powerful emotional pull that can be exerted by and in local places.

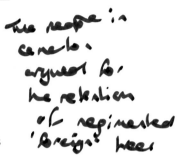

The people in Canada argued for the retaliation of regimented 'foreign' beer

Activity 7.3

Using the material in previous chapters, think about how you might respond to the argument made in the second point above. In particular you might think back to the chapter by Owain Jones (Chapter 5). (You will find hints towards an answer in the rest of the section.)

It is, perhaps, understandable that sometimes it seems that the only, or the best, or the easiest response to the pressures of living in a globalised world is to become a 'localist'. Chapter 6 explored the efforts to which people may go to preserve attachments to places and communities, even though they are no longer in those places and the communities may themselves be globalised. And indeed, many of the struggles against the dominant current forms of global forces are, as we saw above, actually locally based and locally organised. For, although globalisation can often seem to embody a set of forces that is unreachable (global, 'up there' somehow, always arriving from somewhere else), as we have seen in previous chapters (especially Chapters 2 and 3; see also **Allen, 2006**; **Robinson, 2006**), those global forces always have to be produced; they do not actually come from nowhere, they too are produced 'on the ground' in a whole range of local places. It is around such local moments in the making of these global relations that many local struggles have arisen. Nonetheless, that does not mean that the struggles are necessarily local*ist* (that is, only concerned with their own little territories).

Look back at your answers to Activities 7.2 and 7.3, and reread the argument just made. There are a number of reasons why this eruption of protest can be understood as *not* being a confrontation of local and global. First, as many of the protesters argue, this is a battle not against the globalised world, but over the *way* in which the world is globalised. So, in response to Activity 7.2: although people may be defending their local territory against invasion by global flows, they may not wish to exclude *all* global connections, only these particular ones. It is not 'the global' as such that they are against. Second, as we have just seen, the globalised world is built on local foundations; the global is made locally. Third, as was argued in Chapter 5, even before we began to use the term 'globalisation', local places were thoroughly interconnected; there was never a world of isolated territories. The local place itself is, in part, a product of global (that is, wider) flows and practices. Thus, in response to Activity 7.3: local places (local territories) are always in part a product of wider flows – the real question should be what *kinds* of wider flows we want to be open to.

These are really important points. In arguments about globalisation, it is often implied that local is necessarily 'good' and global 'bad' (or in some cases the other way around); or that territory is 'bad' and flow is 'good' (or, again, sometimes the other way around). The argument here is that this is the wrong way to look at things. It is not the geographical form of things, in itself, that is good or bad (whatever your political point of view), but the particular social form of things (such as the power relations involved or the equalities and inequalities). What should be at issue in political debate, in other words, is the way in which particular territories and flows are *made*, together.

Summary

- In recent years, there has been an eruption of protest at the current form of globalisation and an insistence that a different architecture is possible.

- One of the things at issue here is the way in which territories and flows structure the globalised world: what kinds of territories and flows do we want?

3   Challenging connections

3.1   Taking a stand

All of the movements, campaigns and debates that we are considering in this chapter are, in one way or another, about intervening in the way in which the world is currently made. They are attempts not to go along with the world as it is, not to participate in and thereby reinforce the constant process of its making along the same old lines, but to challenge and even change some of the dominant, more settled trajectories.

Of course, the territories and flows of the globalised world are continually being made and remade. As we have seen in earlier chapters, they are frequently contested. The financial interests investigated in Chapter 2 had to change the way their world was made when the old architecture was deemed inappropriate. What is different about the groups we are discussing here is that they would see themselves as (or as representing) those who are relatively powerless in the normal run of things. Look back to the forerunners of 'resistance' claimed in the quotation in Section 2.1, and pick out the terms 'the indigenous', 'working people', 'colonized countries' (Notes from Nowhere, 2003, p.22). These are evocations of 'the little people'; they set the campaigns in a lineage of 'popular' dissent (where 'popular' means 'of the people'). These actors are not those who normally run the world. Indeed, a central contest is precisely over 'who' should have such power, and how it should be distributed.

The quotation in Section 2.1 (Notes from Nowhere, 2003, p.22) also used the term 'resistance' (twice) and, in the same section, I used the term 'the powers that be'. Such terminology could give an impression of two big blocks, facing each other: those with power who run the show and the power*less*. That surely would be an incorrect picture. On the one hand, within the financial sector (often portrayed as the most significant capitalist, globalised industry), the power (and responsibility) is distributed along long chains of command (as explored in Chapter 2), so that even quite lowly functionaries are participants in the production of neo-liberal globalisation. On the other hand, as consumers, almost all of us are implicated in some way or other in this neo-liberal globalisation **(Allen, 2006)**. We buy into it; we go along with it. The global protesters wear classy trainers, use the internet and travel around the world on major airlines. Therefore, maybe it is not a big clash of forces – us versus them (whichever side you would be on).

However, neither is it the case that we are all equal in this. The campaigns we are investigating would see themselves as representing those who are not in a position of great power in the current situation, and that can make challenging the current form of globalisation seem like a daunting proposition.

Activity 7.4

Use the arguments that have been made so far to say why changing things can often seem so daunting. Try to come up with a number of distinct reasons.

The process of getting something changed when the power seems to rest in the hands of the rich + powerful corporations

A first set of obstacles to changing the architecture of things is thrown up by the highly differential robustness and fragility of the forms and forces through which the world is made. The new social movements draw their strength from collectivity, yet the contrast between them and the states, the companies and the international organisations they contest is great. However, even here it is useful to push the question further: quite what is this differential robustness based upon? Some of it is the result of the huge inequalities in the resources that can be brought to bear. Some of it derives from the way things come to seem like common sense, and therefore fail to be questioned; they fall outside political debate. Globalisation itself has sometimes seemed like this, and this is one of the things the new social movements have tried to destabilise – simply by putting it on to the political agenda.

A second reason for the seeming impossibility of changing things is precisely what seems like their global nature. We addressed this in Section 2.2 – the 'global' itself has to be made and it is made in places, in specific activities and in specific locations; it is thereby addressable.

A third difficulty in changing things is that of pinning down responsibility for the production of globalisation. Responsibility seems to be diffused, to be everywhere (see Chapter 2 and also **Allen, 2006**). One way to address this is to focus on symbolic practices, or companies or things that seem to encapsulate the whole bundle of issues you are concerned with, which seem so difficult to pin down at one place or in one form. The targeting of the WTO is one example of this and we shall explore others.

Nevertheless, the difficulties of mounting a challenge reside not only in these things, not only in the powerful forces that must be addressed nor even in the inevitable political conflict over the aims of any change, and the ethical frameworks within which we make judgements. The difficulties also reside in the formulation of the very principles that might be the basis for intervention, its justification; furthermore, they reside in the problem of putting principles into practice.

As we have seen, the geographical concepts, such as those of territory and flow, that have been explored throughout this book are often mobilised as principles in political argument. Thus, an argument about migration, for instance, might want to appeal to the idea that the planet belongs to us all; that there should be no borders and no exclusions – we should be hospitable, and people should be allowed to migrate. Arguments in favour of free trade hail the same kind of principle in support – this should be a borderless world with no restraint (often in consequence labelled 'artificial') on trade. At their limits, what such arguments are relying upon when they call upon this general principle is the idea that flow is good and that territory is bad. In contrast, those who argue for the rights of local people over their local places or for the rights of nations to have autonomy over their own political decision making are placing the principle of territory over that of flow.

There are a number of points to explore here. First, the two background principles outlined above are in tension with each other; at their extremes they simply contradict each other. However, many of us – individuals, political groupings, parties and activists – do find ourselves holding both of these principles at the same time. Perhaps in one part of our minds we do believe that there should be no borders, that the planet belongs to everyone and that all flows – of migrants, of goods and services, of investment (and consequently also of disinvestment), of cultural forms and social norms, and so forth – should be allowed, in truth welcomed. This is one earth. Yet, at the very same time, in another part of our minds we might value very highly the specificity of local places, the differences between local cultures, the rights of nations to make their own decisions, and so forth, and feel that the long histories of the negotiation of relations that has made these places and cultures what they are deserves both recognition and, indeed, protection.

Second, this raises an important point about intellectual rigour and political honesty. Let us take our example further, in slightly caricatured form perhaps, in order to examine an issue. People on the right wing of the political spectrum often advocate free trade as the best means of generating development around the world, and they often back up this position with an appeal to an ideal (and often, it is implied, *ha! Good point!*

inevitable) world of unlimited flow. The very word 'free' in free trade helps to bolster the power of this particular principle. It is a principle embodied in a geographical imagination of a world without borders. Yet the same people, when engaged in a quite different argument – this time about how many migrants from abroad should be allowed to enter a country – might find themselves appealing in justification of their position to a quite different, indeed contradictory, geographical imagination, one in which territory and the rights to territory are what is important and what must be protected. The argument for the necessity to restrict immigration is often backed up by an appeal to the rights of a local people (here a nation) to its own place, and to the fruits of what it has produced. Regardless of other arguments, the problem here lies in the inconsistency of the legitimating principles. It is an inconsistency that is neither intellectually rigorous nor politically honest. Moreover, it is by no means only this particular pair of arguments that can be held up to such criticism. On the other end of the political spectrum, there are many who argue for the right to international migration on the grounds of an ideally borderless world and yet who also criticise the multinationals, the WTO and many a national government for their promotion of free trade. Countries should have the right, they say, to protect their borders against invasion. These are genuinely difficult issues, so how can we negotiate our way through them? The next steps in the argument will take us some way.

Third, if we do find ourselves in such a situation of tension between guiding principles, the aim should be to recognise that tension. For instance, to abandon all borders on the principle of universal hospitality would certainly enable more migration from the poorer countries of the world to the richer (let us say you are in favour of that), but it would also render aboriginal lands defenceless in the face of, to take an extreme example, invasion by multinational mining corporations (to which you might be opposed). The entry of logging companies into Papua New Guinea is a case in point. What is at issue in differentiating between these two situations is the inequality of distribution of power and resources. Maybe in both cases you would wish to take a position on the side of those with less power. This reinforces an important point that I have already made in Section 2.2: that territory and flow (geographical form) cannot *in themselves* be appealed to as our guiding principles. What is really at issue is the politics of the particular situation. Whatever your political position, territory may sometimes be a good thing and sometimes not; likewise with flow.

Fourth and finally, the world in which we are struggling to apply our principles is an endlessly specific one. Indeed, and this is the global anti-capitalists' point, it is a violently unequal one. One message upon which a geographical perspective insists is the inevitable particularity of any place and any situation: each place is unique. And this must affect how we address political questions; it makes it very difficult simply to apply 'rules'. Rather, what is inevitably involved is *judgement*: the necessity of coming to a position, taking a stand in the light of this difficulty and in the best way that one can. In that sense, the stand you take will always be provisional – as the global protesters often say, it will be part of a work in progress. We have to put our principles to *work*. The next section explores a situation which entails just that.

3.2   A case in point

We are constantly faced with issues about which, even if we are not going to campaign around them, we at least feel we ought to have an opinion.

Activity 7.5

Turn now to Reading 7B by John Carvel (2004) entitled 'Nil by mouth', which you will find at the end of the chapter. The reading is an article from a newspaper. You will probably have to read it a number of times. Take it slowly and concentrate first on pulling out the broad structure of the situation.

1   Try to identify some of the principles at stake (the most obvious ones, I think, relate to things I have already mentioned in this chapter).

2   Try to use your understanding of territory and flow to begin to make sense of some of the complexity of the issue.

The issue in the reading concerns migration of health workers from a range of countries to the UK. It is, of course, only 'an issue' at all because individuals and campaigns at both ends of the migration have made it so, pointing out that the sending countries are poorer than the UK, and that a richer country is depriving poorer countries of much needed medical staff that they have trained themselves. It is an issue centred around global inequality.

These are significant flows of people. Often highly trained individuals are leaving health systems where they are sorely needed. Reading 7B says that 'the loss of even a handful of key staff could be enough to destroy a rural maternity service or Aids clinic' (Carvel, 2004). This is an issue with utterly material effects; it concerns people's lives and bodies. Dr Kwadwo Mensah, who has been involved in and carried out research on this question, writes of 'the grim cumulative decline migration can trigger. The Centre for Spinal Injuries in Boxburg, South Africa was the referral centre for the whole region. On the same day in 2000, a Canadian institution recruited the two anaesthetists at the centre. The Boxburg centre has been closed ever since' (Martineau et al., 2002, quoted in Mensah, 2005). More generally, the loss of medical staff results in the deterioration of health systems, dramatic effects on the lives of individuals, and repercussions thereby through the wider economy and society. So, should these medical professionals be stopped from migrating?

In the receiving country of the UK, the government is under great political pressure to improve the National Health Service (NHS), and Reading 7B says, 'it is clear that ministers could not have achieved their targets for expanding the workforce without this influx of talent' (Carvel, 2004). Therefore, in the UK this is also an issue that reverberates through questions of the national economy to the health prospects of individual people.

Two of the principles at stake are:

1   The right of individual people to migrate.
2   The need to address inequality between countries.

Put like this, the question would seem to be one of territory versus flow, and maybe that is one place to start. The flows are making the territories more unequal. Nevertheless, we know from our previous argument in Section 3.1 that this is a common tension which must always be negotiated in a specific context. We also know that territory and flow do not exist in pure form, nor are they static. Moreover, each is involved in the formation of the other. Rather, what we should be thinking about are *processes* – of the formation of territories and of the building, changing and breaking of connections – and these processes are always specific. We must, therefore, set this situation in its particular context.

Let us consider the case of Ghana, a country that was explored a little in Chapter 6, and mentioned in Reading 7B as having lost 660 nurses in one year to the UK health system. There is a long history of connection through flows between Ghana and the UK, stretching from the slave trade, through colonialism and to the Commonwealth. The character of each of these territories is already in some part a product of the history of flows between them. Indeed, that is one reason why the current flow of nurses from Ghana to the UK in particular became so strong. Furthermore, the degree and nature of the relations between these territories, and thus the effects they have had on each other, have changed over time (see Chapter 6). Perhaps bearing all this in mind might help to reconceptualise the issue beyond one of territory versus flow, and open up possibilities for a way forward.

A recent research report for the health charity Medact has confronted these issues in an innovative way (Mensah et al., 2005). It sets the inequality between the UK and Ghana at the centre of the investigation:

> The core of the problem is that international recruitment by the UK of health professionals from countries such as Ghana worsens an already ethically intolerable inequality in health care between the two countries ... The hiring of, for example, Ghanaian health care staff improves health services in the UK at the expense of worsening them in the much more disadvantaged context of Ghana. It does this because:
>
> - both health systems are experiencing staff shortages, in the sense of vacant posts;
>
> - however in relation to needs of health care users, the staff shortage in Ghana is vastly greater, and is a blockage on even basic health care for all;
>
> - the health care professionals who have migrated to work in the UK were trained in Ghana at Ghanaian public and private expense; the benefits of that training are being experienced however in the UK, and lost to Ghana;
>
> - the UK has not had to expend resources for training of the overseas staff it recruits.
>
> (Mensah et al., 2005, p.31)

Table 7.1 sets out some aspects of this situation. Follow the relationships and the comparison of Ghana and the UK.

Table 7.1   New registrations of nurses in the UK, number of doctors on the UK register and two health indicators for selected African and other countries

Country	Nurses: no. joining register (2003/04)	Doctors: no. on register 1 January 2004	Life expectancy at birth (2002)	Total health expenditure/head ($) (2002)
Sub-Saharan Africa				
South Africa	1689	6208	50.7	222
Nigeria	511	1661	48.8	15
Zimbabwe	391	117	37.9	45
Ghana	354	293	57.6	12
Zambia	169	76	39.7	19
Kenya	146	60	50.9	29
Botswana	90	0	40.4	190
Malawi	64	18	40.2	13
South and Southeast Asia				
Philippines	4338	14	68.3	30
India	3073	18,006	61.0	24
Pakistan	140	3807	61.4	16
Sri Lanka	36	1903	70.3	30
High income Commonwealth				
Australia	1326	2648	80.4	1182
Total overseas (non-EU)	**14,122**			
Total overseas (non-UK)	**15,162**	**61,551**		
UK	19,465	150,805	78.2	1,508
Total registrants	**34,627**			
Total on register	**660,480**	**212,356**		

Source: Mensah et al., 2005, p.8, Table 1

The situation in Table 7.1 creates what is known as a perverse subsidy. That is, 'there is a flow of resources from *users* of poor country health care systems – whom those staff would otherwise have been treating – to users of rich country systems who would otherwise face staff shortages' (Mensah et al., 2005, p.31). An immediate response might be to stop the flow. But no, the Medact report (Mensah et al., 2005) argues that there are basic issues of human rights here: the rights of Ghanaian medical professionals to leave Ghana; the rights of Ghanaian medical professionals to decent working conditions either in Ghana or elsewhere; and the rights of people to health care. Moreover, the Medact report argues that these rights are equal between people:

> We root our arguments in the proposition that there are no differences in human rights between human beings; the human rights of each person must be treated on an equal basis regardless of accident of birth and therefore of nationality. The basic question addressed by the paper is: *'How would policy towards health service professional migration look if one starts from these principles?'*
>
> (Mensah et al., 2005, p.5)

However, the achievement of these different rights can sometimes be in contradiction. Ghanaian staff leaving their country, or staying but going on strike to improve their working conditions, can negatively affect the rights to health care of people in that country: 'More generally, in these conditions the migration of health workers can pit the human rights of health workers against the human rights of communities in countries of origin, and the human rights of this latter group against the human rights of communities in countries of destination' (Mensah et al., 2005, p.6). In other words, the Medact report recognises that (i) the achievement of the basic principles may be in conflict and that fact must be addressed, and (ii) these principles operate in a world of inequality and that needs also to be addressed (Mensah et al., 2005). In other words, this is a specific situation.

After detailed analysis of the migratory flows and their effects, the Medact report presents an overarching argument that is of particular interest to us here. Perhaps surprisingly, it presents a case for *increased* connections between the two countries and their health systems; however, it also argues for a *change in the nature* of those flows.

There are two elements to these recommendations. First, the Medact report argues that the migratory flows should not be stopped (impossible anyway), but that there should be *restitution to compensate for the perverse subsidy created by those flows*. This would take monetary form and would have the double effect of aiding improvement in the Ghanaian system and, in the longer term, encouraging Ghanaian medical professionals to stay or to return (as the UK and Ghanaian health care systems became more equal). Second, the report recommends that there should be *positive collaboration* between the two health systems:

> This [restitution] would be best done within a political framework that accepted that health professional migration blurs the boundaries between countries' of origin and destination countries' health services. In the case of the UK and Ghana these boundaries

were already permeable. The best way forward is therefore to build on current links between institutions, professional associations, trades unions and individuals so that, for example, Ghanaian and UK professionals increasingly accept that they are colleagues in a joint enterprise of health service development that can only be done ethically if it explicitly addresses, over time, inequalities of services and conditions.

(Mensah et al., 2005, p.41)

We could understand these two proposals together as advocating a form of solidarity in the face of inequality. However you respond to the detail of the proposals, what is of interest here is that they derive from an understanding that territory and flow are ongoing processes and that what might be necessary is a radical reworking of those processes themselves. Both the connections between Ghana and the UK, and the territories at either end, will be changed by such an approach.

Finally, a reflection. 'Restitution' is a term used for one kind of reparation for historical wrongs **(Lambert, 2006)**. Such historical reparations bear some similarities to the proposed restitutions in the Medact report. In both cases, there is recognition of the longer histories within which the particular situation is set; in both cases, too, the concern is to treat the issue in a collective way. Yet there are also differences. First, in the case of historical reparations, one difficulty is what David Lambert called 'historical distance' **(Lambert, 2006)**. This is not so in the case of migration today where the crucial 'distance' is geographical in a world divided into territories. Second, as Lambert points out, cases for reparations for historical wrongs require a demonstration that the past wrong continues to have effects. The present inequality between Ghana and the UK in part arises because of such past wrongs. Nonetheless, the stance is different: the restitution proposed in the Medact report on health inequality is not, as it is in the case of historical reparations, primarily to compensate for some past wrong; it is concerned with altering the dynamics of what is happening in the present, to change the way the world is being made *now*. Third, reparations for historical events single out those events as having been abnormal (slavery, the holocaust, and so forth); they are deemed worthy of reparation precisely because of that abnormality (which, as Lambert points out, creates difficulties – should we judge 'normality' by historical or present standards, for instance?). Calculations of reparations for the past use counterfactual history to think about what would have happened 'in normal circumstances' as their baseline (for instance, as 'if enslaved people had been paid as waged workers for their labour' **(Lambert, 2006, Section 5.1)**). In the case of this restitution in the present, however, it is precisely 'normality' itself that is being challenged. 'Normal market forces' are central to the production of the problem.

This, then, takes us back to the arguments of **Allen (2006)** and of Young (2003). 'Political responsibility questions "normal" conditions,' as Iris Marion Young claims (2003, p.41), and, we might add, sometimes tries to change them.

Summary

- 'Taking a stand' will involve carefully addressing a range of issues particular to each situation.
- The power relations through which territories and flows are constructed are what are important to a political analysis.
- The inequalities between the Ghanaian and UK health systems are made worse by the flow of medical professionals from the former to the latter.
- One way to address this situation is to recognise how territories and flows form each other, and to try to change the way this happens.

4 Global anti-capitalism

4.1 Flows and enclosures

The question of the remaking of the territories and connecting flows of the Ghanaian and UK health systems posed problems of practical solidarity between people in two places. As a politics, it addressed the relations between the two places and how those flows had effects on the territories they connected. The new social movements introduced in Section 2 are different in a number of ways. For one thing, together they aim to be global. In one collection of writings they describe themselves as 'the largest globally interconnected social movement of our time' (Notes from Nowhere, 2003, p.21). They have certainly succeeded in linking protests around the world, and the practical significance of that international solidarity was clear in the interview with Stanis Kaka from Papua New Guinea in Reading 7A (Notes from Nowhere, 2003, pp.412–14). The very title of the interview, 'We discovered we weren't alone' is a reference to this, and the whole interview makes clear how important and empowering was this process of becoming aware of what was going on around the wider world. Moreover, this incredibly complex and multifarious 'movement of movements' has, in the process of its own construction, generated a very particular geographical imagination of solidarity. It is an imagination that lays stress on the tearing down of borders, that emphasises the productivity of flows and interconnections, but also argues that we must rethink our notions of flow and connection.

In their stress on flow over territory, those in the social movements are in tune with other theorisations of how the geographical configuration of the world may be changing. Manuel Castells, in his book *The Rise of the Network Society* (1996), proposed that a 'space of flows' was being superimposed upon, and gradually becoming more powerful than, a 'space of places' **(Silverstone, 2006)**. It is as though territories no longer tame space for us; instead there is an increased feeling of being bombarded by flows from all sides. But it can also contribute to a feeling of exhilaration in positive engagement; we really can talk across continents. We have also seen – for instance in Chapters 2 and 3 – how, even in the midst of an increasingly globalised world, new borders are erected, and new stabilisations and new territories are established, and that the two processes constantly work together, indeed are necessary to each other.

Nonetheless, the basic premise of many within the new social movements is that territories must be scrutinised and challenged. They start from a position of challenging the borders put up by the powerful. This is one earth. The term they often use for territory is 'enclosure' (see, for instance, Reading 3B in Chapter 3 – the Rural Advancement Foundation's 'Enclosures of the Mind'). The term harks back to the Enclosure Acts in the UK which, by privatising what had been common land and thus depriving the majority of local people of a basis of their subsistence, helped to pave the way both for capitalist agriculture and, by producing an army of landless workers, for industrial capitalism. The aspects of territory that are being stressed by the protesters here, then, are those of the exclusivity of ownership, control, entry or use. In other words, enclosure here refers to the aspect of exclusive boundary-drawing, rather than that of interweaving (see Chapter 1). Enclosures are often counterposed to commons, which Klaus Dodds talked about in their global form in the

Introduction to Chapter 4. The enclosures of the powerful, whether in gated communities, through the privatisation of land or through the privatisation of water, provide a common term for many of the protests of these movements: 'This process, known as "enclosure", remains one of the most powerful concepts in understanding contemporary capitalism, just as tearing down fences is one of the most powerful symbols of resistance to enclosure' (Notes from Nowhere, 2003, p.27). In exemplification of this stance, the collection of material edited by Notes from Nowhere (and entitled 'We are everywhere: the irresistible rise of global anticapitalism') does not claim copyright on the material. Instead it offers *copyleft* (see Figure 7.4).

The texts in this book are **copyleft** (except where indicated). The authors and publishers permit others to copy, distribute, display, quote, and create derivative works based upon them in print and electronic format for any non-commercial, non-profit purposes, on the conditions that the original author is credited, *We Are Everywhere* is cited as a source along with our website address, and the work is reproduced in the spirit of the original. The editors would like to be informed of any copies produced.

Reproduction of the texts for commercial purposes is prohibited without express permission from the Notes from Nowhere editorial collective and the publishers.

All works produced for both commercial and non-commercial purposes must give similar rights and reproduce the copyleft clause within the publication.

© All photographs in this book are **copyright** of the photographers, and may not be reproduced without permission.

The labour of the authors and the editors of this book was given freely. All royalties received by Notes from Nowhere from sales of this book are being donated to the social movements featured in *We Are Everywhere*.

Contact us directly at: info@weareeverywhere.org
www.WeAreEverywhere.org or via Verso

Figure 7.4   Copyleft and copyright

This statement is a working example both of Notes from Nowhere's (2003) attempt to refuse enclosure and of the imaginative presentation of its position (note the reversal of the copyright symbol to copyleft at the start of the text).

Activity 7.6

Read Figure 7.4 carefully. There *are* exceptions (enclosures) even in copyleft. In actuality, Notes from Nowhere (2003) is quite strict – note the distinction between commercial and non-commercial use, for instance. Copyleft conforms, most certainly, to its anti-capitalist principle, but what of the anti-enclosure principle?

In reality, it is difficult to be against *all* enclosures. Naomi Klein, in her collection *Fences and Windows* (2002), recognises just this. While some fences, she argues, must be pulled down, others may need defending: 'Meanwhile, some very necessary fences are under attack: in the rush to privatisation .... Every protected public space has been cracked open, only to be re-enclosed by the market' (Klein, 2002, p.xix). The issue is not fences as such.

There is an attempt in parts of these new social movements to come up with a particular way of thinking, a very different way of imagining a potential geography of the world. There is much talk of bees, of ants and of birds: the evocation of birds, swooping in coordination but apparently without the leadership of any one among them, their colour changing from dark to light as a whole flock turns as one against the sky. 'The flock is clearly more than the sum of its parts. But how is this possible?' (Notes from Nowhere, 2003, p.67).

The proposition is of bottom-up organisation, where direction is not imposed from above but emerges from the activities of millions. Those who subscribe to this understanding term the participants in the movement 'the multitude'. (You might recall Reading 5A from Chapter 5, 'The attentive heart: conversations with trees', which had the sub-heading 'A multitude of voices'.) Here, the aim is for there tobe no centres of command, no top-down organisation, no one big story laid down in advance – no big plan already known. Diversity and multiplicity are strength, and local knowledge and local activity are fundamental: it is out of them that common enemies are recognised and common aims produced. The emphasis is on horizontal relations of working together, in explicit contrast to pyramidal structures of power. This is illustrated in Figure 7.5, where the mask is crucial: the leader is anonymous. SubComandante Marcos (note the 'Sub') is one of the few figureheads of the Zapatista movement. But his identity is unknown in the normal sense. He says that he is not himself: he is an example of many.

This is a political/geographical imagination of the world that has links with changing ideas in the natural sciences, philosophy, political sciences and geography. It also argues that this is the way the world is, or at least the way it is going. It mirrors the global connectivity of neo-liberal capitalism, the complex flows of multinational corporations. Two sets of flows – of capitalism and of the campaigners – oppose each other. What the protesters challenge are the claims to power of neo-liberal capitalism, its constant enclosures, its production of increasing inequality, of exclusion from democratic participation in the economy, the despoliation of the planet. It might seem an unequal contest, against the long-entrenched capacities of the 'normal' workings of the global market economy, but the protesters might respond that they have flexibility and people power on their side. Figure 7.6 illustrates an example of people power, which involved another use of masks.

Figure 7.5   SubComandante Marcos

This form of organisation is certainly difficult to pin down. The protesters face a capitalism that appears to be everywhere, so much so that not only does it seem impossible to attack, but people have even forgotten they are living within it. For those who would defend the current system, the problem is how to pin down this opposition which seems to sprout up everywhere like a virus, that is so difficult to decapitate because it has no organising centre of command. The exasperation of the forces of (present) law and order has exploded time after time.

If capitalism is everywhere, how do you attack it? If responsibility for the production of what the campaigners see as the iniquities of multinational corporations is dispersed through the innumerable links of global neo-liberal capitalism, how are they to pin it down? One of the answers produced through this movement of movements has been to focus on iconic moments. That is to say, to select events, buildings, companies or organisations that symbolise the whole thing; crucial symbolic nodes in the networks of flow. As with the dropping of flags on Antarctica (see Section 4.2 of Chapter 4), this is a way of

Figure 7.6   *Nosotros no somos nosotros* (we are not ourselves): masked in order to be seen

using something material, visible, to carry a wider meaning. Thus, the meetings of the WTO became one focus for the social movements: not only for the form and the actions of the organisation itself, but in particular for what it symbolises. Other summits and international organisations have been similarly targeted. They have been the focus of protests and also of 'parallel summits' – fora where alternative ways of organising the world economy might begin to be thrashed out.

Now, there is something here that is significant for our argument. This geography of campaigning also produces a different kind of geography of solidarity. In the case of the immigration of nurses from Ghana to the UK discussed in Section 3.2, the solidarity was built (or, one of the aims was that solidarity *should* be built) as a result of and through the remaking of the flows between the two places. In the global social movements, something rather different is going on. In this case, the argument is that what connects the different struggles around the world is their common enemy, and that enemy is 'the system as a whole'. This is what emerges from the horizontality of communication

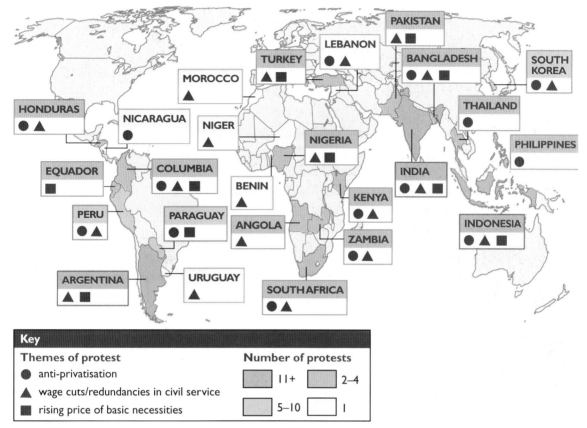

Key

Themes of protest	Number of protests

● anti-privatisation

▲ wage cuts/redundancies in civil service

▮ rising price of basic necessities

11+   2–4

5–10   1

Figure 7.7   States of unrest, January–December 2002

Source: World Development Movement, 2003

between the movements. In these moments of coming together – at Seattle, Prague or Genoa – there is a solidarity of shared opposition. We saw that in the Papua New Guinea case. 'One no and many yeses', is a common refrain.

However, these proliferating social movements are not all about flow. They are, after all, composed from a multiplicity of local and particular struggles. Some of these are based in particular places and concerned with the fate of those places; others are built around particular issues – privatisation, aboriginal rights, combating large dams or being vocal against the arms trade. This is a movement of movements. Diversity is one of the characteristics most frequently proclaimed (hence the 'many yeses'). The constant formation and shifting of these local groups is a form of making and remaking territories (collectivities). Yet these are territories that claim not to have boundaries; they are constellations of concerned people. They are also, in some ways, distinct from the kinds of communities and attachments examined in Chapters 5 and 6. In the cases explored there, it was emphasised that such attachments are developed and made, and can change; rarely are they an automatic product of 'a primordial belonging' (see Chapter 6). The trees for which there is such affection are not 'local'; national loyalties have to be forged; the transnational and diasporic groups work to create more complex attachments. Nonetheless, at the basis of these loyalties is a kind of rootedness. The political groupings under discussion in this section are different again. In many cases they are *elective*: that is to say, attachment to such a group does not arise from any pre-given characteristic or identity trait (for instance, that you live in or come from a particular place or that you were formed in a specific cultural attachment). There are certainly particular interests at play, but in these groups, membership (though possibly that is too strong a term) is also a matter of political commitment, of taking a position. It is interesting to consider whether that makes these groupings more robust or more fragile. Certainly, in the activities, slogans and writings of many of these groups, there is, alongside the elective politics, a leaning towards some notion of organic attachment, in particular through local place. I think there are elements of that in Stanis Kaka's evocation of his village and the community organisation, Kasalapalou, in Reading 7A. So although there are differences we should not make distinctions that are too hard and fast.

4.2   Linking locals

The challenge within the new social movements, of course, is how all those small groups can link up. How can they share experiences, how can they avoid being parochial or localist and how can they be open in interrelated 'territories', constellations within a wider network? Let us discuss two ways in which this challenge has been approached.

The first way in which the challenge of linking up is tackled is through *communication*. Communication between the myriad autonomous groups around the world has been vital. It is integral to the form both of the larger movement and of the local groups themselves – for debate, for information, and for the vast amount of organisation and coordination that has to be done before a social forum or a major protest. In this, the various technologies including the new media technologies (see **Silverstone, 2006**) have been vital. What has been attempted is, however, not conventional. Most obviously, this is an attempt to create an alternative media. The social movements themselves are largely invisible to the dominant corporate media channels except for the occasional big set piece event (such as Seattle in 1999) or if violence breaks out (and even then it usually only makes the global media if it is in the West). The continuous and multifarious protests in the rest of the world usually pass unnoticed by those who receive only the conventional media. This has been one impetus to the development of such alternatives as *Undercurrents, Squall, Schnews* and *Indymedia* – all of them forms of alternative media. Beyond that, there has been an emphasis on developing software and other mechanisms for open access to open up the form of the medium itself. This too is about breaking down enclosures: between reporter and reported; between expert and amateur; and between producers of events and audience. Read the leaflet reproduced in Figure 7.8 and note the language. The aim is often expressed through phrases such as: to reclaim or build 'the virtual commons of the web', 'the physical commons of the streets' or 'the global commons of knowledge'.

This alternative media, then, is not the hegemonic media which controls the news, nor is it the constant bombardment to which life in a globalised world can sometimes seem subject. It does not bombard you – you have to go and find it – but you can access it, and contribute to it, if you wish. A collection of writings by SubComandante Marcos of the Zapatistas is entitled *Our Word is Our Weapon* (2001), and many of the words in this alternative media communicate new imaginations, make known otherwise 'invisible' experiences and speak in the language of dreams – dreams not of a perfectly fitted kitchen or the perfect car but of another possible world.

Nevertheless, the emphasis in this alternative media world is not only on *new* technologies. There is a strong awareness of the digital divide (of the global inequalities of access to the new media, for instance), and a commitment to linking up new technologies with old so that as many people as possible can join in. The internet, then, has been vital to the organisation and spread of these movements, but it has been developed and used in particular ways to reflect their goals. Nonetheless, the digital divide still exists, and greatly affects which groups can, and which cannot, participate in these 'global' communications. Moreover, this brings home the physicality of communication; it does not just happen through some ethereal realm. As well as the need to have all the physical equipment, access to this heterogeneous system may involve a lot more than simply sitting in front of a screen. All kinds of means of communication are enrolled. Remember Stanis Kaka in Papua New Guinea from Reading 7A? On the one hand, using the internet opened up the world for him (it was

seize the media
Reports direct from the streets
www.indymedia.org.uk

No login, no password just press the publish button

Want your action reported? It's up to you, write it and post it to the website - direct from the streets!

Have you ever tried to get your demos broadcast on BBC, your issues discussed in national or local newspapers? Did you ever wish you had access to the corporate media machine? Charities and action groups, campaigns and community groups as well as individuals can publish their own news on indymedia: without interference of editors, without having to streamline your news with the need to generate a profit.

Did you ever wish to make your video clips, your audio recordings or your written reports accessible to a wide and active audience? Indymedia is made by its readers, and viewed by people who strive for social change, who are ready to reclaim the virtual commons of the web and the physical commons of the streets.

Did you ever look out for reports on the struggles and achievements of action groups and campaigns in your local community? Make them yourself: Indymedia is

an open platform and welcomes your contributions.

Ever wished to interfere with the repetitive reporting of media monopolies? Ever wanted to apply your media-making skills to a radically open project? Look out for an imc collective near you.

The "united kollectives" of indymedia uk communicate through open email-lists, and welcome new volunteers . You can write to them at imc-uk-contact@lists.indymedia.org

much easier than overcoming the obstacles he faced in actually travelling to Cochabamba, and access to his local newspaper and radio station had been denied); on the other hand, Kaka had to walk two hours to a friend's house to use the internet; to communicate locally, in addition to establishing an alternative radio station, it was necessary to go round the local villages *talking*.

Reclaiming the Commons

Inspired by the Zapatista movement, Indymedia is a decentralised and open network of counter-information, run by volunteers on five continents. It makes communication technologies available to local and global movements for social justice.

Since the first independent media centre covered the WTO protests in Seattle 1999, the project has grown fast. Today, more than 130 independent media centres are supporting each other with free software, knowledge and other resources. The biggest collaborative radical blog in the internet, indymedia welcomes every contribution. It only draws the line at trolling, racism and similar abuse.

Indymedia is experimenting with the empowering potential of technology as a contribution to the global commons of knowledge. Free, opensource software is at the heart of the project: adaptable and freely available. Kit like digital cameras, mobile phones, laptops and old machinery multiplies if shared. Art, activism and technological knowledge have melted into a new means of political articulation. A multitude of local nodes connected to specific struggles is challenging the levelling power of profit-oriented globalisation.

Indymedia uk stands for "United Kollectives". From Edinburgh to London, from Oxford and Cambridge to Leeds Bradford and Liverpool, in Sheffield, Manchester and the West Country, volunteers have formed collectives to maintain their own local newswires, to produce their own features, and to run the backend of the imc-uk website collaboratively. The collectives work closely with local campaigns and grassroots scenes, and constantly build connections with projects around the globe. They produce printed versions of the website, make and distribute videos, put on radical screenings and are broadcasting local and web-radio shows.

Indymedia is bridging the gap between reporter and reported, producers of events and audience. In the face of capitalism, racism, state-oppression and control, **Indymedia is a massive media carnival: pro-active, assertive, tactical, fun, and political.**

How to publish your own reports on the Indymedia UK Website:

Step One: Hit the 'PUBLISH' link on the frontpage (www.indymedia.org.uk).

Step Two: If you want to upload pictures, video or audio files, enter the number of files you want to upload in the "Media Items" box.

Step Three: Fill in the publish form. Enter your **name** or a pseudonym, a **title** and a short **abstract** for your contribution. Email addresses, phone numbers etc are optional. Your article will be published automatically on the imc uk newswire. If you tick the appropriate boxes, you can also make it appear in 2 **regions** and up to three **topics**.

Step Four: Enter data
- Text: Type or paste straight into the field **"artide"**.
- Photographs/ Audio/ Video: To upload media-files, go to the last section of the publish form, and select the file from your hard drive using the 'Browse' button. Enter a subtitle for your file. Indymedia UK supports 20MB maximum file size in jpg, gif, mp3, avi, qt, mpeg formats.

Step Five: Finish
Hit the 'Contribute' button at the bottom of the form - That's it! your contribution will now be added to the imc uk website.

Bypass the corporate media, publish your own news on imc

From Edinburgh to London, from Oxford and Cambridge to Leeds Bradford and Liverpool, in Sheffield, Manchester and the West Country, there is a local collectives near you - if not set up your own - write to us for details.

Figure 7.8   An Indymedia leaflet

Indeed, talking is also vital to the development of these new social movements. Great stress is laid on face-to-face contact. However, while this reinforces the commitment to the local, it has also led to the development of new kinds of *meeting spaces*. Perhaps chief among these are the social fora outlined in Section 2. The major set piece fora are huge open gatherings, sometimes of a hundred thousand people; they function through a multiplicity of smaller workshops organised by the different groups, and the point of them is communication. Unlike, say, a political summit of 'world leaders' where the point is the outcome and the 'final communiqué' has often been agreed in advance, social fora are movements within a work in progress. Within these fora, many sessions are organised in ways that encourage participation. Between the global social fora, more local social fora exist in thousands of places around the world as spaces where different groups can discuss what they are up to. Geographer Paul Routledge (2002, 2003) has called such spaces 'convergence spaces'.

What are the strengths and weaknesses of these particular arrangements and meeting spaces of the new social movements? One point, again, concerns inequality of access. For reasons of resources, of the difficulty of acquiring visas and so forth, it is more difficult for some than for others to attend such meetings (remember Stanis Kaka's problems). There is also a fragility in the frustration from these endless discussions which may seem never to 'go anywhere'. Certainly, there is a commitment to open-endedness and to making decisions through consensus, but doing that is very difficult. Moreover, there is a vulnerability to domination by particular groups. This is something that the World Social Forum recognises, and the terms for the constitution of a forum are quite explicit: there can be no representation of organised political parties. Think about this for a moment. On the one hand, it is a form of exclusion: the institution of an *enclosure*. Sometimes, perhaps one needs mechanisms of enclosure in order to protect internal openness – once again it is necessary to consider the power relations in the particular situation. On the other hand, such rules of enclosure do not prevent domination by determined groups who may enter as individuals but in actuality work in clandestine coordination. It is difficult to guarantee closure. Yet there are strengths in these particular arrangements and meeting spaces too: the unpredictability, the variety and the creativity that can sometimes be sparked make these spaces, for those who join them, spaces of possibility.

Summary

- A central aim of many of the movements of global anti-capitalism is to challenge the enclosures of the powerful.

- One question that the challenge of new social movements raises is: what kinds of enclosures – if any – may nonetheless be necessary in an alternative globalisation?

- Solidarity against a common enemy is built through linking local struggles, by taking advantage of new communications technologies and by constructing new kinds of meeting spaces.

- The aim of the new social movements is to rethink entirely the architecture of territory and flow that characterises today's neo-liberal capitalist globalisation.

5   A chain of differences

In this chapter so far, we have explored a geography of solidarity constructed around the connection between two places (Section 3.2) and another constructed through getting together against a common enemy (Section 4). There are many other solidarities, but we shall explore just one more to see how territory and flow are part and parcel of the politics in yet another way.

There are many international organisations that bring together groups around the world on the basis that they are campaigning around similar particular issues. The international organisation we shall look at here is concerned with the problems of peasant and small farmers and the localities in which they are set. The organisation is called Via Campesina, and it is introduced in Extract 7.1 below.

Extract 7.1

Via Campesina

Via Campesina is an international movement made up of small and medium-sized farmers, agricultural workers, women and peasants as well as rural communities in Asia, Africa, America and Europe. It is an autonomous, pluralist organisation, independent of any political, economic or other movement. It organises in seven regions: Europe, North-West Asia, South-East Asia, North America, the Caribbean, Central America and South America. It also undertakes joint work with African farmers' organisations.

The creation of Via Campesina goes back to 1992 at a meeting in Managua. In 1993 the first Via Campesina international conference was held at Mons in Belgium. It established the movement as a world organisation, defined its constitution and developed its first strategic orientations. Its second conference was at Tlaxcala in Mexico in 1996, where 70 organisations from 37 countries participated. Questions of agrarian reform, debt, development, technology and food sovereignty were discussed. Then it was Bangalore in India that hosted the third conference. There Via Campesina condemned unequivocally the integration of agriculture and food into the WTO Accords and demanded that they should be taken out of the negotiations. It wants the concept of food sovereignty to be recognised in international law. This claim for food sovereignty, accepted as legitimate in certain international bodies, notably the FAO [Food and Agriculture Organisation], affirms the right of peoples to decide their level of food security both quantitatively and qualitatively. It also affirms the right of countries or groups of countries to control imports at their frontiers when the circulation of surplus agricultural produce has destructive effects on producers and on local markets. In its view, dumping by the rich countries serves to reduce the level of self-sufficiency of the poor ones and to enlarge the gap between them and the rich.

Finally, Via Campesina calls for a world audit to evaluate the serious consequences of the introduction of genetically modified organisms (GMOs) into agriculture and emphasises that the constraining policies of structural adjustment imposed by the IMF and the World Bank amplify themechanisms which impoverish populations and rural milieus. Via Campesina wants to respond to the globalisation of markets and the ever-increasing powers of the transnationals with the globalisation of the trade-union struggle and the adoption of the slogan: 'Let us globalise hope'. Let us envisage another globalisation, that of peoples, of a plurality of cultures and of fair trade.

(Herman and Kuper, 2003, pp.62–3)

Read carefully the introduction to Via Campesina in Extract 7.1. Apart from the potential importance of such a struggle, one thing that struck me was the sentence beginning: 'It also affirms the right of countries ... to control imports'. This is not, then, a politics that is simply against 'enclosure'. In fact, to return to the land of the Zapatistas from Section 2.2, a number of Mexican peasant organisations have joined Via Campesina in response to the opening up, under NAFTA, of the Mexico–US border to flows of corn. Subsidised US corn has undercut the small Mexican producers. Yet should rich and powerful territories have the same rights to protectionism as poorer ones?

What Via Campesina aims at, in its 'autonomous, pluralist organisation' (Herman and Kuper, 2003), is connecting a set of local 'autonomous' organisations in such a way that the differences between them can be respected even while they get together around particular issues. José Bové and François Dufour, leaders of the organisation of small farmers, the French Confédération Paysanne, itself a member of the Coordination Paysanne Européenne and thence of Via Campesina, have described it thus: 'You can't talk about factions within *Via Campesina* ... what holds for Santiago or Bamako doesn't necessarily hold for Rome or Paris. The exchange of opinions and experiences makes this a wonderful network for training and debate' (Bové and Dufour, 2001, p.158). This is an attempt to hold together autonomy (territory in our terms; local coherence) and flow (connection through alliances) in such a way that the connections between them can certainly change the character of local organisations (for instance, through 'training and debate'), but where that local character and local determination are not lost. It is this active connection, of mutual respect and autonomy, that produces this particular geography of solidarity. Let us explore some aspects of it in more detail.

First, how is this form of solidarity not simply the local versus the global? Or even local*ist* in the terms of Section 2.2? Take the case of Bové and Dufour and the French farmers. Their group first came to international attention when, in 1999, along with a crowd of local people, they systematically dismantled a branch of McDonald's that was being constructed in Millau in the *département* (district) of Avéyron in southern France. Immediately, many in the media interpreted this as a defence of territory: as a defence of France and, more specifically, as anti-USA. In reality, Bové and Dufour have gone to great lengths to

[handwritten margin note:] Globalisation benefit the rich countries at the expense of the poor

refute these interpretations. At the very moment of Millau, Dufour was planning an intervention at a US film festival at Deauville, where he:

> wanted to explain to the American Festival-goers that it was not their culture we objected to: that it was very welcome in our regions, but that the multinational companies had to respect our differences, our identity. We don't want hormones in our food; they're a risk to public health, and go against our farming ethics. At a more fundamental level, imposing hormones on us means that our freedom of choice in the food and culture we want is seriously restricted. Agricultural exchanges have existed for a long time: we don't advocate exempting agriculture from the politics of international trading, but we want something different from freedom of the market and the liberal economy.
>
> (Bové and Dufour, 2001, pp.20–1)

Bové and Dufour have, moreover, made many links with like-minded farmers' groups in the USA.

Second, even if this attacking of McDonald's – the purveyor of standardised burgers – is not anti-Americanism, it could still be a defence of French food. After all, French cuisine is something to be proud of; perhaps it is legitimate to want to defend it against foreign influences. This would be another kind of defensive closure. Yet consider: French cuisine is not concocted entirely from influences, products or procedures which are indigenous to France; it is already a hybrid. Therefore, if French food is already a mixture of products and influences from elsewhere, does that not mean that this latest potential entrant should be allowed in too? What arguments might there be against this? Think back to the arguments of Chapter 5, for instance, about 'native' and 'alien' UK trees.

Bové and Dufour (2001) argue against this too – no, they say, what we are against is *bad* food. They call it *malbouffe*:

> **Bové**: 'Malbouffe' implies eating any old thing, prepared in any old way ... For me, the term means both the standardization of food like McDonald's – the same taste from one end of the world to the other – and the choice of food associated with the use of hormones and GMOs, as well as the residues of pesticides and other things that can endanger health. So there's a cultural and a health aspect. Junk food also involves industrialized agriculture – that is to say, mass-produced food; not necessarily in the form of products sold by McDonald's but mass-produced in the sense of industrialized pig-rearing, battery chickens, and the like. The concept of 'malbouffe' is challenging all agriculture and food production processes.

...

Dufour: Today the word has been adopted to condemn those forms of agriculture whose development has been at the expense of taste, health, and the cultural and geographical identity of food. Junk food is the result of intensive exploitation of the land to maximize yield and profit.

(Bové and Dufour, 2001, pp.53–4)

The above quotations are worth studying closely. Before beginning the analysis, however, we should note some important points. Few political statements or positions are entirely consistent; people are constantly working out ideas, maybe trying to hold different principles together. In my analysis, that is what is going on in the statements from Bové and Dufour. Looking at the long history of their political actions now (for instance by reading other statements of theirs), it is possible to detect shifts and modifications in their positions, perhaps provoked at least in part by some of the misinterpretations which they felt they must counter. (Remember the shift from anti-globalisation to global justice discussed in Section 2.)

Perhaps now it is possible to address our earlier question: if French food is already a mixture of products and influences from elsewhere, does that not mean that this latest potential entrant (McDonald's) should be allowed in too? One part of an answer is that this is not a politics of the closure of territory; it is a politics which seeks to challenge the nature of connections. What is at issue is the nature of the relations of interconnection – the map of power of openness, of flows. French food can continue its long history of absorbing new influences: the question is which ones, why and on what terms. The choice of McDonald's to protest against rested upon it being seen as an iconic symbol of the kinds of connections that Bové and Dufour oppose.

Yet many of the groups in Via Campesina are determinedly in favour of the 'local' and especially of diversity. They display a real concern about the potential homogenisation of the world which they see as a result of neo-liberal globalisation. In their case, this emphasis on local diversity seems often to be based on the natural world. They lay great stress on geographical variations within nature and on the need to respect them. One of the many arguments of Mexican peasant farmers about NAFTA, for instance, is that it will eradicate the diversity of Mexican corn production (Herman and Kuper, 2003). This recalls the arguments in favour of local diversity made by Common Ground in Chapter 5.

In the Avéyron in France, the dominant local product is Roquefort cheese, made of ewes' milk. The immediate spark that provoked the Millau protest in 1999 was a US surcharge of 100 per cent on imports of Roquefort. The EU's refusal to import US hormone-fed beef had been declared by the WTO to be against its rules, and a time limit had been set for its lifting. When the EU failed to comply, the USA retaliated with a series of surcharges. Among them was the one on Roquefort. Bové's defence, however, was not made on the basis of a nostalgia for an idyllic local past. Rather, the talk was of the 'farm of the future', and of how that demanded a different kind of locally sensitive negotiation with nature. Bové and Dufour argued against intensive farming because: 'In intensive farming the object is to adapt the soil to the crop, never the other way round' (Bové and Dufour, 2001, p.67). Their argument was that it *should* be the other way around, and that local sensitivity would draw on local knowledge. This then is a defence of the diversity of territories which sees that diversity as constructed out of the weavings of human and natural relations.

There are also other claims for these territories. For instance, Bové and Dufour argue at one point that: 'The people who live in an area have to decide how its resources are to be used' (2001, p.134).

Activity 7.7

Consider the Bové and Dufour (2001) quotation above. Is it realistic? Is it even democratic? What about the claims that arise in a globalised world from a wider connectivity? What about 'local' people who are rich and powerful?

There were hints of this kind of local claim in the Papua New Guinea case too (see Reading 7A). In that instance, there were claims for local economic independence. What might this mean in a twenty-first-century globalised world?

The point here is not to be critical. The issues are almost insuperably difficult, and it is all too easy to point to inconsistencies in engaged political practice. The lessons we should draw are perhaps different ones, and relate back to the discussion in Section 3.1: working out political positions is genuinely difficult, and it is an ongoing process, developed in political engagement.

The third point in a sense returns us to our example of the UK and Ghana discussed in Section 3.2. To talk of autonomy and pluralism is all very well, but what if the interests of groups actually conflict? This was potentially the case between farmers in the EU and farmers in the global South. The French farmers were at the heart of this, for the EU Common Agricultural Policy (the CAP) was important for maintaining farming in France, but hugely discriminatory against farmers of the South. This posed a serious challenge to solidarity, and was overcome only by a completely radical rethink in which the whole nature of 'farming' in the EU was redefined. Stressing the reorientation of agricultural production away from intensive methods, and making a clear distinction between small farmers and large conglomerates, the Confédération Paysanne argued that Europe should cut down its subsidised exports, and that support for farming should be part of a wider policy for rural development. This was, in other words, yet another radical rethinking of the nature of territories and flows which, it argued, could be 'a solidaristic citizens' and farmers' CAP' (Herman and Kuper, 2003, p.xix).

Summary

- Making links between local places and struggles entails rejecting local*ism*, accepting differences and facing up to potential conflicts of interest.
- At best, territory and flow can be mutually supportive, enabling both differences and flows of mutual influence.

6 Conclusion

Living in a globalised world can provide opportunities and challenges. Certainly, it does so for those who would try to change the nature of that globalisation. Building solidarity in such a context is both necessary and difficult. This chapter has explored a range of campaigns and proposals that have taken on such challenges. They represent just a few of many possible engagements with the currently dominant form of globalisation. The ones explored here have, in different ways, attempted to confront some of the power relations through which human globalisation is produced, and the inequalities that can result. However, these proposals and campaigns themselves have to confront difficult issues: what kinds of architecture of territory and flow do they want in this globalised world? Through what mechanisms could such an architecture be built? How can different places and struggles be linked together to indicate the possibility of a different globalisation? Each of the cases examined has involved specific challenges to, and mobilisations of, territory and flow. What have resulted are distinct potential geographies of solidarity. None of them have succeeded in totally changing the world, but perhaps what can be pointed to by way of achievements is that they have put some issues firmly on the political agenda, thought about them in innovative ways and insisted on the possibility that we could make the world otherwise.

References

Allen, J. (2006) 'Claiming connections: a distant world of sweatshops?' in Barnett, C., Robinson, J. and Rose, G. (eds) *A Demanding World*, Milton Keynes, The Open University.

Bové, J. and Dufour, F. (2001) *The World Is Not for Sale: Farmers Against Junk Food* (trans. A. de Casparis), London, Verso. (First published as *Le Monde N'Est Pas une Merchandise* in 2000, Paris, Editions la Découverte & Syros.)

Carvel, J. (2004) 'Nil by mouth', *The Guardian*, 27 August.

Castells, M. (1996) *The Rise of the Network Society: The Information Age, Economy, Society and Culture*, vol.1, Cambridge, MA, Blackwell/ Oxford, Blackwell.

Herman, P. and Kuper, R. (2003) *Food for Thought: Towards a Future for Farming*, London, Pluto Press. (First published as *Changeons de Politique Agricole* for the Confédération Paysanne in 2002, Paris, Mille et Une Nuits.)

Klein, N. (2002) *Fences and Windows: Dispatches from the Front Lines of the Globalization Debate*, London, Flamingo.

Lambert, D. (2006) 'Making the past present: historical wrongs and demands for reparation' in Barnett, C., Robinson, J. and Rose, G. (eds) *A Demanding World*, Milton Keynes, The Open University.

Martineau, T., Decker, K. and Bundred, P. (2002) 'Briefing note on international migration of health professionals: levelling the playing field for developing country health systems', Health Sector Reform Research Work Programme, Liverpool School of Tropical Medicine, http://www.eldis.org/static/DOC12324.htm (accessed 21 October 2005).

Mensah, K. (2005) 'International migration of health care staff: extent and policy responses with illustrations from Ghana' in Mackintosh, M. and Koivusalo, M. (eds) *Commercialization of Health Care: Global and Local Dynamics and Policy Responses*, Basingstoke, Palgrave.

Mensah, K., Mackintosh, M. and Henry, L. (2005) 'The "skills drain" of health professionals from the developing world: a framework for policy formulation', London, Medact, http://www.medact.org/content/Skills%20drain/Mensah%20et%20al.%202005.pdf (accessed 21 October 2005).

Notes from Nowhere (eds) (2003) *We Are Everywhere: The Irresistible Rise of Global Anticapitalism*, London, Verso, http://www.weareeverywhere.org (accessed 21 October 2005).

Robinson, J. (2006) 'The geopolitics of intervention: presence and power in global politics' in Barnett, C., Robinson, J. and Rose, G. (eds) *A Demanding World*, Milton Keynes, The Open University.

Routledge, P. (2002) 'Resisting and reshaping destructive development: social movements and globalizing networks' in Johnston, R.J., Taylor, P.J. and Watts, M.J. (eds) *Geographies of Global Change: Remapping the World* (2nd edn), Oxford, Blackwell, pp.310–27.

Routledge, P. (2003) 'Convergence space: process geographies of grassroots mobilisation networks', *Transactions of the Institute of British Geographers*, vol.28, no.3, pp.333–49.

Shultz, J. (2003) 'The water is ours, Dammit!' in Notes from Nowhere (eds) *We are Everywhere: The Irresistible Rise of Global Anticapitalism*, London, Verso, pp.264–77.

Silverstone, R. (2006) 'Media and communication in a globalised world' in Barnett, C., Robinson, J. and Rose, G. (eds) *A Demanding World*, Milton Keynes, The Open University.

Subcomandante Insurgente Marcos (2001) *Our Word is our Weapon*, selected writings edited by J. Ponce de León, London, Serpent's Tail.

World Development Movement (2003) *States of Unrest III: Resistance to IMF and World Bank Policies in Poor Countries*, London, World Development Movement, http://www.wdm.org.uk/campaigns/cambriefs/debt/States%20of%20Unrest%2011104.03.pdf (accessed 21 October 2005).

Young, I.M. (2003) 'From guilt to solidarity: sweatshops and political responsibility', *Dissent*, spring, pp.39–44.

Reading 7A

Notes from Nowhere, 'We are everywhere: the irresistible rise of global anticapitalism'

The third conference of Peoples' Global Action (Against 'Free' Trade and the WTO), held in Cochabamba Bolivia, began on 14 September 2001 – a dangerous time to be fighting the 'free' trade agenda with one of its most potent symbols – the World Trade Center – in ruins. George W Bush made it clear: you are with him, or with the terrorists. The Governor of Cochabamba District absorbed these instructions rapidly and announced to the press that the PGA conference was a meeting of 'international terrorists'. On arrival in La Paz, many activists heading for the conference were interrogated and detained by intelligence officials. Dozens were threatened with deportation.

Stanis, an unflappable Papua New Guinean, had the longest, strangest journey of all. It began, in a sense, when he started using the internet, which required walking to a friend's house two hours from his village in New Guinea. In this way he discovered, to his delight and astonishment, that many others around the world are, like him, opposing the policies of the World Bank. After a long trek to the capital, Port Moresby, he took a plane to Sydney. Flight disruption after the 11 September attacks delayed him there for three days, and then he caught a plane to Los Angeles. Despite being in transit, he was held in a hotel under armed guard for two nights by US immigration officials who didn't believe that a large, affable rural Papuan with radical literature in his luggage could be anything other than a terrorist.

Stanis was finally sent on to La Paz, where he was detained for two more days, sitting in a small office in the customs lounge with no bed, no food, and $10 in his pocket. Having been jailed in the past for organizing protests against the World Bank in Papua New Guinea, he merely sat there and implacably refused their hamburgers. Eventually he was released, and he came to Cochabamba to share his story. This is an edited transcript of an interview.

We discovered we weren't alone: surfing the net in Papua New Guinea

An interview with Stanis Kaka by Notes from Nowhere

Economic independence struggle

In Papua New Guinea we got our independence from Australia in 1975. It was given, as a gift. We never struggled for independence. They just gave it to us, and we accepted. But it wasn't an economic independence, it was only political independence. But without economic independence we can't run our country. And what is actually happening now is they are trying to take over our lives.

The World Bank and the IMF [International Monetary Fund] came in [in 1991] and offered 'assistance', and the Papua New Guinean Government accepted. Since then we have been told that we are millions of dollars in debt to them, but we can't afford to repay. In 1995 the World Bank and the IMF declared our debt unpayable, and came up with 27 policy conditions that the government had to implement by 1996, or Papua New Guinea would not be able to access any more loans.

[Those policies] include the Customary Land Registration Act – 97 per cent of our land is customary [tribal or collective] land. Most of the people cannot afford to register land, and so are losing it to the state.

We were against those policies and we led a strike in 1996, in which two people were killed. There followed a general strike against the World Bank then, and the government gave orders that the people who were leading should be arrested – including myself. We thought that we were the only ones who were controlled by the World Bank and the IMF. And I, too, thought that when I was leading the strike.

We were waiting to see if our government would continue pursuing these policies. And what happened was in 2001 the World Bank and IMF pushed for the same conditions for the next loan. As a result, all of the university students went on a peaceful sitting protest, and four of them were killed on 25 June 2001. They were sitting all day in front of the parliament building, and that evening the police asked them to leave, but they refused. The police came and used firearms to disperse them, and killed four of them, and 17 were hospitalized.

And since then I've opened my eyes, collected information. Concerned people were getting in touch with me, writing letters and saying, 'That's what the World Bank is doing to Malaysia, to Africa, and to other parts of the world.' And I thought, wow, other people in all these different countries are struggling – well that is not a bad thing.

And so I'm interested in making international links. Earlier this year when I was using my friend's internet I began to realize the internet is access to everything. I find it very easy, instead of waiting two to three months to get a letter. So when I was invited to come [to the PGA conference], it was a great opportunity for me to see what people from other countries are experiencing and get experiences from them.

Burgers from Interpol

Since 1993/1994 when we began the campaign against the corporate take-over of Papua New Guinea by the World Bank/IMF, the struggle has been long and bitter ... And it has also been bloody, with our students paying with their lives ... We know too, that our struggle and campaign is the same being waged all over the world by those of you who, like us, are opposed to the take-over and domination of our world by multinational and transnational corporations.

– Powes Parkop, Anti-Privatization Alliance, Papua New Guinea

When I arrived in La Paz the immigration officer asked me where I was going and I said to travel 'round'. They started saying to me, 'You're not going there, you don't have a place to stay.' I said that someone was picking me up at the airport, and they rang Cochabamba to check. Then I said I was going to a hotel and they could get in touch with me there and they said, 'No you're not, you're going back to Papua New Guinea.' And I said, 'Why am I going back?!' And they said, 'You don't have any legitimate reason to be here. And you are going to that PGA conference so we are sending you back.' The man who interrogated me was working with Interpol [the international police force] and I gave him my telephone number and told him everything, and said, 'If you want to ring my family, ring them and they will tell you the truth.' They were trying to see if there was space on the plane to deport me but there were no seats. Finally, a lawyer rang and came and bailed me out.

I stayed in that airport office for two nights – sitting and sleeping. They sometimes came with burgers but I didn't take them. I just ate one piece and left it on the shelf, saying, 'I didn't come all this way to sit here and eat this kind of food.' The man who came to bail me out shook my hand and said 'Good luck.'

I will tell my people

I work with Kasalapalou, a community organization which raises awareness campaigns about our land, and fights the appropriation of our land through the Land Registration Act. We have a lot of mineral resources in our province. The experience of many provinces in my country is that corporations come in and log and mine – but they don't care about the environment, they just do what they like. That's why we formed our group. It wasn't made with outside influence or help, it just consists of village people.

Despite the fact that the university strikes came out against the World Bank, many village people think these policies are only to do with the educated people, like the students, and that it won't affect them. They say, 'That's nothing to do with us, we enjoy our life here, we have food and shelter.' But they don't know that the government is making laws that will affect them, everyone, not just the few people struggling.

Most village people are not educated but we communicate well with them. There are no telephones or other forms of communication; we use word of mouth and we have a local radio program. There are six districts in the Inga province in which we go around talking to people.

Eighty-five per cent of our population live in the villages. We live in extended families and most of us are pretty happy. Like me, I had a job, but left it and for the last 15 years I've been in the village. But I can survive. I have land there. I can grow my own food. I have three houses in the village, whereas in the city I would have to rent a place! But in the village I have three houses and I own them. I don't have to pay for anything! I don't have electricity bills and I don't have water bills and I don't pay rent. Actually I find it very easy! And that's what I judge things by. Because I see people are struggling under the rules of the World Bank and the IMF, and I find out that the world's people in other countries are struggling also and seeing them as enemies, and then I know there must be something wrong with these institutions.

When I go back home I will tell my people, 'Listen, we think we are helpless, but we're not.' My people normally come and they say, 'You're nobody. You're not a politician. You're nobody special. You're just a village person and you are struggling out here and these people are coming with money. These people have all the power. And they can kill you.' And what I'm telling the people now is that what I am doing will have a big impact in the future. That's what I tell them. So when I was invited to come here, they realized that something was happening across the world.

We can outnumber them

> We are like rats fighting the elephants. People struggling for the land are being killed for it, but the word is more important than violence ... We the people are going to make a big hole for the elephant to fall in.
>
> – Stanis Kaka at an international climate change gathering, 2002

Awareness and distribution of the message in Papua New Guinea is slim. A Malaysian logging company runs our second newspaper, so when we put anything about mining or logging in the newspaper they will never publish it. I have tried to write about this ten or twenty times and when I ring them to find out what has happened to my article they say the Chief Editor has refused to publish it. So when I go back I am going to put my program on a provincial radio station. Now they are banning our form of awareness-raising through the radio station. The radio station manager is my friend, so he lets me speak. But gradually they will stop it. That is why I am looking at ways to set up my own community radio station, so awareness will carry on being built there. We have no other means of communicating so we put our programs out to let people know what the mining and logging people are doing – every fortnight.

We have lots of mineral resources in our ground and thick rainforest, and the big companies are coming in and taking out our resources in raw form without them even being processed in Papua New Guinea. [These 'rip and ship' policies prevent the development of manufacturing in resource-rich countries, while avoiding higher *tariffs* or import taxes for Northern corporations.] So it's going out raw, not even as timber. Some big companies – especially Japanese and Malaysian ones – are logging. And our government can't pay back the money to the World Bank.

And yet our government is inviting them in. I don't know why. I don't know what's wrong with the governments of this world. We normally vote our representative into the parliament, and before they get elected we educate them, question them, and all that. We ask them, 'Are you going to fight for us?' But they promise us everything, and once they get into the parliament they are 100 per cent different. They just dance to the tune of the IMF and World Bank and the government. So when they come back we say, 'When we elected you, you told us different things, but since you got into the parliament you haven't raised your voice and you haven't done anything.'

They say, 'I am only one person myself and I can't do anything. We have got a democratic system, but this is what happens.' But the population of Papua New Guinea is four million. And if four million of us stand up for what is right – there are, I think, only 109 members of parliament – we can outnumber them. That's what I say to them when I go to the villages. I say, 'There are four million of us, four million people of Papua New Guinea; we can speak for our own rights better than those people. Our elected members in parliament don't have any authority – we do.' That's our message. We have got a right. That's what I believe in.

So I would say that this is the real independence struggle of Papua New Guinea. Political independence was gained, but we are struggling for economic independence now. And so far two people died in 1996, four died in June – and probably we are looking at 1,000 people dying before we get economic independence. With the blood of those people, we will get economic independence.

It's not that I am going to end it. When I become old and die, that's not the end. I have children. And I have told them, 'Fight to the end of your life.' So I am training them. I am educating them so they will say, 'What my father fought for, I am fighting for too'.

I used to work for an Australian company doing mining in my own province, but I pulled out. I was working in a laboratory analyzing everything for them and I saw the amount of the waste going in the water system. I didn't agree with this and so I pulled out. And that is the reason for me being really active. People said to me: 'You had a job there! You had a good wage! Why don't you just close your mouth and just go along with them?' I replied that this is my province, and I know what is actually happening. And if I close my mouth and enjoy what is given to me, when I am dead my children will just take out my bones and throw them away. That's why I resigned my job and am now telling my people what is actually happening.

(Notes from Nowhere, 2003, pp.412–14)

Stanis Kaka can be contacted at kakastanley@hotmail.com

Interview by Notes from Nowhere/Katharine Ainger

Resources: Interviews from the Cochabamba conference make up the book, *Desire for Change – women on the front line of global resistance*, LARC, 62 Field Gate Street, London E1 1ES, UK or pgabolivia@yahoo.co.uk

---

Reading 7B

Nil by mouth

Analysis

John Carvel

It is good news that health ministers in England have accepted this week that they should not rebuild the NHS by stripping developing countries of their scarce supply of qualified nurses. What a shame they have not had the courage to find a robust solution to the problems of medical migration.

The figures speak for themselves. Over the past four years about 40,000 overseas nurses have registered to work in the UK, mostly from the Philippines, South Africa, Australia and India. The government has no clear information on how many came to work in the NHS, private hospitals and the more shadowy world of independent care homes. But it is clear that ministers could not have achieved their targets for expanding the workforce without this influx of talent.

Some of the exporting countries appear not to mind. For example, the Filipino authorities plan to train a surplus of nurses in the expectation that many will go to work abroad, remitting part of their income back to their families.

But the drain is a real problem for the countries of sub-Saharan Africa. Latest figures from the Nursing and Midwifery Council show that 6,028 South African nurses registered to work in Britain over the four years to April 2003. Thembeka Gwagwa, chief officer of Denosa, the South African nurses' association, told the Royal

College of Nursing's annual congress in May that her country's health service was short of 1,000 nurses and losing 300 a month. The loss of even a handful of key staff could be enough to destroy a rural maternity service or Aids clinic.

Other countries suffering from poaching are Zimbabwe, which had 1,561 nurses join the UK register over the past four years, Nigeria (1,496), Ghana (660), Zambia (444), Kenya (386), Botswana (226) and Malawi (192). Health ministers have been well aware of the problem and, to their credit, took a lead in offering solutions. Three years ago, in response to pressure from Nelson Mandela, the former president of South Africa, they banned the NHS from running recruitment fairs in developing countries.

A code of practice on ethical recruitment was brought in to stop NHS organisations hiring from developing countries unless there was an intergovernmental agreement to permit it – as there is, for example, with India.

More than 170 agencies supplying the NHS with staff were required to sign up to the code if they wanted to stay in business with the health service – supposedly stopping them poaching on the NHS's behalf. But this did not stop the flow. There was nothing to prevent private hospitals and care homes recruiting in the banned countries. And nothing to stop nurses moving from those private institutions into the NHS at a later date.

The NHS could argue that its hands were clean. The nursing unions, which were anxious about the immorality of poaching, were firm believers in the right of nurses to seek professional development in another country. Any attempt to deny individual mobility would have been seen as an outrage.

But it mattered little to Aids patients in South Africa or Botswana whether their clinic closed because the staff were hoovered up directly by the NHS, or because they left on a more circuitous route via the private sector. A simple answer might have been to impose the code on the private sector. But John Reid, the health secretary, said that would not be possible 'without a complex and intrusive legislative programme'. As he sought rapprochement with the private firms, he was in no mood for that. So the exodus continued and – until health minister John Hutton's visit to South Africa this week – looked set to increase.

Bizarrely, the government ruled that foundation hospitals should be exempt from the anti-poaching rules and merely be 'invited' to adopt an ethical approach. Since all acute NHS trusts are due to gain foundation status within four years, the compulsory ban looked set to wither away.

On Wednesday, Mr Hutton went some way to revive the policy. As an incentive to behave more ethically, private employers will get access to the government's overseas recruitment channels if they sign up to the code. The NHS will not be allowed to recruit nurses from developing countries on renewable temporary contracts to evade the ban on hiring permanent staff. About 200 agencies will be told they cannot supply the NHS with British staff if they are poaching for the private sector.

The Royal College of Nursing says this fails to tackle the real issue. It wants the private hospitals to be made to operate by the same rules as the NHS, thereby closing the back door that has allowed poaching to thrive. Since ministers have no intention of conceding, there appears only one other way forward. It is to accept that developing countries exporting scarce staff should be compensated for doing so through transfer of technology, skills and financial assistance.

The Department of Health does not like the sound of this. Less than half the Commonwealth agrees, it says. Some developed countries might end up compensating each other. And if we compensated for poaching nurses, why not for builders, plumbers and other skilled workers? Why not indeed? The choice is between stopping our unethical behaviour or compensating for it.

And the story may yet have a sting in the tail. Until now, Britain has been the most powerful player in the poaching game, but that role is set to pass to the US. The NHS may be about to lose staff – both British and overseas – to the lure of the dollar.

John Carvel is the Guardian's social affairs editor

(John Carvel, 2004)

Chapter 8

Good food: ethical consumption and global change

Sarah Whatmore and Nigel Clark

Contents

1   Introduction

Markets might seem an unpromising starting point for thinking about ethics and questions of conscience. Though Giles Mohan, in Chapter 6, has shown that some global trading is undertaken by individuals, economic theories and current affairs programmes commonly depict markets as the preserve of large institutions like multinational corporations (MNCs) and the World Trade Organisation (WTO). These often seem remote from the actions and feelings of ordinary people, in which the cold logic of market forces leaves little room for social justice, environmental concern or any other 'extraneous' ethical consideration. Yet the question of our responsibilities towards others with whom we are connected through our consumer activities is always in play. Our shopping habits and lifestyle choices have social and environmental consequences and generate ethical connections between consumers and producers, whether we consciously acknowledge these consequences and connections or not.

There are a growing number of organisations determined to bring these consequences and connections home by generating new senses and practices of spatial proximity and distance as, for example, in the case of campaigns against the use of sweatshop labour in the production of global brands of sportswear **(Allen, 2006)**. Using the internet and other media, such campaigns seek to prick the consciences of trainer wearing consumers around the world by bringing the sweatshop conditions of the otherwise 'faceless' people who stitch their fashionable footwear in 'faraway' places too close for comfort. The mobilisation of consumers to boycott goods tainted with social injustice is not new. Some of you may recall, or have participated in, the boycott of South African food exports during the Apartheid era, for instance. The pamphlets and public meetings of organisations like the Women's Anti-Slavery League in the early nineteenth century, which mobilised popular boycotts of sugar and other commodities produced by slave labour, carry the trace of this connection between markets and ethics back beyond memory, even if the technologies of connection that they employed now seem rather quaint.

The argument which has been developed through the preceding chapters in this book is that paying close attention to how global connections are made in practice, and what they are made of, provides a useful way of bringing powerful forces of globalisation down to earth. This focus on practices, on work or on making, helps us to see globalisation as a process that is the outcome of activities grounded in particular practices and in particular places. This sense of a world in the making is important both analytically, for the ways in which we make sense of living in a globalised world, and politically, for empowering us to feel able to make a difference.

As Doreen Massey noted in Chapter 7, many heterogeneous and diffuse social movements around the world are now coming together, fused in the belief that it is possible to organise a globalised world in ways very different from those that now predominate. Challenging the way that 'free' market forces currently operate is one of the central strands linking these diverse groups and engagements. In this chapter, we look more closely at attempts to reorganise the flow of things around the world, focusing on strategies and campaigns that attempt to harness markets themselves to help transform processes of globalisation.

Our focus is on the networks that have been set up to enable people to consume foodstuffs in ways which promote more just and sustainable forms of food production. Alternative food networks (AFNs) are organised flows of food products that link up those who wish to consume more 'ethically' with those who wish to get a better deal for the food they produce, or who prefer to produce food in ways that market forces currently discourage. How do such AFNs realise ethical connections between consumers and the social and environmental conditions in which the foodstuffs they enjoy are produced? Taking food as its vehicle, the chapter explores how ethical connections between consumption and production are fashioned through the interplay between movement or flow and settling or territorialisation, which can be seen at work on a variety of scales from the global networks through which food commodities circulate to the bodily metabolisms that transform the flesh of animals and plants into that of humans through the foods they eat.

The first step, in Section 2, is to set out some of the general features of AFNs by looking more closely at what is 'alternative' about these food networks both in terms of the 'conventional' food production and trading practices against which they define themselves, and in terms of their distinctive ways of making global markets differently.

Defining ethics

This chapter discusses ethical consumption, ethical premiums and ethical practices – but what do we mean by ethics? Ethics is the concern with what is right, what is good or what should be done. Ethical concerns tend to settle into a set of norms or rules to live by (thou shalt not ..., thou shalt ...). Yet there is another dimension of ethics or ethical concern which is the more spontaneous sense of compassion a person may feel for someone or something else that is suffering or in need. This is a kind of affect, or emotional impact, which moves people to enter into relations of care and responsibility for others. This does not depend on clearly defined norms or rules, though it may later come to be organised through such codes.

The next step, in Section 3, is to intensify the focus on how responsibilities towards others are articulated through the market by means of a case study of a particular AFN – Cafédirect. The oldest and most successful of a host of Fairtrade coffee networks, Cafédirect demonstrates the importance of certification practices to the articulation of ethical connections between the buying and drinking habits of consumers in the supermarket or café and the working and living conditions of small-scale coffee farmers in a global market.

At the same time, the sense of a world in the making which is adopted in this book extends our responsibilities as consumers beyond our fellow human beings towards non-humans. Section 4 involves a second case study of an AFN, this time the case of organic eggs, to help you to address the question: 'what are ethical connections made of?' Highlighting the role of the production standards and protocols set by the Soil Association in creating an organic egg market in the UK, the section shows how questions of responsibility extend beyond social justice among humans to environmental and animal welfare concerns.

With regard to the interests of the non-human world, the apparently individualised issue of what food to buy turns out to have rather significant and far reaching repercussions. As Nick Bingham showed in Chapter 3, the cultivation of plants and animals for food, and the way this is currently organised by the dominant economic system, has a big effect on biological life. The production and consumption of plants and animals is part of how plants move or flow, and on how they settle or territorialise. As we will see in this chapter, the aim of maximising economic returns has a profound impact on the conditions under which animals are raised and their everyday welfare. This also plays a big part in determining what kinds of animals and plants are most profitable, with important repercussions for the diversity of biological life.

In Section 5, we explore this 'bigger picture' and look in more detail at the claim that the 'ethical consumption' of food can contribute to the remaking of the global. To what extent, we ask, can ethical consumption really make a difference to the way in which global markets operate? Returning to Chapter 7 and José Bové and François Dufour and the French farmers' campaign against *malbouffe* – bad food or junk food – we tease out some of the connections between changing eating practices in one place and its implications for the 'food sovereignty' of other places. Food sovereignty, as we shall see, is not simply about economics or social justice, it is also about caring for plants and animals and for the local environment.

Having just seen, in Chapter 7, some of the ways in which large numbers of dispersed people are beginning to act collectively, it may at first appear to you that consumption, however ethical it may be, is a little too personal or individualised to have much impact on the powerful structural forces at work in the contemporary world. Nevertheless, as this chapter sets out to show, changing habits or patterns of consumption are small acts that can add up to much larger consequences. Moreover, practices of ethical consumption can also open the way to other forms of political engagement.

Ethical consumption, organised and promoted through AFNs, is a pathway through which ordinary, concerned people can find their way into more collective action. Consequently, 'responsible' practices of shopping and eating can be steps towards new forms of solidarity with others, which do not simply take advantage of existing market forces but offer a challenge to how these markets are presently arranged and structured.

Chapter aims

- To look at the way in which shopping for food is part of the making of a globalised earth.

- To show how market forces can be utilised by AFNs in ways that also raise issues about the injustice or inequity of global markets as they are currently organised.

- To consider how participation in ethical consumption can offer a pathway to more collective forms of political engagement.

- To explore the implications of food production and consumption for animal welfare, biological diversity and environmental conditions.

- To understand how everyday involvements in territories and flows can change the shape of the world.

2   Food and global markets

In this section, we examine how markets for food operate in a globalised world. As you will recall from Chapter 7, inequalities can be embedded in flows, and this was shown in the example of medical professionals moving from Ghana to the UK. The trade in foodstuffs, as it is currently organised, offers a further example of unequal flows. A sense of the injustice of this trade is one of the main rationales behind more ethical consumption of food, and the setting up of AFNs to facilitate and promote this form of consumption. Before we look more closely at the origins and operation of AFNs, it is important to think a little more about what is meant by the term 'consumption'.

2.1   Shopping for change?

In the case of food, 'consumption' generally refers to the activities of both provisioning and eating. In a highly urbanised world, provisioning (getting hold of food) principally involves market transactions for the vast majority of people in affluent societies and for affluent social groups in poorer societies in less developed countries: transactions that take place in markets, shops and supermarkets. Like provisioning, eating is a socially conditioned and variegated activity that takes place primarily in people's homes, spaces structured by diverse family and household arrangements. Other more collective contexts like restaurants and the canteens of schools, hospitals, prisons, offices and factories are also important spaces of food consumption (Bell and Valentine, 1997). While this framing of consumption serves reasonably well for the purposes of this chapter, it is important to note at the outset that it assumes a world of relative plenty and, hence, is inappropriate to places and people living with food scarcity and insecurity, historically and today.

When it comes to understanding how global markets work and the forces that shape them, consumption has been relatively overlooked until recently in favour of the activities of production and trade. Common-sense mappings of the journeys of foodstuffs from field to mouth make it easy to see consumption as little more than the 'end of the road' for products which have already been fully fashioned. Economic accounts of the making of global markets tended to focus attention on the large corporate players and international institutions that organise the production or distribution of goods and services. By comparison, consumption seemed a rather mundane activity undertaken by myriad individuals every day which was just too disorganised, too trivial or too much of a chore for consumers to be taken very seriously as a force for change. For similar reasons, consumption has also been treated as something of a poor relation in the political arena, at least by the standards of organised forms of political resistance and change such as labour unions, political parties or, even, pressure groups and protest movements.

We have seen this change recently through, for example, the efforts of the anti-sweatshop campaigns discussed by **Allen (2006)**. In relation to food, consumption has come into its own analytically and politically as a force for change in the wake of a succession of high-profile food scares like 'mad cow disease' (BSE) and genetically modified (GM) foods. Through such events, public anxieties about industrial foodstuffs have gathered political and economic force as innumerable individual shopping and eating decisions accumulate through supermarket tills, unsold stock and acts of civil disobedience to register as resistance to industrially produced foods and as demands for 'alternatives' (see Callon et al., 2002).

It is in this context that Arjun Appadurai, a well-known commentator on globalisation, has observed that: 'the small habits of consumption, typically daily food habits, can perform a percussive role in organising large-scale consumption patterns ... made up of much more complex orders of repetition and improvisation' (Appadurai, 1996, p.68). What Appadurai is suggesting here is that, like a chorus of voices or drops in a pool of rainwater, the aggregation of innumerable individual decisions about what food to buy and eat can swell the effect of those decisions into a significant shift in shopping and eating patterns. This effect can be simply a matter of coincidence – large numbers of people independently making similar changes in their food choices or habits at roughly the same time. Nonetheless, increasingly, the aggregation of consumer decisions or acts is influenced by public controversies, the competing demands of commercial advertising to launch new products or reinforce brand loyalty, health scares and/or dietary advice by government health agencies, and campaigns run by pressure groups and charitable organisations asking consumers to put their money where their consciences are in the name of some social or environmental claim (Barnett et al., 2004).

AFNs have been set up in order to mobilise consumer buying power in pursuit of such ethical agendas. For, without the organisation and infrastructure that AFNs provide, it would be next to impossible for individual consumers to connect in more ethical ways with the producers of foodstuffs that they enjoy. By facilitating such links,

AFN
Alternative food networks

MNC
Multinational Companies

AFNs attempt to make a difference to the way in which global markets operate.

2.2   The 'free' market and the globalised food trade

By definition, AFNs position themselves against the practices of mainstream or conventional food markets. Food, like many other global commodities today, is the product of highly industrialised systems of production in which farming finds itself squeezed between two other sets of activities. On the one hand, there are those activities associated with the production and marketing of the chemical and biotechnological inputs on which farming increasingly relies, such as fertilisers and pesticides, growth hormones and antibiotics, artificial insemination of livestock and genetic modification of crop plants. On the other hand, there are the activities associated with food processing and retailing, such as homogenisation and radiation treatments, convenience products and 'cool chain' delivery systems (that is delivery of perishable products, which must be kept cool at every stage of their journey), branding and 'own label' marketing.

In both cases, these activities are more profitable than farming and are concentrated in the hands of a limited number of large MNCs. By contrast, and despite some concentration of farm business and land ownership, farming itself continues to be a relatively dispersed activity involving large numbers of small and medium sized producers, often managed and worked by family members. In this context, it is perhaps unsurprising, but nevertheless ethically questionable, that the price we pay for food in the shops is unequally distributed between the key players through whose hands it has travelled in these different sectors of what is known as the agri-food chain.

One of the core characteristics of mainstream food markets that AFNs set out to challenge is the inequalities of 'who gets what' in the distribution of costs and profits between these different activities. This is illustrated in Figure 8.1, which is a composite diagram produced from a Christian Aid report on the global supermarket (Christian Aid, 1996). A leading charity concerned with alleviating world poverty, Christian Aid was one of the first to campaign for a change in the organisation of global food markets. Taking four popular food commodities – instant coffee, bananas, grapes and tea – Figure 8.1 shows how the retail price of these foods is distributed between those involved in getting them to market. The figures are only estimates and you need to treat them as no more than indicative of who is at the sharp end of this distribution. What is clear, however, is that the diverse community of so-called 'primary' agricultural producers – peasant farmers, plantation workers and small-scale growers living for the most part in Africa, Asia and Latin America – tend to receive only a modest share.

Manufacturer's profit
17p

Jar, label and boxing
21p

Distribution
3p

Retail mark up
53p

Grower
30p

Shipping to Europe
8p

Processing, production, overheads
33p

Transport and preparation or export
10p

(Based on a £1.75 jar of own-label instant coffee, with figures average across sectors.)

Producer
14%

Warehousing, packing and export fees
4.5%

Importer wholesaler
28%

Retailer
7%

Shipping and unloading
16%

Plantation workers
5.5%

(Percentages based on a banana from Costa Rica, figures from Foro Emaus, Costa Rica and Bananalink, UK.)

Transport, taxes distribution and other UK costs
40p

Workers
2.5p

Plantation
25.5p

Other Brazil costs
27p

Supermarket mark up
47p

(Figures based on a 1 lb bunch of grapes from Brazil retailing at £1.42.)

Plantation worker's wages
7%

Plantation costs and profits
9.5%

Supermarket mark up
30%

Packaging
7%

UK manufacturer's costs and profits
45%

Transport, warehousing and taxes
1.5%

(Figures based on a box of own label tea bags.)

Figure 8.1   Social justice: who gets what?

Source: Christian Aid, 1996

To make more sense of this pattern of unequal (or, as some would say, unjust) distribution of the rewards of production, we need to look in more detail at how this trade is currently organised and regulated in global markets. The prevailing terms of trade in global food markets centre on a tension between the rhetoric of free trade and the practice of imposing tariffs. Free trade, you will recall from Chapter 7, represents an 'ideal' of completely unconstrained movements of goods around the world which is regularly promoted by the governments of rich nations and international organisations like the WTO. In this sense, free trade is a cornerstone of the broader project of neo-liberalism, the reorganisation of the international economy described by Michael Pryke in Chapter 2.

The notion of territorial openness, unboundedness and unlimited flows implied by the principle of free trade reveals its limits – or contradictions – when the same freedom to cross borders is denied to people from relatively poorer countries who wish to migrate in search of better economic opportunities, as Doreen Massey noted in Chapter 7. Yet this is not the only way in which the actual practices or policies that are part of the neo-liberal organisation of the global economy diverge markedly from its rhetoric.

Another way that 'free' flow in the global economy is quite deliberately and regularly restricted is through the selective setting up of tariffs. Tariffs are a duty or tax added to imported goods in order to raise revenue but also, in many cases, to decrease the competitiveness of imports in relation to locally produced goods. As a territorial practice, the raising of tariffs (sometimes termed 'tariff barriers'), as employed by nation states and trading blocs such as the European Union (EU), serves to protect the market position of producers and produce within their borders against those from outside. Due to the relative or comparative advantage that many countries in the global South have in producing food cheaply, foodstuffs are a particularly common target for the imposition of tariffs.

Moreover, as we first heard in the discussion of Via Campesina in Chapter 7, protection by tariffs is often supplemented by subsidisation policies for local producers, which cushion them from market conditions and further tip the terms of trade in their favour. Therefore, a combination of subsidy and protection can give these producers (generally in the North) an advantage over non-subsidised and unprotected producers (usually in the South), allowing the former to export against the tide of lower production costs that would otherwise give relatively poorer countries an advantage. This often results in a flooding of the markets of these countries with cheap produce, undercutting their own local producers.

Thus, as numerous commentators and campaigning organisations point out, far from being a fully open system or a level playing field, global food markets are systematically skewed against the producers and produce of relatively poorer nations and regions, particularly in Africa and parts of Asia (Oxfam International, 2002; Watkins and Fowler, 2003). Or, to put it another way, inequalities are embedded in flows of trade in foodstuffs and in the territorial practices of regulating these flows. This specific structuring of flows is then manifested in the territorial effects of food markets, namely, a reinforcement or exacerbation of economic inequalities between relatively wealthier and poorer parts of the world. At this point, you might find it helpful to refer back to Section 2 of Chapter 2, which sets out the arguments for and against financial liberalisation. These closely parallel debates about trade liberalisation and will help to prepare you for Activity 8.1 below.

Activity 8.1

Now look at Figure 8.2 and the newspaper extract overleaf. Figure 8.2 is a Christian Aid campaign advertisement that appeared in various UK weekend newspaper colour supplements in September 2004, taking the form of a postcard to be signed and sent to UK Prime Minister Tony Blair. The newspaper extract is a critique of this Christian Aid campaign written by Stephen Pollard a 'fellow at the Centre for the New Europe' (we are not told what this is) that appeared in *The Times* newspaper the same month (Pollard, 2004).

1   As you are reading, jot down what you think Figure 8.2 and the newspaper extract are saying about free trade. What are the differences and what, if any, are the similarities?

2   How might the two positions of Figure 8.2 and the newspaper extract be articulated in terms of territories and flows?

Dear Tony Blair,
You might think Free Trade is fair, but
I think poor countries must be allowed
to protect their vulnerable farmers.
I believe that to end poverty and protect
the environment we need Trade Justice, not
Free Trade. I vote for Trade Justice.

Title: Initial:

Surname:

Address:

                        Postcode:

Tel no:

Email:

Send to Christian Aid and we'll make sure
Tony Blair knows how you feel.

We will not give your details to any other organisation.
If you do not wish to receive additional information on
Christian Aid's work, tick this box ☐

Christian ⅰⅰAid
We believe in life before death

Registered charity no. 258003

Using
a stamp
saves us
money.

Christian Aid
FREEPOST
London SE1 7YY

GN2509

Our Government claims Free
Trade is the solution to
the world's problems. But
that's exactly what you
would expect them to say
when it allows them to
profit. It's the
Millions of Farmers
          in poorer nations
who, with Free Trade
forced upon them, are
unable to sell their produce
because their local
markets are flooded with
imports from Europe.

STOP THIS MADNESS.
Help us to
          get Tony Blair to listen.
Send off this postcard to show you
support Trade Justice. If your postcard is
missing, vote online at

www.votefortradejustice.org

Christian ⅰⅰAid
We believe in life before death

Registered charity no. 258003

Figure 8.2   Free trade: some people love it; others just want trade justice

Source: Christian Aid, 2004

Aid like this is fatal

Stephen Pollard is a senior fellow at the Centre for the New Europe

Do you want to help to kill an African? It's very easy. Just sign Christian Aid's petition against free trade.

According to the charity's current campaign: 'Millions of farmers in poorer nations are being gradually ruined by free trade.' As evidence for this, it cites 'the onion farmers of Senegal. With free trade forced on them, they're unable to sell their produce because their local markets are flooded with onions imported from Europe.'

That statement is true, apart from one detail: it is not a description of free trade but of its opposite, protectionism.

The EU foodstuffs market is warped by the subsidies of the common agricultural policy (CAP). When EU farmers export, they sell products which would not have been grown without subsidy. The EU spends €2.7 billion a year paying farmers to grow sugar beet, for example, while it imposes high tariff barriers against sugar imports from the developing world.

The CAP generates immense surpluses that cannot be sold within the EU. Much of these are exported at low prices that undercut those charged by the developing world's unsubsidised producers. And when they attempt to export to the EU, their access is blocked by trade barriers. The EU's agricultural tariffs are as high as 250 per cent. Free trade is the solution, not the problem.

According to Oxfam, if Africa could increase its share of world trade by just 1 per cent, it would earn an additional £49 billion a year — enough to lift 128 million people out of extreme poverty. That will happen only if trade barriers are lifted.

There are two possible explanations for Christian Aid's misguided campaign. One is that those behind it are so stupid that they simply do not know that free trade involves abolishing subsidies, pulling down trade barriers.

The other is that they know that full well, but have an anti-globalisation, anti-prosperity agenda that they are attempting to disguise with an apparent but misleading concern for the developing world.

A recent paper by the Centre for the New Europe calculated that one person dies every 13 seconds somewhere in the world — mainly in Africa — because of the EU's protectionism. The Christian Aid campaign's stated aim would make that figure even worse.

(Pollard, 2004)

It may be easier to start with what Figure 8.2 and the newspaper extract above have in common. Both, in their very different ways, highlight the inconsistencies within the current organisation of global trade in agricultural produce. Although Pollard (2004) offers more detail than Christian Aid (2004), both point towards the tension between a principle of free trade and a practice of subsidies and protection. However, there is a big difference, in that Christian Aid (2004) implies that this contradiction is inherent in the ideal (or myth) of free trade, leading it to a stance of opposing free trade in favour of a notion of 'trade justice' which affords poorer countries the right to impose their own forms of trade protection. Pollard (2004), on the other hand, maintains his faith in free trade and believes that the 'ideal' should be pursued with all the more rigour, to the extent of doing away with subsidies and tariff barriers everywhere. To put this in terms of the concepts we have developed in this book, Pollard (2004) believes in the overall advantage of breaking down territorial boundaries in favour of unimpeded flows (though recalling what you have read in Chapter 7, you might wonder what his view is on the free movement of migrants from Africa to Europe, for example). Christian Aid (2004), by contrast, seems to be suggesting that territories need to maintain their own control over certain sorts of flow. Nonetheless, the notion of 'justice' itself indicates a kind of equalisation between territories which, in its own way, implies a continuation of flows

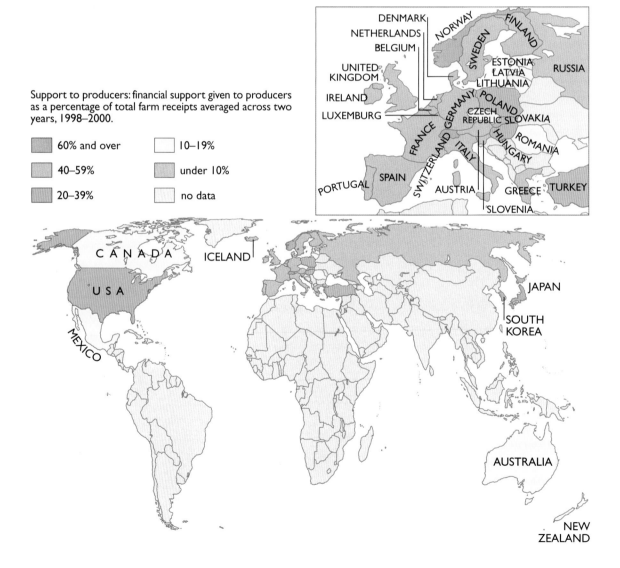

Support to producers: financial support given to producers as a percentage of total farm receipts averaged across two years, 1998–2000.

60% and over

40–59%

20–39%

10–19%

under 10%

no data

although it suggests a change in the nature or terms of these flows such as that proposed in the report for Medact in the Ghana example in Chapter 7, Section 3.

The distribution of practices of tariff protection and subsidy, as was suggested above, is significantly slanted in favour of producers in countries like the USA and regional trading blocs like the EU. The maps reproduced in Figure 8.3 illustrate this skewed distribution of tariffs and subsidies very clearly. In the first map, subsidies are

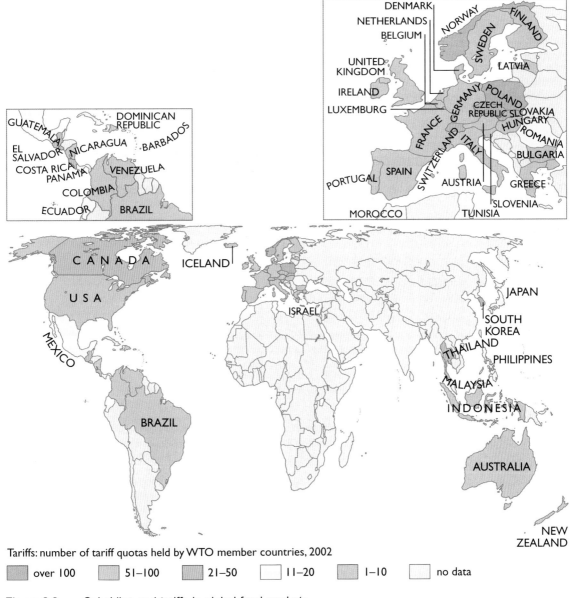

Tariffs: number of tariff quotas held by WTO member countries, 2002

| over 100 | 51–100 | 21–50 | 11–20 | 1–10 | no data |

Figure 8.3   Subsidies and tariffs in global food markets

Source: Millstone and Lang, 2003, p.67

concentrated in the relatively rich countries that are members of the Organisation of Economic Cooperation and Development (OECD), with particularly high levels of subsidy being paid to farmers in Japan, Norway, the EU and Switzerland.

In the second map in Figure 8.3 it is evident that particularly high numbers of import tariffs are being imposed by the EU, the USA and Canada, and a handful of countries in Latin America and Asia. In making sense of these maps, you should pay close attention to the countries and regions that are described as having 'no data' as well as to those which are shaded. These 'no data' countries are those whose local producers are very rarely protected by tariffs or propped up by subsidies. They are therefore most likely to suffer from the effects of skewed terms of trade, including market undercutting by incoming floods of subsidised products and barriers to their own exports.

Summary

- AFNs are premised on the understanding that patterns of consumption have important impacts on global markets.
- Inequalities are imbedded in the flows of global food markets as they are currently organised, particularly through the territorial practice of tariff protection.
- The territorial effects of the global free market in foodstuffs are controversial, but critics argue that they tend towards reinforcement of economic inequalities between wealthier and poorer parts of the world.

3 Fairtrade: consuming with a social conscience?

In this section, we look in detail at the way AFNs have been set up to address what they see as the injustice of the uneven terms of the global trade in foodstuffs. Through the example of Fairtrade and the case of Cafédirect coffee, we explore how ethical food consumption expresses a sense of responsibility to distant others – that is, producers in relatively poorer countries – which is articulated through the market.

3.1   Fairtrade coffee

Coffee, like tea and chocolate, is a drink that is globally commonplace today, fuelling all manner of social situations, relationships and interactions from business meetings and office coffee breaks to café cultures and home comforts. This is illustrated in Figure 8.4 by an advertising hoarding for a cyber café in Bangalore, India.

Figure 8.4   'Sip coffee. Surf internet', Bangalore, India

Coffee, tea and chocolate drinks are derived from plants that are native to tropical and semi-tropical climates, and now grow widely through Africa, Asia, Latin America and the Caribbean as a result of the kinds of colonial movements of plant resources discussed in detail in Chapter 3. The mainstream global markets in these crops are characterised by three features. First, production takes place primarily on plantations, typically involving a concentration of large areas of land in the hands of relatively few owners employing a large number of low-paid labourers who are often dependent on their employer for housing too. Second, plantations replace the mixed ecologies of the land area they cover with a single commercial crop, a so-called 'monoculture', which is dependent on intensive chemical treatments to sustain fertility and control disease. Third, the price of these primary agricultural commodities is unprotected on world markets because they are generally produced in countries of the South, where protection and subsidies are rare. This means that these commodities can experience dramatic price fluctuations, both as a repercussion of major climatic or disease events and as a consequence of the activities of MNCs in the primary coffee market or other corporate players involved in speculating on commodity price movements in the financial futures markets (see Chapter 2). Some sense of the scale of coffee consumption, the size of the coffee market and the share taken by Fairtrade coffee can be gained from the summary analysis of the situation in the UK given in Extract 8.1.

Extract 8.1

UK coffee consumption: the Fairtrade share

Coffee break: the UK market

- 31 billion cups of coffee are drunk in the UK every year.
- In 2000 the UK imported 3.1 million bags of coffee worth US$423.3m. Comparable figures for 1995 show the dramatic fall in coffee prices: 2.8 million bags were imported then worth $671.9m (1 bag = 60kg).
- Between 1993 and 2000 the *volume* of the UK coffee market declined by 1.6% while the *value* of retail sales leapt from £652m to £798m, an increase of 22%.
- In 2000 coffee surpassed tea, taking more than 51% of the hot beverages market by value.
- Instant coffee accounted for 76% of market volume and 87% of the market value, with roast and ground accounting for the remainder.
- Among the manufacturers, Nestlé and Kraft Jacobs dominate the instant coffee market, taking 50% and 21% respectively; supermarkets' own label brands come a close third.
- The UK coffee shop market grew by 55% between 1997 and 2000 and is not expected to reach saturation until 2003.
- Sales of Fairtrade roast and ground coffee grew by 27% in 2001 with an estimated retail value of £10.5m, and accounting for 10.5% of the total volume of the roast and ground market.
- Fairtrade coffee took a 3% share of the total coffee market in 2001 (soluble and ground coffee).
- Twenty-five companies market Fairtrade coffee; it is available in most supermarkets as well as in Costa Coffee and Starbucks outlets.

(The Fairtrade Foundation, 2002a, p.7)

Fairtrade coffee is the only sector of the coffee market that has grown over the last decade, against the overall trend towards decline in world coffee consumption. Europe is the largest market for Fairtrade coffee, with the UK coming third in the national league table behind Germany and the Netherlands in terms of market share. The Fairtrade movement began as a dispersed set of parallel initiatives by charitable and non-profit organisations in different countries, principally in Europe. Coffee was one of the first commodities to be targeted by these organisations as they set about buying directly from producers in the global South, paying them more than they would get for their beans on the conventional world coffee market, and selling the coffee to consumers through charity shops and informal networks at a higher price than conventional equivalents. In other words, the common strategy of Fairtrade organisations has been to generate an 'ethical premium' which redistributes the value of the higher prices paid by consumers to the prices paid to producers.

It is important to be clear that ethical consuming practices do not simply come about through the spontaneous actions of consumers. The AFN for coffee had to put in place new lines of flow between producers in the South and Northern consumers. As is the case with the organisations campaigning for a different kind of globalisation which we looked at in the last chapter, work has to be done to forge global connections that enable ethically motivated consumers and alternative food networkers to act at a distance, or 'act globally', as effectively as those in mainstream organisations.

The capacity to act at a distance, to do something in one place that produces an effect in another, is achieved as a result of much effort. Connections that extend the reach of an action in time and space have to be worked at: work that involves the combined energies of people skilled in particular ways; devices that enable things and information to travel; and codes of conduct hard-wired in written regulations or computer software that routinises behaviours. We should also keep in mind that MNCs have to work just as hard at fashioning global food markets as do the charitable or non-profit organisations promoting Fairtrade foods; it is their (both MNCs and AFNs) objectives and, sometimes, their methods as well as the social and environmental impacts of their activities that differ (Whatmore and Thorne, 1997). In addition to using some of the same practices as these corporations to forge linkages and persuade customers to buy their products, AFNs have also been highly inventive in devising new ways of fashioning markets differently.

3.2   Certification and the FAIRTRADE Mark

As Iris Marion Young (2003, p.43) argues, an important aspect of taking responsibility for others in a globalised world is to 'challenge the assumption that market exchange processes are or ought to be untraceable'. Rendering products and their patterns of flow visible and traceable in this way is a key strategy of organised opposition to unfair or exploitative production practices, as in the case of the antisweatshop movement **(Allen, 2006)**, and it is just as important when it comes to setting up alternative, ethically motivated networks.

One of the biggest challenges for AFNs is to make the ethical credentials of a product conspicuous and credible throughout the often long distances travelled on its journey from where it is produced to where it is consumed, a journey that can involve significant physical transformations in the product as, for example, from beans to freeze-dried granules in the case of instant coffee. Convincing people that a product is reliable – that it is what it says on the label – is vital, and difficult to achieve. AFNs build trust through two main strategies that mark out their activities from conventional markets.

The first of these strategies is what has become known in the food marketing world as 'product traceability' and involves being able to track each step in a product's journey to the market, and to make these tracks accessible or visible to consumers so that they can, if they want to, trace a product's entire biography. This is important to guarantee the fairness of the conditions under which the coffee has been produced, and it is just as vital in the case of organic foods, which we will examine in Section 4. (Organic foods require meticulous record keeping so that a piece of meat, for instance, can be traced to a particular animal from an identifiable farm, herd or parentage in order that the husbandry regime under which it was raised in terms of feed and veterinary treatment can be ascertained.) New tagging protocols are needed to ensure a food product's 'clean' passage through any transportation or processing facilities such that its ethical claims remain undiluted by being mixed with other produce.

The second strategy characteristic of how AFNs make the ethical credentials of their products reliable in order to secure consumer trust involves the development of labour intensive certification practices. Certification is the process that guarantees the ethical claims: it involves establishing contractual codes of practice that set strict standards to which producers and processors must conform, reinforced by advisory, monitoring and inspection regimes.

In the case of Fairtrade coffee, certification is signalled by the Fairtrade logo. This logo gained its current prominence after the profusion of organisations and products involved in fair trade initiatives began to consolidate their efforts. By the 1990s, after first agreeing common criteria for what counts as fair trade, they had come together under an international umbrella body – Fairtrade Labelling Organisations International (http://www.fairtrade.net) and adopted a single international FAIRTRADE logo.

Today, over 250 different products are bought and sold in the name of Fairtrade, including tropical fruits and juices and a whole range of non-food products. In the UK, the various charitable organisations which had taken the first steps in fair trade in the 1970s (for example, Oxfam, Traidcraft and Christian Aid) set up the Fairtrade Foundation to administer the FAIRTRADE Mark as their common logo. As the Foundation declares: 'Fairtrade guarantees a better deal for third world producers. This is the guarantee that the Fairtrade Foundation makes to consumers and that is an integral part of the marketing symbol of Fairtrade – the FAIRTRADE Mark' (The Fairtrade Foundation, 2002b).

The Fairtrade Foundation applies this general guarantee by setting and monitoring two sets of generic producer standards: one for small farmers and one for workers on plantations and in factories. The first set applies to smallholders organised in cooperatives or other organisations with a democratic, participative structure. The second set applies to the employers of waged workers who are required to pay decent wages, guarantee the right to join trade unions and provide good housing when relevant. Fairtrade standards stipulate that traders must:

- pay a price to producers that covers the costs of sustainable production and living;
- pay a 'premium' that producers can invest in development;
- make partial advance payments when requested by producers;
- sign contracts that allow for long-term planning and sustainable production practices.

As in the case of the logos associated with mainstream brands, such as Nike's 'swoosh' or McDonald's 'golden arches', the FAIRTRADE Mark induces consumer recognition of the 'brand' and of its market 'identity' as well as guaranteeing the standard or quality of the goods bearing the logo. As shown in Chapter 7, even radical groups resisting the tendency of 'enclosure' by the dominant forces of globalisation set certain restrictions on the material they have marked with the 'copyleft' logo. In this sense, any logo or trademark, even one that inverts the legal device of 'copyright', works by a form of territorialisation, which is to say that it clearly defines and differentiates an object from its surroundings in order to facilitate its movement or flow (see Chapter 3, Section 2).

In the case of the FAIRTRADE Mark, this territorialisation stabilises a particular set of social and technical arrangements which both assists the flow of products and strengthens the reliability of the ethical claims that they embody as they travel between the spaces of production and consumption. By contrast to the 'copyleft' strategy, however, the Fairtrade Foundation uses the conventional legal device of copyright and goes to considerable lengths to regulate the use of its Mark by commercial and other organisations. The Foundation produces two manuals: one stipulating how the Mark should be used in promotional materials; the other giving detailed instructions for its use on packaging. These manuals specify and restrict every aspect of the appearance of the Mark – from size and position to colour and layout. Some indication of the laborious business of fixing the FAIRTRADE Mark can be gauged from the opening description of the logo that appears in these manuals and is reproduced in Figure 8.5. Note too that in order to write about the Mark here, we must also observe the capitalisation of FAIRTRADE stipulated in the copyright specification.

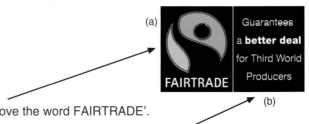

Logo

The FAIRTRADE Mark consists of two parts:

(a) The FAIRTRADE symbol (human figure) above the word FAIRTRADE'.

(b) A qualifying statement, 'Guarantees a better deal for Third World Producers'.

- **The two halves of the Mark must always appear together and unaltered**.

- The Mark must not be redesigned, amended or re-proportioned in any way.

- The typeface and spacing of type should not be altered.

Figure 8.5   The FAIRTRADE Mark

Source: The Fairtrade Foundation, 2002b

3.3 Cafédirect: a Fairtrade coffee network

Cafédirect coffee was the second fair trade product to receive the FAIRTRADE Mark in the UK and is now the top-selling brand in the fair trade coffee market in the UK. However, its success today belies humble beginnings. Cafédirect is a consortium that grew out of informal cooperation between the trading arms of four non-profit or charitable organisations which have been active the longest in the Trade Justice Movement in the UK – Oxfam trading, Twin Trading, Traidcraft and Equal Exchange. In the early days, these organisations each engaged independently in setting criteria for what constitutes fair trade: negotiating contracts with coffee producers; monitoring their compliance with the terms of the contracts; and selling fair trade coffee to UK consumers through their networks of charity shops, market stalls and community or church support groups. In 1993, all this changed with the consortium's registration as a private non–profit company, the appointment of a managing director and the recasting of the partner organisations as 'shareholders'.

This reorganisation marks a significant shift in the stability and reach of AFNs in which coffee became the ethical medium of connectivity between consumers in the UK and primary producers in Latin America, Asia and Africa. First, the practices of contract negotiation and compliance monitoring with producer organisations dealing with Cafédirect have become more standardised under the common rubric of the FAIRTRADE Mark, administered by the Fairtrade Foundation, increasing Cafédirect's capacity to deal with a larger number of more varied and complex forms of producer organisation. Second, Cafédirect coffee is no longer a uniform product but is differentiated by various types or blends of beans which are marketed according to differences in their flavour and strength, and with reference to their region or country of origin. Third, Cafédirect products are now sold through mainstream food retail outlets as well as charity shops, hugely increasing the size of the market. In the 1990s, Cafédirect marketed the ethical credentials of its coffee under the byline: 'The aroma of fresh coffee without the whiff of exploitation' (see Figure 8.6 overleaf).

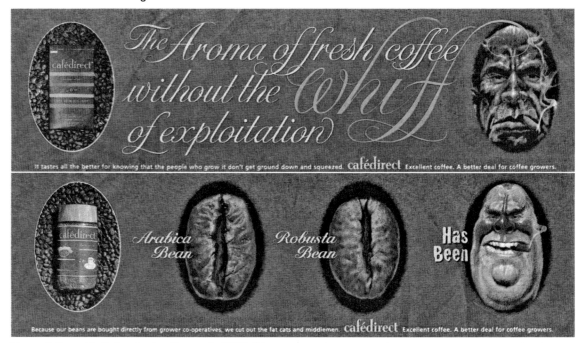

Figure 8.6   Cafédirect advertisement, 1996–97

Source: Cafédirect, 1996–97

This explicitly political message was reinforced by the imagery of these early advertisements, which played on the wrinkled oval shape of the coffee bean and its likeness to a caricature of corporate greed in the shiny face and cracked smile of a corporate 'boss'.

Today, much more of the work of differentiating Fairtrade from mainstream products is done by the FAIRTRADE Mark itself, while the primary imagery deployed in advertising and packaging is more concerned with conjuring the places where Cafédirect coffees are grown. A useful way to gain a stronger sense of the considerable work, the multiplicity of organisations and the material arrangements involved in making a Fairtrade coffee network work is to trace a specific product from the range on the supermarket shelf via the particular network through which it has journeyed to the place or region in which it began life. Indeed, this strategy is a staple of the efforts of fair trade organisations to engage consumers through their marketing and promotion materials.

Activity 8.2

Now turn to Reading 8A by Cafédirect (undated) entitled 'Peru' and Reading 8B by the Fairtrade Foundation (undated) entitled 'Alejandro', which you will find at the end of the chapter. These readings are two accounts of local producers and production. Reading 8A is an extract from one of the 'grower' profiles on the Cafédirect website in 2005. Reading 8A tells of the role played by the fair trading network in the regeneration of the cooperative movement of coffee producers, with particular reference to one cooperative: Central de Co-operativas Agrarias Cafetaleras (COCLA). Reading 8B is from the Fairtrade website, and briefly tells the story of the working life of a coffee producer. We have chosen a Peruvian grower, Alejandro.

1 As you are reading and looking at the illustration, think about the intentions of these accounts and how they work. What sort of information are we given? Do you find that the accounts have an emotional impact on you?

2 Try and think more generally about the way these accounts set about creating a sense of connection between far-flung consumers (or potential consumers) and particular communities or families of producers. What kinds of 'geographies of responsibility' do they embody? And what do they say about our capacity, as 'ethical consumers', to make the world otherwise? Think also about the role of technology in conveying this sense of connection.

It seems that these accounts are trying to help to make ethical connections across distance, not just by giving information about the benefits and achievements of trade justice, but by opening up a personal or 'face-to-face' link between consumers and producers. Combining third-person information with first-person accounts and photographs is a common way in which campaigning organisations attempt to enrol people in changing the globalised world **(Rose, 2006)**. You may also recognise this strategy from Fairtrade products – where it often takes the form of small images and stories of producers featured on the outside of packets.

It would also appear that these accounts seek to appeal to our emotions: not only is the tale of the regeneration of the COCLA cooperative a rousing and hopeful story, but in the case of Alejandro the coffee grower, we are privy to his 'passion', including his 'enthusiasm and love' for his work (Cafédirect, undated). In Chapter 5,

Owain Jones spoke about affective territorialisation, drawing our attention to the way in which emotional attachments can play a powerful part in rallying people to defend the places with which they identify. In these trade justice producer stories, what we can see are attempts to inflect flows with a similar affective charge, so that our connections through consumption are experienced as meaningful as well as morally sound and economically viable.

We could also view this strategy of telling producer stories as a part of a bid to construct consumption as potentially much more than a personal or individualised activity. Through the establishment of an affective link or flow, we are drawn into a kind of identification or solidarity with distant others. Clearly, the internet plays an important role (along with packaging, leaflets and other sources of trade justice stories). However, we need to remember that, unlike the use of the internet by movements for global justice that we heard about in Chapter 7, this communication is a one-way flow. We see producers' faces, and read their stories, but they do not see or read about us. Yet, in another sense, the geography of responsibility that these accounts seek to reinforce and convey is very clearly one in which both parties – consumers in the North and producers in the South – have their own responsibilities (Young, 2003). If we, on our home ground, are implored to consume ethically, they on their ground, are seen to be working hard, organising and innovating. Accordingly, in their respective parts of the world, consumers and producers are depicted as working successfully, in connection and with solidarity, to make the global world in a new and different way.

There is also something else being encouraged on the Fairtrade website. The reader or net surfer is invited not only to become more informed, but to become more involved. There is a 'get involved' heading on the Fairtrade site which opens on to campaigns and events. Under these headings, we hear about the expansion of fair trade practices and certification to incorporate institutions or whole towns, as well as about invitations to get more actively involved in the Trade Justice Movement. This sense that ethical consumption can act as a pathway to more active and more collective participation in campaigns to change the globalised world is a theme that is continued in Section 5.

Another point that you might have picked up from Readings 8A and 8B is not directly about trade or justice. We read that COCLA promotes organic farming, and we also heard that Alejandro believes that 'all farmers should look after the environment and have organic, sustainable production methods'. In reminding us that fair trade and concerns with the environment (or with the quality of non-human life) are often entangled, this leads us into another important area of ethical consumption and alternative food networking. In Section 4, we shift away from coffee – and trade justice – and examine the issues of organic food and animal welfare.

Summary

- AFNs address the uneven terms of the global trade in foodstuffs.
- Much work has to be done by AFNs to set up and sustain new lines of flow between producers in the global South and consumers in the global North.
- Certification and trademarking are important territorialising practices through which AFNs guarantee the ethical credentials of their products.
- Producer stories and images add an affective dimension to fair trade promotion which seeks to generate solidarity between consumers and distant producers.

4   Organic food: more than human ethical concerns

You should now have some sense of an AFN at work, engaged in the laborious business of product certification and copyright licensing to ensure the reliability of its envoy – the FAIRTRADE Mark. It is through territorialising practices like these that responsibilities towards others are articulated through the global market, and goods mobilised in ways that make a difference in the world. Nevertheless, as the Introduction to this chapter indicated, the question of responsibilities, or of the ethics of consumption, can be posed slightly differently in terms of: what are ethical connections made of?

4.1   Chickens and eggs

One of the ways in which the question of ethical connections is being addressed by the ethical concerns and practices of AFNs is to expose how human well-being and the well-being of other living things that become our foodstuffs are intimately connected through our shared bodily vulnerabilities and metabolisms. Perhaps the most potent reminders of these 'non-human' connectivities in recent times was the outbreak of so-called 'mad cow disease' in the UK in the early 1990s, during which scientists confirmed that a degenerative brain disease affecting large numbers of cattle could be (and was being) passed to human beings through infected meat products (Ridley and Baker, 1998). Nonetheless, a sense of the routine and often overlooked enactments of the intimate connections between animal and human health and well-being can be found in an example closer to the everyday experience of shopping and eating (for some of us at least): the raising of chickens and the production of eggs.

In this section, we look at how the interplay between the spatial practices of territorialisation and flow that shape global food markets simultaneously plays through the intimate designs of the food industry on animal bodies. The AFNs that we will be focusing on here are not only concerned with the consequences of intensive animal husbandry for human health, although this is a cornerstone of their strategies for enrolling consumers to their ethical agenda. Rather, their primary concern is to extend the company of others with which our activities as consumers connect us – to address the implications of industrial food production and distribution for animal welfare and the environment as matters of ethical import on their own terms. Here, you will learn about some of the market practices through which these connections are made in the conventional food industry, and made differently by AFNs concerned with animal welfare and/or environmental sustainability, not simply in terms of the kinds of certification and copyright practices illustrated in Section 3 but also in terms of how the market practices are made flesh in the animals (and plants), and the environments they inhabit, through a case study of eggs produced to organic production standards set by the Soil Association.

Intensive methods of livestock production have led to spectacular
increases in the productivity of meat, milk, eggs and other animal
derivatives, but at a very high price in terms of animal welfare (http://
www.compassioninworldfarming.org). Taking the case of chickens,
there are approximately twenty-nine million egg laying hens in the UK,
over 70 per cent of which are housed in battery cages. Most battery
cages house four or five birds, each having 550 cm^2 of space – about
as much room as an A4 sheet of paper. Think about that for minute.
Figure 8.7 may help you to picture it. At these densities, movement is
severely restricted and levels of aggression and fearfulness high,
resulting in raised incidences of stereotypical feather pecking
behaviours and disease infection. To deal with these consequences,
intensive production methods routinely include: keeping battery
chickens in semi-darkness; without litter; beak 'trimming'; wing
clipping; and incorporating antibiotics and yolk colourants in chicken
feed. Every day it is estimated that some 100,000 chickens die

Figure 8.7   A battery chicken: real cage dimensions

prematurely in UK factory farms as a result of these intensive methods of production (http://www.rspca.org.uk).

The consequences of these intensive production methods for human health, among both poultry workers and the consuming public, can be measured by the regularity of incidences of food poisoning resulting from salmonella and other bacterial pathogens passed from contaminated chicken meat and eggs. While some of these incidences are undoubtedly the result of consumers or caterers failing to follow basic hygiene and cooking instructions, the routine presence of the pathogens in these products cannot be so easily explained.

The industrialised methods are associated with a significant concentration in the organisation of poultry production. Historically, chickens have been kept as vital sources of both eggs and meat by millions of households around the world from peasant farmers to urban dwellers, and still are today. In the modern (conventional) poultry industry, these functions are separated out, with chickens either reared for the production of eggs (layers) or raised for the production of meat (broilers). Over time, these birds and their living conditions have been scientifically redesigned through breeding, feeding and housing regimes, such that their body shape, behaviour, lifespan and quality of life have become tailored to serve their industrial function ever more 'efficiently'. In the USA, for example, just eight chicken processors now supply about two-thirds of the US poultry meat market – a mainstay of the global fast food diet in the guise of highly processed meat products like 'chicken nuggets' (Schlosser, 2001).

While egg production is not so centralised, the trend is broadly similar. In the UK, for example, where just 5 per cent of laying hens were kept in flocks with more than 1000 birds in 1950, by 1995 this was 95 per cent. Today, three-quarters of the UK's eggs come from fewer than 300 units, each with more than 20,000 layers and the largest with over 500,000 birds (Soil Association, 2003, p.32).

Several charitable and non-profit organisations have been involved in challenging the animal welfare and environmental consequences of these conventional market practices. These include organisations concerned with the broad issue of animal welfare such as the Royal Society for the Prevention of Cruelty to Animals (RSPCA); those concerned more specifically with farm animal welfare such as Compassion in World Farming; and others for whom animal welfare concerns are an integral part of a wider philosophy of environmental sustainability in farming systems such as the Soil Association, which is a leading player in the international organic food movement based in the UK. While the latter are much older organisations than those involved in the Fairtrade networks that you encountered in Section 3, their active participation in establishing AFNs likewise dates to the 1970s, experiencing significant market growth from the 1990s onwards.

However, whereas we have seen a consolidation of the organisations and standards involved in the certification practices of Fairtrade networks, the same cannot be said of the AFNs addressing the more than human concerns of animal welfare and environmental ethics. In the case of eggs, the consumer faces something of a minefield of competing logos and trademarks, certification standards and organisations, all making different ethical claims that have very different consequences for the chicken.

4.2   What is in an egg? Setting animal welfare standards

If you browse the shelves of any supermarket, the chances are that you will come across a bewildering variety of differently packaged eggs from the vaguely reassuring 'farm fresh' or 'farm assured', to the more specific sounding 'barn', 'free range' and 'organic' eggs. This order roughly follows the price gradient of these categories. How are you to tell the difference between the ethical claims of these terms and their accompanying logos? How are you to tell what, if any, difference they make to the bodily experience of the chicken? If you want to know the answer in detail, Compassion in World Farming (2003) provides a useful review and guide.

The key point to bear in mind is that, in the UK, all eggs, whatever their marketing names and logos, are regulated under UK and/or EU legislation on trading standards and/or animal welfare standards. That is, unlike the social conditions of agricultural production, there are minimum standards of animal husbandry to which even conventional producers are required to adhere. This reflects long-standing policy concerns with the public health implications of animal products and, to a lesser extent, with questions of animal cruelty. These standards vary according to the different terms or logos outlined above and, in most cases, it is up to trading standards authorities to enforce these standards by checking that the production regime from which the eggs are sourced meets the stipulated minimum requirements. In the case of conventional egg production, it is worth underlining that the kinds of practices associated with battery systems, outlined above, meet these minimum requirements. No matter how misleading they may appear to the consumer, neither the 'farm fresh' nor the 'farm assured' labels signify anything other than that these minimum standards have been met.

The baseline definition of what constitutes farm animal welfare in the UK derives from what are now known as the Bramwell Five Freedoms, as set out in the report of the Bramwell Committee in 1965 and subsequently enshrined in the codes of recommendation on animal welfare standards set by the UK Government's advisory body on farm animal welfare in 1979. These five freedoms are:

The Bramwell Five Freedoms

- Freedom from hunger and thirst
  By ready access to fresh water and a diet to maintain full health and vigour.

- Freedom from discomfort
  By providing an appropriate environment including shelter and a resting area.

- Freedom from pain, injury or disease
  By prevention or rapid diagnosis and treatment.

- Freedom to express normal behaviour
  By providing sufficient space, proper facilities and company to the animal's own kind.

- Freedom from fear and distress
  By ensuring conditions and treatment which avoid mental suffering

(Farm Animal Welfare Council, 1979)

These recommendation codes are 'aspirational' guidelines rather than legally enforceable standards but, over the years, in response to persistent public disquiet and campaigning by animal welfare organisations, some elements of these codes have been translated into binding regulations through UK or EU legislation. However enforceable they may be in practice, what is important from the point of view of this book is that these standards (which are themselves a form of territorialisation) represent a concerted effort to put limits on the territorialisation of animal bodies and behaviours which intensive animal husbandry seeks to impose. Principles such as the notion of 'freedom to express normal behaviour' suggest an acknowledgement that the territorialisations characteristic of industrialised livestock raising constitute, for some, an acceptably restrictive channelling of the 'flow' of the energies and expressiveness of non-human life.

In this context, the ethical claims of AFNs are less readily distinguishable from conventional food networks by the practice of fixing, or territorialising, logos. AFNs have to work harder to differentiate the reliability of their trading mark, as an envoy of more rigorous animal welfare and/or environmental standards, from that of conventional producers if they are to succeed in winning consumer trust as intermediary organisations. These more rigorous standards cover livestock conditions ranging from the environment (including stocking density, environmental design and air quality) and food and water provision to management practices (including regularity of inspection and monitoring, and treatment of health problems) and reproduction and treatment of young. Yet even here, the situation is not straightforward. For example, the RSPCA, a highly respected animal welfare organisation, launched the 'Freedom Foods' trademark backed up by an inspection and monitoring regime to promote 'higher welfare standards and conditions for farm animals' (http://www.rspca. org.uk). As the advertisement reproduced in Figure 8.8 shows, 'Freedom Foods' draws an ethical connection between the monetary price consumers pay for animal products (in this case chicken) and the price paid in animal suffering – the cheaper the one, the more expensive the other. Nevertheless, the mark has been criticised for 'setting its standards too low' in a review of quality assurance schemes conducted by Compassion in World Farming (Lymbery, 2002). Certainly, if one looks at the detailed documentation of what is stipulated by the RSPCA Freedom Foods regime in the case of egg production, it retains some controversial aspects of conventional farm assurance schemes, such as allowing beak trimming (Royal Society for the Prevention of Cruelty to Animals, 2003).

The trademark that gains the highest number of 'first' places for different categories of livestock (including laying hens) in the same review of animal welfare standards (Lymbery, 2002) is the Soil Association's 'organic standard'. The organic egg market in the UK is estimated at some 150 million eggs produced from some 700,000 laying hens. It is distinctive compared with other organic products because it does not depend on imports but is entirely derived from domestic producers (Soil Association, 2003).

Figure 8.8   The more you save, the more the chicken pays

Source: Royal Society for the Prevention of Cruelty to Animals, 2003

Summary

- AFNs have helped to extend ethical concerns of consumers to include the conditions under which animals are raised.

- Intensive, industrialised animal husbandry territorialises both animal bodies and production processes in novel ways.

- Standards for the treatment of livestock seek to impose limits on the territorialisation of the energies and expressiveness of animal life.

5   Niche market or force for change?

In this section, we move on from the practices of specific AFNs to address some of the larger claims made about their achievements and potential. In particular, we are interested in the possibility that ethical consumption, while taking advantage of markets, can also operate as a force which challenges the way that global markets currently operate. Pushing this logic, we explore the broadest possible ramifications of extending the trade and production of 'good food' through its impact on the well-being of local producers or individual non-human lives, and on to its implications for biological life in general and the global environment.

5.1   Ethical consumption as pathway to participation

You have now had a chance to see the ethical claims for Fairtrade and animal welfare in action. It is important in making an assessment of these strategies to be aware of some of the counter-arguments that are made. One of the most common arguments is that fair trade or organic products will never amount to much more than a niche market. This claim is usually based on one of two, somewhat contradictory, arguments. The first is that the higher price of ethically produced and traded products vis-à-vis their conventional equivalents restricts the market for them to relatively wealthy consumers who can afford to pay the extra to 'salve their consciences'. Some critical, or radical, commentators raise this issue as a way of implying that ethical consumption is a 'soft' substitute for more engaging and 'genuine' forms of political activity. The second counter-claim that has often been made is that, as they become more successful, the ethical credentials of AFNs are diluted through their integration into the mainstream food market – for example, by dealing with corporate supermarkets.

With regard to the first claim, it can be noted that Fairtrade coffee costs on average some 5–10 per cent more than conventional equivalents, while the price premium on organic over conventional ('farm assured') eggs in UK supermarkets is somewhere in the region of 10–15 per cent, and around 10 per cent free range over conventional eggs. The social profile of consumers of these products does not support the assumption that only 'wealthy' people buy them. For instance, in Europe (itself a relatively wealthy region by global standards), purchasing patterns suggest that households across the income profile choose Fairtrade over conventional coffee. This means that some households are paying more as a percentage of their household income to support the ethical objectives of Fairtrade than others, but it does not mean that price is an absolute determinant of who engages in ethical consumption.

The claim about the impacts of AFNs being 'mainstreamed' is more complex, and may be seen as an attempt to make something negative out of what may be one of the strengths of ethical consumption and its organising networks. In response, it is important to realise that one of the features of organic and animal welfare food networks is that they operate through a number of outlets other than supermarkets, from farmers markets and box schemes to wholefood stores and consumer cooperatives (where the price differential may also be lower). Moreover, the capacity of AFNs to work with, and influence, more mainstream institutions and networks can equally be read as a refutation of the 'expensive and elitist' charge, and as indicative of the successful promotion of their message and means.

One measure of the success of Fairtrade coffee, for example, is that several of the leading MNCs in the conventional global coffee market are actively looking to introduce 'ethical' brands to compete with Fairtrade coffee. In this vein, Kraft (which owns household coffee brands such as Kenco, Maxwell House and Carte Noire) has begun to introduce sustainably produced coffee into several of its brands. Some of these are certified by the Rainforest Alliance, a New York based NGO, as sustainable both ecologically and socially. Use of a different certification standard will pose difficult questions for consumers and only time will tell whether mainstream suppliers like Kraft will convert their whole operations to the principles of fair trade.

Another indicator of the expanding uptake or mainstreaming of fair trade practices is the development of collective initiatives such as setting up Fairtrade regions (The Open University is a member of one) and the conversion of institutional catering outlets to Fairtrade goods, for instance the adoption of Fairtrade coffee as standard in the House of Commons or in commercial coffee outlets like the AMT franchise that now populates so many railway stations and other public places in the UK (http://www.amtcoffee.co.uk). Food provisioning policies in these institutional settings can have significant impacts on patterns of consumption in society more broadly. Whether or not they do so is in the hands of those who inhabit these spaces as workers, members or customers. A good example is the University of York in Canada which, under pressure from staff and students, converted campus coffee outlets to its own brand of fair trade coffee – 'Las Nubes' – a brand that is now also being sold in an independent Canadian coffee chain (see the following article).

Fair-trade coffee earns York a bean

Philip Fine

Montreal

Canada's York University has unveiled its own brand of fair-trade coffee.

Las Nubes, the Costa-Rican-grown coffee, will give the Toronto-based university a buzz while offering a novel way of fundraising for research.

York is pumping extra money into environmental pro-jects, supporting fair trade and ecologically sound practices.

Timothy's, a coffee chain, will sell the product with the York logo at its 140 stores. A dollar per pound of coffee sold will fund the university's con-servation research in the Costa Rican rainforest.

Lorna Marsden, York pre-sident, said the coffee would allow consumers 'to demon-strate their commitment to the environment and social jus-tice'.

(Fine, 2004)

As in the case of the Fairtrade initiative, AFNs concerned with animal welfare have succeeded in converting a number of institutional caterers to using free-range eggs or, rather less frequently, organic eggs (and sometimes other food products) as standard. In changing the prevailing register of publicly acceptable ethical standards, some unlikely shifts in global sourcing protocols among some of the biggest food corporations have come about. A good example is the introduction of tighter animal welfare specifications by McDonald's in its supplier contracts with meat producers, including improvements in the size of battery cages and the cessation of debeaking chickens (see the article on the opposite page).

As AFNs promoting animal welfare foods are quick to point out, even with bigger cages this is still factory farming, and doubtless these changes are part of a concerted effort to improve McDonald's public image and recover profitability in difficult times.

By the same token, buying Fairtrade goods, useful as it is, is not enough to bring about the changes in the global food trade that many campaigners wish to see. Rather than seeing ethical consumption as inherently limited, however, some researchers have suggested that it may be more helpful to view it as a first step, an opening to a pathway that has the potential to lead to other forms of political involvement and participation (Barnett et al., 2005). Once sparked by a concern over what they are buying or eating, consumers may then be mobilised for more ambitious and collective projects. One prominent example of this is the support attracted by the Fairtrade Foundation's fair trade town and city campaign in the UK. As Barnett et al. tell the story:

> In 2000, a group of Oxfam activists in Garstang announced that their town was the first Fairtrade Town in the world. The Fairtrade Foundation (FTF) immediately seized on the campaign strategy as a device they could formalise into a national campaign. By Fairtrade Fortnight in 2005, 100 towns and cities in Britain had been awarded Fairtrade Town/City certification, with more than 200 others currently campaigning for certification.
>
> (Barnett et al., 2005, p.5)

As well as encouraging consumers – or net surfers – to back the Fairtrade towns and cities initiative, the Fairtrade website also directs people towards the Trade Justice Movement. This is a broad alliance of organisations, including Oxfam and Christian Aid, which campaigns to transform the organisation of international trade in the interests of both trade justice and environmental protection in the global South. The Trade Justice Movement has in turn fed into the larger Make

McDonald's orders its suppliers to phase out de-beaking of hens

By Mary Dejevsky in Washington

The fast-food giant McDonald's has ordered all its egg suppliers in the United States to improve the treatment of their hens, including phasing out the practice if de-beaking and providing much bigger cages. The company also wants to ban forced moulting, when farmers withhold food and water to make the hens lay more eggs.

The new standards were recommended by a panel of scientific experts appointed by the company to address concerns from lobby groups, including animal rights campaigners, about the way animals are treated. That McDonald's has decided to require the improvements, and made them public, is evidence of increased public concern about food quality and animal welfare in the US. It is the first American food supplier to introduce such regulations.

Robert Langert, senior director of public and community affairs for McDonald's, said: 'This is our pathway to be a leader on this issue.'

Bruce Friedrich, a spokesman for the animals rights group People for the Ethnical Treatment of Animals, said that the new rules were an improvement, but 'it's the bare minimum of bare minimums that you refuse to starve and dehydrate animals to death'.

The move was also believed to reflect concern among scientists that the current treatment of hens could increase the risk of diseases that can spread to humans. Recommendations along the lines now adopted by McDonald's were made to all egg producers recently by the industry's own scientific advisers.

McDonald's, which uses 1.5 billion eggs a year, has recently been the target of action by animal rights campaigners in Europe, and US observers were frank about the degree to which European concerns about food safety and animal welfare are starting to influence US consumers. Several of the practices that McDonald's wants outlawed are already banned or in the process of being phased out in Europe.

McDonald's appears also to see a market advantage in the US from being regarded as a pioneer in a move away from factory farming. The company has already tightened regulations for the treatment of livestock and is renowned for its strict quality control from farm to table. It conducts regular inspections of slaughterhouses and farms to monitor compliance with its regulations, and the new rules will be enforced in the same way.

The company had no comment on whether the changes would raise prices in its hamburger outlets. Increasing the size of cages by 50 per cent will be the most expensive improvement.

(Dejevsky, 2000)

Poverty History campaign, which drew some 225,000 protestors to Edinburgh in the UK in July 2005 to demand trade justice, debt cancellation and increased aid for the world's poorest countries from the leaders of the world's most powerful states gathered at the G8 Summit. Meanwhile, working on the other side of the fence (the G8 now meets behind fences to avoid demonstrators), Cafédirect supplied coffee and tea to the G8 Summit participants, for which they were warmly thanked by Number 10 Downing Street (Cafédirect, 2005).

5.2   Global solidarity for local agriculture

Ethical consumption can serve as an opening to forms of solidarity which extend well beyond the realms of consumption. In other words, it can be a vital first step towards participation in those international movements intent on transforming the globalised world, movements we encountered in Chapter 7. By establishing new forms of connection between food producers and food consumers, most AFNs position themselves as part of a broader movement that aims to transform not only what we eat, but the whole weave of activities and processes that come under the rubric of 'agriculture'.

As we saw in Chapter 7, international organisations that seek to transform rural or agricultural life play a significant part in the wider campaign for a more just and sustainable globalisation. These movements bridge the global North and South: the protests of José Bové and the French Confédération Paysanne finding common cause with the many small- and medium-scale agricultural producers worldwide which make up the international movement Via Campesina (see Chapter 7). What Bové advocates in his attack on *malbouffe* (bad food or junk food), and Via Campesina advocates more generally, is the right of agricultural producers to a degree of protection with regard to standards of food production. This is a struggle for justice for local producers and local communities; it is about getting fair prices for their crops and not having local or national markets distorted by the unrestrained market forces of neo-liberalism, which currently forbid consideration of the ethical origin of traded foodstuffs.

Nonetheless, it is about something more than this, as Doreen Massey showed in Chapter 7. It is also a defence of the particularities of the local in the face of the potential homogenisation which Bové and Dufour and many fellow critics and campaigners see as one of the main effects of neo-liberal globalisation. What Bové refers to as *malbouffe* has an inherent unhealthiness that derives from its intensive, industrialised production. Furthermore, it is also food that is standardised or uniform. 'Good food', by implication, draws on local knowledge: it embodies the traditions and rhythms of a particular place (Bové and Dufour, 2001, Chapter 4).

It is in this sense that we can see how the promotion of ethically sound and healthy produce by AFNs resonates profoundly in theory and practice with Bové's critique of *malbouffe* and everything it stands for. AFNs seek to put those people who want to produce 'good food' in touch with those people who want to consume 'good food'. Like Bové (and the much broader Via Campesina campaign), AFNs and the ethical consumption they promote involve defence of place, locality, community – or what we have been referring to in this book as 'territory'. Nonetheless, this call is being made in a globalised world of flows. In such a context this must be a defence of place not as closed or bounded, but as potentially nourished by certain carefully modulated flows – namely the trade in 'good food'. It cannot realistically be a politics simply of closure. We saw in Chapter 7, Section 5 that while Bové and Via Campesina do call for some closures (for instance to protect local food producers against 'dumping' of produce from rich countries), they are not opposed to globalisation as such. Rather this is a politics that seeks to challenge the current nature of flows.

Activity 8.3

Take a pause now and go back to Chapter 5 for another look at the cover of Common Ground's book *Local Distinctiveness* (Figure 5.16), which featured in Activity 5.5.

1   Which squares relate to agricultural products? What message do you think they are trying to get across about farming?

2   How do you think this message relates to Bové's and Dufour's critique of *malbouffe* and AFNs' promotion of 'good food'?

Many of the squares on the book cover give examples of locally or regionally specific produce: cattle, pigs, sheep, potatoes and apples (Acklam Russet, etc.). The cover as a whole gives an impression of localities giving rise to diversity: different places with different traditions of growing food; different livestock breeds and crop strains; and different ways of processing food. The message would seem to be that rural life is, or at least should be, composed of a whole weave of connections between local conditions, local farming traditions (gates, railings) and local food specialities (such as Cornish pasties). There is no suggestion here that 'good food' should not travel, or that we should not go in search of it, but there is certainly a sense that food and eating, to use the words of Bové, should be one of 'the ties that bind us to the land or place where we live' (Bové and Dufour, 2001, p.56).

By way of the ethical food consumption promoted by AFNs, and Bové's and Dufour's notion of good, healthy, local food, we have come back to one of the core themes of this book: the vital entanglement of human and non-human processes. While this chapter may have approached the issues of trade justice and animal welfare as relatively distinct aspects of ethical food consumption, we have also come across numerous indications that the conditions under which human producers live and work, and the predicament of other life forms and the environment, are mutually implicated in important ways. While farm animals and crops, along with agricultural landscapes, have been shaped in many ways by human practices, they also retain significant elements of their own force and integrity. Farm animals and crops play an important part in global biological diversity, for the particular weave of human interests and non-human biological processes has given rise to many new breeds and strains. In this way, it has been argued, small farmers have historically been guardians of genetic diversity (Herman and Kuper, 2003, p.42).

As Bové puts it: 'farmers work with what is alive and on the land ... Choices made by farmers directly affect the land and the environment' (Bové and Dufour, 2001, p.124). Certain practices, organic farming in particular, but also other procedures that respect soil and natural flows, can actually enhance biodiversity on farmland; they help preserve and even restore biological fertility of soil, as the Soil Association, for instance, has long argued.

Through participation in AFNs, people's everyday consumption practices can have benefits for the integrity and richness of territories far away, with potential impacts that reach all the way down into the soil that has accumulated over geological time. In this regard, it is interesting to note that in 2003, the Soil Association and the Fairtrade Foundation announced a new agreement about ways of working together. This included a proposal 'to work together closely to improve the speed and ease of certification for producers in the developing world who wish to sell products that are both Fairtrade and organic' (The Fairtrade Foundation, 2003).

5.3   From Alternative Food Networks to new global architectures

Effectively, people are mobilising around the world in order to protect the local 'sovereignty' of territories, to win them the right to protect their own agricultural practices and local environments. As we saw in Chapter 5, the integrity of the local should not be taken for granted; it is always made rather than given or preordained. More than ever, in an increasingly globalised world, the integrity of places – communities, localities and regions – needs to be worked at. With the understanding of the interplay between territories and flows that you have developed throughout this book, it should come as no surprise that, in a globalised world, global solidarity is needed to protect the local.

But you may also wish to push this argument further. First, there is the question: what is 'the integrity of the local' in today's world? Certainly it cannot mean either a closure of the local against the outside world or a rejection of any change at all. The debate must be around what *kinds* of connections and what *kinds* of change. Secondly, you might think back to the discussion in Chapter 7, Section 3 of how we come to political judgements. There it was argued that spatial form is not in itself enough. 'Local' is not necessarily 'good' any more than 'global' is necessarily 'bad' (or vice versa come to that). There are powerful 'local' places as well as ones struggling to defend themselves (check back here to Activity 7.7). So even the claim for 'local control by local people' will have different force (and imply a different politics) in different situations.

For the organisations concerned with AFNs, as well as the movements more directly focused on the struggles of small farmers and peasants, it is clear that international trade regulations put profound limits on what local farmers or even national governments can achieve. As Oxfam puts it: 'a systematic, not a niche, solution is needed' (Oxfam International, 2002). Initiatives to promote ethical trading and consumption, in the sense of a systematic solution, soon find themselves confronting the question of what kinds of architecture of territory and flow would make possible more sustainable and just practices of food production. For many of the groups involved in AFNs, the ultimate aim of sparking the concern of people in their role as consumers is to mobilise them in support of changing the ways in which markets are structured and regulated. According to the terms we have used in this book, AFNs are a step on the way to alternative 'global architectures' of trade and food production.

Those who confront the existing architectures which organise the territorialisation and flow of food stuffs are not only seeking structural alternatives to the current trade system. They are also challenging the way in which human beings currently relate to other living things, the soil, air and water. The point that Bové and Dufour (2001) and others make about farmers' knowledge of the living things they work with and of their local environments is not simply that such historically accumulated experience can be ignored, but that it can be obliterated by the powerful structural forces that currently organise global production and trade. In this light, the 'level playing field' metaphor that is often evoked in neo-liberal promotion of free trade needs to be critically addressed in relation to the profound irregularity or unevenness of local conditions. Farming practices, including the plants and animals that agriculture depends upon, often encapsulate centuries, even millennia, of adaptation to local conditions of soil, life and weather. More than this, these activities have helped to form the soil and shape local microclimates into the weave to which we have been referring throughout this book as a 'territory'.

There are many grounds on which to take issue with neo-liberal architectures, as we saw in Chapter 2 and again in Chapter 7. Nevertheless, as Herman and Kuper (2003) point out, the inability to take adequate account of the dynamics of climate, which remains an important aspect of agricultural production, is a particularly powerful reason to question and contest the dominant way of organising markets. As they argue:

> According to neo-liberal dogma, agricultural markets are self-regulating. This claim is not supported by the facts. ... Contrary to the neo-liberal credo, agricultural markets have a spontaneous and chaotic character. While demand may be stable in the ... short run, agricultural production fluctuates according to climatic vagaries. Agricultural prices and incomes fluctuate even more, as do consumer prices. This is why all countries since the time of the Pharaohs have had agricultural policies to regulate agricultural supply, both at the level of imports and by having some storage policy to minimise price fluctuations. The world market, given its domination by agri-food oligopolies, is unable to provide the regulation needed. Rules of international coordination other than the free trade fostered by the WTO are required.
>
> (Herman and Kuper, 2003, p.13)

Herman and Kuper's point about agricultural production varying according to 'vagaries' of climate should remind you of the point we made in Section 3.1 about price fluctuations of coffee as a result of climatic and disease events. We need to keep in mind, as Nigel Clark suggested in Chapter 1, that human activities may well be rendering climate still more unpredictable across the globe. Such changes may present challenges to local knowledge, but the need to adapt to climatic flux might also mean that a deep and intimate understanding of local conditions, in all their variability and unevenness, becomes even more important. In addition, maintaining soil fertility takes on a new significance. Industrialised agriculture is an important source of greenhouse gases, but healthy, well-maintained soil is also a sink for carbon, effectively absorbing greenhouse gas emissions. Restoring the productivity of degraded soil, in this light, is high on the Intergovernmental Panel on Climate Change's list for mitigating the effects of human-induced climate change.

The point that needs stressing here is that global architectures which are put in place to organise the flows and territorialisations of human economic activities also have immense implications for the flows and territorialisations of the non-human world. Farming for food is one of the most ancient and enduring ways in which human beings have taken responsibility for channelling the flows and reorganising the territories of other species. This is unavoidably a power relationship, and a far from balanced or symmetrical one, in that human agents — working in their own interests — impose controls on the behaviour and bodily form of other organisms. The concern for the welfare of intensively farmed animals (see Section 4) reflects a view shared by many people that this power relationship has been extended and intensified in ways that too severely limit the capacity of other life forms to flourish or express themselves. In this regard, the call for alternative architectures to organise food production and trade are both a challenge to the current structuring of relations of power between relatively poorer and wealthier sectors of global humanity, and a challenge to existing power relations between our species and other forms of life (though not necessarily at the same time or in the same context).

Although the well-being of other species (usually animals) takes us down to the level of individuals, as Figures 8.7 and 8.8 showed, the question of restructuring food trade and production returns us to the broader issue of the flows and territorialisations of biological life in general, along with the soil, air and water upon which it depends. As with the cases of responding to climate change or the contest over medicinal plants, the issue of transforming architectures of food production and trade in an increasingly globalised world requires us to think through the global implications of a great many localised or place-bound activities. Thinking about what makes 'good food', in this sense, leads to some profound and complex questions about the human responsibility for sustaining the physical systems of the planet in ways that are conducive to the flourishing of human and non-human life.

Summary

- Despite criticisms of its elitist or niche characteristics, it has been argued that ethical consumption has the potential to lead to more collective forms of political participation.

- Many AFNs are part of a broader global movement which aims to transform the whole weave of activities and processes that constitutes rural life and agricultural production.

- Global solidarity over the production and consumption of 'good food' can impact locally on the well-being of producers and on their relationships with non-human life and the environment.

- Challenging the existing global architectures that organise food trade and production has important implications for the power relations both between the global North and South, and between humankind and non-human life.

- Food trade architectures have implications for the flow and territorialisation of biological life, soil, air and water, all the way up to the global scale.

6   Conclusion

In this chapter, we have looked at how shopping for food is part of the making of a globalised earth. We have seen that changing our habits of consumption — what we choose to eat — can have an impact on distant lives both human and non-human, on soil and on the environment more generally. Indeed, the lesson of those who promote ethical food consumption is that in a globalised world, whether we are aware of it or not, our eating habits contribute to the making and remaking of territories both near to and far from those we inhabit. Accordingly, we have gained an understanding of some of the ways in which everyday involvements in territories and flows change the shape of the world.

In Chapter 7, we saw how issues and campaigns can arise out of a deep questioning of the way that the globalised world is currently organised. In this chapter, we have discussed how some of those who take issue with current patterns of globalised trade and production have come together to forge alternative connections. By promoting food which has been grown and processed in just or sustainable ways, such people and organisations offer an everyday and tangible way of raising these questions for other people, a way which might foster a sense of our entanglement with and responsibilities to others.

We have seen how small acts of ethical consumption, when they take root, can be woven into larger and more encompassing projects such as institutional fair trade initiatives or whole cities or regions declaring their interest in fairer trade. Consuming 'good food' is also, as this chapter has argued, an opening for individuals to become further involved, to be drawn into more organised and collective efforts to transform the world. In fact, it is difficult to advocate ethical consumption, whether for fair trade or organic and other less industrialised forms of agriculture, without sooner or later confronting the powerful structural forces which organise most other forms of trade.

Far from being a merely individualised gesture, ethical consumption implicates consumers in AFNs – many of which are deeply involved in campaigning for structural change in the architectures that organise global trade. The struggle for institutional change, at this level, expresses and enacts the idea that 'we' are not necessarily more responsible for what goes on inside our own country than for what happens in other countries (Young, 2003). It also suggests that this responsibility might extend towards species other than our own; this can take the form of a consideration for the day-to-day welfare of animals as individual beings, or of a concern for the broader issue of biological diversity and for the state of the physical environment more generally. Calls to eat well and eat differently embody a challenge to the power relations that structure our interactions with other people and those that structure our interchanges with other species.

The architectures that organise the global trade in foodstuffs, as this chapter has argued, have important implications for the flow and territorialisation of wealth and economic opportunity between different human groups. We have also seen some of their repercussions on the flow and territorialisation of animal bodies and behaviour. However intensive or extensive these impacts are, we need to remember that particular human actors with particular interests have set up these architectures (though, clearly, not always with all the actual outcomes in mind). This makes it quite conceivable that such architectures could be set up in radically different ways – a point we have been making in a range of ways and in a variety of contexts throughout this book. The establishment and spread of AFNs are at once proof of the possibility of organising things differently, and a potential step in the direction of much more profound changes.

References

Allen, J. (2006) 'Claiming connections: a distant world of sweatshops?' in Barnett, C., Robinson, J. and Rose, G. (eds) *A Demanding World*, Milton Keynes, The Open University.

Appadurai, A. (1996) *Modernity at Large: Cultural Dimensions of Globalization*, Minn., University of Minnesota Press.

Barnett, C., Clarke, N., Cloke, P. and Malpass, A. (2004) 'Consuming ethics: articulating the subjects and spaces of ethical consumption', *Antipode*, vol.37, no.1, pp.23–45.

Barnett, C., Clarke, N., Cloke, P. and Malpass, A. (2005) 'The political ethics of consumerism', *Consumer Policy Review*, vol.15, no.2, pp.2–8.

Bell, D. and Valentine, G. (1997) *Consuming Geographies: We Are Where We Eat*, London, Routledge.

Bové, J. and Dufour, F. (2001) *The World Is Not for Sale: Farmers Against Junk Food* (trans. A. de Casparis), London, Verso. (First published as *Le Monde N'Est Pas une Merchandise* in 2000, Paris, Editions la Découverte & Syros.)

Cafédirect (undated) 'Peru', http://www.cafedirect.co.uk/growers/peru.php (accessed 3 September 2005).

Cafédirect (1996–97) 'The aroma of fresh coffee without the whiff of exploitation', http://www.cafedirect.co.uk/about/ads_1996.php (accessed 25 October 2005).

Cafédirect (2005) 'G8 Summit: a thank you letter from Downing Street', http://www.cafedirect.ie/news.php/000114.html (accessed 22 August 2005).

Callon M., Méadel, C. and Rabeharisoa, V. (2002) 'The economy of qualities', *Economy and Society*, vol.31, no.2. pp.194–217.

Christian Aid (1996) *The Global Supermarket*, London, Christian Aid.

Compassion in World Farming (2003) *The Compassionate Shopper's Guide*, available at http://www.ciwf.org.uk/publications/reports/ shoppers_guide_2003.pdf (accessed 4 November 2005).

Dejevsky, M. (2000) 'McDonald's orders its suppliers to phase out de-beaking of hens', *The Independent*, 24 August.

The Fairtrade Foundation (undated) 'Alejandro', http://www.fairtrade. org.uk/suppliers_growers_coffee_alejandro.htm (accessed 21 August 2005).

The Fairtrade Foundation (2002a) 'Spilling the beans on the coffee trade', http://www.fairtrade.org.uk/downloads/pdf/spilling.pdf, p.7 (accessed 3 September 2005).

The Fairtrade Foundation (2002b) 'The new FAIRTRADE Mark', http://www.fairtrade.org.uk/about_new_mark.htm (accessed 26 October 2005).

The Fairtrade Foundation (2003) 'Update on the discussions with the Soil Association', http://www.fairtrade.org.uk/pr130603.htm (accessed 29 August 2005).

Farm Animal Welfare Council (1979) 'Codes of recommendations for the welfare of livestock'.

Fine, P. (2004) 'Fair-trade coffee earns York a bean', *Times Higher Education Supplement*, 2 April.

Herman, P. and Kuper, R. (2003) *Food for Thought: Towards a Future for Farming*, London, Pluto Press. (First published as *Changeons de Politique Agricole* for the Confédération Paysanne in 2002, Paris, Mille et Une Nuits.)

Lymbery, P. (2002) *Farm Assurance Schemes and Animal Welfare: Can We Trust Them?*, Hampshire, Compassion in World Farming Trust.

Millstone E. and Lang, T. (2003) *The Atlas of Food. Who Eats What, Where and When*, London, Earthscan.

Oxfam International (2002) http://www.maketradefair.com (accessed 27 October 2005).

Pollard, S. (2004) 'Aid like this is fatal', *The Times*, 27 September.

Ridley R. and Baker, H. (1998) *Fatal Protein: The Story of CJD, BSE and other Prion Diseases*. Oxford, Oxford University Press.

Rose, G. (2006) 'Envisioning demands: photographs, families and strangers' in Barnett, C., Robinson, J. and Rose, G. (eds) *A Demanding World*, Milton Keynes, The Open University.

Royal Society for the Prevention of Cruelty to Animals (2003) *Freedom Foods Welfare Standards for Laying Hens and Pullets*, Horsham, RSPCA.

Schlosser, E. (2001) *Fast Food Nation*, London, Penguin.

Soil Association (2003) *Batteries Not Included: Organic Farming and Animal Welfare*, Bristol, Soil Association.

Watkins, K. and Fowler, P. (2003) *Rigged Rules and Double Standards: Trade, Globalisation, and the Fight against Poverty*, Oxford, Oxfam.

Whatmore, S. and Thorne, L. (1997) 'Nourishing networks: alternative geographies of food' in Goodman, D. and Watts, M. (eds) *Globalising Food*, London, Routledge.

Young, I.M. (2003) 'From guilt to solidarity: sweatshops and political responsibility', *Dissent*, spring, pp.39–44.

Reading 8A

Cafédirect, 'Peru'

Cafédirect suppliers:

Central de Co-operativas Agrarias Cafetaleras (COCLA)

Central de Cooperativas Agrarias Cafetaleras de los Valles Sandía (CECOVASA)

Co-operativa San Juan del Oro

Co-operativa Bagua Grande

The Peruvian landscape includes areas of desert, a stunningly beautiful stretch of the Andes and the tropical rain forests of the Amazon basin. The ancient Inca civilisation has left its traces in cities such as Cuzco and the ruined Machu Picchu, and in the customs of the Incas' Quechua-speaking Indian descendants.

In 2000 Peru was the 10th largest producer of coffee in the world. Out of a total population of 23.9 million, over 1 million Peruvians are involved in the production, transport, processing and export of coffee, making it Peru's biggest agricultural earner. To many farmers it is their only viable alternative cash crop to coca.

Until the late 1980s the co-operative movement was strong, with farmers receiving substantial financial and technical assistance from the government. The situation changed drastically in the 1990s when all but the strongest co-operatives fell victim to a combination of intense terrorist activity, the removal of state support, and low prices following the collapse of the International Coffee Agreement.

Terrorist activity has now subsided throughout Peru and the situation for the co-operatives is improving, although there is still a long way to go. Farmers are realising that they must join forces to improve their situation and compete against private traders.

'Co-operativism is the only way producers can work and survive. We should keep up the struggle to consolidate our organisations with a spirit of solidarity with all co-operatives.'

Felipe Huaman, General Manager of Bagua Grande Co-operative

COCLA

COCLA was founded in 1967 and in common with many of Peru's co-operatives suffered a period of decline in the late 1980s and early 1990s, following the liberalisation of the Peruvian coffee industry. The turning point came in 1995 with the appointment of a new management team and the establishment of COCLA's own export office in Lima. As a result of increased efficiency and training programmes for staff and farmers, COCLA has seen its organisation strengthen and the membership grow. Now COCLA is comprised of 24 primary societies and has a membership of 4,500 farmers spread out over an area of 40,000 square kilometres.

The Quillabamba region, where COCLA is based, produces some of Peru's finest coffee. COCLA has promoted organic farming since the early days, providing technical training for its members in organic conversion and improved farming methods. Currently about half of COCLA's societies are organically certified.

Cafédirect's Producer Support & Development team has worked closely with COCLA to identify the zones where the best coffee is grown, and has offered advice on techniques for improving quality. This led to the launch of Cafédirect Organic Machu Picchu Mountain Special in September 1999 – the first ever Fairtrade organic gourmet Peruvian single origin coffee.

The farmers involved in the development of the Organic Machu Picchu Mountain Special saw their incomes effectively double during 1999 – taking into account premiums for Fairtrade, gourmet and organic production, as well as the prices paid by local buyers.

COCLA has decided to spend some of its Fairtrade premiums on a training programme, employing agronomists to provide technical assistance to farmers. The results have been outstanding – in 1997 only 30% of the coffee delivered to COCLA was of export quality, but by 2000 this figure had risen to 76%.

'We all want to improve the quality of our coffee, which we never used to do because we lacked the economic means or coffee prices were low or because we did not have a good market for our coffee. Now we have buyers who give us a better price and we have an incentive to keep improving the quality of our coffee.'

Rogelia Figueroa Gabera, wife of Alberto, a COCLA farmer

The producers themselves decide collectively how the Fairtrade premiums that COCLA receives are spent. In the case of one of COCLA's primary societies, José Olaya, the farmers unanimously decided to spend the premiums to buy a truck.

'The farmers decided to give part of the premium towards the purchase of a truck. This transparency and the democratic process for deciding how the premium would be spent have created trust in the co-operative. Since then more farmers have joined, which means more coffee, more premium and so more benefit for all.'

Augusto Tirade Bejar, President of the José Olaya Co-operative

(Cafédirect, undated)

Reading 8B

The Fairtrade Foundation, 'Alejandro'

Alejandro is a coffee producer from Peru. He is married, with two children, and is 41 years old.

Dedicated to coffee since he was ten years old

His passion

Alejandro works his coffee with enthusiasm and love because he knows that by producing a high quality coffee there will be people who drink it and be happy to support the farmers.

His daily life

Alejandro has dedicated himself to coffee since he was 10 years old, helping his parents with their agricultural work. Alejandro was the youngest of four sons and at 20 was left to look after the farm when his parents died. One of his brothers also died and the other two went to find work in other cities, since the farm was too small to support them and their families as well. Alejandro's wife is called Elvira Camacho Cruz, 30 years old and from the same area. They have two children, Alfrán who is 7 years old and a daughter called Camila who is 2 years old.

Alejandro has been a member of the Cooperativa Huadquiña since he was 16, and producer of organic certified coffee since 1995. Being a member of Cocla means great benefits for him. Cocla marketing the coffee means getting a better price, and he also receives on-farm technical assistance, training in cooperativism and pre-financing.

A better deal

Alejandro believes that cooperativism is one of the best ways to organise to sell your products and that fair trade has helped him to better his standard of living. Alejandro works his coffee with enthusiasm and love because he knows that by producing a high quality coffee there will be people who drink it and be more willing to support them. He believes that all farmers should look after the environment and have organic, sustainable production methods.

(The Fairtrade Foundation, undated)

Conclusion

Nigel Clark and Doreen Massey

The making, unmaking and remaking of the world is a constant and ongoing process. It is taking place all around us, all of the time, and on many different scales. Yet it is not just happening *around* us: everything we do, or choose not to do, is caught up in this making, in its own little way. When we make a cup of coffee, to take an example from Chapter 8, we use an agricultural product that has been planted, tended, picked, processed, packaged, shipped and marketed. Accordingly, we play a small part in the 'life' of a commodity: we enter into flows of trade that link our lives as consumers, living in one part of the world, with those of producers who are likely to live very different lives elsewhere in the world. And even when we choose to drink a different brand of coffee, a fair trade brand, for instance, or pass over our coffee for a glass of orange juice, we do not so much opt out of such complex connections as enter into an alternative chain or circuit of events.

As we have seen in this book and its companion volume, **Barnett et al. (2006)**, many of the paths which connect us with other people, other places and other things have stretched and grown more tangled over the recent past: a complex and variegated process which the term 'globalisation' seeks to convey. Some approaches to the issue of globalisation take this as evidence that the world is moving, as if in a single direction, from a state of fixity and boundedness to a condition of borderlessness and constant motion. In this book, however, we have taken a rather different approach. Through the examples and stories we have investigated, we have shown that life in a globalised world involves settling down as well as moving on, and entails new forms of enclosure or boundary making in addition to novel ways of moving across borders and boundaries. We have also demonstrated that people or things which appear to have been where they are now 'for ever', usually turn out, at some time in the past, to have come from somewhere else, a place that is often a surprising distance from where they now seem to 'belong'. To put it in the terms we have used in this book, in order to understand the condition of life in a globalised world, we have to take into consideration both processes of 'territorialisation' and processes of 'flow'. We need to look at territories and flows in interplay, working with or against each other in dynamic and constantly shifting ways.

One important implication of viewing the world through the play of territories and flows is that it helps us to recognise that the planet which we inhabit is 'in the making', even without our own human contributions – and has been, throughout its long existence. As Chapter 1 illustrated, there were both flows and territorialisations of the physical stuff of the world billions of years before the emergence of human beings. In an important sense, some of these forces and processes – such as weather systems or movements of the earth's crust – have been fully 'globalised' from early in our planet's formation. The International Geophysical Year (IGY) of 1958–59, centred on Antarctica and discussed in Chapter 4, was a milestone in this regard, for it gathered new evidence about the way that the earth's physical processes operate globally – as parts of a single, integrated system.

One aspect of this idea of the planet as a 'geophysical' system, highlighted by the IGY, was the cautionary note that physical changes in one part of the world could have serious impacts far away, as in the case of the melting of the Antarctic ice cap which would affect sea level throughout the world. These speculations, as Chapter 1 pointed out, have since become serious concerns for many ordinary people worldwide. Recent decades have seen a growing awareness about the physical interconnectedness of the planet, and a rising acceptance of the idea that human activities are now transforming the earth's physical systems in their entirety. By this logic, even the energy used to boil the water for our cup of coffee, if it was not from a renewable source, would be adding its own small incremental change to the composition of the earth's atmosphere, and in this way contributing to changes in the circuits or flows that make up the global climate.

A global-scale issue like climate change calls for a response which draws together people across all the territorial divisions of the planet. The sheer demands of such a task – all the physical and social obstacles which need to be overcome – are daunting, and it is hardly surprising that many people take a resigned or fatalistic stance towards some of the problems of a globalised world. Nevertheless, one of the themes weaving its way through this book is that we are not thrust into such situations suddenly, without precedent or prior experience. Global issues like climate change, the inequities of trade or the governing of global commons call for new ways of mediating between territories and flows. And mediating between territories and flows, if not necessarily couched in these terms, is not something new to human beings. Finding new ways to work with and through flows and territories is a challenge that human actors have taken on at many different scales, in many contexts, under many different circumstances.

Among other things, each of the chapters in this book has looked at different ways in which groups of people have sought, or are seeking, actively to intervene in the flows and territories that make up their world. These are experiences which we need to learn from and build upon, and that is what this book has set out to do. While each of the examples we have looked at has its own unique blend of elements and events, and its own particular lessons, you will also have noticed a number of shared strands or unifying themes. The point of using concepts like territory and flow, and of gaining a grasp of the dynamic ways in which they interact, is that it enables us to generalise. These concepts are meant to travel: you should be able to use them to help make the shift from cases which are by now familiar to new areas of concern. They are intended to help you grapple with the sort of issues and challenges that life in a globalised world will no doubt place in your path.

One of the themes we have emphasised in the book, then, is that human beings put a great deal of effort into the making and remaking of territories and flows. Each of the chapters, in its own way, has stressed action: the constructing or enacting of territories and the setting up or transforming of flows. Some of the 'work' we have looked at entails the bolstering of territorial boundaries through practices of enclosure and exclusion or through attempts to control and capture flows. Conversely, some of the efforts we have addressed serve to open up or even dismantle borders, or to free up and disperse flows. As you may have noted, none of the authors in the book has tried to pinpoint the perfect balance of openness or closure, or to set down precisely the ideal interplay of any specific territory and flow. Yet there is a shared sense, across the various chapters, that efforts to totally enclose territories are counterproductive, or perhaps doomed to failure, by virtue of the fact that all territories need to be nourished and enlivened by flows. Moreover, such attempts at enclosure are often experienced as unethical because of the way in which they seek to shut down or capture flows that others may have deep-seated investment in or reliance upon – as in the case of attempts to patent certain medicinal plants (see Chapter 3), or in the bid to privatise water (see Chapter 7). Similarly, we have seen that proposals to totally efface territorial borders in favour of unrestricted flow tend to be no less problematic. Whether it comes in the guise of economic liberalisation (Chapters 2, 7 and 8) or in the form of politically radical assaults on barriers to migration (Chapter 7), we should be suspicious of strategies which fail to acknowledge that all territories rely, to some degree, upon the regulation of flows in order to preserve their integrity and coherence.

However, as we indicated above, human beings do not do the work of shaping and refashioning territories alone. A second theme running through a number of the chapters is that human exertions are part of a much more encompassing process in which the wider world makes and remakes itself. To some extent, all human activity has to work with other forces: we work in and on a non-human, physical world which is itself constantly in flow and endlessly forming or transforming its own territories. This widening of the sense of what it is to be active, and what it is to be global, encourages us to be attentive to a great range of spatial and temporal scales. Where did these trees come from? What was weather like in this place thousands or millions of years ago? To what extent has the earth beneath our feet shifted over geological time? The dynamism of the physical world, we have suggested, is immensely challenging. It can often confound and belittle human endeavours, as we saw in the case of the extreme weather and shifting ice of Antarctica in Chapter 4, or the catastrophic Indian Ocean tsunamis encountered in Chapter 1. Yet these dynamic qualities of the physical world also help to make life on our planet rich, diverse and fascinating – they give rise to an immense variety of plant and animal life, landform and weather conditions, and in this way contribute to the blend of ingredients that makes every place unique.

An appreciation of the non-human forces at work all around us should serve as a reminder that the human ability to act or assert ourselves varies greatly in different contexts or circumstances. While there are few indications that human agency will take control of tectonic plate movement, we can observe a growing human capacity to transform the bodily make-up of other living things, as we saw in the case of plants in Chapter 3 and animals in Chapter 8. However, there are huge differentials among human actors in their power to assert themselves in the making of their worlds. Throughout this book, and its companion volume **(Barnett et al., 2006)**, we have explored some of the ways in which people are connected with others, near and far. Depending on how they are positioned within these relationships, some individuals or groups have far more ability than others to influence the processes in which they are entangled. In the post-war period, as discussed in Chapter 2, a relatively small group of powerful actors was able to set the rules, for a time, for the operation of financial markets on a global scale. We have also seen, in Chapter 8, how the opportunity to gain reward for the production of goods is profoundly restricted by inequalities structured into the flow and territorialisation of global trade. Nonetheless, these arrangements which organise power or capacities to act can themselves be worked upon, as several chapters noted – they can be challenged and they can be changed.

When we are dealing with human processes of territory and flow building, it is not only the capacity to act which is important, but also the desire to act: not just what we can do, but how we feel about different things, places or events. We have seen that certain objects, such as special trees or familiar forests, for which people feel affection and attachment can come to symbolise belonging to a particular place or territory (Chapter 5). Yet we have also seen that objects which carry a strong emotional charge can also circulate, like the kente cloth of the Ghanaians (Chapter 6), nourishing a sense of attachment to a territory even when people have travelled far beyond its borders. Strong feelings about an object, a place or other people can be a powerful incentive to act, to get involved, to try and transform the way in which the world works. This can operate in an affirmative way, as in the case where images and stories encourage us to care about the working conditions of the people whose products we consume (Chapter 8), but it can also happen with negative associations, such as when a corporate image, like the golden arches or burgers of McDonald's, are singled out by campaigners as the epitome of all that they wish to change (Chapter 7). We should also keep in mind that affect or desire need not necessarily be restricted to our species and that, as shown in the argument of the animal welfare campaigners encountered in Chapter 8, animals too have feelings and ways in which they prefer to express themselves.

All these themes come together in the possibility of reorganising the interplay of territories and flows at a structural level. At various points throughout the book, we have referred to what we have called 'architectures': the frameworks which human actors, working collectively, set up with the intention of regulating the dynamic interrelationship between territories and flows. Increasingly, in an ever more globalised world, these architectures must deal with flows that pass through numerous territories, and territories which are, by the same token, linked by flows to a great many other territories. Furthermore, these architectures are also called upon to incorporate both human and non-human processes. Though the flows and territories they deal with need not be human-made, these architectures themselves are indeed human constructions, and as such they are open to being rethought, revised or totally restructured.

One of the more remarkable features of the current state of our globalised world is not simply the growing recognition that existing architectures can be challenged and changed, but the breadth of the human voices that wish to have a say in their remaking. No longer can a handful of countries club together to determine the fate of Antarctica, for instance. Now a chorus of other nations, from all over the planet, demands to participate in its governance, as Chapter 4 recounted. No longer is it possible for select representatives of the most powerful nations to meet to discuss global trade or financial regulations, as we saw in Chapter 7, without a multitude of spokespeople from citizens groups, peasant groups and tribal groups gathering from all over the world to talk up and present their alternatives.

One of the main lessons we can draw from a geographical imagination that stresses the dynamic between territories and flows is an understanding of the way that a myriad of small, often quite ordinary, acts can come together to produce large and consequential effects. What we may be seeing with some recent forms of campaigning and activism is a conscious attempt to harness this power of many small acts to help bring about larger scale or structural transformations. This, in itself, may not be so novel, but it does seem to be happening in new ways. Whether it is the convening of broadly inclusive international social forums (Chapter 7) or the establishment of alternative food networks (Chapter 8), activists seem to be increasingly aware that a wide variety of actors and different kinds of activities have a potential to contribute to social change. These political activists also seem to recognise and take advantage of the fact that a globalised world offers pathways of movement and communication which make it more possible to bring widely dispersed social groups together than at any previous time.

As this book and its companion volume **(Barnett et al., 2006)** have been arguing, facing up to life in a globalised world means acknowledging that our everyday acts can have profound consequences for other people and other things, others who may well be spatially and temporally distant. It is now becoming apparent that, as we make our way in the world, we are often contributing to the undoing or unravelling of the worlds in which others are trying to make their way. For many people in many different contexts, this means that finding new ways to organise our activities is more than just a possible option, it is an obligation or responsibility. The examples we have looked at in this book are all, in a sense, experiments in responding to the challenges raised by living in a globalised world. Some of these experiments are small and local in focus, while others are global in scale and ambition; some may involve means or goals with which you might empathise, while with others you might feel strongly at odds. Nevertheless, if there is cause to be hopeful in a world of pressing global problems, it is perhaps in the way that these experiments in organised responsibility are proliferating around us, and in the manner that all of us, in one form or another, are invited to participate.

Reference

Barnett, C., Robinson, J. and Rose, G. (eds) (2006) *A Demanding World*, Milton Keynes, The Open University.

Acknowledgements

Grateful acknowledgement is made to the following sources for permission to reproduce material within this book.

Chapter 1

Text

Reading 1A: Lynas, M. (2003) 'At the end of our weather', *The Observer*, 5 October 2003. Copyright © Mark Lynas; Reading 1B: Conisbee, M. and Simms, A. (2003) *Environmental Refugees: The Case for Recognition*, New Economics Foundation; Reading 1C: 'Tiny Tuvalu sues United States over rising sea level', Reuters, 29 August 2002. © Copyright. All rights reserved. Distributed by Valeo IP. Valeo Clearance Licence 3.5398.4811156-93063; Reading 1D: 'Tuvalu seeks help in US global warming lawsuit', Reuters, 30 August 2002. © Copyright. All rights reserved. Distributed by Valeo IP. Valeo Clearance Licence 3.5398.4811156-92295.

Figures

Figure 1.1: copyright © Peter B. Bennetts/Lonely Planet Images; Figure 1.3a: copyright © Digital Globe, Eurimage/Science Photo Library; Figure 1.3b: copyright © Digital Globe, Eurimage/Science Photo Library; Figure 1.4: copyright © Mark Lynas/Still Pictures; Figure 1.5: copyright © Peter B. Bennetts/Lonely Planet Images; Figure 1.6: copyright © Steve Pile; Figure 1.8: copyright © 2001 Dirk H.R. Spennemann; Figure 1.9: copyright © Ken Preston Mafham/ Premaphotos/Nature Picture Library.

Chapter 2

Text

Reading 2A: Sassen, S. (2004) 'The continuing utility of spatial agglomeration', in Bevir, M. and Trentmann, F. (eds) *Markets in Historical Context*, Cambridge University Press. © Cambridge University Press, reprinted with permission of the author and publisher; Reading 2B: Campbell, D. (2004) 'Havens that have become a tax on the world's poor', *The Guardian*, 24 September 2004. Copyright © Guardian Newspapers Limited 2004.

(International; Cooperative Biodiversity Group-Peru)', *Pharmaceutical Biology*, vol.37, Swets & Zeitlinger; Figure 3.10: by courtesy of Washington University at St Louis; Figure 3.11: courtesy of Bell Museum of Natural History, University of Minnesota Herbarium; Figure 3.12: Balick, M.J. and Cox, P.A. (1996) *Plants, People, and Culture: The Science of Ethnobotany*, Scientific American Library.

Chapter 4

Text

Reading 4A: Gould, L.M. (1958) *The Polar Regions in Their Relation to Human Affairs* (Bowman Memorial Lecture), American Geographical Society. Copyright © American Geographical Society.

Figures

Figure 4.1: copyright © US Geological Survey/Science Photo Library; Figures 4.3 and 4.4: Herbert Ponting. copyright © Royal Geographical Society; Figure 4.6: copyright © Frank Hurley/National Library of Australia; Figures 4.7 and 4.8: copyright © Nigel Clark.

Chapter 5

The research used in this chapter was conducted as part of an ESRC funded research project – R000237983, 'Arbori-Culture: The Importance of Trees to Place'. Thanks to the people of Camerton and those interviewed during the research. Thanks to Professor Paul Cloke with whom this work was conducted in the School of Geographical Studies, University of Bristol.

Text

Reading 5A: Kaza, S. (1996) *The Attentive Heart: Conversations with Trees*, Shambhala Publications; Reading 5B: Skinner, J. (1984) *Journal of a Somerset Rector 1803–1834*, Oxford University Press; Reading 5C: Woolf, V. (1965) *Two Parsons, The Common Reader, Series II*. The Society of Authors as the Literary Representative of the Estate of Virginia Woolf.

Figures

Figure 5.1 (top left): copyright © Bob Gibbons/Ardea; Figure 5.1 (top right): copyright © Maurice Nimmo/FLPA;Figure 5.1 (bottom): copyright © Ken Day/FLPA; Figure 5.2: copyright © Cheryl Gibson/Sheffield Wildlife Trust; Figures 5.3, 5.4, 5.5, 5.9, 5.10, 5.11,

5.12, 5.13, 5.15 and 5.17: copyright © Owain Jones; Figure 5.6: Down, C.G. and Warrington, A.J., *The History of the Somerset Coalfield*, David & Charles Publishers; Figure 5.7: courtesy of Radstock Museum; Figure 5.8: courtesy of Tim Hughes; Figure 5.14: courtesy of Camerton Parish Council; Figure 5.16: reproduced from a poster with permission of Common Ground. www.england-in-particular.info and www.commonground.org.uk. See Clifford, Sue and King, Angela, *England in Particular: a Celebration of the Commonplace, the Local, the Vernacular and the Distinctive*. Hodder & Stoughton, 2006.

Chapter 6

I would like to thank the following people for their help and advice. Addie Trude for her critical insights into Ghanaian cloth in the diaspora, Leroi Henry for assistance in researching Ghanaian migrants in the UK, and Esther Fiscian for her agreement to be interviewed and to use her testimony in this chapter.

Figures

Figure 6.1: copyright © Jacob Crawfurd/Crawfurd Media; Figure 6.2 (top): copyright Basel Mission Archive, Reference No. D-30.62.003 'King Prempe after his reinstatement' photograph taken at Kumase, 1926; Figure 6.2 (bottom): copyright © Fiona Hanson/PA/Empics; Figure 6.6: copyright © TopFoto.co.uk; Figure 6.7: copyright © Associated Press, WHITE HOUSE; Figure 6.8: copyright © Giles Mohan; Figure 6.9: copyright © Ebenezer Antwi-Nsiah.

Chapter 7

Text

Reading 7A: Ainger, K. (2003) 'We discovered weren't alone: surfing the net in Papua New Guinea', from *Notes from Nowhere* (eds) *We are Everywhere: The Irresistible Rise of Global Anticapitalism*, Verso; Reading 7B: Carvel, J. (2004) 'Nil by mouth', *The Guardian*, 27 August 2004. Copyright © Guardian Newspapers Limited 2004.

Table

Table 7.1: Mensah, K., Mackintosh, M. and Henry, L. (2005) 'The "Skills Drain" of health professionals from the developing world: a framework for policy formulation'. Medact.

Figures

Figures 7.2 and 7.3: copyright © Tom Kruse; Figure 7.5: copyright © Sipa Press (SIPA)/Rex Features; Figure 7.6: copyright © Pedro Valterierra; Figure 7.7: Ellis-Jones, M. (2003) *States of Unrest III: Resistance to IMF and World Bank Policies in Poor Countries*, World Development Movement www.wdm.org.uk; Figure 7.8: www.indymedia.org.uk.

Chapter 8

I should like to acknowledge the helpful advice and information on egg production standards provided by Anna Bassett, Agricultural Advice Manager at the Soil Association.

Text

Page 375: Pollard, S. (2004) 'Aid like this is fatal', *The Times*, 27 September 2004; Page 401: Dejevsky, M. (2000) 'McDonald's orders its suppliers to phase out de-beaking of hens', *The Independent*, 24 August 2000. Copyright © The Independent; Reading 8A: Cafédirect, Peru, www.cafedirect.ie/growers/peru.php; Reading 8B: The Fairtrade Foundation, 'Alejandro', www.fairtrade.org.uk, copyright © Fairtrade Foundation.

Figures

Figure 8.2: Christian Aid © 2004; Figure 8.6: Cafédirect plc; Figure 8.8: copyright © RSPCA; Page 399 cartoon: copyright © Andrew Birch.

Cover illustration

Copyright © Patricia & Angus Macdonald/Aerographica.

Index

Page numbers in **bold** refer to definitions of terms.